NATION-EMPIRE

Studies of the Weatherhead East Asian Institute, Columbia University

The Studies of the Weatherhead East Asian Institute of Columbia University were inaugurated in 1962 to bring to a wider public the results of significant new research on modern and contemporary East Asia.

NATION-EMPIRE

Ideology and Rural Youth
Mobilization in Japan
and Its Colonies

Sayaka Chatani

CORNELL UNIVERSITY PRESS   ITHACA AND LONDON

Cornell University Press gratefully acknowledges receipt of grants from the Faculty of Arts and Social Sciences and the Department of History, National University of Singapore, which aided in the production of this book.

First published 2018 by Cornell University Press

Printed in the United States of America

Library of Congress Cataloging-in-Publication Data

Names: Chatani, Sayaka, author.
Title: Nation-empire : ideology and rural youth mobilization in Japan and its colonies / Sayaka Chatani.
Description: Ithaca : Cornell University Press, 2018. | Series: Studies of the Weatherhead East Asian Institute, Columbia University | Includes bibliographical references and index.
Identifiers: LCCN 2018011988 (print) | LCCN 2018015970 (ebook) | ISBN 9781501730764 (pdf) | ISBN 9781501730771 (epub/mobi) | ISBN 9781501730757 | ISBN 9781501730757 (cloth: alk. paper)
Subjects: LCSH: Rural youth—Political activity—Japan—History—20th century. | Rural youth—Political activity—Taiwan—History—20th century. | Rural youth—Political activity—Korea (South)—History—20th century. | Young men—Political activity—Japan—History—20th century. | Young men—Political activity—Taiwan—History—20th century. | Young men—Political activity—Korea (South)—History—20th century. | Nationalism—Japan—History—20th century. | Nationalism—Taiwan—History—20th century. | Nationalism—Korea (South)—History—20th century. | Japan—Colonies—History—20th century.
Classification: LCC HQ799.8.J3 (ebook) | LCC HQ799.8.J3 C45 2018 (print) | DDC 305.253/091734—dc23
LC record available at https://lccn.loc.gov/2018011988

For Zeno, Ash, and Colm

MAP 1. The Japanese Empire in the mid-1930s

Contents

Illustrations

Acknowledgments

It sounds like a cliché, but I really had no idea what I would find—or whether I could find anything—before I started my field research for this project. I feel extremely lucky that things came together in the end. During my journey of research, writing, and rewriting, I incurred many debts of gratitude.

First, I would like to thank all of my interviewees and informers. This includes Huang Rongluo, Huang Yuanxing, Xu Chongfa, Chen Meizhu, Chen Jiakang, Wen Qingshui, Jiang Zhaoying, Kim Yŏng-han, Kim Hŭng-nam, Pak Kyŏng-jung, Katō Haruhiko, Yūki Tamiya, Katō Minoru, Taira Eishō, Yamashiro Shigemi, Fukuchi Zenji, and a number of anonymous interviewees. Their stories are the heart of this book.

I relied on the expertise and hospitality of many researchers and institutions across East Asia. In Japan, I was repeatedly helped by Kōichi Okamoto at Waseda University, Tani Teruhiro at the Tsuruga Junior College, Kakeya Shōji at the Japan Youth Center, Teshima Yasunobu and Adachi Hiroaki at Tōhoku University, Kanehira Kenji then at the Miyagi Prefectural Archives, Nakamura Kazuhiko at Ōsaki City Hall, Sasaki Ritsuko and Takeuchi Mitsuhiro at the Furukawa-Shida community center, Nara Hiromi at the Ōgimi village history office, Nakamura Seiji at Meiō University, and staff at the Nago local history office. In Taiwan, I owe thanks to the staff at the Center for Chinese Studies, librarians at the National Library of Taiwan at Yong'an, Shu-ming Chung at the Academia Sinica, Huang Zhuoquan at the National Central University, and Lien Juichih at the National Chiao Tung University. In Korea, Do-Hyun Han at the Academy of Korean Studies; Jong-Soon Kim of Naju City Hall; and librarians and archivists at the National Library of Korea, the National Archives of Korea, the Yonsei University Library, and the Seoul National University Library helped me greatly.

A number of scholars shared information and their sources with me. I thank Itagaki Ryūta, Miyazaki Seiko, Christopher Nelson, Brandon Palmer, David Ambaras, Matthew Augustine, Neil Waters, and Miyagi Harumi for their generosity. I am also grateful to a large number of fellow East Asia historians who inspired me and offered me help in various ways during my research and writing years—my apologies for not listing their names, as that would take a whole chapter. My cohort in the Max Weber Postdoctoral Programme at the European University Institute and colleagues in the Department of History of the National University of Singapore also gave me warm support during the time of revising the manuscript.

In practical terms, my field research required a little more money than that of an average first-book project. I am grateful for receiving generous funding from the Canon Foundation in Europe Research Fellowship; the Center for Chinese Studies in Taiwan; the Harry Frank Guggenheim Foundation; the Japanese American Association-Honjo in New York; the Konosuke Matsushita Memorial Foundation; the Shincho Foundation; the Social Science Research Council; and Howard and Natalie Shawn; as well as the Department of East Asian Languages and Cultures, the Department of History, the Weatherhead East Asian Institute, and the Graduate School of Arts and Sciences at Columbia University. I also thank the NUS Faculty of Arts and Social Sciences and Department of History for providing a generous book subvention grant.

I had never realized how precious friends, mentors, and advisers of my graduate school years would become, until recently. Carol Gluck, Charles Armstrong, Susan Pedersen, and Kim Brandt guided me through the ups and downs of my graduate work. The assistance of Noguchi Sachie at Starr Library was essential. Konrad M. Lawson, Arunabh Ghosh, Sujung Kim, Alyssa Park, Tim Yang, Christopher Craig, Colin Jaundrill, Reto Hofmann, and many other friends from those years continue to be my best sources of wisdom and support. Christopher, in particular, helped me multiple times on materials on Miyagi. I am blessed to have the inspiring mom-scholar allies, Yumi Kim, Chelsea Szendi Schieder, Liza Lawrence, and Gal Gvili, whose presence has been indispensable to my mental health and professional pursuits. Similar thanks go to friends in Singapore. I would especially like to thank Akiko Ishii, Masuda Hajimu, Naoko Shimazu, and Taomo Zhou.

I owe the team at Cornell University Press for helping me through the process of editing and publishing. I am also grateful to Nanju Kwon, Anlin Yang, and Kumiko Reichert for their assistance on the transliteration and romanization of Korean, Chinese, and Japanese titles and sources, respectively. Their professional work made this book much more readable. An earlier version of parts of chapters 1 and 2 came out as a chapter "Youth and Rural Modernity in Japan, 1900s–1920s" in *Transnational Histories of Youth in the Twentieth Century*, ed. Richard Jobs and David Pomfret (Palgrave Macmillan, 2015) and a version of chapter 6 was published as "Between 'Rural Youth' and Empire: Social and Emotional Dynamics of Youth Mobilization in the Countryside of Colonial Taiwan under Japan's Total War" in *The American Historical Review* 122, no. 2 (April 2017): 371–398. I thank Springer and Oxford University Press for the permissions to reproduce them.

I am permanently indebted to my family. I thank my parents in Japan for their never-failing support. I thank Abby and Umi for their loving care for my family. Colm, Zeno, and Ash are the single most important element that makes me appreciate and savor my life at the end of each day. I thank Zeno for being proud of his mama's working on "all about long long time ago things!!" and Ash for her frequent visits and happy giggles at my desk every day. I dedicate this book to them.

Note on Transliteration and Translation

I used the Revised Hepburn for Japanese terms, names, and titles, the McCune-Reischauer for Korean, and the Hanyu pinyin for Chinese. Exceptions were made whenever I found that the individuals preferred using different spellings for their names. In those cases, I attached the romanization in the McCune-Reischauer or the Hanyu pinyin in the notes. I followed the standard order of Asian names (the surname followed by the given name) except for the names of scholars who publish mainly in Western languages. For example, Katō is the surname and Einojō is the given name in Katō Einojō.

I used widely accepted English place-names, including Tokyo, Seoul, and Taipei. To be historically accurate, Seoul was called Keijō and Taipei was Taihoku during the colonial period. I consistently used "Seoul" and "Taipei" in citations as well. Likewise, I used today's place-names mainly instead of colonial-era names. In today's Taiwan, however, Wade-Giles is more commonly used.

	Pinyin	**Wade-Giles**	**Japanese**
新竹	Xinzhu	Hsinchu	Shinchiku
國民黨	Guomindang (GMD)	Kuomintang (KMT)	

I used the same English terms for administrative units in Japan, Taiwan, and Korea. The administrative system changed over time, but to avoid confusion, I consistently used the terms below:

Japan: 県 [*ken*] prefecture
 –市 [*shi*] city
 –郡 [*gun*] county
　–町 [*chō*] town
　–村 [*son*] village
　　–部落/大字/小字 [*buraku, ōaza, koaza*] hamlet
　　　　　　　(e.g., Miyagi prefecture—Shida county—
　　　　　　　Shida village—Aratanome hamlet)

Taiwan: 州 [*zhou*] province
 –市 [*shi*] city
  –郡 [*jun*] county
   –街 [*jie*] town
    –庄 [*zhuang*] village
     –大字/小字 [*dazi/xiaozi*] hamlet

> (e.g., Xinzhu province—Zhudong county—
> Beipu village—Beipu hamlet)

Korea: 道, 도 [*to/do*] province
 –市, 시 [*si*] city
  –郡, 군 [*kun/gun*] county
   –邑, 읍 [*ŭp*] town
    –面, 면 [*myŏn*] village
     –里,리 [*ri*] hamlet

> (e.g., Sounth Ch'ungch'ŏng province—Nonsan county—
> Kwangsŏk village—Ch'ŏndong hamlet)

I used the term *elementary school* consistently, but the original terms varied as follows:

Japan: 小学校, 國民学校 (1941–1945)
Taiwan: 公学校 (小学校 for Japanese settlers), 國民学校 (1941–1945)
Korea: 普通学校 (小学校 for Japanese settlers), 小学校 (1938–1941), 國民学校 (1941–1945)

NATION-EMPIRE

NATION-EMPIRE AS GLOBAL AND LOCAL HISTORY

On October 7, 1943, a twenty-one-year-old man living in the countryside of colonial Taiwan wrote in his notebook, "I am turning into a passive person working at the institute. I have to become a volunteer soldier next year!"[1] The man's name, in Mandarin Chinese pronunciation, was Xu Chongfa, and his family was of Fujian Chinese descent. Working as an instructor at Xinzhu province's youth training institute, Xu used that notebook primarily to record—in Japanese—his daily activities and his impressions of wartime youth training. In the midst of work-related details, these two sentences abruptly appear. This little, and almost accidental, introspective note provides a glimpse of Xu's worldview. And it puzzles us. What did he see in the idea of volunteering for the Japanese army?

Xu's expressed frustration makes sense, considering how extremely difficult it was to become a volunteer soldier. The Japanese Empire launched the volunteer program in Taiwan in 1942, a year before Xu's diary entry. In its first year, 425,961 young people applied for just one thousand open spots. That number rose to 601,147 in the second year, and then to 759,276 for two thousand available spots in the third year. According to the 1940 census, the total male population in the main age group targeted for this program (seventeen to thirty years old) was 633,325—this means that virtually everyone in the target age group, as well as those outside of it, applied by the end of the war. The majority of applicants, particularly in its initial phase, came from farming families, who constituted 42% of Taiwan's total population, despite the fact that volunteer soldiers were paid far less than porters hired by the military.[2] The highly competitive nature of the

1

program produced the phenomenon of "volunteer fever" across the island and even created a "blood-application culture," so named because many individuals signed applications in their own blood to express their "pure loyalty."[3] Although to a lesser degree, the volunteer fever seen in rural areas of Taiwan was paralleled in colonial Korea, where the same program began in 1938. In the first year, 2,946 Korean men applied for four hundred open spots; by 1943 there were 303,394 applicants for sixty-three hundred slots.[4]

Undoubtedly, these figures in official statistics included many cases of deception and coercion hidden beneath the word *volunteer*. But many testimonies in both Taiwan and Korea give evidence of the widespread desire among youth to become volunteer soldiers. An eager response like Xu's was not uncommon, although he might have been more passionate than most because he considered himself an exemplary Japanized youth. Xu was in charge of training hundreds of other Taiwanese youth to become qualified as volunteer soldiers. His students, in their personal and public writings, expressed firm support for the Japanese war effort and belief in the Japanese moral virtues, seeking to demonstrate their heartfelt loyalty to the Japanese emperor. Today, academics have been attempting to record and analyze the experiences of colonial soldiers in the Imperial Japanese Army.[5] However, when it comes to the volunteer soldiers, we have very little record of the motivations and attitudes of the great majority of candidates who applied but were turned down.

We can raise a variety of questions about the phenomenon of the volunteer fever and postcolonial recollections of it. But the questions central to this book are the most basic of all. How did young men in the colonies become passionate about their colonizer's nationalism? Why did they feel compelled to apply to the volunteer soldier program? In fact, why on earth did *anyone*, whether in the metropole or the colonies, embrace a presumably imposed ideology and express willingness to fight for a cause so irrelevant to their immediate interests?

Half of the story is easily traced. State bureaucrats, politicians, and activists devoted a great amount of time and energy to guiding young generations in that direction. In the Japanese Empire, the *seinendan* (village youth associations) became the main vehicle of top-down youth mobilization. The seinendan began as hamlet social organizations, widely seen in rural Japan, that governed peasants' lives for centuries. Thanks to the prior spread of these groups, the Meiji government (1868–1912) not only found a way to organize and educate young people (roughly age twelve and twenty) but also gained access to even the most remote rural communities. In colonial Taiwan and Korea, Japanese imperialists did not initially find any equivalent of these traditional youth associations, but they copied the seinendan format of youth organization, trying to make it as deeply rooted in rural communities as possible. By the 1930s, across the empire, seinendan groups were expected to serve state and social leaders' goals to transform the young rural masses into ideal Japanese imperial subjects—hardworking, healthy, and productive modern farmers loyal to the state and the emperor. During its military expansion on the Asian continent and then in the Asia-Pacific War from 1937 to 1945, the imperial state relied on these "youthful pillars of the empire," Japanese and non-Japanese, to supply military and industrial manpower. Its obsessive effort to organize native youth was extended to the newly occupied territories in Southeast Asia during the war.[6] To state officials, agrarian youth represented the grassroots forces that would resolve the rural poverty and national predicament, bind Asia together, and shoulder the empire's heavy burdens.

What Japanese officials hoped to achieve in youth mobilization is not the primary focus of this book, however. My foremost goal is to shed light on a less clear dimension of the story, namely the local social dynamics that determined the value and meanings of youth programs from the viewpoints of participants. The operations of the seinendan were heavily conditioned by rural social contexts, resulting in a unique dynamic distinct from that of the urban-based Boy Scouts or competitive middle schools. The seinendan carried the idealized image of "rural youth" (*nōson seinen*), which embodied masculinity, modernity, and moral superiority over urban culture. Such an image of rural youth had great appeal for many average-class young villagers. But within the vast imperial network of the seinendan, young people lived in diverse social and cultural contexts that gave different meanings to the rural youth discourse and their membership in the seinendan. What value did they find in imperial youth programs? How did youth training affect their social relationships? How did it lead to colonial volunteer fever? Ultimately, what did the adoption of Japanese nationalism mean to youth in the Japanese and colonial countryside?

A large portion of this book examines the histories of young men and their changing social surroundings in villages of northern Japan, Okinawa, northern Taiwan, and southern Korea from the late nineteenth century to the mid-twentieth century. I hope that a comparison of local histories will bridge some chasms that bizarrely exist in the studies of Japan and its empire. The most obvious one is a geographical divide. Despite the classic calls to consider the deep link between the metropole and its colonial societies, studies that cut across the Japanese Empire remain rare.[7] The imperial spread of the seinendan not only offers a useful anchor that brings together different parts of the empire; it also underscores the importance of transcending today's national boundaries to flesh out the larger dynamic of empire building. Another gap is a conceptual twin of the geographical divide. Modern nation building, empire building, and totalitarian wartime mobilization have been compartmentalized as different themes. In the Japanese Empire in particular, they were inseparable from one another. The processes and experiences of youth mobilization show the close overlap of these dimensions.

The result of bridging these gaps is a major remixing of historiographies and the uncovering of previously ignored links. The rise of youthful rebelliousness in 1920s Japan has not been juxtaposed with the spread of anticolonial youth groups during cultural rule in Taiwan and Korea. One might never have imagined that how ex-conscripts in Japanese villages wrote their résumés in the late 1920s could have anything to do with how hundreds of thousands of young men in the colonies would apply to the volunteer soldier program later. Even stark differences between these societies, such as in the schooling and literacy rates, are accorded new meanings when we compare their consequences. The new linkages offer some suggestive implications for studies of other colonial empires. But they are especially important in the case of Japanese imperialism, because close linkage was *the* defining characteristic of the Japanese Empire, which had an extremely strong drive to homogenize diverse populations into a category of "Japanese."

Japan's Nation-Empire

This translocal study of youth mobilization takes a new look at Japan's assimilationism. A number of scholars have already analyzed the intellectual genealogy of the assimilationist principles envisioned by Japanese politicians and theorists, along with their policies full of dilemmas, contradictions, and fluctuations.[8] Here, instead of unpacking debates about Japanese assimilationism, situating Japan in the global context will explain why Japanese leaders and colonialists from top to bottom, despite their diverse positions and disagreements, widely shared a drive to homogenize imperial subjects and aspired to form a nation across imperial domains—or what I call a "nation-empire."

For policymakers in Meiji Japan, building a nation and building an empire meant essentially the same thing. They commonly believed that the empire was a powerful version of the nation-state. In his lecture on Japanese colonial policies in 1914, Gotō Shinpei elaborated on the relationship between nationalism and imperialism. Educated in Germany, Gotō had established the colonial administration in Taiwan in 1898 and became the first president of the South Manchuria Railway Company in 1906. He was thus one of the most qualified experts of his time on Japanese colonial policies. Gotō viewed imperialism as something that grows out of nationalism and argued that Japan finally joined the trend of European "national imperialism":[9] "Nationalism, having arisen in the nineteenth century, became truly a major political force. This force provides the strong with a supreme weapon, but it is clear that, for the weak, it is rather a suicidal weapon. The result of competition for survival among European powers is that weak states were forcefully assimilated as nationalism arose. The extreme cases include Ireland, Finland, Poland, Bosnia, and Herzegovina."[10] Arguing that population pressures turned strong nations into colonial empires, Gotō continued, "Japan was unaware of the trend of the nineteenth century in which the transition from the rise of nationalism to national imperialism generated the need for colonial policies." As a result, in his view, Japan was improperly prepared to enter the world of empires.[11]

Gotō was not alone in his view that a modern empire developed from a nation. We can see a similar assumption in the social Darwinist perspective, which spread across the world during the nineteenth century. In Japan, Katō Hiroyuki delivered a theory of "survival of the fittest" as the basic character of world politics and influenced many leaders in Japan and Asia by the 1880s.[12] A Chinese reform activist, Liang Qichao, for example, used a similar conception of national imperialism and the social Darwinist view to explain China's situation under European imperial powers.[13]

Both Gotō's understanding of national imperialism and the social Darwinist worldview reflected two dominant political trends of the late nineteenth century: aggressive imperialism and racial theories. When Meiji Japan was established in 1868, the dismemberment of Africa and the Pacific was violently accelerating. Jennifer Pitts has argued that European imperialists in the nineteenth century, compared with their predecessors, shared a widespread sense of "cultural or civilizational confidence."[14] They had long developed an ideological legitimation for overseas expansion, drawing on the language of liberalism and universalistic morality to claim that they were bringing civilization to non-European "barbaric" peoples. But by the late nineteenth century, the "nation" came to be defined increasingly in terms of racial or ethnic coherence, leading to anticolonial nationalisms and challenging the earlier logic of legitimacy for European imperialism.[15] Meanwhile, in imperial capitals, theories of racial differences came to dominate colonial policymaking as well. Even a presumably "color-blind" assimilationist empire like the French in Algeria increasingly viewed colonial populations in racial terms.[16] In this environment, Japan embarked on modern statehood as a new nation and an empire simultaneously.[17] Not only that, the crosscutting forces of empires and racial and ethnic nations pushed Japan in one particular direction: toward the nationalization of its colonial empire, or "nation-empire" building.[18]

Born out of the late nineteenth-century global context, Japanese assimilationism stood upon its own racial-ethnic assumptions, somewhat different from those of the French Empire. For many Japanese colonial rulers, racial, ethnic, and cultural assimilation (*dōka*) was a sui generis logic of legitimacy.[19] In the French *mission civilisatrice*, the avowed goal of assimilation was the implementation of French republicanism, which the French claimed was universally applicable. In Japanese colonies, racial and ethnic descriptors defined the goal of assimilation; in other words, the goal was to integrate colonial people into the "Yamato race."[20] For this reason, intermarriage, especially between Japanese women and Korean or Taiwanese men, was officially encouraged as a way to expand the Yamato race. The definitions of "Japanese nation" and "Yamato race," the envisioned degrees of assimilation, and the advocated means to achieve it lacked consistency. Nevertheless, Japan's assimilationism presumed the goal of making the colonized *similar* to the colonizer rather than making the colonized *better* in the universal scale of civilization—although the difference between the two disappeared when empires measured the "cultural level" of the colonized.[21]

Most of the Japanese colonial strategists assumed a continuation between the integration of Ezo (Hokkaidō, 1869), Ryūkyū (Okinawa, 1879), and Karafuto (1905) and the acquisition of "outer territories," including Taiwan (1895), Korea (1910), and Nanyō (South Seas or islands in the Southern Pacific) (1919). They envisioned Korea as a colony of agricultural settlements similar to Hokkaidō.[22] Okinawans often heard the phrase "Okinawa is the eldest son, Taiwan the second, and Korea the third."[23] In speeches and essays, the sameness of racial and ethnic origins across these domains was emphasized repeatedly. The first governor-general of Korea, Terauchi Masatake, defined the assimilation policy in the 1910 Proclamation of Annexation: "It is the natural and inevitable course of things that the two peoples [of Korea and Japan] whose countries are in close proximity with each other, whose interests are identical and who are bound together with brotherly feelings, should amalgamate and form one body."[24]

This discourse of sameness increased in importance and became the premise for Pan-Asian unity over time. The *kōminka* policy implemented in Taiwan and Korea between 1937 and 1945, often translated as "imperialization" or "imperial subjectification" policy, sought to achieve racial and ethnic reprogramming, or "Japanization." Aggressive Japanization policies were already familiar to Okinawan people in the Meiji period, to the extent that historians call it Okinawa's *kōminka*.[25] The *kōminka* demanded that Okinawans, Taiwanese, Koreans, and many more imperial subjects in other places speak, eat, walk, think, and die like ideal Japanese subjects.

The aspiration for nation-empire building was also evident in the large ruling apparatus constructed, which resembled that of the nation-state. Among the empires, Japan deployed by far the largest number of colonial bureaucrats per capita. Colonial bureaucrats in Korea numbered 103,225 in 1942 for a population of roughly twenty million and 86,212 in Taiwan for a population of about six million in 1940.[26] By contrast, slightly more than 1,200 British bureaucrats worked in the elite administrative division of the colonial service in Africa, governing for an estimated population of forty-three million. The Indian Civil Service had 1,250 covenanted members for a population of 353 million.[27] In French West Africa, the colonial bureaucracy averaged five hundred French officials for a population of fifteen million in the 1920s. Indochina, with nearly 21.5 million people, had a larger bureaucracy, but it still numbered only five thousand.[28] In addition to government officials, schoolteachers and semi-governmental organizations facilitated intense rule over colonial people. Moral suasion (*kyōka*) groups operated simultaneously in Japan and its colonies to teach emperor-centered nationalism and modern living customs. Youth training programs were considered a part of this dense ruling apparatus.

Japan's deviation from the European norm of colonialism became clear particularly during the interwar years. All empires became increasingly sensitive to their international reputation in the system created under the League of Nations, in which they set standards for ethical colonial rule and monitored one another's practice. In this new international arena, indirect (associationist) colonial rule, a policy propagated by Lord Lugard in his 1922 *The Dual Mandate in British Tropical Africa*, became the norm even for non-British empires. Imperial propagandists depicted indirect rule as more humane, more feasible, more far-sighted, and less costly than assimilationism or segregation.[29] Amid this shift in the global norm, however, the Japanese government paradoxically confirmed its assimilationist stance.[30] The "Wilsonian moment" of 1919—the Korean mass demonstrations for independence and the Taiwanese movement for self-rule—propelled Japan to seek more sophisticated means of assimilation rather than turning to indirect rule.[31] In response to the Korean independence movement, Prime Minister Hara Takashi argued that "the desire of most Koreans is not for independence, but to be treated as equals of the Japanese. I intend to see to it that the Koreans have such equal opportunities in education, industry, and government position, as well as to undertake reform of local government along the same lines it has proceeded in Japan."[32] During the total mobilization for World War II, Japanization became a moral goal that would distinguish Japanese from Western imperialism. The governor-general of Korea, Minami Jirō, argued that the initiation of military service in Korea was another step toward fully uniting Japan and Korea. He declared, "Our country's rule of Korea is fundamentally different from colonial policies of Western powers."[33]

The bottom-up analysis of youth mobilization in this book evaluates how this stubborn orientation toward assimilationism was experienced by ordinary people at the grassroots level. Going beyond the overlay of national discourse, the juxtaposition of village cases shows the continuity and simultaneity, as well as fundamental gaps, between "domestic nationalization" and "colonial assimilation" with great concreteness. The premodern roots of the seinendan appealed to Japanese imperial leaders, who emphasized their departure from the Western model of imperialism. But at the same time, it meant imposing a Japanese method of social engineering onto the alien environments of colonial villages. How seinendan-style youth groups were received and translated in their local contexts gives us a glimpse of the diverse local reactions to Japan's assimilationist drive.

Switching our viewpoint from the empire to mobilized youth also helps us to reexamine our assumptions about the powerful imperial state. The strong drive for nation-empire building and the signs of successful mobilization tend to create the image of a domineering, controlling, and hegemonic state machine. However, the processes of youth mobilization in villages, even in the metropole, were full of unexpected and convoluted results. We will see how clueless and ineffective officials and activists often were in their effort to influence village societies. The real puzzle of Japanese assimilationist rule is thus not why Japanese policymakers pursued that goal contrary to the global norm, but how the Japanese Empire achieved a degree of success in Japanizing young men across its colonies despite its fragile status as a mostly foreign colonizer.

Assimilation as Ideological Mobilization

Japanese assimilationist policies were lopsided in stressing the homogenization of people's behaviors and the fostering of loyalty among imperial subjects. Education was the primary means used. Japanese teachers in the countryside, whether in Japan or its colonies, made every effort to instill national consciousness by teaching children the "correct" Japanese language and preaching to them about the ancient lineage and glory of the emperor. From the viewpoint of students, Japaneseness was measured mostly by their demeanor alone. They were expected to show their blind worship for the emperor, speak accent-free Japanese, and be hardworking, hygienic, thrifty, and obedient. Among colonial populations, Japanization required an acquisition of prescribed Japanese habits so that they would become automatic reactions, not the result of processed thoughts.

Transforming people's behaviors and possibly consciousness was not a politically neutral act, to be sure. Postcolonial scholars of Taiwan and Korea emphasize the enforced subjugation of colonial peoples under policies of assimilation, especially during the Japanization period. Leo T. S. Ching has pointed out that Japanization concealed the inequality between "natural" and "naturalized" Japanese with regard to political and economic rights.[34] Korean historians often use the term *ethnic cleansing* to express the oppression of Korean collectivity.[35] Subjugation and differentiation through Japanization were not limited to the formal colonies. For ethnic minorities and rural women in Japan, nationalization and assimilation meant a construction of the category of barbaric selves, such as "primitive Okinawans," contrasted against the idealized "Japanese." It also meant turning themselves into cheap and productive laborers useful to Japanese labor markets.[36] For young men in villages of marginalized northern Japan, nationalization triggered dual feelings of self-loathing for being backward peasants and self-worth as pillars of Japanese agrarian ideals. On all fronts of assimilation, as Ching argues, the category of "Japanese" was constantly being negotiated.

If we view the issue of Japanese nationalization and assimilation as power politics engaged in the transformation of individuals, we can discern new opportunities for comparison with different kinds of polities beyond colonialism. Most of today's scholars of modern histories view the concept of power not in terms of the means of violence exercised but as a measure of the control exerted over people's hopes and desires. The role of the modern state in power politics in particular has become the center of scholarly investigation. We have adopted a variety of concepts, such as hegemony, discipline, persuasion, and governmentality, to identify the modern state's invisible control over individuals. These concepts have yielded new avenues by which to analyze even the most brutal totalitarian regimes in history. Studies of fascist and communist regimes have shown how the state exercised a pervasive cultural power in addition to violence and terror: Fascist Italy established what Victoria de Grazia has called a "culture of consent" through Opera Nazionale Dopolavoro, the national leisure organization;[37] the Nazis promised happiness and success to the members of the *Volksgemeinschaft* (community of the people);[38] and Stalinism offered a utopian socialist civilization to industrial workers.[39] Historians have also been eagerly locating the agency of individuals in their maneuvers, support, or resistance vis-à-vis the state.

This approach has been attractive to historians of Japan's colonial assimilation as well. Todd A. Henry, who offers a nuanced ethnography of public spaces in colonial Seoul, for example, views Japanese assimilation as "contested experiments of colonial governmentality" and frames his analysis in the binary of "the structures of Japanese rule" and "the multivocal agency of the subjects who filled its cracks."[40] Takashi Fujitani also regards wartime integration policies in Korea as an extension of governmentality.[41] The application of state power theories to Japanese colonial rule, especially Fujitani's juxtaposition of Koreans in the Japanese Empire and Japanese Americans in the United States, has broken the conventional "imperial–colonial" divide and opened up a new possibility for comparisons with various kinds of rule.

This book goes a step further. Instead of assuming the dichotomy between the power of the modern state and the individuals who maneuver within it, I situate both the state and people in ever-changing, intertwined layers of social relationships. Here I join the recent revival of scholarship that asserts the importance of social dynamics in studying totalitarian governance. Since Alf Lüdtke's call for documenting the "everyday history" of ordinary people under Nazi Germany in the 1980s, the field has expanded and revealed the vibrant sphere of people's activities.[42] More recent scholarship has not only sharpened the analytical edge, by investigating people's social identity, bonding, grudges, and aspirations, but has also expanded the geographical scope, reaching Mao's China and Kim Il Sung's North Korea, for example.[43] These studies have shown the heterogeneity of the social sphere and led us to sometimes question the "totalitarian" nature of these regimes. This book will not settle for revealing the wide social appeal of the state ideology or diverse social activities hidden beneath seemingly domineering state control over private lives. It will claim that the transformation of individuals to make them extremely useful to the state, even their internalization of a state ideology, was a product of changing social relationships.

By *internalization of a state ideology*, for lack of a better phrase, I refer to the phenomena in which people became emotionally attached and committed to a set of beliefs and a value system that the state strongly promoted. Other scholars might prefer using different terms, such as *identity conversion*, or even *brainwashing*. But the former of these alternatives presumes the mutually exclusive nature of (ethnic) identities, and the latter neglects the fluidity of people's attitudes. My own expression could be misleading, too, if it gives the impression that people swallowed static ideas imposed from outside. Rather, they actively shaped the ideology by appropriating the ideas to their personal and social contexts.[44] But it was still quite obvious to the subjects of mobilization, especially in the colonies, that a large part of the ideology came from the imperial state. Whatever co-optation ensued, there remained an awareness that by using the rhetoric of the imperial state, the subjects made themselves increasingly available to the state mobilization machine.

The word *internalization* might also invite epistemological critiques. Can we gain access to people's inner thoughts, and if so, how? People's mindsets could be impossibly fragmented. Just as Jan Plamper warns researchers of popular opinion in Stalinism about "the mind-boggling diversity of human thought, utterance, and action," it is impossible to measure the degree of ideological belief in any individual.[45] This is why I look for signs of emotional attachment, instead of searching for people's "true voice." Close attention to social relationships is central in teasing out the formation of emotions surrounding Japanese imperial nationalism in specific local contexts. I hope that a comparative study like this one can rescue us from both the sea of suprahistorical individualistic particularities and the predetermined dichotomy between the state and its subjects and allows us, however incompletely, to uncover the social mechanisms of ideological mobilization.

The Social Mobility Complex

This decentering of the state in our inquiry is not intended to deemphasize the political nature of nationalization and assimilation. But it shifts the locus of politics down to people's eye level. Various kinds of social tensions specific to geographical and economic conditions, gender, and generations emerge as central in this type of investigation.

One critically important social tension arises from the perception of urban dominance widely held by rural residents. As in many other parts of the world, the city-country binary became a dominant trope in Meiji Japan. Louise Young has observed that in contrast to those who cherished the ideological value of the countryside during the Tokugawa era, Meiji leaders firmly believed in urban supremacy. Cities, particularly Tokyo, became the face of modernity, and the countryside was considered "modernity's Other."[46] I argue that as important as visions of urban modernity (and urbanites' rural nostalgia) was the new sense of being backward and being neglected shared by rural residents. After all, the majority of people lived in rural areas—roughly 70% of Japanese and 80% of Taiwanese and Koreans lived in the countryside in the 1930s.[47] They viewed urban modernity and urban culture as their "Other." Such perceptions by rural populations were transnational. It is not a coincidence that in the early twentieth century, precisely when symbols of urban modernity dominated popular media and discourse, agrarianism gained currency as a powerful form of nationalism across the globe.

Despite the pervasiveness of the urban-rural binary, few historians have given much thought to the psychology of rural residents confronting urban-centric development as an element that defined the era.[48] A mere focus on the rural sphere does not necessarily reconstruct that aspect. For example, Richard Smethurst argued in a classic work that the rural seinendan and army reservist groups provided robust support for militarism in prewar Japan. He attributed this fact to the unchanging, feudalistic, and obedient nature of village communities, reinforcing the image of the backward and problematic countryside.[49] The tendency to perpetuate urban hegemony is more blatant in writings on colonialism in general. David Prochaska, in his work on settler colonialism in French Algeria, explicitly stated, "Cities are more important relative to the countryside, and the European urban dwellers are more important than the European *colons* of the Algerian *bled* (countryside)," because "the urban centers of Algeria played a disproportionately important role in the history of the colony. It was here that settler society was first and most fully elaborated, it was here that Algerian nationalism arose and took root. In short, what went on in the cities largely determined what went on in Algeria as a whole. Whoever controlled the urban centers . . . controlled to a large extent what went on in the colony itself."[50] Although not as explicitly expressed, this mindset seems to prevail among many historians of Japanese imperialism. There is a heavy emphasis on colonial capitals in the English-language historiography, and "colonial modernity" often refers to advanced technologies, urban landscape, intellectual discourses, middle-class lifestyles, and mass media, all of which were distant images for the majority of colonial populations.[51]

For sure, colonial capitals were fascinating places. But unless we look beyond the urban centers, we cannot even interpret the position of the capital in colonial society, let alone grasp the larger picture of colonial dynamism. As a historical fact, Prochaska's view of cities as a microcosm of the entire colony was not shared by Japanese colonizers of the 1930s. Colonial agents keenly studied how rural populations lived under Japanese rule. Villages experienced colonialism in many different ways. On the one hand, as many Marxist scholars have emphasized, the exploitation of peasants was systemic.[52] On the other hand, with fewer interactions between the locals and Japanese settlers, the boundary between "us" and "them" revolved less around the colonizer–colonized divide. As we will see, more than their hatred of the colonizer, their antagonism toward urban residents and intellectuals occupied many village youths' minds. In the 1930s, their convoluted feelings of envy, resentment, and rivalry vis-à-vis their urban counterparts became a social glue among seinendan members across the empire. By appropriating the global and imperial discourse of agrarianism, many youth in the countryside attempted to imagine a rural modernity—defined fluidly by the denial, transformation, or imitation of urban modernity. In short, the trope of an urban-rural binary created a specific social dynamic and sentiment among young people in the countryside, one that enormously affected how imperial policies of nationalization and assimilation reached them.

Another social tension worth emphasizing is that between generations. The elevated status of "youth" (Japanese: *seinen*, Mandarin Chinese: *qingnian*, Korean: *ch'ŏngnyŏn*) since the late nineteenth century and during the most of the twentieth in East Asian public discourses coincided with the global emergence of "modern youth" as the main protagonist of modernization and revolutions. Before that global moment, different classes, occupations, locations, and genders had developed their own ways of conceptualizing age progression and organizing age groups. But in most parts of neo-Confucian societies, the idea of youth, expressed in various terms, was locked within the spectrum from childhood to seniority and was rarely highlighted as the most important part of a lifespan or the most noteworthy age group. The hierarchy of generations was highly important in regulating people's everyday lives because it specified the status and roles of individuals in familial, social, and sexual relationships.[53]

"Youth" came to life as an independent category when society underwent massive changes in the late nineteenth century. The use of the Japanese term *seinen* to specifically refer to the new category of "modern youth" is said to have originated in an 1880 translation of the name of the Young Men's Christian Association. Although the term itself had appeared in earlier texts, its use for the YMCA dramatically changed its connotation, soon generating a whole genre of seinen magazines and theories about seinen.[54] This attention to new youth grew rapidly by absorbing various concerns of the time. Youth was primarily viewed as the main driver of modernization by social commentators like Tokutomi Sohō, who encouraged them to develop a national consciousness and acquire Western knowledge. For state officials, "youth" also became a graspable category that gave legibility to the abstract masses. They regarded guiding this impressionable section of the population as key to mass control. People living under national and imperial formations and rapid industrialization were also experiencing an unfamiliar and unexpected social phenomenon: a distinct divide between generations.[55] A decade of difference in birth years now meant a substantial difference in experiences and mindsets. In short, the mixture of hope and anxiety about living under dramatic social changes was reflected in the growing discourse of youth.

The modern concept of youth thus had a universalizing effect across classes and locations but created a new social tension between generations. The imagined universality of youth was a driving force behind various uniformed youth groups in the twentieth century, be it the imperial and colonial Boy Scouts, Mussolini's Opera Nazionale Balilla, the Hitler Youth, or the Soviet Komsomol. Studies of these groups observe that the new generational perceptions were the cause, not the result, of their popularity, although the groups themselves further widened generational divisions.[56] At the same time, as we will see throughout this book, the idea of youth itself was also heavily modified according to the particular social and individual context. The seinen discourse certainly awakened many village youth in the Japanese Empire, but how young people digested it and how it changed their lives varied significantly. Young villagers' engagement in the politics of becoming modern youth was another factor that determined the processes of nationalization and assimilation.

Finally, another major source of social tensions, regrettably not examined thoroughly in this book, was gender. Becoming a modern youth, which specifically had a male connotation, presupposed departure from the previous way of reaching manhood. Because manhood and manliness had been closely intertwined with the hierarchy of age, redefining the statuses of age groups inevitably affected gender formations. In Japanese villages, the premodern hamlet male youth groups already functioned as a place where young men who had come of age (around fifteen *sai*) experienced and developed masculinity.[57] Participation in social duties, group entertainment, and control of the sexuality of female villagers—all activities carried out through the local youth group—elevated the masculine quality of individual men and confirmed overall male domination in village affairs.[58] In establishing the modern seinendan, many became extremely eager to reform the previous customs of the hamlet youth groups, including how their sexuality and masculinity should develop; premarital sex came to be abhorred in public discourse, and the introduction of army conscription in 1873 redefined the source of manliness.[59] Nonetheless, both in practice and as a symbol, the masculinity-producing character of the seinendan was barely changed from before the Meiji period. At the same time, the construction of masculinity was no longer constrained by village boundaries but was influenced by national, imperial, and global elements. Mastering and deploying the rhetoric of Japanese imperial nationalism became a part of the gender-defining process. Similarly, the seinendan formed in the colonial countryside intervened in the processes of gender construction specific to individual localities.

The reason why I have not been able to undertake a more thorough analysis of gender politics surrounding rural youth mobilization is that manliness was defined by too many contradictory factors. Being youthful and disciplined and having experienced military service, being rural rather than being an effeminate urban and intellectual youth, prizing hard work and thrift in contrast to the popular image of *modern girl*, and being knowledgeable, eloquent, quiet, and cosmopolitan all boosted a young man's masculine qualities. Although young men had various kinds of "Other" conceptions against which they asserted masculinity, young rural women rarely became the opposite pole. Men occasionally gave women a space in which to participate in the construction of "rural" and "youth" and to express female views, but men usually did not have to negotiate with women about how masculinity was attached to being either "rural" or "youth." In short, the politics of constructing manliness overlapped too many social battles while engaging too little with the opposite gender. This characteristic of the politics of masculinity prevented me from demarcating its contours. I hope that future studies with other vantage points will present a more critical analysis of rural politics of both masculinity and femininity.[60]

The case study chapters of this book (chapters 2,3, 5–8) focus on how various social tensions, including the ones described above, affected the lives and worldviews of young men in the countryside, and how they shaped the processes of nation-empire building at the grassroots level. I use the term *social mobility complex* to refer to the mechanism in which many social elements came together to push young men into the embrace of Japanese imperial nationalism. I have chosen this name because the core of the mechanism was the perception of upward social mobility. But this mechanism was not derived from a pragmatic calculation of material interests. Rather, the emphasis rests on the *sense* of one's self-transformation from perpetual peasant to success-seeking modern youth. This was usually triggered by the availability of new jobs or opportunities to graduates of youth training institutions that enabled them to continue building up their credentials as "model rural youth." Tangible benefits were important because they changed the psychological state of young farmers. For the same reason, class mattered. The main protagonists of the social mobility complex were young men in the "middling class" in each village society. In the Japanese, Korean, and Taiwanese countrysides, new methods of agricultural production, land reforms, the decline (or consolidation) of traditional landlords, and many other factors gave birth to this new social class especially around the mid-1920s.[61] Those in the middling class cultivated a sufficiently large area of land and secured a relatively stable source of income. They were wealthy enough to send their sons to at least six years of elementary school and often the additional two-year upper-level program. But they were not affluent enough to be able to pursue higher education in cities. In subsequent chapters, I sometimes use the phrase *minimally educated* or *little educated* to describe this group in contrast to those who continued further in their formal education. However, the reader should remember, as the historian Yoshimi Yoshiaki argues, that those who graduated from the upper-level program "had quite a high level of knowledge" and "were probably better at writing than those who go on to university nowadays, and the proportion of graduates was also roughly similar."[62] Sons of middling-class families equipped with high levels of literacy formed the most ambitious group in each village during the interwar years. Not coincidentally, this group of young men provided by far the largest supply of soldiers, exceeding its demographic proportion.[63]

Accompanying the perception of social mobility was the collective identity of "rural youth" that spread across the countryside. This was made possible through the expansive communication sphere in newsletters and other publications that circulated among seinendan members. The shared identity and confidence of rural youth in turn implanted a sense of moral superiority relative to intellectuals, urban youth, and older generations among participants. In the construction of this moral superiority, Japanese agrarian nationalism became the common token. Young men enthusiastically appropriated it in their local contexts and internalized it when they deployed the rhetoric in their writings and speeches.

The emergence of this mechanism was perhaps not clearly noticed even in contemporaries' eyes, yet it rendered a quiet revolution in many young villagers' lives. Far from being obedient and feudalistic as they are often labeled, these supporters of Japanese militarism and agrarian nationalism in the countryside were subversive, career-seeking, and outward-looking modern beings.

The writings of those who thrived in the social mobility complex show that the process was filled with emotions, including joy, a sense of bonding, resentment, grievance, envy, and jealousy. Their emotional attachment to Japanese nationalism—which I view as synonymous with their internalization of the ideology—transpired through their experience of sharing these emotions by using the prose of the state. This might remind historians of emotions of the formation of what Barbara H. Rosenwein calls an "emotional community."[64] Our inquiry does not concern the boundaries of emotional communities or youths' peculiar emotional discourse, however. In this study, the widespread sharing of emotions proves the centrality of social relationships. In youth training institutions, youth were defined as the target of discipline—the opposite of emotional beings. But their iron discipline was a product of their emotions, shared in their local social complexities. In other words, emotions not only indicate young people's strong embrace of the ideology but also underscore the grassroots, haphazard, fluid nature of ideological indoctrination.

Villages and Individuals

This book offers multiple comparisons. One of them is between representation and people's experiences. I analyze the discursive construction of "rural youth" among national leaders in Japan and among colonial intellectuals in Taiwan and Korea in chapters 1 and 4, respectively, in order to provide a contrast with village experiences. How that representation ceased to function in empire-wide programs, including soldiering in the Japanese military, is explored in chapter 9. Throughout, "rural youth" indicates the discursive entity, and "village youth" and "agrarian youth" signify actual people living in the countryside.

Most of the book consists of a comparison of three villages: Shida village, Shida county, in Miyagi prefecture, Japan (chapters 2 and 3); Beipu village, Zhudong county, in Xinzhu province, Taiwan (chapters 5 and 6); and Kwangsŏk village, Nonsan country, in South Ch'ungch'ŏng province, Korea (chapters 7 and 8). These concrete cases demonstrate how discourse interacted with people's real-life desires and emotions. Implied in the village cases is a comparison between "inner territories" (*naichi*), as the main islands of Japan, including Okinawa, Karafuto, and Hokkaido, were called, and "outer territories" (*gaichi*), or the formal colonies. I have placed the word *so-called* before these terms in the part titles because the naichi–gaichi divide is not necessarily useful in understanding the lives of village youth. This was particularly the case in Okinawa, which I explore in the Interlude following chapter 3.

One might wonder how representative of Japan, Taiwan, and Korea these villages are and how comparable they are to one another. I did not aim to find a representative village for each country, although I believe that these villages share characteristics with many other villages. Nor did I seek perfect comparability among the three villages beyond the observation that they were equally small and peripheral in national–imperial politics. The primary goal of comparing villages is to suggest a new way to dissect the empire. These villages exhibit the diversity of experience within present-day national boundaries and even within a single village. Equally important, they show patterns that prevailed across the empire. Unless we recognize microlevel patterns, we will remain puzzled as to how the empire could, despite its coercive character, ideologically mobilize such a huge proportion of young populations across its domains.

Individuals' accounts are useful because they reveal subtle changes in their social positions. I introduce one or two men in each case study. In the Shida chapters, I discuss the case of Katō Einojō (1904–1987). Katō was the eldest son of a landlord, and thus not an example of an average farmer. He kept detailed records of his private youth group, called the Aratanome 4-H Club, as well as documents on village administration and wartime mobilization. Personal accounts of average farmers of the 1920s and 1930s are hard to obtain, but his group journal and local administrative documents provide the voices of some farmers in his vicinity.

In Taiwan, I focused on the stories of Xu Chongfa (1922–) and Huang Yuanxing (1925–). Huang and Xu belonged to the average class of village youth in Xinzhu. After elementary school, both went to a number of youth training programs in the late 1930s and early 1940s. They insisted on speaking Japanese during the interviews, even though I spoke with their families in Mandarin Chinese. In the aftermath of the war, Xu, who (as noted at the beginning of this chapter) had been an instructor at Xinzhu province's youth training institute, brought home a library of personal letters from trainees, instructors' notes, attendance records, newsletters, and photo albums the night before the Guomindang force came to confiscate the facility. Thanks to his collection, I was able to examine an unusually abundant amount of personal details.

In Korea, I was fortunate to locate and interview Kim Yŏng-han (1920–).[65] Kim grew up as the eldest son of a family in Kwangsŏk village, South Ch'ungch'ŏng. After elementary school, he participated in youth programs and obtained jobs in local administration as a model rural youth. He kept a few photos and records of his youth training and, as a local historian, collected a large number of materials from the colonial period. During our interviews, we constantly switched between Korean and Japanese. In comparison with the interviewees in Taiwan, Kim was far more cautious in narrating his involvement in colonial mobilization; he had remained in touch with few friends from this period partly because many left the region during and after the Korean War. At the same time, he emphasized the importance of youth training in the formative years of his life. He sang Japanese military songs in public and wrote down the lyrics without any request from me. He also criticized Korean Marxist historians, saying, "They don't know the real situation of the countryside," thereby illustrating confidence in his firsthand knowledge of village affairs.

Altogether, the stories from these individuals and villages show us how micro-level social tensions and relationships formed the social mobility complex and haphazardly came to support Japan's goal of nation-empire building. Having embraced the national–imperial ideology, however, village youth encountered a major challenge once they joined pan-imperial programs. During their military service in particular, many of colonial youth paradoxically aspired to "become truer Japanese" in order to prove their non-Japanese ethnic pride (chapter 9). The mobilized youth continued to face turbulence after the demise of the Japanese Empire. The individuals' stories again offer a stable anchor in our analysis of the dramatic shifts in the postwar period, as described in the Epilogue.

I am fully aware that, along with their questionable generalizability, the materials I use, particularly oral histories, have a risk of inaccuracy and require consideration of how memories were constructed and narrated. My role as an interviewer—a female Japanese researcher studying (at that time) at an American institution—might have influenced what interviewees said and how they phrased it. I assume that postcolonial situations, especially interviewees' relationships with the new rulers and the growth of Taiwanese and Korean nationalisms, affected their narratives. Despite these issues, the interviewees provided a vivid picture of everyday life in the countryside that we could not hope to gain from archival materials. Being able to see their expressions and hear their voice tone helped me discern more than I could through colonial official reports and newspapers—and besides, printed sources have their own issues of questionable accuracy and reflect the intentions of unidentifiable authors. The personal histories contained herein reveal a wide range of emotions formed in interviewees' immediate social relationships. They give us a clue to the puzzle of why these people aspired to become model rural youth and how the youth mobilization of the Japanese Empire operated with such intensity and scale.

Part 1

THE SO-CALLED INNER TERRITORIES

NATIONAL TRENDS

Among the many semi-governmental institutions that Japanese bureaucrats supervised in the pre–World War II era, the *seinendan* (village youth associations) were among the most impressive successes in terms of their scale. By the 1920s, almost every village had a seinendan, which included virtually all eligible people—young men between their early teens and late twenties who had completed elementary school. Their national network spread like a cobweb, and county-, prefecture-, and nation-level federations regularly organized sport and training events.

For state officials eager to reach the rural masses, the seinendan were both a means and a goal. Unlike uniformed youth groups in other countries, the seinendan were deeply rooted in village communal life. They organized labor sharing during farming seasons, took charge of seasonal festivals and volunteer work, imposed rules and regulations on their members, disseminated news, and gathered spontaneously after a day of farming. Traditionally, the village youth associations were also where young men entered the age of sexual interests and conduct, reaffirmed male dominance in village society, and enjoyed a great degree of autonomy that was tacitly approved of by other villagers. In the twentieth century, the seinendan received more supervision from officials and functioned as the major venue of top-down mobilization of farm youth. The state depended on village seinendan groups to discipline youth, who were often labeled as impressionable and immature, and create ideal Japanese subjects. Through the political and economic upheavals of the 1930s, seinendan members carried the heavy burden of agricultural production increases, unpaid infrastructure maintenance, and military service, and with devotion they lived up to the reputation as the bastion of nationalistic ideology. The influence of the seinendan in rural life was so widely recognized that they even challenged the centrality of academic instruction provided by the school system.

Institutions like the seinendan, locally grounded and nationally controlled at the same time, were indispensable in state officials' pursuit of nation building, not only in Japan but also in colonies such as Karafuto, Taiwan, Nanyō, and Korea. In their minds, the development of the seinendan was analogous to the consolidation of state domination. The government began promoting village youth associations after the Russo-Japanese War in 1904–1905, during which many villages observed youths' substantial day-to-day support for the war. After World War I, the army urged the government to standardize the associations under the name of *seinendan* and established the Seinendan Chūōbu as their overall headquarters. By the late 1910s, the scale of the seinendan reached its height, numbering eighteen thousand groups and 2.9 million members; these figures remained roughly steady until World War II. In 1921, the seinendan constructed the building of the Japan Youth Center (Nippon Seinenkan) in Tokyo with donations created by the labor of seinendan members across the country. Legally a public foundation that collected financial contributions, managed investments, and operated hostel facilities, the Japan Youth Center became the new headquarters of the seinendan, and it has been providing the largest amount of funding for regional and national seinendan activities ever since. In April 1925, the seinendan network was turned into the Greater Japan Seinendan Federation (Dai Nippon Rengō Seinendan), which officially incorporated the seinendan federations in Taiwan and Korea in 1938.[1] It was renamed the Greater Japan Seinendan (Dai Nihon Seinendan) in 1939 and was merged with similar national organizations of younger boys and young women to form the Greater Japan Seishōnendan (Dai Nihon Seishōnendan) in 1941.[2]

Behind the familiar story of state-led mass mobilization were, of course, diverse motivations embraced by everyone involved. Even the government's desire to control village youth was far from monolithic, as different ministries, such as Home, Education, Agriculture, and Army, envisioned their own goals. Intertwined with officials' interests was the enthusiasm of intellectuals and social activists who applied ideas of developmental psychology, imperial youth mobilization, and agrarianism to seinendan training programs. What miraculously unified the diverse voices was the unique and capacious concept of "rural youth" (*nōson seinen*). This term connoted healthy, masculine, and patriotic national "pillars" (*chūken*) and became an essential symbol in everyone's rhetoric. Soon it became a weapon for young farmers themselves. By internalizing the symbolic power attached to rural youth, young men in remote hamlets imagined a new community extending beyond the village and even the nation, and they sometimes challenged established authorities.

The success of the seinendan in becoming a national movement thus owed much to the fluid discourse of rural youth. By embodying the image of model rural youth, the seinendan made it possible for various groups to pursue contradictory sets of interests—creating strong soldiers while deemphasizing the presence of the army, keeping young people in the remote countryside while fostering their desire to connect with the global community of modern youth, and teaching them self-discipline while allowing them to rebel against the establishment. This multidimensionality and flexibility contained in the function of seinendan institutions attracted almost all factions of national leaders, village notables, and young people themselves.

Yamamoto Takinosuke's *Inaka seinen*

Despite the intensive state oversight, the seinendan always maintained an image as grassroots institutions. The main reason for this was their rural and communal character inherited from pre-Meiji hamlet youth groups (often called *wakamonogumi* or *wakarenchū*). But the bottom-up image also was attributable to Yamamoto Takinosuke, a young country dweller who founded the national seinendan movement at the turn of the twentieth century. His career as the "mother of the seinendan" started in 1896, when he was a twenty-four-year-old schoolteacher in Hiroshima. He gave birth to a massive movement by self-publishing a small book, *Inaka seinen* (Rural youth).[3]

Yamamoto's life at the time of writing the book was typical of that of aspiring young men in the countryside. Like many others, he had failed the conscription exam, probably because of poor vision.[4] Poverty forced him to abandon his dream of either continuing on to middle school or going to Tokyo. Instead, he had to settle for working at a village administrative office and elementary school. *Inaka seinen* begins with a lament about the life of youth in the countryside, expressing Yamamoto's growing frustrations after six years of trying to inject life into local youth groups. In his writing, rural youth became a distinct category separate from their urban counterparts: "Although [the youth of the city and the country] are both youth, one kind is embraced warmly and the other is abandoned on the street. The so-called 'rural youth' are the ones who have been abandoned. They are without school name or diploma. . . . Even though they constitute the majority of the youth of the nation, they are neglected and left out of the discussion."[5]

Yamamoto was reacting against what he viewed as a growing focus on students in urban areas. The late 1880s and early 1890s saw the burgeoning of commercial magazines targeting urban youth. The scholar Kimura Naoe argues that *seinen* (youth) became a new category as an alternative to *sōshi*, the mob-like youth who had engaged in violent political demonstrations during the Freedom and Popular Rights movement of the 1880s. The most influential source of the new understanding of seinen was the popular journalist Tokutomi Sohō and his magazine, *Kokumin no tomo* (The nation's friend). This magazine was named after the American publication *The Nation*, which Tokutomi read avidly while attending Dōshisha English School in Kyoto.[6] In 1887, it featured a series of articles titled "The Youth of New Japan and the Politics of New Japan," which Kimura calls "a manifesto for the magazine."[7] In these articles, Tokutomi, only twenty-four years old at the time, envisioned high school and college students as the engine of a new Japanese politics. He claimed that youth had been principal agents in historic events, including the Meiji Restoration, and that their energy should not be misguided as had been the case with the violent *sōshi*.[8] The voice of *Kokumin no tomo* echoed around the country and reached far beyond urban intellectuals. Many young men formed associations in cities and provincial towns, ranging from small groups of ten to fifteen people to large organizations with thousands of members. They produced youth magazines, many of which imitated the design, format, and language of *Kokumin no tomo*.[9]

Yamamoto was one of many inspired by the new discourse on seinen. Less than a decade later, however, when he wrote *Inaka seinen*, the widening gap in status between urban and rural youth made this discourse appear hypocritical. "Most of the so-called youth magazines published in the cities have no argument, use beautiful and well-crafted language, and yet do not convey sincerity or inspiration," Yamamoto complained. "They use the phrase 'for the sake of the youth of the whole nation,' but they consider only their [urban] consumers. . . . No one is really passionate about inspiring the youth in the countryside."[10]

Despite his frustration, Yamamoto still perceived "youth" as an identity of utmost importance that should transcend the urban–rural social divide. He called on the reader neither to detest nor to fear urban youth. The real cleavage was between the young, "progressive reformers by nature," and the old (*rōbutsu*, literally "old things"), who were backward, conservative, corrupt, and indecisive.[11] To fulfill their responsibility together with urban youth, rural youth needed reform and guidance. In his eyes, they lacked a national consciousness and were "wasteful, lazy, weak, sly, obscene, servile, undetermined, reckless, and irresponsible," although he blamed the social circumstances of farm villages for making them that way.[12] Yamamoto proposed reorganizing traditional hamlet youth groups, which had existed for several centuries but which he thought had lost their ability to educate and train young people. Simple but concrete guidelines—rising early, climbing mountains, taking cold baths, wearing only cotton clothes, reading newspapers, and avoiding early marriage—would bring new life to rural youth.

In his conclusion, Yamamoto earnestly encouraged village youth to discipline themselves and develop a region-wide community. "I believe in a great new movement of the nation in which, from the corners of the Kurile Islands to the tip of Taiwan, hundreds and thousands of rural youth groups and millions of strong village youth will unite, communicate with one another, mutually associate, and mutually collaborate."[13] Even though Japan was still fighting battles to conquer the mountains of Taiwan, Yamamoto's book already presented the blueprint of an imperial network of rural youth. Through his writing, the birth of the seinendan movement was embedded in the imagination of Japan's nation-empire.

Agrarian Nationalism

Yamamoto's activism is usually considered the starting point of a nationwide movement to revive old hamlet youth groups and transform them into modern seinendan. But the main reason why the seinendan gained wide support and grew rapidly over the next half-century was that many leaders in Japan's modernizing society viewed developing strong rural youth as crucial. One important group among these leaders was the advocates of agrarian nationalism. Although the origin of anti-urban pastoralism can be traced to earlier eras, rapid modernization and industrialization during the Meiji period raised new concerns about social changes. As a flip side of urban supremacy widely embraced by Meiji leaders, many bureaucrats, urban intellectuals, and landlords developed various strains of agrarianism (*nōhonshugi*). They believed that urban culture and industrial capitalism corroded national spirit, that agriculture was the basis for prosperous and harmonious nation, and that the purity of the nation was preserved in the countryside.[14] One of the most influential agrarians, Yokoi Tokiyoshi, a professor at the Tokyo Agricultural College, emphasized the moral, ethical, and physical strength of farmers. He argued:

> In my opinion the vitality of a country is fostered by its middle-class families; it is particularly well developed among farm families. Such qualities as innocence, sincerity, obedience, vigor, fortitude, trustworthiness, earnestness, and robust health are appropriate for soldiers and for defending the country. Don't farmers excel in these qualities above

all? Although you cannot make a country out of land alone, the country must not become separated from the soil. Therefore the farmers, who have the closest connection with the land, love it the most and thus love the country the most.[15]

Already apparent in this passage from 1897 was the view of farmers as the basis of the nation's military strength. Yokoi even argued that the Way of the Farmer was the heir to Bushidō, the Way of Warrior.[16] Army officials had already identified the simple way of life in the countryside as preferable to urban living styles for preparing healthy and obedient soldiers, and Yokoi's agrarianism corroborated their belief. Not all agrarians agreed with Yokoi, but as the army grew confident in its power to influence domestic and international politics after victories in international wars—in 1895 against Qing China, 1905 against Russia, and 1915 against German troops in China—agrarians and army officials increasingly shared common interests and goals. By the early 1930s, when Japan launched its aggression on the Chinese continent and established Manchukuo in northeast China, agrarianism provided the ideological basis that facilitated Japanese farmers' support for imperial expansion. Katō Kanji, the main proponent of agricultural migration to Manchuria, argued in 1936:

> Nothing is more important than hardening the spirit of Japan, the spirit of Yamato. Accordingly, precisely by taking charge of agriculture as Japanese and devoting themselves to increasing the prosperity of the country, the true farmers living in this faith will for the first time be able to become imperial farmers. For this reason the farmers must for a time spring up, lay aside their sickles, and take up swords. The unity of agriculture and the military is a natural thing. The true farm spirit is the spirit of Yamato.[17]

Other agrarians criticized this alliance between agrarian and militaristic goals. At the same time, however, they also envisioned communalism and collectivism in farm villages—the values emphasized by army leaders—as a powerful antidote to the poisons of urban corruption and moral decay.[18] Yanagita Kunio, the founder of modern Japanese ethnology, though he criticized Yokoi as an extremist, also viewed the countryside as the repository of Japan's native culture. Yanagita, as a bureaucrat in the Ministry of Agriculture and Commerce, was dismayed by the widening gap in material development between urban and rural society. His agrarian romanticism grew stronger as he went on a "pilgrimage" to rural villages and began to write more as a folklorist. Popular Meiji novelists also romanticized rustic life and waxed poetic about the superiority of farming villages over cities. Tokutomi Roka, Miyazaki Koshoshi, and Kunikida Doppo exalted the pure and moral life of rural society in contrast to the emptiness of urban life. "Freedom is found in the mountains and forests," Kunikida wrote in 1897.[19] The folkloric turn and pastoral romanticism in Meiji fiction—both of which were produced mostly by urban intellectuals—contributed to the deepening stream of agrarianism in imperial Japan.

Yamamoto Takinosuke's *Inaka seinen* reflected both an embrace of agrarianism and a critique of pastoral romanticism. For him, the discourse of a morally superior countryside had done little to boost the self-confidence of rural populations. Yamamoto described the mindset of villagers that detested everything "rural":

> The worship of cities among country people has remained unchanged now and in the past. . . . People consider it the greatest shame to be called *inaka mono* (country bumpkins); they have changed the name from *inaka* (countryside) to *chihō* (local) without notice, and they avoid uttering the word *inaka*. . . . When discussing the budget for education of one village I know, some argued that, in determining the qualifications of elementary schoolteachers, since local teachers do not have correct pronunciation, we should abolish [the recruitment of local people] and recruit teachers from Tokyo. Our language in the countryside has been gradually corroded by shallow urban language— no *inaka* language, no *inaka* morals, and in the end they even deny being *inaka*.[20]

Vividly voicing his exasperation, Yamamoto's writing reveals the psychology of many rural residents who internalized the urban–rural binary and self-imposed shame as the backward "Other" of Meiji modernity.

The feeling of being left behind was exacerbated by the extreme poverty of many rural areas. Due to the new tax system, the effects of the monetary economy, and the deflation of the 1880s, tenancy increased from about 27% of arable land in 1868 to 45% in 1908.[21] Famine repeatedly struck Japan's northern regions, where poverty was widespread.[22] Although conditions in Hiroshima, where Yamamoto lived and wrote, were not as severe as those in northern Japan, the nation-wide deflation of the 1880s had already forced many small farmers to sell their land and revert to tenancy.[23] The poverty of farming villages alarmed the government, especially after the Russo-Japanese War drained national resources. In addition to measures taken by the Agriculture and Commerce Ministry, the powerful Home Ministry launched the Local Improvement Movement (1906–1918) and implemented a number of programs to boost agricultural productivity and farmers' morale. Agrarianism, as a means to promote diligence and discipline among farmers, was invoked every time Japan faced a rural crisis throughout the decades before 1945. The village youth associations were considered the perfect carrier of such agrarian ideals.

Youth as the Target of Reform

Another social force that contributed to the spread of the seinendan was the global trend advocating that youth should be exposed to nature. Around the turn of the twentieth century, many industrializing societies witnessed the formation of youth groups. Robert Baden-Powell launched the British Boy Scouts movement in 1908 to respond to the epidemic of "the weak, stunted, over-excited, and too often diseased" children in urban cities.[24] The Boy Scouts spread across the British Empire and beyond (including Tokyo), together with the idea that going back to nature would bring healthy bodies and masculine patriotism to decadent urban youth. A less structured movement, the German Wandervogel, resembled the Boy Scouts in their pursuit of a clearly anti-urban, anti-materialist mission. The rise of these youth groups reflected concerns that were present worldwide: elites' fear of moral decay, sexual promiscuity, and juvenile delinquency among urban students, as well as the boredom felt by middle-class youth themselves. In Japan too, "bad youth" in large cities came to be recognized as a social problem by the second decade of the twentieth century. Behaviors of both slum children and the students at prestigious middle schools were scrutinized by middle-class reformers, becoming the target of "correction."[25]

Globally, youth groups shared a tendency to embrace pastoral romanticism and the assumption that young people have universal traits across regions. One irony for seinendan supporters was in these experts' observations, "youth" usually meant urban youth. Japanese social reformers drew on the world-famous, cutting-edge theorist of the time, G. Stanley Hall, the American founder of the field of child psychology. In 1910, scholars translated into Japanese Hall's 1904 seminal work, which explained stages of children's development by using the recapitulation theories of social Darwinism, moving from savagery to civilization. "Adolescence," a new key term that referred to young people, was considered a dangerous and turbulent period that determined whether children return to their primitive ways or are transformed into civilized people.[26] The theory of adolescence triggered pedagogical discussions about possible interventions by adults and gave academic legitimacy to youth-tutelage organizations. Despite their view of rural youth as the antithesis of urban "bad youth," social reformers in Tokyo, too, categorized seinendan members as "adolescents." After all, they based their idea of adolescence on little empirical analysis of Japanese youth, let alone Japanese village youth.[27] Nonetheless, advocates of the seinendan gained strength from the global "scientific knowledge" that developed in the field of child psychology.

Moral Suasion, Self-Cultivation, and Social Education

Agrarians held various opinions regarding the role of army and state officials in fostering harmonious rural communities. Experts on child development also debated how adults should intervene and prevent the crisis of adolescence. All their lectures to seinendan members, however, delivered the same message: you must work hard, and hard work is sacred. Yanagita Kunio argued retrospectively in 1930 that "what brightened the future of new Japan [in the Meiji period and the Taishō era of 1912–1926] was the development of the seinendan," and that their foremost strength was their work ethic. "They demonstrated robust and pleasant labor for road repairs, tree planting, or rescue operations," Yanagita wrote. "The pleasure of engaging in collective labor with a cheerful mind was a healthy interest and stimulation for the members as well."[28] "Hardworkism" (*kinrōshugi*) characterized seinendan activities and was reinterpreted countless times during cycles of economic and wartime mobilization in the first half of the twentieth century. To ensure that the principle of hardworkism would prevail, state officials and social activists used various campaign terms, such as *kyōka* (moral suasion), *shūyō* (self-cultivation), and *shakai kyōiku* (social education).

Hardworkism became the core principle of the seinendan mainly through the advocacy of the Hōtokukai (Society of Repaying Virtue). The Hōtokukai began in the late nineteenth century in the form of local organizations seeking to implement the teachings of Ninomiya Sontoku (1787–1856), a philosopher and practitioner of agrarian morality. His followers preached honesty, diligence, frugality, communal values, and most importantly, harmony between moral and economic incentives by emphasizing the virtue of labor. Top officials in the Home Ministry established the movement's national body, the Chūō Hōtokukai, in Tokyo in 1905 to merge Ninomiya philosophy and daily life reforms pursued by the government. Hōtokukai branches quickly spread through the nation to such an extent that, by 1911, there was reportedly no local area without one.[29] The Chūō Hōtokukai had deep institutional connections with the seinendan. It established its youth division in 1916, which quickly became an independent body, the Seinendan Chūōbu. This organization functioned as the headquarters for the local seinendan between 1916 and 1922.[30]

The emphasis on discipline preached by local Hōtokukai groups was useful, from state officials' point of view, in promoting governmental kyōka campaigns. Originally a Buddhist and Confucian term, kyōka in Meiji Japan meant ideological education to create diligent and loyal subjects dedicated to the cause of the nation.[31] In the Local Improvement Movement after the Russo-Japanese War, local officials and leaders conducted various moral suasion campaigns in both urban and rural communities.[32] The movement's ideological principles were summarized in the Boshin Imperial Rescript (1908): emperor-centered nationalism, hardworkism, and the spirit of frugality. Through kyōka campaigns, these values became familiar rhetoric in people's everyday lives. The Hōtokukai took charge of designing many kyōka programs and regarded the seinendan as the engine of kyōka in rural villages.

In order to turn young farmers into reliable pillars of Hōtokukai-led kyōka programs, seinendan leaders and schoolteachers conducted *shūyō* (self-cultivation). As an umbrella term for nonacademic youth education, shūyō usually meant reading and listening to tales of "the spirit of sacrifice, beautiful morals of obedience, good customs of simplicity and thrift, and an ethic of discipline and moderation."[33] Through shūyō, seinendan members were supposed to understand the importance of agriculture and develop a passion for improving the conditions of rural villages. Shūyō was also considered a measure to curb mass migration by youth to large cities, a grave concern for officials and agrarian activists alike. "City fever" (*tokainetsu*) was harshly criticized by seinendan advocates because of the way in which urban life changed the body and personality of the migrant: "Those who migrate to cities soon experience a deterioration of their health. . . . Moreover, those who have already acquired the taste for urban life do not return to the village no matter how difficult their lives are, and even if they move back, there is little possibility that they will become good farmers."[34] Thanks to their internalizing of Hōtoku discipline through shūyō, seinendan members were expected to remain in the countryside and undertake kyōka campaigns in the village.

In the 1920s and 1930s, kyōka campaigns and shūyō programs further expanded under the title of social education (*shakai kyōiku*), a term coined by officials in the Ministry of Education in 1920 to promote education among working teenagers.[35] Officials had been recognizing the need for academic guidance outside school ever since the Russo-Japanese War. A survey of the academic achievements of elementary school students in 1905 Tokyo showed how quickly their abilities deteriorated after they graduated from school, leading to their low success rate on the conscription exam.[36] In the 1920s, facing increasing political activism by socialist and communist leaders, widespread tenant disputes, and growing labor movements, the Ministry of Education set up a bureau of social education (1924) to expand the education of working teenagers outside school.

The ministry then launched a program called Kyōka Total Mobilization in 1929 to take a stronger initiative in kyōka campaigns rather than leaving them to activists and semi-private organizations.[37]

The emphasis on social education reflected a conscious effort by state officials to engage with an increasingly complex society. Norisugi Yoshihisa, an education official who founded the social education administration, theorized about society and the purpose of social education in many of his writings. "A critical discovery in modern scholarship, an equivalent of the discovery of a new continent by Columbus, is that of the fact and concept of 'society,'" he argued. He considered it miraculous that social education became part of the ministry's work in 1920, because "until several years [before then], government authorities did not have a good feeling about the word 'society' itself."[38] For him, society was "an organic group consisting of people who share a collective purpose." Thereby merging the concept of society with public and state interests, he defined the goal of social education as helping individuals to attain the qualities to be good members of society, including the spirit of social cooperation, public service, and self-reliance.[39] In effect, social education represented a continuation of previous kyōka and shūyō programs in a more institutionalized fashion, and both of these terms remained central in social education. Norisugi and other education officials continued to regard the seinendan as the main institution of social education. They viewed the deep roots of youth groups in village societies as best suited for the goal of transforming the members and villagers into modern social and national citizens.

The Influence of the Military and Taishō Democracy

The rising importance of the concept of society, as expressed in the term *social education*, reflected state bureaucrats' urgent concern to reformulate the government's relationship with the people. In the 1920s, the public sphere expanded and challenged Japan's old statesmen-dominant polity, particularly in the forms of contentious politics—rivalries between political parties, tenancy and labor disputes, and growing socialist and communist activities—that arose during the period of "Taishō Democracy." Rural problems were at the heart of these tensions. All the major political parties advocated the "revitalization of farming villages" during electoral campaigns, politicizing the anti-urban and anti-capitalist sentiment that was widespread among rural residents. Unable to differentiate their policy goals, parties created a situation of a "competition of enthusiasm" and further propelled the rhetoric of agrarian ideals.[40]

Another aspect of the Taishō Democracy was that intellectuals and liberal activists criticized the developing influence of the military over politics and society. The seinendan played a unique role in this milieu. Born out of Japan's war against Russia, the seinendan were the key institution bridging the army and the rural population. At the same time, however, many village seinendan members saw their groups as a means by which to participate in contentious politics. Because of this apparent dual role of the seinendan—shouldering the army's goals and bringing democratic activism to the grassroots level—historians' evaluations of the function of the seinendan are also divided. Scholars such as Ōe Shinobu and Richard Smethurst regard the spread of the seinendan as an indicator of rising militarism, whereas others, including Kanō Masanao, Ōkado Masakatsu, and Ōgushi Ryūkichi, see it as a sign of growing democracy.[41]

Without a doubt, the army's involvement was indispensable in the development of the seinendan. A top Meiji leader, Yamagata Aritomo, was hoping to promote the socializing effect of military training when he set up the army conscription system in 1873. Yamagata's protégé Tanaka Giichi, who would later serve as both army minister and prime minister, established the Army Reservist Associations (*zaigō gunjinkai*) in 1910, linking former conscripts throughout the country. These leaders viewed the army as "the final national school" that teaches loyalty, discipline, and patriotism among the population.[42] World War I prompted Tanaka, then the chief of the Administration Bureau within the Army Ministry, to strengthen and nationalize the seinendan. Tanaka studied the mobilization of various youth groups while visiting Europe during the Great War, and he was convinced that a firm grip on youth was of critical importance to help the nation avert a major ideological upheaval during wartime. He energetically promoted this view in his writings, including his 1915 book, *Social National Education*: "Youth education is not just an issue of pedagogy, but that of national survival. On this large point, all nations share the same conclusion. Therefore, people in every nation have realized that youth, who shoulder the future of the nation, must be guided with special purpose and caution, not overly emphasizing academic or physical education. It is a trend to believe that this is most needed to develop the nation. At the same time, all nations also share the conclusion that guiding them appropriately strengthens the national defense."[43] Tanaka's experience abroad and his concerns at home facilitated the nationalization of the seinendan.

The strength of German troops in particular left a deep impression on Tanaka and other government leaders despite these troops' eventual defeat in World War I and Japan's confrontation with them in China. Norisugi Yoshihisa was in awe of the degree of mobilization of students and youth in Germany: "In the prewar period, there were 60,346 college students [in Germany], of whom 38,400 went to war, which amounts to 64%. Moreover, most of these students volunteered to join the military." By contrast, in Japan during the wars of 1894 and 1904, "college students who volunteered to fight were extremely few." In Germany, even elementary school students became "soldiers fighting in the farming fields." Norisugi quoted a German slogan, "The ridges of the farming fields are your trench, the potatoes that you plant are your supply, the weeds in the fields are your enemies to defeat, and we are German soldiers who know no fatigue!"[44] Officials such as Tanaka and Norisugi envisioned that the network of seinendan, along with the Army Reservist Associations, would similarly ensure national sentiment and produce healthy soldiers in the countryside.[45] This belief was strengthened in the face of radicalizing leftist activism among urban college students in the 1920s.[46]

The army's active involvement in youth education did not stop with the seinendan and Reservist Associations. Ugaki Kazushige, who succeeded Tanaka Giichi as army minister, established youth training centers (seinen kunrenjo) in 1926. Attached to elementary schools, youth training centers targeted working male youth between the ages of sixteen and twenty. In close collaboration with the village seinendan, they provided eight hundred hours of instruction in academic subjects, vocational training, and military drills. They were considered a part of the expanding emphasis on social education and strongly stressed shūyō. Although enrollment was not mandatory, the army encouraged farm youth to participate by allowing shorter conscription terms for graduates. Touting agrarian nationalism as a core principle, youth training centers, like the seinendan, spread mainly in the countryside. Their goal of "improving youth's qualities as superior national and public subjects" and their methods of agricultural and military training showcased the fusion of agrarianism, military goals, and social education.[47] In the early 1930s, the idea of governmental youth education traveled to colonial Korea with Ugaki. As governor-general in Korea from 1931 to 1936, he launched an agrarian campaign with a strong emphasis on rural youth training, including the establishment of village youth associations and youth training centers.

Under Taishō Democracy, however, the extension of the army's influence over youth education in the name of shūyō alarmed many politicians and seinendan advocates. The 1915 decree on the seinendan, issued after Tanaka Giichi's powerful lobbying, stirred controversy because it limited seinendan membership to those between the ages of twelve and twenty. Even though the decree defined the seinendan strictly as an institution of self-cultivation designed to spread patriotism, to many people the age limit signaled a link to conscription. In the National Diet, a Seiyūkai politician, Hikita Eikichi, harshly criticized the army's intentions: "I cannot help but oppose the attempt to put more than thirty thousand youth associations in Japan under the control of military officers." He argued that the village seinendan often included men up to age forty, or even over fifty, and that therefore the age standardization would destroy these groups.[48]

In the face of such criticism, army leaders tried to tone down their interest in youth education and emphasized the development of physical strength in young citizens instead. Tanaka Giichi himself argued, though not convincingly, that preparatory military training would potentially harm the army (because youth might lose their earnestness by the time they entered the army) and that youth education should focus instead on enjoyable physical exercise and the building of bodily strength.[49] Army officials constantly denied that they were seeking to foster a military ethos in youth training centers. For instance, Nagata Tetsuzan, an army officer who had written a famous report on the prospect of all-out war mobilization in 1920, argued that youth training centers "were not born out of a stupid idea to turn people into incomplete soldiers through incomplete military education" but rather "to prepare youth with robust bodies and mentalities instead of teaching them battle techniques in peacetime, and to send those of best quality to the military camp and educate them according to the needs of the time."[50]

Other advocates of the seinendan also attempted to establish an image of them as disassociated from the army. One successful form of public advertisement in this regard was the construction of the Meiji Shrine (Meiji Jingū) in Tokyo by seinendan members. Tazawa Yoshiharu, a top official in the Home Ministry (later called the "father of the seinendan"), organized this project between 1919 and 1923. A total of 16,443 volunteer youth traveled from seven prefectures, camped outdoors, cooked for themselves, and engaged in strenuous construction labor for ten to fifteen days at a time. The construction was more dangerous and tougher than the volunteers had originally imagined. Many were injured or became sick during their service. Yet in the eyes of Tazawa and top leaders, this project not only provided free construction labor to the government but also "spiritually linked the Meiji Shrine to the seinendan."[51] The Meiji Shrine symbolized the direct and deep connection between the emperor and rural youth, and this symbolism gained increased importance during World War II. Even village youth in the colonies learned about the construction project as a model case of youths' hardworkism, and the shrine became a must-see site during their study trips to Japan.[52] Through this project, as well as sports festivals and other events held at the Meiji Shrine Stadium, the seinendan emphasized their tie to the imperial household—a presumably more acceptable kind of patriotism than militarism among Taishō-era populations. The historian Hirayama Kazuhiko argues that it had the effect of concealing the military's involvement in youth programs under the surface of emperor-centered nationalism.[53]

In addition to these efforts, some policy changes took place in response to public concerns about the military's influence on the seinendan. A 1920 government decree emphasized the "autonomy" of seinendan members and changed the upper age limit to twenty-five. "People-centered and people-based (*minshu minpon*) ideologies—or the so-called ideologies of democracy" triggered this change, Moriya Eifu, another official of the Home Ministry involved in seinendan nationalization, later explained.[54] In fact, this decree marked the beginning of a new phase called the "autonomy movement" in the institutional history of seinendan. Although the army did not loosen its grip on farm youth, the rise of socialist and communist activism gave many young people more political leverage in local and national politics. Some seinendan groups, most famously those in Nagano prefecture, sought greater independence from the bureaucratic national network for young people and local branches, and others attempted to increase youths' responsibility within the given institutional framework.

The Popularity of the Seinendan in the "Success" Paradigm

It is hard to know, and impossible to generalize about, how young people in the countryside viewed the heightening ideological and political interests—agrarian nationalism, moral suasion and self-cultivation, and military needs—that converged in the village seinendan. But we do know that the number of youth groups skyrocketed after 1905. Maeda Ujirō observed the figure increased by about one thousand every year and reached more than seven thousand by 1912.[55] In 1918, the Ministry of Education recorded the total number of seinendan as 18,482, with almost 2.9 million members.[56]

The rapidity and scale of the expansion of seinendan cannot be explained merely by the fact that the army and state officials encouraged the formation of seinendan groups. One catalyst was the widespread excitement about Japan's hard-won victory against Russia in 1905. The nationwide sense of exhilaration motivated young men to pass the conscription exam. Joining local seinendan and attending their study sessions raised the chance of becoming successful conscripts. At the same time, the rapid rise in seinendan groups was also a sign of their continuity with pre-Meiji hamlet youth groups. Although Yamamoto Takinosuke argued that traditional youth groups no longer functioned effectively, they were still an important governing institution in many rural hamlets. In fact, the Meiji government initially banned traditional hamlet youth groups because they appeared too autonomous, taking charge of community policing and fire control and sometimes engaging in violent mob-like political acts. These hamlet-based youth groups did not suddenly disappear; rather, they changed their names and adjusted their activities in accordance with the new policies of the Meiji state (as will be discussed in chapter 2).[57]

On the surface, seinendan groups appeared to share a uniform set of activities and purposes. They typically consisted of elementary school graduates and were headed by schoolteachers. The "Report on Conditions of Youth Groups in Western Prefectures," compiled by the Ministry of Education in 1910, argued that all fifty-six groups cited as models had similar programs: study sessions, monthly meetings, contests involving agricultural goods, physical exercise, and kyōka activities aimed at improving public morals.[58] Other lists of "model seinendan" also showed standard goals: study sessions designed to raise the success rate on the conscription examination and regular meetings intended to build communal spirit.[59]

These national surveys, however, failed to register the popularity of one particular activity promoted by the seinendan: night study groups, or *yagakukai*. Gunma prefecture alone, where the total population was less than one million, had 11,061 night study groups in 1909.[60] A booklet of night study group regulations from Shinjō in Akita prefecture, also produced in 1909 and written with brush and ink, provides a glimpse of its goals and study plan. A new form of the Shinjō seinendan, this night study group unanimously agreed to require mandatory participation by all male residents under age twenty in the village. It had two teachers: one was responsible for teaching classical Chinese texts and composition, and the other taught arithmetic. Twelve organizing members took responsibility for management, and another twenty-one members co-signed the new regulations. The study group functioned almost as a regular school, except that it adjusted its hours to the farmers' schedule. The teachers offered roughly forty-eight hours of classes a month, dividing students into three levels: preparatory, regular first year, and regular second year. The regulations required members to take graduation exams and expelled them if they missed class more than three times in a year. Members had to pay a form of tuition every month, consisting of either a batch of homespun straw rope or six pairs of straw sandals.[61]

None of the standard reasons given in the national surveys to explain youth group activity appeared in Shinjō's night study group regulations—no mention of conscription or public morals—although the age limit matching the conscription age corresponded to the military's need. The Shinjō night study group's goal was phrased in larger terms: to catch up with the trends of the time and be ready for Japan's new exposure to international society. The section outlining its purpose argued, "Now, along with the postwar [i.e., following the Russo-Japanese War] development, the need for learning is even more evident. Despite that, what is this condition in which we still cling to the obsolete system?"[62] Transforming the entire group into a study group was a way to bring modernity to the village. For youth in Shinjō, the goals of improving the conscription rate and abandoning old customs were means to the end of achieving rural modernity. They felt that the key to modernity lay in opportunities to learn. Education defined success in Meiji society, and this fact caused many village youth to migrate to the cities in the first place. Shinjō youth studied classical Chinese texts, which national leaders considered an antiquated body of knowledge. Despite such gaps in their conceptualization of what constituted "modern," the night study group provided a possibility—no matter how slight—of pursuing an alternative path of education for those who lacked the means or time to continue attending school.

The aspiration to succeed remained the main source of energy for many seinendan groups in the 1920s. Youth in the countryside criticized the prevalent "city fever" because the "real road to success" was hard work, not formal schooling. "I would like to say to youth who study by themselves [without going to school]— Never despair, carry out your original goal!"[63] One town's seinendan newsletter in Akita quoted the politician Nagai Ryūtarō, who pointed to the biographies of such well-known figures as Lenin, James MacDonald, and Mussolini as evidence that youth could become powerful leaders by working hard, even if they could not attain a formal higher education.[64] Many young people wrote essays that called for patience and diligence. Titles such as "A Youth's Roar: Life Is Effort" and "Success Comes from Hard Work" appeared in almost every issue of their newsletters.[65]

These essays show that village youth reimagined *risshin shusse* (rising in the world) to accommodate their own paths as modern farmers and villagers. The phrase *risshin shusse* usually described social mobility pursued through education and positions in bureaucracy in the cities. The popularity of the phrase reflected Meiji's "success" paradigm, in which individuals' morality and success were interlinked with the nation's prosperity. But success soon ceased to be monopolized by upper-class men who had access to higher education. In the discourses created in mass magazines, middle-class men and women, through their devotion to shūyō, could also experience success.[66] Likewise, in their writings, seinendan members turned themselves into the truer protagonists of the success paradigm. Now success was no longer an urban affair. Deeply immersed in agrarian ideals, village youth claimed the centrality of the rural sphere in the success of individuals and the nation alike.

Youth Identity and Rural Modernity

In the institutional history of seinendan associations, World War I marked the start of the rapid nationalization of village seinendan groups. Government officials supervised their training methods, ideologies, awards, and communication across the country. The standardization of the seinendan did not necessarily work against youths' personal interests, however. It expanded the sphere of communication among them, thereby providing village youth with the rare opportunity to develop their own discourses.

The forces of standardization that operated during this period are hard to miss. Government funding encouraged many youth groups to adjust their goals to closely match those proclaimed at the national level.[67] The Shūyōdan (Self-Cultivation Group), a rapidly expanding network of educators led by Hasunuma Monzō, offered blueprints of new youth training programs for seinendan activities. The Shūyōdan emphasized youth initiatives and group exercises. In August 1915, for example, it gathered eighty-three village youth for the first "mock self-rule village" training at Lake Habara in Fukushima over eight days. The participants were assigned to small tents representing households, and they governed the households and the village through consensus-building exercises. Shūyōdan educators adopted the use of tents from German Wandervogel activities and torches from the British Boy Scouts, and also taught Shinto-style *misogi* (purification) prayers in the lake water.[68] Tazawa Yoshiharu, one of the founding leaders of the Greater Japan Seinendan Federation, enthusiastically incorporated the training approach of Shūyōdan. Its methods defined seinendan activities, to the extent that Yamamoto Takinosuke argued that the Shūyōdan were the executive leaders of the seinendan.[69]

Although the impact of these forces of standardization on the lives of farm youth varied, one phenomenon stood out. Young people in the villages began writing. Seinendan members all over the country produced an enormous number of newsletters (*seinendanhō*) during the 1920s and 1930s. They took different forms: some were collections of handwritten essays; others were better-formatted works that had obviously been edited by professional publishing companies. Some had a larger number of essays written by youth themselves, compared with others that functioned mainly as a news bulletin board. Today, 1.3 million issues of *seinendanhō* produced in various locations have been archived.[70]

The medium of seinendan newsletters gave rise to a new practice of identity construction, that of "rural youth." This phenomenon was analogous to the proliferation of youth magazines in the 1890s. Kimura Naoe describes the importance of the act of writing in creating the concept of seinen, arguing that for these youth, the act of writing itself—filling the easily accessible media with youthful slogans—rather than the content of the writing, nurtured seinen identity.[71] Similarly, seinendan members used the act of writing and the space available in their newsletters to practice their social identity as rural youth. One commonality in their writings was their view of youth as a distinctive group that had always existed in history. As one newsletter put it, "Now society, which had forgotten about seinen for a long time, has recognized the power of seinen again. Whether it was thanks to the seinen's own power or the force of the time, either way the seinen who have been quietly thinking and quietly disciplining themselves are now expected to take on the grave responsibility of carrying out social reforms."[72] Members also used seinendan newsletters to develop more abstract philosophies. The appearance of essays like "Why Thou Dost Live" and "Hope Is the Life of Youth," which had no reference to practical problems, revealed that, in addition to the act of writing, such acts of philosophizing was becoming another attribute of rural youth.[73]

Gaining knowledge about foreign counterparts also became an important feature of modern rural youth. Leaders and bureaucrats in Tokyo often introduced German and other European youth groups in the national seinendan journal *Teikoku seinen* (Imperial youth), flooding almost every issue with their feelings of admiration for and rivalry with these groups. The hierarchical passage of information from the center to localities was not the only path of foreign influence. Many farm youth spontaneously adopted foreign movements at the grassroots level. Another youth newsletter in Akita, for example, published a letter from Mussolini addressed to Japanese youth. Mussolini praised the Japanese Empire for absorbing Western culture and introduced Italy's own Blackshirt Fascist youth to readers.[74] Young newsletter writers often used expressions from foreign literature, and Goethe and Tolstoy were two of their favorites. "As Goethe says, the fate of Germany rests on the shoulders of German youth. ... The development of our desperate village now rests on our shoulders, the shoulders of youth," wrote a seinendan member.[75] They absorbed the information coming from outside their living space—whether national or international—eagerly.

Adding to these participants' intensifying identity as rural youth was the destruction of the urban capital in the Great Kantō Earthquake of 1923. Witnessing the devastation of metropolitan Tokyo, many writers began to question the value of material wealth and the definition of national strength. One young farmer wrote in his diary that this natural disaster had been destined to happen to punish a sinful urban culture:

> Of late the vainglorious striving of [those] city people had reached extremes that caused poor, simple farmers no end of anxiety. With their elegant clothes and their gold teeth, gold rings and gold watch chains, they flitted from one lavish social affair to another. They would go off on trips to the seashore or the mountains to escape the heat . . . and tour the famous sites. But now all that has vanished as if in a dream, consumed by fire, and suddenly they find themselves reduced to misery.

It seems that Heaven found it necessary to chastise them with a natural disaster in order to protect the nation.[76]

In a surprisingly elaborate manner, this diarist recorded his surging anti-urban sentiment instead of a feeling of national unity in the face of a massive disaster, as if Tokyo had been his ultimate enemy.

The government policy of seinendan standardization, the ruination of urban modernity in the earthquake, and young people's ability to make contact with the outside world gave village youth a new sense of belonging at the national and global levels. Many elements associated with nationalization affected their new consciousness. New military-style uniforms, flags, and seinendan songs created by nationally famous composers embodied the network of modern youth. Although the earlier youth groups struggled to bring modernity to the countryside, by the 1920s, they had turned the definitions of modernity and success from an urban-centered phenomenon conditioned by higher education to a rural-based lifestyle, displaying new assertiveness in their sphere of communication.

The Politics of Age

The rise of rural youth as a new social category in and outside the seinendan encouraged young farmers to engage in various social confrontations in the 1920s. Many participated in tenant disputes, rice riots, and socialist and communist activities, directly challenging the police and national seinendan leaders. In the institutional history of the seinendan, these confrontations are considered parts of the "autonomy movement." Despite the broad scope of their activities, both youth themselves and seinendan bureaucrats viewed the new assertiveness of these farmers in terms of generational conflicts, rather than as rural residents opposing urban dwellers, local branches confronting the central bureaucracy, or leftist ideals challenging capitalist–industrialist state goals.

Most famous in the autonomy movement were the members of the Shimoina county youth group in Nagano prefecture. They argued that their youth group was a voluntary, autonomous group not controlled by bureaucrats or military cliques and that youth, "the engine of social progress and creation of history in any era," shared "the same stance with the general masses." They incorporated the arguments of Ōyama Ikuo and Yamakawa Hitoshi, liberal and socialist thinkers of the 1920s, in asserting that youth education should adopt "scientific research methods" and that youth deserved "freedom to study social issues of all regions, past, present, and future."[77] The Shimoina youth group was greatly influenced by the Liberal Youth League, formed in 1921 to put Yamakawa's socialism into practice in the Shimoina region. With this league's members, the youth group organized demonstrations to demand universal suffrage and oppose the Peace Preservation Law, and it invited Ōyama Ikuo, Fuse Tatsuji, and other high-profile social activists to speak about youth's autonomy.[78] To resist bureaucratic control, the Shimoina youth group refused to join the Greater Japan Seinendan Federation for more than a year after the federation was established in 1925. Shimoina's example inspired some seinendan groups in other regions, particularly those in provincial towns that were already exposed to leftist activism, to resist official control as well.[79]

The issue of age limits again became a central point of contestation in the autonomy movement, but from a different perspective from previously. Now the youth, seeking to block the potential influence of older leaders, insisted that membership be strictly limited to those under age twenty-five. The Shimoina youth group articulated a strict generational principle, stating that "the seinendan have to be for the youth and by the youth" during a discussion on "Methods of Establishing Autonomous Seinendan" at the Second National Seinendan Convention held in 1923. At the 1925 convention, Okano Kenzō, a representative from Kanagawa prefecture, criticized Tazawa Yoshiharu's presence and participation in the discussion: "We would like someone who has children or grandchildren to refrain from making comments. We would like, just among us young people, to discuss things slowly and thoroughly and proceed with the convention spiritedly." His remark was met with applause from the audience. The argument for a maximum age limit was presented at multiple conventions, but the bureaucrats voted it down each time.[80]

The initiative among young people to politicize their age shows how the category of youth had become a force of its own by the 1920s. At the beginning of the twentieth century, education experts and government officials had defined the stage of life between childhood and adulthood—adolescence or youth—as something distinctive. By the time of the autonomy movement in the 1920s, both youth education experts and seinendan bureaucrats had realized that this demarcation of youth and adolescence as a separate and independent category had become a double-edged sword, now providing a weapon for youth themselves. Many young people rejected the prevailing culture of seniority, no longer worshipping the model of "experienced farmers" (rōnō), exemplified by Ninomiya Sontoku, as agrarians and Hōtokukai activists had envisioned.[81] They started to believe that being under twenty-five years old granted them a particular legitimacy and power to challenge the establishment in the spheres of family, village, and state.

By the mid-1920s, the national seinendan movement and the discourse of rural youth had come a long way since Yamamoto Takinosuke's publication three decades before. The neglected and abandoned rural youth of Yamamoto's conception had now attained an unshakable reputation—with ample self-confidence—as the vanguard of rural-centered modernity and the major source of national strength. Many state officials, activists, scholars, and political parties had a stake in the ways in which the seinendan were growing. Operating mostly from the headquarters and working at the national level (with the exception of Shimoina's autonomy movement), however, these facilitators of the national trends had little sense of how village-level seinendan actually affected young people's worldviews and daily lives.

When examining Japan's assimilation policy in its colonies, scholars rarely question how assimilation or nationalization occurred within Japan in the first place. Tracing the path of the national seinendan movement sheds light on a few little-known elements.

Most important, the spread of emperor-centered nationalism, which itself was simultaneously a device and a goal in creating a national consciousness, did not happen simply because it was imposed on people through the Boshin Imperial Rescript, school curricula, and propaganda. Rather, it resulted from intermediary concepts like "rural youth," which not only carried the ideology but directly attracted people and groups with differing visions. The capacious idea of rural youth often mediated conflicting interests but also generated new tensions. One example is the overlap of interests between the army and youth in adhering to the age limit. The army's demand for an age limit on seinendan membership generated a new consciousness about age among young people, eventually triggering the autonomy movement against bureaucratic control. The concept of rural youth remained extremely fluid, being deployed for and against the establishment by various parties.

Another element apparent in the seinendan movement is that ideological education was a continuous process. Such terms as *kyōka* (moral suasion), *shūyō* (self-cultivation), and *shakai kyōiku* (social education) flooded Japanese society throughout the pre-1945 period. The increasing emphasis on these terms, as well as the rapid institutional expansion of the seinendan, mirrored state officials' perceived need to counter the rise of society in the 1910s and 1920s. Exactly at the time when colonial governments were redesigning assimilation policy in Taiwan and Korea through cultural rule, the home government was experimenting with new strategies to assimilate youth in Japanese rural peripheries.

The seinendan movement also confirms the ties between the military and rural societies, but not as Smethurst has explained them. Rather than representing feudalistic traditional communities, the seinendan symbolized a break from them. The attraction of the seinendan for village youth derived from the possibility of achieving rural modernity, for which the presence of the army was essential. Specifically, the military pressured state officials to allocate resources for youth education in the countryside. The military's influence, however, was not limited to institutional support, the type of education given to pre-conscripts, or the modern uniform and discipline that impressed so many people. In a world of aggressive empires, where military capability determined a nation's strength, Japan's series of victories in war created the hegemonic image of a world-class military in the countryside. When army officials called on rural youth to shoulder the burdens of the empire, many village youth responded enthusiastically, imagining their new role as exceeding their village boundaries, reaching toward the empire and the world.

However, these national trends, already full of intertwining interests and unintended consequences, were all merely background items to the young people who actually participated in the village seinendan. Major institutional changes, such as the 1925 establishment of the Greater Japan Seinendan Federation, did not necessarily mean much to them. How the seinendan functioned and what they meant to the lives of youth in the village context will be our focus in the following chapters.

2

FROM MOBILIZATION TO THE
SOCIAL MOBILITY COMPLEX

At the beginning of the twentieth century, Japanese national leaders viewed Japan through multiple lenses. The country was a newly centralized nation-state lagging behind the Western powers, an emerging empire in East Asia, and a potential liberator of nonwhite colonized peoples. Focusing on a small village in northern Japan, Shida in Miyagi prefecture, we see how politics was even more multilayered. Japan's imperial expansion, its state policy to boost rice production, and Miyagi's position as a regional leader among the often marginalized northeastern prefectures (Tōhoku region) generated a mix of hope, pride, self-designation, and feelings of both superiority and inferiority in the minds of local leaders.

The central goal of this chapter is to show how the changing political and economic surroundings affected the lives and psychological states of village youth during the first three decades of the twentieth century. This has to begin by confronting the conventional perspective that flattens Tōhoku regional history in a singular narrative of stagnation. Unlike Japan's western region, where the rural social hierarchy based on landholding largely collapsed by the early 1920s, Tōhoku saw the persistence of landlords' power and the lack of diversification of cash crops. Such a structural profile has created an image according to which the social hierarchy in the Tōhoku countryside resisted change even in the 1920s.[1] On the other hand, it is old news that the countryside experienced modernity in its own way.[2] What we need here is a perspective that sensitively accounts for diverse elements, including the location and industries of the village as well as factors of class, generation, and gender, that created a complicated mosaic of people's experiences.

The age relationship gives us one such angle that reveals significant shifts in village politics. In the mid-Meiji period, the public discourse on youth as agents of modernity reached even the most remote areas of Tōhoku. New youth groups emerged by absorbing the nationwide energy and discourse of modern youth. Yet the term *youth* (*seinen*) obtained specific meanings only through the filter of village dynamics. Naturally, both village society and the connotations of "youth" underwent multiple changes. In their early stages, Meiji's village youth groups served landed leaders in their modernization projects. After World War I, youth gained more leverage against established authorities. In Shida village, a relatively wealthy young man, Katō Einojō, captured this moment of the rise of youth. Katō's initiatives and his private youth group, called the Aratanome 4-H Club, embodied the simultaneously conservative and rebellious characteristics that defined these groups led by relatively privileged youth.

A critical change in the social environments for average farm youth also transpired in parallel to the development of Katō's movement. Many elements came together to generate a mechanism, which I call the "social mobility complex," that greatly altered young men's social prospects and worldview. It started as a side effect of a governmental program—namely, youth training centers (*seinen kurenjo*), built by the army in 1926, produced new employment opportunities. This change in social advancement, in combination with the expansive discursive space of the seinendan network where village youth shared their emotions and aspirations, made village youth view themselves differently—no longer as perpetual farmers but as success-oriented career seekers. This powerful marriage between practical benefits and identity construction was likely an unintended consequence from state officials' point of view. But it massively affected young people's lives and consciousness. By the end of the 1920s, youth could confront older generations and the landlord-centered village system from a very different standpoint previously unavailable to them.

Zooming in on one Tōhoku village helps us see the socioeconomic role of young men that the popular concept of adolescence could not possibly capture. It also demonstrates that what we know as the spread of national consciousness—a central component of the process of nationalization or assimilation—did not mean that one's awareness as a national subject overrode other kinds of consciousness. Rather, it depended heavily on the development of other, more immediate, social identities. The case of rural youth mobilization, in which the awareness of being a proud "rural youth" prevailed among young men, showcases such a social process of creating national beings.

A focused social history also tells us how ideologies operate at the grassroots level. Even in the Japanese countryside, the *content* of the emperor-centered national ideology has less power to explain how and why young people were mobilized than the social *function* of the same ideology. Exposed to teachings on the myths and glory of Emperor Meiji, young men in the countryside naturally exhibited a variety of responses and nonresponses. But nationalism, often interpreted freely, was passionately deployed when they fought social battles—whether the goal was to challenge older generations, overturn urban centrism, or advance their career prospects. This attitude, seemingly a pragmatic use of a state ideology, was nonetheless a product of their psychological and emotional reaction to a rapidly modernizing society. Identifying the emergence of the social mobility complex clarifies how people's pragmatic and emotional incentives were intertwined amid the spread of Japanese agrarian nationalism.

Shida Village, Miyagi, and Tōhoku in Modern Japan

Although remote rural villages evoke an image of old, conservative forces resistant to change, they were as much the products of modern governance as were the cities. Shida village came to life as a community only after modern centralized rule reached the countryside. In the local government system constructed in 1888–1889, the Miyagi prefectural government amalgamated thirteen hamlets between and adjacent to two small rivers, the Shibui River in the north and the Tada River in the south, to create the new administrative village of Shida. This village was at the northeast edge of Shida county, twenty-eight miles (forty-five kilometers) north of the prefectural capital, Sendai. From 1889, the village head, village administrative office, and electoral village assembly governed Shida until it was absorbed into Furukawa city in 1950.[3]

Shida was often labeled a typical "pure farm village." Geographically, it was mostly flat with good access to water and transportation thanks to the Tada River. Its population grew from 505 households and 4,428 residents in 1888 to 1,145 households and 7,710 residents in 1950.[4] More than 80% of the villagers engaged in rice production. As of 1950, rice paddies covered 70% of the total land.[5] The northern half of Miyagi prefecture (called Senhoku) was, and still is, one of the major rice-producing centers in Japan. But even relative to other areas of the prefecture, Shida village's industry and landscape were markedly rice-centered.

The region had been exporting rice to Edo (now Tokyo) even before the beginning of the Meiji period in 1868, but that did not mean that it would become a large production center in the new era. Only after the Meiji state, with the 1873 land tax law, began to collect taxes from uncultivated land did landowners become keen to use every bit of their land.[6] Miyagi-brand rice became synonymous with "coarse and bad rice," the staple food for lower-class urban

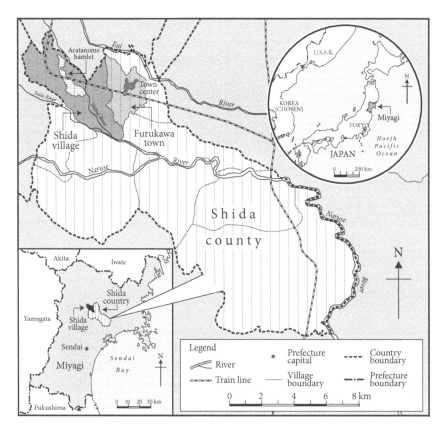

MAP 2. The location of Shida village

populations during the Meiji period.[7] This was partly because natural disasters, particularly cold weather and floods, often affected the harvest.[8] The low quality of rice also resulted from the lack of good drying techniques, which caused the product to deteriorate rapidly in quality during transport.[9] Nitobe Inazō, a prominent agricultural economist, once argued that the northern part of Japan was not suitable for cultivating rice.[10] Yet new agricultural policies demanded that northern prefectures concentrate on rice production from the 1890s onward.[11] The process of overcoming these obstacles to meet the national goal of *fukoku kyōhei* (enrich the country, strengthen the military) appeared to lie at the heart of landlord-tenant relationships, the frictions between villagers and the Miyagi prefectural government, the expansion of (agricultural) education, and the spread of youth training institutions in this area.[12]

Political leaders in the Tōhoku region often harbored feelings of inferiority as the nation marched toward modernization. The establishment of the Meiji state in 1868 and rapid nation and empire building only highlighted the region's misery. Tōhoku was on the wrong side during the Boshin War, a civil war in which new forces seeking to dismantle the Tokugawa shogunate and build an emperor-centered polity defeated their opposition in 1868–1869. Tōhoku (in an alliance called Ōu Reppan Dōmei) fought what would become the national army, led by the "Seinan" (southwest) forces of the Satsuma and Chōshū domains.[13] After this defeat, the domains of the region were dissolved and virtually colonized by the new centralized state. Many among the samurai–bureaucrat class had no choice but to migrate to Hokkaidō as agricultural settlers. Those more fortunate became landholding farmers at home, and Shida and its surrounding villages had a number of these former samurai landholders. "Despite the fact that those who were called 'rebels' in the Seinan War [of 1877] now receive preferential treatment, the 'rebels' in the Tōhoku war have not had their names cleared even today.... Nothing is more telling than this single fact," Sugawara Michiyoshi, a politician from Sendai, lamented as late as 1933.[14] The memory of the Boshin War and Tōhoku's low status in Meiji politics haunted Tōhoku intellectuals for decades.

Even the celebratory year of Japan's victory against Russia, 1905, was a time of devastation for the Tōhoku region, making local intellectuals resentful of the new empire. A series of unusual weather patterns—a warm winter, a cold spring, snowfall in May, followed by harsh summer heat, continuous rain, and early frost in September—battered the region, severely damaging the crops and causing famine. Shida county had exported 46,200 *koku* of rice outside the region in previous years, but in 1905, it produced only 8,790 *koku*, not enough to feed the county's residents even for a few months.[15] Hangai Seiju, an intellectual from Fukushima, the main source of rebels in the Boshin War, expressed his anger at the abandonment of the region in his 1906 book *Tōhoku of the Future*. Hangai contrasted the lack of interest in Tōhoku with the excitement given to the outer territories. "Rather than the exploration of Hokkaidō, the management of Taiwan, or intervention into Korea, the recovery of Tōhoku should be the first priority," he argued. He attributed Tōhoku's misery to Tokyo's inferiority to Osaka, viewing the expansion of the empire as driven by the centuries-old aggressiveness of Osaka merchants.[16]

Resentment regarding the country's southwest-centric development was not the only reaction among Tōhoku leaders. They themselves also embraced many of the backward images attached to them. "Laziness" was the feature most commonly pointed out, even by the future prime minister Hara Takashi, who was initially elected to office from Miyagi.[17] The *Miyagi Educators Journal* often discussed the problematic characteristics of Tōhoku people. One teacher listed twenty-five deficiencies: lacking time consciousness, ignorant of the sacredness of physical labor, lacking a spirit of cooperation, poor in public morals, finding little value in trust, having wasteful customs, incapable of self-rule, and so on.[18] Revealing the attitude of social reformers toward the Tōhoku masses, this list resembled many descriptions by Japanese colonizers of the people of Okinawa, Korea, and Taiwan.

Among Tōhoku populations, Miyagi residents developed a complex dual self-image, positioning themselves at the center and periphery of politics at the same time. Miyagi, of the six prefectures in Tōhoku, did not view itself as solely a marginalized periphery. Its people often expressed great pride in Miyagi as the cultural and historical center of Tōhoku. The Mutsu Sendai domain had been the third largest in the country during the Tokugawa period, and its founder, Date Masamune, was a legendary military hero of the late sixteenth century. In the name of Date, Miyagi residents were proud of the Sendai garrison's reputation as one of the strongest in the army. This recognition of Miyagi as the center of Tōhoku created a perceptual gap between leaders in Miyagi and those in the rest of the region. This mixed reputation and self-image drove Miyagi's social leaders to attempt to break out of their geographical constraints and place themselves in a larger framework of imperial Japan. "Miyagi prefecture should not remain in the position of 'Tōhoku's Miyagi prefecture,'" another author in *Miyagi Educators Journal* argued, continuing, "[It is,] indeed, 'a Miyagi prefecture of the Greater Japanese Empire.'"[19]

The Elementary School Youth Group under Landlord-Led Reforms

The year 1905 was a key moment for farm youth in Miyagi and around the country. The simultaneous occurrence of the Russo-Japanese War and a large-scale famine brought about a notable change in the villages of Tōhoku. The Miyagi prefectural government adoted an act to promote youth groups in 1906, hoping thereby to both strengthen the military and restore rural economies.[20] Inspired by Yamamoto Takinosuke's call for revitalizing rural youth groups, advocates exalted the power of young leadership and the autonomy of youth groups. But in reality, young generations in villages obtained neither leadership nor autonomy. Rather, they were integrated into the landlord-led reforms of labor relationships and rice production.

The Russo-Japanese War triggered a surge of new youth groups in the countryside in the first decade of the twentieth century. Miyagi, too, witnessed an expansion of various youth organizations—groups of elementary school graduates, youth clubs, and night study groups—as the war unfolded. Youth gatherings and night study groups had existed even before the war, but in the prefectural report compiled in 1905, the officials noted that their nature had shifted. War-time youth groups sent off the conscripted soldiers and welcomed the returnees, provided manual labor for the families who had lost men in the military, helped illiterate families to exchange letters with their fathers and sons in the battlefield, and organized collective funerals for the war dead.[21]

These youth groups had already been preparing their members for the conscription exam, but becoming successful conscripts now moved to the forefront of their proclaimed goals. From its 1873 implementation, army conscription had been receiving ambivalent reactions from populations. On the one hand, obtaining an upper grade (*kōshu*) on the thorough conscription exam was a rare honor that the state bestowed on only a handful of applicants in each village. Doctors tested recruits on over a hundred physical disorders. The recruits were also required to take an academic examination, which included reading a given passage and performing arithmetic calculations using an abacus.[22] Even in the late 1930s, when the army was frantically recruiting soldiers, only about 15% of its entire cohort consisted of upper-grade recruits. No family wealth or status altered one's chance of achieving this honor, and the label, once achieved, remained attached to a man for the rest of his life.[23] One's exam performance thus had an enormous impact on one's social identity.

On the other hand, the prospect of serving in the army horrified many. In reality, because the army used a lottery to choose draftees from among those who passed the exam, despite the title of universal conscription only 10% of the age cohort had to serve in the Russo-Japanese War.[24] But precisely because the odds were fairly low, the conscription system created a sense of unfairness among those who had to bear a three-year disruption in their lives.[25] As a consequence, morale posed a problem. During the Russo-Japanese War, many youth in Miyagi evaded conscription; officials reported that eighty-nine young men in Shida county's registry had somehow disappeared.[26] The regional newspaper *Kahoku shinpō* regularly reported "unpatriotic" incidents and "people with sunken spirits" in the military. In the battles, soldiers rebelled against their superiors, generals "shamelessly" surrendered when their subordinates were being killed, and officers committed suicide.[27] The news reports on these incidents concluded that the government needed soldiers of better quality and greater morale. Youth groups were supposed to serve this goal.

But the other urgent need, for devoted farmers who could restore rural economies, was the one that mainly defined the nature of youth groups in Tōhoku villages following the Russo-Japanese War. Immediately after the war, the Home Ministry launched the Local Improvement Movement, on behalf of which village officials and schoolteachers implemented various kyōka (moral suasion) campaigns. Two new youth groups emerged in Shida village in this context. One of them, the "Shida elementary school youth group" was organized by the school's principal, Mikami Hajime. He restructured a previously existing study group of graduates into this new "youth group" designed specifically to nurture "the spirit of hard work and thrift." With Mikami as head of the youth group, schoolteachers as directors, and local notables as accountants, the youth group adopted the moral teachings of the Hōtokukai (Society of Repaying Virtue) and educated fifty-four graduates of the elementary school in that year.[28]

Agriculture and academic studies were two pillars of their activities. The members cultivated forty thousand square meters of rice paddies and ten thousand square meters of vegetable fields to earn their collective profits. After the first year, they deposited fifty yen of profits for future use. The participants also created a pool of money to buy books, paper, ink, and oil lamps for their night classes by selling straw products that they produced together over twenty days of labor. Night classes were offered between October 15 and December 24, when farming was off season. The young men were divided into three levels and studied reading, composition, shūyō (self-cultivation), abacus arithmetic, and agriculture. For those who would soon take the conscription exam, the teachers offered two months of intensive sessions on Japanese, mathematical calculation, and the handbook for new conscripts.[29]

Award ceremonies honoring model youth were important occasions for boosting awareness of the kyōka campaigns. In Shida, Kadowaki Chōshirō became an exemplary awardee in 1907. A twenty-year-old farmer at the time, Kadowaki had lost his parents when he was nine and could not afford to finish even the upper-level years of elementary school. When his grandfather fell ill as a migrant worker in Iwate, Kadowaki traveled to bring him home and take care of him. By "studying hard, farming diligently, and contributing greatly to youth group activities," Kadowaki became a model of the agrarian campaign.[30] The whole Shida elementary school youth group was honored by the Miyagi's governor in 1909 for contributing to the improvement of education and living customs.[31]

It is not a coincidence that the new youth group was formed among graduates of the elementary school. Schools were the core institutions responsible for producing subjects of the nation, especially in remote villages.[32] The physical presence of the Imperial Rescript on Education of 1890, usually enshrined in a designated place at each school, symbolized the direct connection between the school and the national authenticity embodied by the emperor. Village notables exercised significant influence in the elementary school's operations. The village administration, consisting of well-off landed families, built and managed the school as an engine of modernization.[33] Established as an attachment to the elementary school, the youth group also took on the modernization effort advanced by village notables.

The youth group, however, was more than just a mere functionary of kyōka campaigns. One of its important functions was to help local landlords transition from traditional to modern landlordship.[34] The 1870s goal to "enrich the country, strengthen the military" created the need for abundant rice that low-paid laborers could afford.[35] To respond to this national need, landlords enforced agricultural innovation while seeking to reduce their financial burden.[36] Reaching the peak of their power from the 1890s to the early 1900s, landed notables found the youth groups useful in promoting reform and securing free labor. In the name of "financial independence through cooperative cultivation," youth groups recultivated abandoned land and became a collective tenant for the village administrative office.[37] The creation of "common land," a widely observed phenomenon from the 1880s to the 1910s, began with the land reform intended to rescue poverty-stricken tenant farmers by providing jobs.[38] The tenants created new rice fields that became the public property of hamlets. Soon the village administration office centralized the hamlet-owned fields and rented them to tenants through written contracts. The profits created, which were usually deposited in the village credit union, went from there into public investments, such as education and infrastructure. This combination of transactions transferred the responsibilities previously fulfilled by the landlords in a private capacity to the village administration while securing continued dominance for the landlords.[39] The youth groups exhibited a microcosm of this transition. Encouraged to create and cultivate the common land and to deposit the profits in the credit union, they helped to transfer the private conduct of the major landlords to the village administration.[40] In fact, the achievement of youth groups was assessed by the size of land they cultivated and the amount of deposits they made in the initial decade. Shida county's 1912 summary of county affairs showed only the area of land occupied, membership, and deposits of each youth group, saying nothing about their night classes or conscription success rate.[41]

The youth groups also assisted the landlords in introducing new agricultural methods. Landlords formed local agricultural associations (*nōkai*) to promote new technologies, such as new varieties of rice and fertilizer, and to implement land reorganization. *Kame no o* became the most popular breed of rice in Tōhoku, since it grew fast, resisted cold weather, and could tolerate a large amount of fertilizer. But adopting new kinds of rice and changing the familiar methods of cultivation often met with resistance from farmers. For them, trying a new method was a life-or-death gamble. To enforce agricultural reforms, the prefectural government enacted a law to allow police coercion and penalties. The use of coercion at sword point, called "saber agricultural governance," made it unmistakably clear that the agricultural reforms had become a policy goal, leading the Miyagi government to intervene in the previously private negotiations between landlords and tenants.[42] To align with this effort, the Shida elementary school youth group used part of its fields for experimental agriculture to test new seeds and fertilizer.[43] In contrast to raw coercion, the youth group gave a positive and progressive image to the adoption of new agricultural methods.

In short, in the eyes of landlords, the Shida elementary school youth group represented the model tenant farmer. Its members were supposed to acquire the virtue of hard work through collective cultivation of common land and an innovative spirit from new agricultural methods. At the same time, from prefectural officials' point of view, promoting new youth groups was a measure to counterbalance the excessive influence of landlords. In the period following the Russo-Japanese War, local landlords, whose power had ballooned as agents of modernization in the past two decades, began seeing a backlash from tenants and government officials. In the increasing tension pertaining to leadership of agricultural reform, the youth group proved useful for the landlords who attempted to maintain their influence, but also for local government offices that wanted to keep their power in check.[44]

The function played by youth groups in the tension between landlords and local governments, albeit central in village affairs, never surfaced in the discourse on rural youth training. Activists who promoted local youth groups emphasized only the educational effect of disciplining adolescents. Tomeoka Kōsuke, the founder of a famous farming school, argued in the *Miyagi Education Journal* that youth groups were useful in providing continuing education, encouraging time-consciousness, and providing leisure to rural youth, but failed to discuss the youth group's position in local power politics.[45]

Transforming Hamlet Youth Associations

In 1905, the year when the Shida elementary school youth group was established, the village administrative office organized a separate, the "Shida village youth group." In contrast to Mikami's group, which gathered select youth, the village youth group cast a wide net, absorbing the traditional youth associations of the hamlets. Its activities overlapped with those of the other group, as both offered night classes and engaged in common land cultivation.[46] These two groups represented opposite characteristics embodied by village youth: Mikami's elementary school youth group had a more modern face, symbolizing the new administrative village unit, whereas the village youth group preserved continuities from the disestablished but deeply rooted hamlets.

During the Local Improvement Movement, the advocates of youth groups emphasized the novelty of those youth groups that emerged in the era following the Russo-Japanese War. They highlighted that these groups differed from the previous groups, particularly the student groups prevalent in urban areas during the 1890s. These student groups were inspired by Tokutomi Sohō's call for youth to be an engine of the modern nation. They imitated Tokutomi's *The Nation's Friend*, publishing essays, stories, and poems in their journals and holding lectures and public speeches to spread enlightenment thought. In Miyagi, the Fudōdō village youth group and the Hoppo youth group exemplified this trend of the 1890s. Both were open exclusively to elite youth; the former consisted of sons of upper-class families, and the latter required two internal references to join the group.[47] These youth groups in Miyagi demonstrated that Tokutomi's influence had reached Miyagi's remote areas, but also that this movement was strictly confined to wealthy, well-educated youth.

The persistence of the pre-Meiji form of youth associations, too, was a concern to new youth group advocates. Yet these associations were more deeply integrated into the local society and did not simply disappear. Fukutake Tadashi argues that Tōhoku's hamlet organizations evolved around a vertical hierarchy with the hamlet landlord (the "main family," or *honke*) at the top and its branch tenant families beneath it, resembling a kind of clan-based community.[48] These farmers governed themselves through multiple community agreements (*keiyakukō*). The local historian Gotō Ichizō, in his fieldwork on various forms of agreements, argued that they were "the supreme decision-making institution of each hamlet." Their agreements were the iron law of mutual support in every aspect of community life—marriages, funerals, irrigation, harvesting, education, festivals, and so on—and being excluded from them meant ostracism from the community.[49] Age and gender associations in the hamlets were organized to support this *keiyakukō*-based governance.[50] The age ranges and names of these groups varied from hamlet to hamlet. Many male youth associations had the old names of *wakashūgumi* and *kuwasukikō* and included those between fifteen *sai* of age and the mid-thirties, or even the early forties. Initiation into the hamlet youth association was a significant moment in a man's life. It meant that he had become a mature and responsible member of hamlet society, gained access to hamlet property, and was allowed to marry.[51] In some hamlets where only the eldest son from each household joined their traditional youth associations, it also meant that he would eventually represent his household in community agreements.

Meiji officials banned these hamlet youth associations in 1877, calling them obsolete and violent. They were considered inappropriate partly because they preserved old customs, such as premarital sexual conduct and costly funerals, which Meiji social activists sought to reform. It was also because these traditional youth groups were the most powerful physical resource of the hamlet. They took charge of hamlet patrols, rescues, and fire control. Meiji officials believed that their degree of autonomy sometimes went too far, especially when they reportedly engaged in political campaigns, ousted certain officials, and forced villagers to provide them with alcohol and meals. "It is of concern if the [new] youth group holds too much power, because youth associations of the past exercised too much power and there were many examples of their causing problems," Tomeoka argued.[52] In its effort to control the means of violence, the Meiji state could not allow local youth groups to maintain such power and autonomy.

Shida village officials' establishment of a village youth group in 1905 reflected their admission that these traditional hamlet youth associations still existed and played an indispensable role in the village. Even though the new village office appeared to have taken over the administrative function from the previously separate hamlets, the hamlets often maintained their basic purpose as organic units of governance, and community agreements continued to regulate villagers' everyday lives.[53] The hamlet youth associations, even after the ban by the Meiji government, continued their gatherings under new names, such as "agricultural society" or "fire-fighting group."[54] The new village youth group absorbed these hamlet youth groups as its branches. As a result, the age range of village youth group members in Miyagi's 1909 survey was notably broader (fifteen to forty years of age) than what government officials in Tokyo expected (fourteen to twenty).[55] Many retained features of the traditional associations, such as hierarchical age relationships within the youth group or the initiation ceremony. The continuity was also manifested in a rapid expansion of group membership on paper. Within five years of its establishment, the Shida village youth group had 635 members. Takeuchi noted that, because of the heavy dependence on traditional hamlet youth associations, "activities of the new [village-level] youth groups lacked originality and inevitably became inactive."[56]

Despite these observations, the emergence of village-level youth groups signified important changes in rural societies. One of them was a further step toward a male-dominant social system. Military conscription had already raised the value of young male bodies, and the effort by the Meiji state to establish new codes of law also institutionalized patriarchy.[57] The village youth group was part of this trend that enhanced the position of men. Unlike the hamlet age groups, which tightly organized both male and female residents, the activities of new youth groups targeted primarily males.[58]

The village youth group also mirrored the transformation of the familial-labor relationship in the hamlet community. For centuries, the main landlord family (honke) did not just rent out rice fields to nearby farmers, but also formed the core of an organic community, blurring the distinction between family and non–family members.[59] A number of young tenants in Tōhoku started their farming life as apprentices of the honke, and their coming-of-age and future land holdings were determined through their relationship with the honke.[60] Especially in Tōhoku, where the practice of agricultural wage labor did not spread as in the western region, the sentimental tie between the honke and its subordinate farmers remained strong in the Meiji period. During landlord-led reforms, the dominance of the honke institution continued. But the new labor relations based on written contracts ended the traditional life cycle of many tenants, and the new youth groups replaced apprenticeship during the transitional period. In other words, while the village office represented the new landlord class and regulated tenant farmers through written contracts, youth education also ceased to center around the familial-labor relationship and became a public enterprise under the supervision of the village administration and the elementary school.

The Influence of World War I

The nature of village-level youth groups shifted again when the political and military role of male youth entered another phase. During the 1910s and 1920s, the younger generation around the country joined in political rallies and demonstrations in line with various ideologies. In the meantime, Japan participated in World War I as an ally of Britain and fought German troops in China. As the Japanese military witnessed the new scale of mass mobilization in Europe during the war, its eagerness to intervene into people's everyday lives expanded greatly.

Step by step, village youth groups were institutionalized. Receiving orders from government ministries in 1905, 1915, and 1918, local governments standardized youth groups and created networks. In 1910, the new Shida elementary school principal unified the previous two groups.[61] The new Shida village youth group was officially named Shida Village Seinendan in 1916.[62] The establishment of the network continued from the village level to the county and prefectural levels. In May 1911, Shida county held a youth association convention for the first time. More than two thousand young men from one town and nine villages of the county gathered in Furukawa town middle school. The county head, Iwabuchi Toshio, gave an opening speech and read the 1890 Imperial Rescript on Education. It was announced that the main purpose of the federation was to "promote unification and communication between all seinendan in the county" through common projects, awards, lectures, sports events, and various learning and discipline-enhancing activities. The army's direct involvement was clear by its presence at the ceremony. An attending army officer gave an hour-long talk, titled "On Military Education," and discussed the "physique, mentality, [and] obedience" that were "demanded in the youth groups from the military's point of view." After talks by the officials, three seinendan members gave five-minute speeches. One of them, Sugawara Rikizō, a fourteen-year-old farmer from Shida village, talked about the Boshin Imperial Rescript of 1908, which preached emperor-centered nationalism and the spirit of hard work. The officials gave him a special prize because "his speaking attitude, intonation, and pronunciation were impressively clear and fluent, and the way in which he moved the audience of more than two thousand people proved his superb performance."[63]

Another sign of the army's influence was the renewed attention to physical exercises and sports events. In November 1916, the Miyagi Prefecture Seinendan was launched; its network extended across 222 village and town youth groups and involved more than thirty-five thousand members. The prefecture-level seinendan's main activity was large-scale sports events. Its inauguration on November 12 accompanied a sports festival, in which five thousand youth who had won their local competitions participated.[64] Sports events held by elementary schools and youth groups had been the most popular entertainment in rural villages since the early Meiji years. These prefecture- and county-level competitions inspired both young participants and spectators and enhanced the popularity of the seinendan.[65]

FIGURE 2.1. The Inauguration of Miyagi Prefecture Seinendan Federation

Miyagi kyōiku (December, 1916): preface. Photo reproduced courtesy of the University of Tōhoku Library.

Military conscription also gained a new spotlight. After the war, national leaders increased the pressure on the seinendan to produce healthy soldiers. At conscription exam sites, the examinees who had a sexually transmitted disease, astigmatic eyes, or poor general health were viewed as disgraces to their village. If they could not read a passage from a school textbook, the examiner faulted their seinendan group by asking the examinees, "Did you go to night classes?" and "Which teacher was in charge?"[66]

Even among well-off landlords, military experience became a new source of prestige. Many landlords enhanced their social status by gaining experiences as military officers, as well as by their commitment to agricultural reform. In Shida village, Kadowaki Yoshio embodied both pathways. He was born into a wealthy family in 1872, joined the military in 1894, and was promoted to private first class in the military police. He fought in Taiwan, seizing aborigine-owned land, and traveled extensively during the Russo-Japanese War. On his return, Kadowaki established the army reservist group in Shida village in 1910 and took charge of veteran affairs for the next thirty years. He became Shida village representative of the agricultural association in 1906, served as the village head from 1912 to 1917, and was one of the strongest forces promoting agricultural reforms during the Local Improvement Movement.[67] Kadowaki represented the modernity in many ways in the villagers' eyes: he had received higher education, visited foreign places, been decorated as a military officer, and promoted new agricultural techniques. As a local notable, Kadowaki preached the agrarian ethos to young farmers.[68] Village leaders of the new generation depended on the dual emblems of military background and agricultural innovation rather than the mere fact of being landholders.

The Rise of Rural Youth in the 1920s: Katō Einojō

After the Russo-Japanese War, the seinendan institutions had experienced multiple rounds of mobilization by the army and other state ministries. The established importance of the agrarian–military ethos appears to have regulated the lives of seinendan members—or so village leaders, army officers, and state officials intended. But in the 1920s, the increasing attention to rural youth education, as seen in chapter 1, paradoxically created an autonomous sphere of activities for village youth. Many young men found empowerment in their improving status in village affairs. For them, youth group activities provided a window onto national and global spaces beyond their hamlets and villages.

Sons of relatively wealthy families could use their new leverage as rural youth more readily than average farm youth could do. Katō Einojō in Aratanome hamlet, Shida village, is a good example. Born in 1904, Katō was the first son of the second-largest landlord family in the village; his family held more than forty hectares in 1928.[69] In 1926, he formed a youth group with over a dozen neighborhood youth between the ages of fifteen and twenty-six, including several family employees and women. Katō always wanted to study in Tokyo and "fly into the larger world," according to his son. However, because Katō's father, Katō Hisanosuke, expected him to take over as head of the family, he was not allowed to pursue a college education in Tokyo as his two younger brothers did. Instead, he was sent to an agricultural school in Sendai after graduating from the upper level of the local elementary school.

Katō Hisanosuke was a leader in agricultural innovation and an admired local notable, but Katō Einojō did not find attractive the chance to follow in his footsteps. Instead, he ran away from home and enrolled in the Tokyo School of Foreign Languages, living with his sister, who was married to an aircraft engineer. After a few years, Katō Hisanosuke came to Tokyo and forced Einojō to go back to Miyagi. Katō Einojō remained bitter about his father's actions throughout his life. Back in Shida, his only outlet for his youthful rebelliousness was to establish a new youth group. At the same time, his knowledge of art, literature, foreign affairs, and agriculture intrigued his peers in Aratanome. So did his knowledge of how to use Western cutlery and play golf. Besides his exuberant charisma, he provided a free space for the neighborhood youth to hang out. His parents resided separately in nearby Nakaniida hamlet, where they started a new rice threshing and shipping company. The Katō family's original house in Aratanome, with its spacious garden, became a perfect place for the neighborhood youth to gather and play various sports.[70]

One fascinating aspect of Katō's youth group was its name, the Aratanome 4-H Club. When Katō discussed with his friends what to call their gatherings, he remembered that his teacher at the upper-level elementary school, Takahashi Gunji, had once mentioned the 4-H club in the United States, which emphasized youth training through rural life. Takahashi was a young intellectual who had just graduated from normal school. Katō deliberately avoided using the common nomenclature, *seinenkai* or *seinendan*. To him, the initiative of youth themselves, not any affiliation with the government, represented the group's core characteristic. He also felt alienated from the official purpose of seinendan training because his short stature had prevented him from passing the conscription exam. The name "4-H Club" expressed his connection to the outside world and his liberation from the rules of a landlord family and hamlet. It also symbolized the cultural leadership of a nonmilitary figure with agrarian ideals. The members held more than sixty evening gatherings during the first fourteen months of operation. Katō gave lectures on scientific developments, international affairs, architecture in Tokyo, Japanese economic policies, and social issues. He assigned two members to give a speech at every gathering. For many members, this was their first experience of speaking in front of an audience. After sharing their knowledge with each other and practicing public speeches, they played cards and listened to music on Katō's gramophone, a rare possession in the countryside.

After five years of these activities, Katō wanted to start a new group project, publishing a journal. He picked the title *Omoto* (Rhodea) an evergreen plant that represented eternal youth. At one gathering, Katō suggested that the members write essays together and watched them struggling with paper and pen. "I feel sorry hearing them sighing deeply in front of the distributed paper," he wrote in his own essay on that occasion, "but it is 'spare the rod and spoil the child.' Opportunities do not come twice. Without struggle, we do not become men with humanity."[71] Group members wrote poems and essays about their work, families, gardens, and daily lives. One member who spelled his name as Naoji in Roman characters wrote about the 4-H Club: "Writing an essay is not easy . . . The leader said, 'try writing anything that comes to your mind as it is' . . . what on earth should I write about? . . . Since the inauguration of the club, the knowledge of the members has improved a lot. We take turns giving speeches, and now we have reached the point of writing essays for a journal. It feels delightful, as if we had become big scholars or something."[72]

Katō Einojō's lack of interest in the Shida village seinendan did not imply that the 4-H Club was antagonistic to the hamlet and village order. In *Omoto*, Katō expressed strong agrarian ideals and respect for those who performed military service, much as the seinendan did. One of the group's first activities was to save money through collective labor, such as selling eggs. The government had been campaigning to promote savings around the country, and Katō believed that labor and savings projects would allow youth to learn self-discipline as well as helping the national economy. The organization of the 4-H Club followed the standard format of the seinendan, despite the club's more voluntary nature. The members agreed on formal regulations and rules, elected executive members with limited tenure, and held three kinds of meetings (regular, convened, and executive). They also worked closely with the patrol group of Aratanome hamlet. The patrol group consisted of the heads of households in Aratanome, who traditionally supervised the pre-Meiji youth group and hamlet affairs in general.[73] Katō's leadership position replicated the teacher's role in the village seinendan. Although the 4-H Club was no doubt an enjoyable and collegial experience for its members, their relationship with Katō was undeniably hierarchical. As such, the 4-H Club in Aratanome was a new phenomenon that occurred outside the official purview, but it combined many features of the old hamlet youth group and the new seinendan.

The Aratanome 4-H Club exemplifies how youth from relatively well-off families incorporated the global and national discourse of rural youth and attempted to create their own groups. In its social context, it mirrored the changing position of landlord classes as well. After the series of famines during the Meiji era, agricultural production steadily increased during the 1920s and expanded the fortunes of the middling farmers, who cultivated between one and five hectares of rice paddies either as landowning farmers or as relatively well-off tenants. Unlike during the Meiji era, agricultural advancement now relied less on the initiative of landlords, and more on public research centers and government investment in larger-scale irrigation and land reforms. The agricultural association, originally the league of landlords, turned into an institution that promoted new agricultural techniques to support these middling farmers. It was not a coincidence that Katō Hisanosuke, witnessing the changing status of his family, felt compelled to start a new business. Furthermore, starting in the mid-1920s, tenant farmers organized large-scale disputes all over the country to secure their tenancy rights. Many of them won permanent cultivation rights, which dramatically limited the landlords' power, increased their tax responsibility, and virtually ended their tight control over village affairs.[74] In the late 1920s, observing the collapse of the organic hamlet communities that evolved around the landholding main family, the village office emphasized the old slogan of "united village" (*zenson itchi*) in an attempt to alleviate class confrontation in the village.[75]

Katō Einojō had a stake in this changing environment. Still holding a grudge against the older landlord system that had forced him to abandon his dreams of living in the city, he might have felt that he was a participant in the new rural dynamism. The strong emphasis on youthfulness in the 4-H Club provided him with a new community to replace the old landlord-tenant hierarchy that had previously dominated hamlet affairs. Perhaps he felt proud of creating new ties with villagers while his father had a harder time maintaining the old ones. Yet, at the same time, Katō Einojō's leadership in the 4-H Club relied on urban experiences that were available only to the sons of landlord families. Regardless of Katō's intentions, the club helped the village administration to mitigate confrontation between different classes and secure the overall status of the landlord class.

The Aratanome 4-H Club's detachment from class confrontation stands out in light of the involvement of many village youth in tenant disputes in the 1920s. Since these conflicts often affected entire village or hamlet populations, many seinendan groups and their members had no choice but to participate. In Toyosato village in Miyagi, for example, the seinendan leader played an active part in bringing the tenants' demands to the village assembly in 1927.[76] In some cases, youth undertook radical leftist activism. For example, Inomata Yūjirō, once famous as a model farmer in Miyagi and winner of a youth speech contest in the early 1910s, turned to socialist activities in the 1920s. Inspired by activists' calls for a peasant uprising, he started a tenant union in his home village. He was arrested and tortured repeatedly during the police crackdown on Communist Party members in 1928.[77] The Shida area was relatively slow in joining these movements, but by 1930, even Shida village had two major disputes, with more to follow in subsequent years.[78] Before the tenant disputes spread, the surrounding region was already a site of contentious politics. Various political parties rallied in adjacent Furukawa town in the 1920s.[79] Furukawa was home to the nationally famous liberal thinker, Yoshino Sakuzō. The same town elected Akamatsu Katsumaro, a Socialist Party leader, to the House of Representatives in 1928.[80] It is hard to imagine that Katō Einojō accidentally could have been unaware of these lively political movements in neighboring Furukawa. He seemed to have deliberately maintained his youth group as a circle of neighborhood young people and avoided getting involved in class struggles of any kind.

Because of the intense confrontation between the government and leftist activists, political polarization appeared to define youth activism in the 1920s and early 1930s.[81] In historians' eyes, the youth groups of the two opposing camps were fighting proxy battles over access to the masses. More noteworthy, however, was the variety of motivations and the strong presence of localized agendas on both sides. Economic and labor relationships were only some of the factors that drove youth to leftist politics. Generational conflicts, anti-urbanism, family tensions, and other divisions in hamlet society motivated their decision to join a youth group of one or another political leaning.[82] As a result, political leaders were sometimes surprised to see former model youth participating in tenant disputes, while, conversely, many rebellious youth ended up in conservative positions. The unpredictable nature of youth had already alarmed the officials during the rice riots of 1918, which were sparked by the skyrocketing price of rice. Top government officials like Tanaka Giichi and Tazawa Yoshiharu expected the seinendan and army reservist groups to help the government maintain social order during the chaos. Yet more than 10% of about eight thousand arrestees turned out to be seinendan members.[83] As we shift our focus from national politics to the social dynamics of young participants, it becomes clear that the apparent political polarization was merely one of many manifestations of an expansive space of freedom that was opening up for village youth. Katō Einojō was rebelling against his own environment too, except that his rebellion took the form of deploying his modern knowledge to create a strong generational community, rather than engaging in political demonstrations.

The Social Mobility Complex

For average farm youth who did not have family wealth or status like Katō, it was the emergence of the social mobility complex, which was triggered by the expansion of youth training institutions in 1926, that altered their social opportunities and allowed them to challenge the established authorities.

Youth training centers (*seinen kunrenjo*), which spread in 1926 and became youth schools (*seinen gakkō*) in 1935, were not the first schools that took charge of training working youth. Since the beginning of the Local Improvement Movement, educators in the countryside had made determined efforts to establish a supplementary vocational school in every elementary school. In Miyagi, 210 vocational schools had been built by 1926.[84] In Shida, the village head, Kadowaki Yoshio, decided to set one up in 1915.[85] At these schools, elementary schoolteachers continued to give a few hours of instruction every week to their graduates, helping them to maintain their academic level and improve their agricultural skills. By the early 1920s, the village had an upper-level elementary program, the supplementary vocational (agricultural) school, and the youth groups to supervise farm youth.[86]

Although the wide array of youth programs had already existed, the army and its minister, Ugaki Kazushige, advocated establishing youth training centers. Because supplementary vocational schools educated only youth under age sixteen, the army sought to strengthen contacts with all youth under the conscription age of twenty through this new institution. To facilitate participation, tuition was free and graduates could shorten their military service requirement from two years to eighteen months. Through youth training centers and their emphasis on shūyō and agrarian education, the army attempted to improve the quality of conscripts while satisfying the public demand for demilitarization that was spreading in the 1920s.[87] Miyagi prefecture quickly established 244 centers in July and August 1926, including one in Shida village.[88]

How did the new youth program affect the life of young villagers in the context of the 1920s? The biggest difference was *not* in the content of education; the combination of military and agrarian ideals was not a novelty, and the new program would not suddenly make it more attractive than previously. More significant was the new means of supplying the education. Hundreds of village youth found employment as temporary instructors in the newly established youth training centers. Supplementary vocational schools already had a chronic problem in finding appropriate teachers. Because of financial constraints, elementary schoolteachers were responsible for vocational classes, but those who had attended normal schools had very little experience in agriculture. "Looking at the reality of agricultural education at the elementary school, [teachers] just

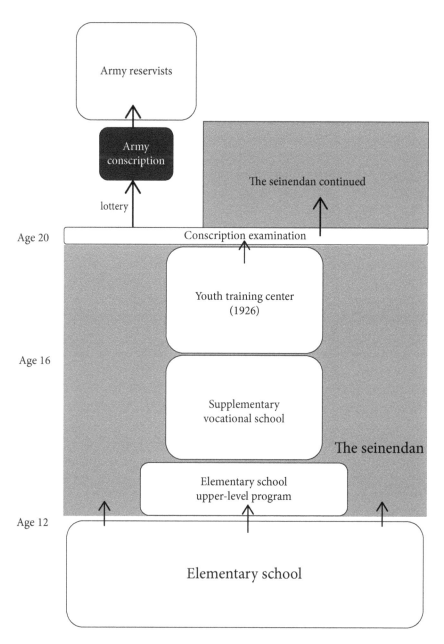

FIGURE 2.2. Rural youth training institutional setup in Miyagi in the late 1920s

After elementary school, most male graduates in the countryside enrolled in the village seinendan. The students in these post-elementary programs thus overlapped with those in the seinendan. The conscription examination was a requirement for all male citizens of twenty years of age, but until the late 1930s, those who actually served the army were a minority, with an acceptance rate of one out of five at best.

follow pages of the agricultural textbook as if it was a reading class, let fifty to sixty students cultivate only one hundred square meters of practice farms in their wooden sandals, . . . or make them clean the campus or water system to kill time," an advocate of vocational education in Miyagi complained in 1925.[89] In the new centers, teachers had to give military-style physical training as well. Moreover, students at youth training centers (and at youth schools, built after 1935) were working-age farmers who were not easy for regular schoolteachers to teach.[90] To solve the problem of finding teachers, villages hired people who had experienced both farming and military service as part-time instructors. Each youth training center usually had about three or four of these instructors in addition to five or six regular schoolteachers. This means that, in Miyagi, more than 750 army reservist members were training younger generations at a time. The centers also switched instructors every few years. Outside Miyagi, the ratio of reservist instructors was 10% higher, creating even more jobs.[91] In national statistics, more than 40% of youth school instructors lacked formal qualification as teachers.[92]

A few elements of this recruitment made "rural youth" into a new career path. More important than the number of job slots created, the requirement to prepare a résumé gave farm youth the first opportunity to apply a narrative of career development to their own lives. The newly hired instructors filed their résumés at the schools, and the schools reported all of them to the prefecture. Thousands of these youth, who would otherwise have remained nameless even in local histories, suddenly appeared as individuals with self-narrated career records in Miyagi's prefectural archives. Their résumés were simple. They were born around the time of the Russo-Japanese War and graduated from the upper level of elementary school. Some attended supplementary vocational school for another year or two. Most continued on directly into family farming and all had passed the conscription exam and served in the military. Some described in detail advances and awards they received during their military service. Within a few years, schools started hiring them. Despite the relative simplicity of these résumés, through compiling them, farm youth began to find meaning in these experiences and to view themselves as career-seeking professionals.

Another element that made a difference in youth's lives was financial reward. Their promised salaries varied between twenty and sixty yen for fifty to one hundred hours of physical training instruction a year.[93] The resulting hourly rate was equivalent to that of full-time substitute male teachers in Miyagi's elementary schools.[94] Although the payment was often delayed, this salary was significantly higher than the payments received for government-provided relief in rural villages of the depression.[95] Accompanying the monetary compensation was social recognition as school instructors. Schoolteachers were often the only intellectuals known to farm youth. To become full-time teachers, they needed a degree from competitive programs in either a middle school or a normal school.[96] With the expansion of youth training centers, farm youth without teacher training were recruited and suddenly gained an opportunity to be called *sensei*.

In effect, the establishment of youth training centers—a typical discipline-building institution from the state's viewpoint—empowered average farm youth in a way totally unexpected by army officials. Fulfilling the dreams of army leaders, it helped to consolidate the route from the seinendan to the youth training center, army conscription, and the reservist group as a ladder of continuous development, but this became meaningful to farm youth only if they had a possibility of reaching the next step. The prospect of developing a career through this route broke open a major crack in the confinement of rural social immobility for average- to-lower-class farm youth. Even though new holes had been appearing in the glass ceiling of rural communities since the late nineteenth century, most seinendan members were still stuck beneath it unless they had either family wealth, some major achievement during their military service, or access to higher education (including local agricultural schools, which became increasingly available to sons of above-the-median farm families in the 1920s). Becoming a cog in army-led institutions was a very different kind of self-empowerment from that sought by Katō Einojō (the son of a landlord) or the "autonomy of youth" envisioned by leftist activists. But they developed an equally powerful sense of self-worth as rural youth and expressed it in the discursive space of seinendan newsletters, which circulated at the village, county, prefectural, and national levels. In these forums, they celebrated the superiority of rural youth and, with greater conviction, reinterpreted *risshin shusse* (rising in the world) in terms of rural-based careers.

I view this mechanism by which farm youth transformed themselves from perpetual farmers into success-seeking modern rural youth and developed a common identity with their peers as a defining component of the social mobility complex. The term *rural youth* no longer meant a sector of the population or an idealized image of national subjects, but instead, became a type of career field that one could pursue. After teaching experience in the youth training center, many young people continued up the career ladder, becoming full-time teachers in elementary schools, technical advisers in agricultural research centers, and seinendan leaders. In addition to holding formal job positions, they could advance their quality as rural youth by participating in short-term training events, lectures, and workshops. Similar to certificates from formal schools, training as model rural youth was widely appreciated, and these youth's records and reputations were readily transferable between localities and jobs.[97]

This alignment of career consciousness, social identity, and shared confidence connected village youth to state ideologies of anticommunism and nationalism and would eventually produce an ideological stronghold for state and military goals. But instead of repeating the prose of the state, young villagers created their own versions of nationalism by combining agrarian, anti-urban, and anti-intellectual elements. Satō Kesao, a seinendan member in Edano village, Igu county (southern Miyagi), was convinced that "today, the city-centered material civilization has already declined, and the time has come for the revival of rural-centered spiritual culture." In his view, leftist activists were urban products. "Have any of the left-leaning thinkers so detested these days come from hardworking rural villages? If there is [one], he is just instigated [by others]. In any period, such thoughts are generated from a corner of the materially and spiritually impoverished city."[98] Mori Shigeshi, another member of the Edano Seinendan, demanded in a handwritten essay a pension for farmers equivalent to that for retired government officials: "Our empire is an agricultural nation as we all learned in elementary school. . . . It is a contradiction in logic and ignorance of humanity that farmers, the foundation of nation building, . . . are left without any pension."[99] Their claims advanced state-sanctioned agrarianism even further and viewed urban-centrism as the fundamental problem. These seinendan members did not shy away from pointing out that the state itself was sustaining that problem.

Through the lens of the social mobility complex, we can observe how local contexts determined the ways in which state programs affected young people's lives. Now that advances in the military could facilitate rural youth careers back home, military service (and not just the conscription exam) gained important new value. Those who were eager to establish their careers volunteered for the navy instead of waiting for army conscription. Many served in the military with greater willingness or enthusiasm, not necessarily because they dreamed of serving the nation or the military, but because a record of military service offered better longer-term life prospects.[100] The village seinendan were also accorded new meanings, as they became young people's gateway to social mobility. State officials continued to attribute youthful enthusiasm for the seinendan to successful discipline and indoctrination, without observing how specific aspects of youth institutions interacted with social dynamics. In fact, officials were desperate to control these youth, as illustrated by the excessive institutional structure in the countryside: by the 1930s, the seinendan, a supplementary vocational school, a youth training center (later a youth school), and an army reservist group existed in each village to supervise only a few hundred young people. These institutions were managed by the same small group of village leaders and teachers, and, in the reality of participants' everyday lives, their activities and regulations were indistinguishable. Even after elementary school education became widespread, and the language of emperor-centered nationalism became hegemonic in public discourse, the state was still compelled to incessantly test the loyalty and national quality of young villagers through the 1920s and 1930s. In the end, an unintended result of establishing career paths for rural youth, not the tightening of the reign, brought a critical change to young people's mindsets and their relationships with state programs.

The example of seinendan development in the Tōhoku countryside reveals a considerable discrepancy between the understanding of leaders in Tokyo about how village youth were being assimilated into the national culture and actual experiences at the grassroots level. The overall success of instilling agrarian and militaristic nationalism in village youth made it appear that plans and programs were functioning as intended. Perhaps national leaders like Tazawa Yoshiharu and Ugaki Kazushige believed that, through the seinendan or youth training centers, they were establishing a direct tie between young men in the countryside and the emperor or the army that transcended hamlet, village, and regional social relationships. But as we have seen in the Shida village case, village youth groups were always conditioned and characterized by the local dynamics of the villages. In the first decade of the twentieth century, the new village youth groups facilitated a transition from traditional to modern landlord-tenant relationships. This process reminds us that despite the discursive tendency to view rural youth as the target of education, or "adolescents" in the language of developmental psychology, village youth actually had a larger socioeconomic presence. In the post–World War I era, the rural youth discourse culminated in the national scene, which was appropriated and aggressively deployed by Katō Einojō as he challenged the previous hegemony of the landlord family represented by his father. It is, however, the emergence of the social mobility complex that brought about a quiet social revolution to the majority of village youth. Drawn by new employment opportunities, they applied a new narrative of career development to their farming lives, consolidated their belief in the central role of rural youth in local and national economy, and shared their identity of being rural youth through the seinendan's print outlets.

This process was, indeed, one of nationalization, as it transformed young people formerly restricted to hamlet-based roles into modern rural youth who transcended multiple local boundaries. Farm youth came to enthusiastically exchange agrarian values and nationalistic expressions. But the mechanism that generated their expressions was more complex and locally grounded than sheer ideological preaching. Here again, the idea of rural youth, which mediated conflicting interests but also generated new tensions among national leaders, spread deep and wide at the grassroots level, playing a part in the transformation of young people themselves.

The local story also suggests an empire-wide simultaneity in some respect. While the colonial governments in Taiwan and Korea were alarmed by the expansion of the public sphere in the 1920s, local and national officials in the metropole were also facing increasingly unruly social movements. Across the empire, officials deployed different means to control populations, balancing tactics of opportunity, discipline, and oppression. In Japan, village youth became the immediate target of control but, at the same time, obtained new social leverage against established powers. Eventually, the social mobility complex produced an ideological support base for state officials fighting socialism and communism. This alignment of the interests of village youth and the goals of state officials was a result of the convoluted interactions among many layers of social relationships, along with associated psychological reactions and counteractions. The detailed causes and effects involved in such a social mechanism can only be imagined at best by fleshing out their local contexts and individual circumstances.

Before we leave this chapter, a brief look at young women's experience is warranted. The social mobility complex was decisively male-dominated in character, but young women were not totally left out in the rise of rural youth, although they experienced it on a smaller scale. Some villages established study groups for female elementary school graduates also around 1905.[101] After World War I, activists and teachers believed that young women should obtain shūyō and the spirit of hard work so that they would become hardworking wives and healthy mothers.[102] In 1917, a national network of young women's groups, called *shojokai* (maidens' groups) was established, and they were transformed into the Greater Japan Young Women's Seinendan Federation (Dai Nihon Rengō Joshi Seinendan) in 1927.[103] The founder of the *shojokai* network, Amano Fujio, argued that the shojokai were the mother of the seinendan, and "if 'young men' (seinen) are the element of national energy, 'young women' (*shojo*) are the source of that energy."[104] In the 1920s, many young women participated in the discursive space of rural youth through seinendan newsletters. Like their male counterparts, young women were hired by supplementary vocational schools and youth schools where female students obtained skills in sericulture, household accounting, sewing, cooking, and other home sciences. Their views and experiences deserve a separate narrative from male-centered ones. But it could be easily imagined that because schooling was less common among female farmers, forms of education that occurred outside the realm of formal schooling had a more significant impact on women in their pursuit of a rural modernity.

3

TOTALITARIAN JAPANIZATION

The emergence of the social mobility complex for young men in 1920s Miyagi was not isolated from Japan's imperial affairs. Time and again, the imperial expansion exacerbated the feelings of marginalization experienced by Tōhoku people, which fanned village youth's burning desire for rural modernity and achievement. Over the course of the 1930s, as Japan entered the era of large-scale mass mobilization, the empire and young people's lives in the countryside became more immediately linked. Not only were more Japanese youth sent to imperial frontiers as soldiers and agricultural colonizers, but the intensive mobilization across the empire also caused the experiences of youth in various localities to converge further. We see more similarity and simultaneity in nation-empire building across wider regions in this period.

It is hard to miss the linkage between global and imperial contexts and the courses taken by the seinendan in Miyagi. The international debate over colonial associationism and assimilationism, for example, was paralleled by a domestic debate about localization and nationalization in youth training. In both debates, the dual goals of emphasizing local culture and spreading national–imperial identity created considerable tension. Over the course of the 1930s, Japan's home and colonial governments simultaneously strengthened assimilationist stance. Once the Second Sino-Japanese War started in 1937, the empire-wide seinendan and other youth programs underwent rapid institutional amalgamation to reflect accelerating nation-empire building. The local seinendan received the most intense supervision from the national–imperial headquarters, and participation by all eligible youth became mandatory at youth schools in the Japanese countryside. Across the empire, whether people called it *kōminka* or wartime mobilization, the state engaged in totalitarian Japanization, frantically endeavoring to shape the thoughts, behavior, and demeanor of village youth.

The degree of ordinary people's compliance and participation is a point of debate in studies of different types of totalitarian regimes.[1] Japan's wartime regime exhibited several common characteristics of totalitarian rule: the state's effort to merge the public and private spheres, forceful imposition of state ideology, oppression of individual opinions, and punishments for even minor dissenters. As in European cases, Japan also enjoyed wide public support for the state's war effort, at least at its initial stage. The empire's expansion was exciting, even for many Tōhoku residents who had previously loathed it.[2] Their everyday lives were colored by news and imaginings of faraway imperial frontiers. Seinendan members—as future soldiers, agricultural pioneers, and peers of Hitler Youth—were the core protagonists of rural-centered imperialism. The phrase *model rural youth* increasingly evoked admiration and prestige in village society. In a way, their reputation mirrored the trust placed in the totalitarian imperial state by wide swaths of the population.

Switching the perspective from structure and discourse to village social environments, however, reveals that the concept of compliance does not grasp people's lived experiences. Given the multidimensional social battles, the resistance–collaboration paradigm, in which compliance and participation tend to be situated in the ambivalent middle, explains so little of people's actions. Nor does the focus on individual agency or freedom capture the issues at stake for village youth. The largest part of village youth's mental struggle seems to have been a battle to establish their self-worth. Amid the chorus of propaganda, their identities were shaped through local, national, generational, or gender tensions. Take Katō Einojō's passionate involvement in wartime mobilization. Because of the political capital he had developed through his Aratanome 4-H Club and his previous use of the images of youth and farmers as symbols of rebellion, Katō viewed the increasing responsibility placed on him during wartime not as a sudden invasion by state power but as a step forward in his ongoing pursuit of social leadership. For younger men, however, the totalitarian environment and their inevitable deployment for battles and in industrial labor in the 1940s complicated their sense of self-worth: they were heroes and dispensable at the same time. Even if they managed to remain in their villages, youth schools no longer presented viable career routes. The space of expression had been diminished. The social dynamics of villages were again undergoing a significant change, removing young men from the driver's seat of social mobility. In short, although the discursive emphasis on rural youth continued until the end of the war, the social mobility complex for young men had already collapsed years earlier.

The presence of such social battles reveals at least two things. First, even when the state seemed to eliminate any private or social sphere and directly controlled individuals, social contexts still produced tangible feelings of joy, pride, resentment, and desperation that affected their attitudes toward state mobilization. Second, constantly changing social dynamics created lingering effects on different generations. Katō's personal synchronization with rural youth discourse in the 1920s led to his home-front enthusiasm a decade later. By the same logic, the demise of the social mobility complex for young men in the early 1940s presaged an eventual collapse of the popular basis for the regime sooner or later. The spiral of shrinking popular support from the pillars of state mobilization and expanding coercive control signaled the beginning of the end for such a regime.

Rural Youth in the Great Depression

Beginning in the 1910s, the discourse of rural youth flourished across the empire. In the 1930s, it reached another peak. People in Tōhoku felt particularly strong sentiments regarding the category of rural youth during this decade, a period when they experienced the dual hardships of economic difficulty and wartime mobilization.

Japan had already been in an economic crisis before the global depression hit in 1929. Rice prices fell in most years of the 1920s, and many banks and businesses collapsed in 1927. The Great Depression delivered another blow to the market, causing the value of agricultural products to plummet by almost half between 1929 and 1931. During the 1920s, a large number of people had moved from rural Japan to urban centers, widening the gap in social environments between cities and countryside.[3] But in the 1930s, unemployment forced many urban migrants to return to their home villages, in turn creating the problem of excess population in the countryside.[4] Frustration born of rural poverty led to an upsurge in tenant disputes. Rural problems were so widespread that after a coup attempt by young military officers on May 15, 1932, one of the arrested officers made a famous statement, attributing his participation to a desire "to help the families of the soldiers from Tōhoku."[5]

Tōhoku, indeed, embodied the nation's economic struggles in a particularly gruesome way. In 1932 and 1934, the region was hit by unusually cold weather, which caused two devastatingly poor harvests. The scale of devastation wreaked by these famines was reported widely as a national tragedy. Photos of starving infants and exhausted mothers and stories of thousands of schoolchildren developing impaired vision because of malnutrition appeared in regional and national newspapers on a daily basis for months.[6] In Aomori prefecture alone, more than twenty-four hundred girls were reportedly sold into the sex industry or factories by their families in 1933.[7] Shida county, Miyagi prefecture, experienced massive rainfall in summer 1932, which worsened the already severe damage to crop yields, leading to chronic food shortages.[8] In 1934, Shida again faced a combination of cold weather and water damage. Particularly hard-hit was Kashimadai hamlet, where 65% of the farmland produced absolutely nothing, driving the farmers to the edge of starvation.[9] This emergency led to another surge of tenancy conflicts in Shida in the early 1930s.[10] After the price of rice plunged during the depression, landlords demanded that tenants compensate for the deteriorating quality of rice by providing a larger amount. *Kahoku shinpō* reported that this demand imposed "blood-sucking pain" on farmers and after the Mass Party's involvement, the Shida area reportedly became "the hottest region of peasant disputes in the prefecture."[11]

Tōhoku received overwhelming sympathy, but this seemed to be another confirmation of the region's inferior status within the empire. In the early 1930s, heavy industry dictated Japanese labor and capital markets.[12] "The famine [of 1934]," the historian Kerry Smith argues, "was in many ways a reminder of just how wide the gap had become between the modern, developed sector and the countryside."[13] Urban intellectuals believed that more modernization—rational and effective farming—was the only remedy for Tōhoku's plight. Agencies, such as the Home Ministry and the semi-governmental Imperial Agricultural Association, conducted various studies of the situation, its causes, and possible solutions. Some of them characterized the tradition of Tōhoku agriculture as the source of the problem, pointing out its "simple management," "primitive land use," "backward use of labor," and "inferior agricultural productivity."[14]

The Farm, Mountain, and Fishing Village Economic Revitalization Campaign was launched nationally in 1932 as a government response. But this campaign's content reflected the gap between still discursively powerful agrarianism and the diminishing influence of the rural economy in the national balance sheet. Agrarian activists, the army, and the Ministry of Agriculture asked the cabinet for a larger budget to help farmers and even prompted the press to make "the village problem" national news in 1932.[15] But Finance Minister Takahashi Korekiyo instead cut the budget for emergency rural relief from 366 million yen in 1933 to 235 million yen in the following year. His decision came from the observation that the countryside had turned from a major source of tax revenue into a large financial burden since World War I. In direct contrast to further investment of national resources, the "self-revitalization" (*jiriki kōsei*) campaign received enthusiastic support from Takahashi and other policymakers. It exalted

the familiar Hōtoku philosophy of moral uplift, which emphasized individuals' responsibility for maintaining sound management in rural households and
village society. The campaign sought to produce maximum results through an
ideological mobilization while spending little money.[16]

In response to this campaign, local leaders in each village and hamlet promoted the spirit of self-help and pushed the limit of productivity through labor-
and fertilizer-intensive agriculture. Shida village's participation in the movement
also emphasized self-reliance and sought to overcome villagers' massive debt
without government help. As one expression of this self-reliance, the village head,
Katō Hisanosuke, father of Katō Einojō of the Aratanome 4-H Club, established
a cooperative called the Two-Eight Society in 1934. He encouraged the villagers
to commit three hours every night to home manufacturing on top of a full day
of farming between fall and spring, save 20% of the profit gained, and use the
remaining 80% to pay taxes. Involving almost all the households of the village,
the Two-Eight Society also tried to reform everyday customs and reduce spending on weddings, funerals, and other ceremonies.[17]

The younger generation took on many responsibilities in the Economic
Revitalization Campaign. Instructors at elementary and youth schools, many of
whom viewed themselves as model rural youth, participated in managing the
campaign.[18] The Agricultural Association targeted youth in the management
improvement projects, and the Ministry of Agriculture called these local programs "youth movements."[19] In addition to their direct involvement in the official
campaign, youth sought to improve village morale by providing entertainment.[20]
In Shida's neighboring village of Ōnuki, for example, seinendan members managed to bring in popular motion pictures for evening screenings. Even though
they could not afford to hire a narrator (benshi), villagers watched new samurai
films in an outdoor theater set up by the seinendan. Youth also presented amateur plays, music, and vaudeville performances at seasonal festivals.[21] The sports
festivals organized and performed by the seinendan remained to be one of the
biggest social events in rural villages, and nearly all residents came to watch and
participate in the games. Ōnuki village youth humorously turned even the government slogan of "self-reliance" into the name of a sport.[22]

At the discursive level, the category of rural youth continued to symbolize
a bright and hopeful future in the eyes of both government officials and villagers. Seinendan activities in each hamlet and news of the conscripts from the
village who were fighting for recently established Manchukuo were often the
only encouraging news helping the villagers to briefly forget the reality of their
rural conditions.[23] In newspapers, photos of young men in military, seinendan,
or youth training center uniforms represented the modern force in the countryside, offering a visual contrast to the reports on the largely unemployed and

starving population. Youth speech contests, usually called *yūben* (eloquence) competitions, were widely reported, often accompanied by photos of a young man on the podium in front of an equally young audience. In the 1929 Miyagi prefecture–level competition, the speeches "A Roar of a Young Man" and "Rescue a Small Rural Village" received the first and second prizes, respectively.[24] Other newspaper reports praised rural youth for helping villagers to complete tax payments, rescuing neighbors from a fire, diligently attending youth training centers and youth schools, and conducting shūyō roundtable discussions.[25]

These symbols of youthful leadership impressed villagers to such an extent that affected the mindset of lower-class farm families. In the late 1920s, the generational and economic class that had grown powerful through the social mobility complex—graduating from the upper level of elementary school, maintaining decent academic ability but without the means to continue an education, and owning or renting farmland to engage in cultivation as farmers—now became the pillars of the new rural campaign.[26] Once their status was solidified in the 1930s, those in the lower strata whose sons had barely finished the six years of elementary school recognized the career of model rural youth as an optimal choice for upward mobility. Between 1930 and 1935, enrollment and graduation rates in the upper level of elementary school suddenly expanded despite the dire financial situation of many villages, demonstrating the robust expansion of education among lower-class farming families.[27] These families prioritized giving an extra few years of education to their children and having them enter the path toward becoming model rural youth over turning them immediately into members of the labor force.

The Hamlet Soldier

Public emotions attached to the category of rural youth also burgeoned in accordance with the expanding military needs of strong soldiers. In the early 1930s, the Economic Revitalization Campaign and military mobilization virtually merged into one. Together they produced a torrent of programs, slogans, and regulations that overwhelmed the rural population. In fact, war was intrinsic to the success of the rural campaign. Scenes of soldiers returning to rural villages, for example, reminded villagers that rural life was part of a bigger imperial effort. Villages organized parades and ceremonies, in which injured soldiers' reunions with their families became a spectacle for public consumption. *Kahoku shinpō* reported the "ecstatic welcoming" happening in every village and town. The reports usually did not discuss where the soldiers fought or what they had done, but focused instead on their returning with honor (and on the deaths of others in battle) instead.[28] In this atmosphere, army conscription began to carry the seriousness of combat as the decade progressed.[29] In 1936, two young men in Shida county submitted blood-signed applications, and other examinees shaved their heads at the conscription exam site to demonstrate their determination. The newspaper described that year's conscription exam as "reflecting the time of urgency."[30]

The army consciously linked rural villages and battlefronts to reinforce the image of the "hamlet soldier." After the Manchurian Incident in 1931, farm youth began participating in daily military drills. The annual army inspection of young men became another local spectacle.[31] Hundreds and thousands of youth, mainly students at youth training centers, engaged in large-scale combat games, reportedly using real weapons.[32] Schoolchildren observed these practices, inflating the excitement about the war and about the prospect of becoming soldiers.[33] Women also took part, serving as nurses.[34] Once conscripted, enlisted men were organized according to their home regions to maintain cohesion of the unit. Soldiers were encouraged to write to seinendan members back home.[35] Schoolchildren also wrote letters of comfort to the soldiers on the front lines under their teachers' instruction. Through these measures, soldiers simultaneously achieved respect in rural society and experienced social pressure to fight and die with honor, and the villagers incorporated scenes of war and death into their everyday lives.[36]

Localization and Nationalization

As the "hamlet soldier" and "village Japan" were being constructed simultaneously through the tie between rural villages and the army, youth training institutions underwent further nationalization. In the late 1920s, the national seinendan network helped young people to imagine themselves as main agents of rural modernity and pillars of the empire. At the same time, the transformation of their consciousness took place within the locally grounded social mechanism of upward mobility. Being closely linked to both national and local levels of Japanese society, the seinendan and other youth training institutions were caught in the vortex of nationalizing and localizing forces. Seen differently, this tension resembled that occurring between associationism and assimilationism as international society debated the new norms of colonial rule. Across the globe, the appreciation of "pure" local and native cultures and the promotion of national–imperial identity grew alongside each other. Japan was not an exception to this trend. Possessing a dual self-image of both leading the regional culture and being marginalized on the national–imperial scene, Miyagi's youth educators exhibited complex reactions to this debate.

In the late 1920s and early 1930s, a wave of localization set the tone. Local history, folklore, and folk art movements became popular across Japan.[37] Especially in educational practices, localization and decentralization arose as a nationwide movement.[38] Many articles published in the *Miyagi Education Journal* argued that one's love for a native place (*kyōdoai*) should be the basis for education.[39] Elementary schools put up slogans such as "Understand one's native place, love one's native place, and develop one's native place" and hung paintings of Miyagi's legendary general, Date Masamune.[40] Authors in the journal embraced a new appreciation of the Tōhoku dialect, which had been a target of correction earlier in the century. Asserting that even "the Tokyo language is another dialect," one teacher stressed the importance of regional dialects, arguing that "it is not standard Japanese that vividly expresses the emotional lives of local people, but the language of the native place, or in other words, the dialect."[41] In this context, the local quality of the village seinendan gained huge traction. "The essence of youth training centers is clearly the educational facility of the state. . . . All the educational methods conducted by the educators there are based on a set of laws. In comparison, the seinendan are completely private groups and are not subject to any legal constraints," Nagato Raizō, a social education official in Miyagi prefecture, contended, adding, "The seinendan, viewed from their history, emerged with various local characteristics of each village and town, as well as of each region."[42]

Nevertheless, despite Nagato's perception, the seinendan's emphasis on the localities owed much to nationalizing forces. The seinendan received as much supervision by prefectural and national officials as did the youth training centers. Government ministries had eagerly intervened in seinendan activities even before 1925, when the Greater Japan Seinendan Federation was established as a national network of local seinendan. In the Shōwa period (beginning in 1926), Emperor Hirohito frequently visited the ceremonies and sports festivals of seinendan members, emphasizing the direct tie between rural youth and the imperial state. The network of seinendan became a single body, the Greater Japan Seinendan, in 1939 and expanded to integrate groups of younger children (*shōnendan*) in 1941. Through these national networks, local cultures represented by village seinendan units were studied, compiled, and presented.[43] The premise of locally driven and centuries-old seinendan was itself a product of nationalization of the seinendan institutions.[44] This dynamic of local characters defined and promoted for consumption by urban intellectuals and bureaucrats reminds us of the production of colonialist knowledge and ethnographical studies.

Conveniently for prefectural authorities, agrarian values concealed the inherent contradiction between the localizing and nationalizing forces. Every nonurban region claimed its value based on its commitment to agriculture and fisheries production, the moral quality of villagers, and the presence of strong, healthy young men. Shida county was no exception. *Kahoku shinpō*'s specialized local report in 1936 featured Shida county "in the throne of agricultural Miyagi." It emphasized that Furukawa city, famous for tenant disputes and political contestations between socialists and the government, had overcome its earlier difficulties and united for the revitalization of Tōhoku.[45] The phrase "pillars of youth" (*chūken seinen*) appeared in the middle of the page, stressing the high morale of young men and army reservists.[46] By emphasizing these typical agrarian elements, local leaders appeared supportive of nationalizing and decentralizing forces at the same time.

The tension came to the fore, however, in the perceived role of rural youth. Whereas the term *rural youth* symbolized local pride and agrarian supremacy when it appeared in the regional newspaper, that same phrase produced a different image for urban educators—the target of reform. A research team measured the levels of intelligence of young people in an academic test in 1938, claiming that scores were significantly lower in the countryside than among city youth. In a case study of Shirai village, Chiba prefecture, the team stated that "81% of male and 78% of female youth have below-average intelligence."[47] Perhaps sensing urbanites' condescension toward rural youth cloaked in the praise of localities, Miyagi educators emphasized the value of local culture in supporting the nation. "Native place *is* the nation (*kokka*)," one schoolteacher emphasized, continuing, "Superior Miyagi people, from the national point of view, are superior Japanese people."[48] In measuring the importance of Tōhoku to the nation, some referred to the rivalry between the east and the west, which Hangai Seiju had highlighted in 1906 when he warned against westward imperial expansion. "We must not make Tōhoku into Kansai-style [Osaka, Kyoto]" because "Tōhoku is, and has to remain, the root of Japan," argued Itō Hyōgo, a schoolteacher in Miyagi.[49] Proud of his origins in Fukushima, the president of the Tokyo Science Museum also claimed in 1938 that "the culture is shifting from Seinan [southwest] to Tōhoku [northeast]."[50]

These claims by Tōhoku educators paradoxically revealed the difficulty of countering the nationalizing trend in youth training. As Nagato Raizō pointed out in an earlier quote, youth schools (previously youth training centers) did increasingly become the vehicle of uniform education over the course of the 1930s.[51] Many young teachers in these schools faced mounting pressure to apply cookie-cutter methods, which quickly diminished their ability to attract younger generations. Each school struggled to raise attendance rates; village administrators had to lure students in and manipulate the numbers. "The primary goal is to raise the attendance rate, and training itself is of secondary importance," argued a schoolmaster in Iwadeyama, Miyagi, in 1934. They achieved nearly perfect attendance by reducing the frequency of training from four to two times per month and by sending reminders to families in advance.[52] Among students, young farmers were still considered exemplary, but teachers had a harder time recruiting youth in other industries. "The attendance of youth in commercial business is nearly zero," *Kahoku shinpō* stated in 1935.[53] As the war progressed, the army demanded greater standardization of training in youth schools. *Kahoku shinpō* reported in February 1941: "To respond to the current international situation, complete the goal of 'all citizens are soldiers,' and overcome the difficulty of the times, the Sendai Army Division's headquarters decided to focus its energy on youth military drill. As a guiding principle in youth schools, it will correct the students' thought and behavior that had varied according to region-specific conditions by adopting the set principle based on encouragement of the Japanese spirit and imperial rescripts."[54]

On the same page of *Kahoku shinpō*, the Sendai garrison boasted that Miyagi had the highest enrollment rate in youth schools among Tōhoku prefectures at 99% of 43,320 eligible youth.[55] Village officials worked so hard to keep up with the unrealistically high expectations to the extent that the numbers on paper ceased to mean anything. Shida village recorded the largest number of youth school students in 1941, with 304 (and 65 graduates), but it had lost track of the size of its enrollment by 1942.[56] At a time of full-scale war mobilization, even modest statistics of the population of young male attending youth schools seem to have become too bothersome to compile. The energy of village officials was redirected from training to the constant allocation of manpower to the military, agriculture, and heavy industries.

By 1943, the nationalizing forces completely overwhelmed the localizing ones. Even the "model farm villages," which used to represent the beauty of the locale at least in theory, were now leveled with the word "standard" (*hyōjun*). Three hundred "standard farm villages" were established throughout Japan to "perform appropriate agricultural management and nurture farming families that conduct robust and long-term agriculture in response to the demands of the nation."[57] The government gave subsidies to these select villages to encourage the standardization of other villages. Local characteristics that were once praised as the basis of national culture disappeared from this new program and, overall, from the wartime planned economy in the early 1940s.

Japanization in All of Life

These forceful nationalizing measures in the Japanese countryside were part of an empire-wide movement to turn all people into ideal Japanese subjects, or what was called *kōminka* in the case of the colonies. Regardless of the location, state officials imposed Japanization in a totalitarian manner in the late 1930s and the first half of the 1940s. One clear empire-wide commonality in the method of Japanization was the emphasis on the bodily acquisition of nationalistic spirit. "Native village education," Miyagi educators' favorite slogan—which was originally intended to shift resources toward developing local identity—became instead a method of inculcating nationalism in young people through everyday life.

Eliminating the boundary between formal training time and private life marked a decisive departure from previous kyōka campaigns toward totalitarian Japanization. Schoolteachers and seinendan leaders had always aimed at influencing the lifestyles of children and youth, but mere influence was no longer enough for a nation in wartime emergency. To merge home and nation, "integration of training and everyday life" (kunren no seikatsuka, seikatsu no kurenka) became a new teaching philosophy in the Funaoka Youth Training Center in Shibata county, Miyagi, in 1935. Army officers of the Sendai garrison applauded its "forward-thinking" training as they viewed the center's activities, mainly "military-style" agricultural practices. They also visited the students' homes to study how their changed behavior at home affected other family members.[58]

The so-called China Incident of 1937, which initiated Japan's all-out war against China, intensified this trend of integrating military training and everyday life. Kahoku shinpō declared in large fonts that the situation of total war was an "Unprecedented National Crisis," which made "Youth's Mission Critical."[59] The Shida County Seinendan held a convention of its two thousand members, just like thousands of other seinendan groups around the empire, to pronounce a state of emergency and take an oath of commitment to the war effort.[60] "All of the activities of youth in Shirai village have to be filled with national significance and penetrated by the spirit of devotion to the state," argued the 1938 previously cited study on rural youth education.[61] This document emphasized that the seinendan should focus on the "collective practice of daily life" (shūdanteki seikatsu jissen) as a means of intensive moral training.[62]

To implement this "collective practice of daily life," many youth training institutions turned themselves into a dojo (a training facility for martial arts), where individuals received strict supervision of every aspect of their daily routine while living together.[63] In December 1938, Katō Hisanosuke made a large donation to build a dojo in the local Hachiman shrine yard, in the hope of "producing youth with iron bodies and iron spirits." The dojo served multiple purposes as a center of youth's self-cultivation: it was an exercise facility for male and female village youth, a venue for lectures and speeches, a place to practice martial arts, and a memorial hall commemorating the China Incident with photos of the village's heroic war dead.[64] As the war front expanded, elementary schools were also turned into dojos that emphasized bodily acquisition of nationalistic spirit over academic learning. "A 180-degree change in education!!," a schoolteacher in Sendai advocated in 1942. "It is extremely outdated if you regard only intellectual instruction as the value of schools." Against the criticism that "school beats bells and drums, having too much religious flavor," this teacher stressed that the "training of all aspects of children's lives" required integration of training and everyday life.[65] Many youth schools adopted the dojo-style training as well. A teacher at a youth school in Kurihara county reported in November 1943 that the school's mission was to "make youth aware of the meanings of their work and their mission at their workplaces and complete their mission, through every possible means, with burning loyalty in response to imperial benevolence." The training content ranged from radio listening comprehension and military marches to monetary savings and lectures on imperial agrarianism.[66] In the 1940s, the prior emphasis on the *local* in native village education was replaced by a stress on the young *body* that knew no separation between private and national spheres. A cornerstone of Japanization programs, this training method was adopted widely across the Japanese Empire.

Rural Imperialism

While the radical Japanization of this period aimed at consolidating the "nation" part of the nation-empire, the seinendan were expected to bring the presence of the "empire" down to villages. Japanese agrarian nationalism had always been linked to Japan's territorial expansion. But after imperial control over Manchuria in the 1930s magnified the discourse of an agriculture-centered imperialism, the link between the seinendan and the imperial frontiers became more direct and robust. Schoolteachers argued that the seinendan in the 1930s differed from those in Meiji times: "Today's Japan displays a superlative presence as a champion of East Asia and world leader, so the seinendan in the Japanese countryside should not remain in the era of *wakarenchū* (hamlet youth associations), *seinenkai* (youth groups in Meiji), or *shojokai* (young women's groups in the 1910s) as in the thought of the early or mid-Meiji period."[67] They envisioned a transformation of the seinendan to match the expanding scale of imperialism in the late 1930s.

In fact, through government programs that encouraged migration to Manchuria, the empire of the 1930s affected the everyday lives of rural Japanese in a novel way. Manchuria was called "the new paradise" and presented as a panacea for widespread rural problems in the 1930s. Japanese villagers had faced a shortage of arable land especially when the rural population expanded during the depression.[68] To ease this pressure, the agrarian activist Katō Kanji, with support from the Kwantung Army (or Kantōgun, the Japanese army stationed in northeastern China) and commanders Ishiwara Kanji and Tōmiya Kaneo advocated and launched the Manchuria colonization program in 1932.[69] The program provided Japanese farmers with military drills and agricultural training at the Uchihara training center in Ibaraki prefecture and then relocated them as armed agricultural colonizers. After sending 423 farmers from the Tōhoku region and Nagano prefecture to Manchuria in the program's first year, the central government planned to send millions of farmers in the following ten years.[70] The media introduced success stories of emigrants in one issue after another, popularizing Manchuria as a destination.[71]

Between 1932 and 1936, the Miyagi prefectural government sent 12,419 emigrants according to its official record, a fifth-largest group in the country.[72] In reality, Miyagi officials, even while they frantically recruited volunteers, had no concrete evidence that Manchuria was the solution to rural poverty. Kimura Tadashi, who headed the Miyagi Prefecture Town and Village Heads Association, did not conceal his lack of confidence in a 1931 speech: "I know nothing about Manchuria. I have been told only that Manchuria has limitless land and limitless resources. There is always an insistence that Manchuria is Japan's lifeline, and that we must protect the rights and interests earned in the battles of 1904–1905. It is a very abstract thing."[73] Nonetheless, mobilization accelerated every year. The prefectural government set up a "Miyagi village" in Manchuria, consisting of a few settlers from each village of the prefecture, so that emigrants had more than immediate kinship to rely on. Some villages promoted migration more enthusiastically than others and created their own "branch villages" in Manchuria. Nangō village, also called the "best migration village in Japan," was the first in the country to plan a branch village.[74] Nangō's move fanned Miyagi's "migration fever" and encouraged other villages to hold lectures, motion picture showings, and hamlet meetings to emulate Nangō's collective colonization of the continent.[75]

Since the target population for emigration was young male farmers, the seinendan played a central role in mobilization. They were the most reliable organization to prepare model migrants from the viewpoint of the government and the Kwantung Army. Bureaucrats, particularly those in the South Manchuria Railway Company, were concerned about the risks of a large number of unemployed youth going to Manchuria with dreams of easy money. The magazine *Ie no hikari* warned that there were an increasing number of waitresses from cafés and bars, as well as prostitutes—symbols of urban decadence—in Manchuria.[76] To encourage the migration of farm youth for agricultural colonization, all levels of government offices worked with the corresponding levels of seinendan associations. At the national level, the Japan Youth Center in Tokyo hosted a large celebration in 1932 to mark the departure of a group of migrants.[77] In 1937, the Greater Japan Seinendan Federation established a "colonization department" to facilitate overseas migration and submitted to the cabinet a policy recommendation to establish the Youth Colonization Volunteer Corps for Manchuria-Mongolia (Manmō Kaitaku Seishōnen Giyūgun, hereafter the Volunteer Corps). The seinendan leaders used every available venue to promote the Volunteer Corps, such as advertising them in the official seinendan journal *Seinen* (Youth), the *Japan Youth Newspaper*, and the popular series *The Youth Cards*, among others. In 1938, more than twenty thousand young men joined the Volunteer Corps and relocated to Manchuria.[78]

The prefectural level of seinendan associations had already been taking youth to the frontier of the empire. Since 1925, the Miyagi Seinendan had been organizing observational trips to Manchuria and Korea. These trips supposedly provided an opportunity to "transcend national borders, reflect upon the state of our empire, feel the customs of the continent, correct our perceptions of Manchuria and Korea, mourn at the battle sites, and see the activities of compatriots."[79] After the Manchurian Incident in 1931, 206 participants from these trips formed the Miyagi Youth Manchuria–Korea Society to show their firm support for those "who risk[ed] their lives defending the lifeline of the Yamato race." The society initiated a variety of publications, lectures, and study groups.[80] *Miyagi seinen* (Miyagi youth), the official Miyagi Seinendan newsletter, was the main forum for its activities. In fact, *Miyagi seinen* and the *Miyagi Education Journal* constantly reported impressions of Manchuria, Korea, and occasionally Taiwan submitted by teachers and youth who visited these places. Their experiences of riding the trains with passengers of different ethnicities, passing through dangerous zones where the Japanese were often attacked by bandits, and walking among the neon signs, bars, and jazz music in Jilin depicted the adventurous atmosphere of their trips from Korea to Manchuria. At the same time, this unfamiliar space filled with flashy hypermodern symbols did not feel completely foreign to these visitors because of the presence of Miyagi settlers there.[81] The travel participants often obtained help from Miyagi business owners regarding accommodations, meals, and tour guides.

Reports on the agricultural settlement in Manchuria similarly employed a combination of the unfamiliar and familiar. "We use the machines of Western nations for agricultural tools, which are unimaginable in Japan," wrote a settler from Miyagi in the fourth migration program.[82] Through having Miyagi's fellow natives introduce their experience, the "unseen scale" of agriculture in Manchuria became more comprehensible to young readers. Hyung Ok Park has argued that the Korean farmers who settled in the Kando region of Manchuria functioned as cells in the "osmotic" expansion of the capitalist empire.[83] Miyagi's emigrants to Manchuria created a similar process of osmosis in that these migrants enlarged not only the literal boundary of the empire but also the conceptual boundary of Miyagi's rural villages.

At the village level, fraternal bonds that grew among seinendan members served to bring the larger imperial state closer to village everyday life. Many young people who immigrated to the colonies continued to submit essays to their home village's seinendan newsletters. Some newsletters allowed overseas contributors to give a "real account" of the empire. Especially in the 1920s, when youth migration was not yet a widely prevalent phenomenon, seinendan members living in outer territories were a rare source of firsthand accounts. In the Akita City Seinendan newsletters, for example, Satō Yūtarō, a member living in northern Korea, shared his observations. Cautioning the reader against the mistaken image of Koreans, Satō described the "real" Koreans as "loyal and humane," although "some have the slyness of the loser of a war." His chauvinism was apparent in his conclusion that "it was sufficient for those in the past to just be the conqueror (*seifukusha*), but we have an additional duty now: the assimilation of the conquered (*hiseifukusha*)."[84] Over time, as rural youth became an established identity category, the concept helped shift the emphasis from foreignness to familiarity. Kanno Sukeo, a settler in Taiwan, submitted his essays to the seinendan newsletter of his home village, Edano, in Igu county, Miyagi, around 1935. Kanno gave no sign of being a settler other than the word "Taiwan" in front of his name. His essay deplored the fact that people with high morals often fell into poverty. It downplayed the unique environment of living in Taiwan by focusing on the universal concerns of rural youth.[85] Essays like this one flattened various experiences in the empire and shrank them into one narrative of struggling rural youth. Through these exchanges and the personal ties that grew among seinendan members, the expansive empire became a familiar, graspable world to them.

In short, Japan's conquest of Manchuria gave rural villages pioneer status, and young generations in the countryside nurtured a deep sense of agrarian imperialism. They came to believe that their responsibilities extended from their hamlets and villages, beyond the Japanese archipelago to the frontier land of northern China and Manchuria. They were told to "love their native place" because "the earnest love for their native place" was "the mother of the development in the continent."[86] They were also told to "raise self-awareness" as imperial settlers in the continent and to abstain from alcohol, violence, and arrogant behavior so as to cultivate admiration for Japan among Chinese locals and Korean settlers.[87] All aspects of their lives, even their weddings, were mobilized to advertise imperial settlement. Nangō village chose thirteen brides for migrant volunteers and conducted a group wedding in February 1937. The wedding ceremony at the

Nangō Shrine was intended to "further propel the accomplishment of the village goal," that of "emigration to Manchuria." The brides wore *monpe* work trousers and "absolutely no makeup," to symbolize the spirit of Manchurian migration.[88] Thus, village seinendan members found themselves in the midst of the emigration campaign, as both mobilizing forces and mobilized subjects.

In addition to their ties to Manchuria, the seinendan symbolized imperial power through their connection with the Hitler Youth. Fascist movements in Europe had already captured the attention of young and old alike, as well as the ideological right and left in Japan in the 1920s and 1930s.[89] Both the national seinendan magazine *Seinen* and village seinendan newsletters viewed Mussolini and Hitler as superior leaders. In September 1938, the seinendan and the Hitler Youth exchanged visits to tour around each other's empires.[90] Twelve members of the Hitler Youth, headed by Reinhold Schulze, were welcomed enthusiastically by Japanese crowds at every stop during their three months of travel in the Japanese Empire. Their brief stop at Sendai on September 11 became a regional spectacle. *Kahoku shinpō* published photos of German youth in the famous Jugend uniform. It declared, "The five hours the Hitler Jugend spent in Sendai, the city of forests, was filled with expressions of Japanese-German friendship by all 220,000 residents. Enthusiasm for the youth of our ally followed and boiled hot. Sendai was plunged into a whirlpool of breathtaking excitement for five hours."[91] The Shida village newsletter also reported on the visit: "The Jugend sang the German national anthem to the Sendai Seinendan musical band, and then [the seinendan] sang 'Kimi ga yo' (the Japanese national anthem) in return." After a series of speeches, "to introduce the local arts, the city seinendan performed a sword dance, the young women's seinendan sang 'Sansa shigure,' and it finished with a children's performance. The Jugend sang the Nazi party song, the Jugend song, and so forth. In a harmonious atmosphere with a stream of solemn feeling, we gave three shouts of *banzai* (long live) for Germany, and Mr. Schulze led three shouts of banzai for the Greater Japanese Empire."[92] The appearance of the Hitler Youth impressed the public and raised the Japanese people's confidence in seinendan associations as representing a global power on a par with Germany. These exchanges symbolized a new vision of internationalism and were reported even in remote villages like Shida.

Individuals and Social Relationships

How did village youth react to these intensifying forces of agrarian, imperial, and military mobilization? This is a difficult question to answer. Wartime state and army officials desired to more directly and hierarchically control young villagers, leaving little space for individual expression of personal views. Local contexts and personal motivations were deeply submerged under nationalistic slogans. Even retrospectively, those still alive today are not willing to share their memories of participating in and supporting state mobilization. In actuality, all generations were physically occupied by the requirements of producing agricultural and industrial goods, conducting military drills, attending neighborhood meetings, and compensating for the loss of manpower to military conscription. One witness who joined the seinendan in 1943 in Shida village recalled that he was too busy with farming and attended seinendan activities only occasionally.[93] The challenge of sheer survival and increasingly paranoid state policies created a dark age for aspiring young villagers. Even when the state seemed to exert perfect control over everyday life, however, we can still detect how social contexts surrounding individuals shaped the ways in which they engaged in the mobilization.

Most noticeably, the generation who lived through the rise of rural youth in the 1920s made the transition to wartime rural imperialism and militarism without a major rupture. The personal records of Katō Einojō, the landlord's son in Shida village, indicate no major shift but only an acceleration of his belief in the power of rural youth. Katō had become a semi-public figure by the late 1930s, and his life revolved around active involvement in war mobilization. His full embrace of wartime rhetoric tells us that public enthusiasm for war mobilization, at least partially, stood upon the foundation of social dynamics that developed prior to the era of all-out war.

Katō Einojō, already thirty-three years old when Japan launched the war against China in 1937, took Japan's "state of emergency" seriously, since he was a pillar of Aratanome hamlet. Having failed the conscription exam in the 1920s because of his height, he remained in the village through the 1940s, serving in many official positions related to agricultural administration, education, and hamlet governance. After completing a lecture course on "the Greater East Asia Co-Prosperity Sphere" in June 1941 and another called "Leadership in the Time of Crisis and Self-Awareness of National Subjects" in October 1942, he became the head of village *sōnendan* (adult associations) in 1943.[94]

Katō had already acquired considerable skill and a reputation as a hamlet leader through the experience of leading his Aratanome 4-H Club. Once he took charge of hamlet affairs, he frequently wrote and circulated hamlet newsletters to report donation quotas, surveys to be conducted, rules of the new national health insurance, venues and quantities for rationing of goods, and detailed plans for agricultural cooperatives.[95] These writings reveal his excitement in playing a leadership role that had already been apparent in his earlier youth group activities. The rebelliousness that had characterized his youth group, however, was replaced by new confidence as a figure of authority. *Kahoku shinpō* reported on

Katō's leadership in promoting the war effort in 1943, as he gathered heads of households to explain the grave national food shortages. Promising to contribute 20% of his own rice holdings to the hamlet's donation quota, he begged others to join him. He also argued that "it is a shame for farmers" to receive rice rations. Under Katō's initiative, Aratanome residents took a collective oath that they would consume other foods in case of a rice shortage in their households.[96]

Slogans about youth and farmers continued to attract Katō's attention. *Omoto*, the youth journal he edited in 1931, had already expressed the feelings of proud young farmers and their determination to work hard in such contributions as "a farmer's poem" and "a letter to the enlisted soldier." When the emphasis on youthfulness and hard work intensified under wartime mobilization, Katō quickly adopted the ubiquitous rhetoric of "fighting rural youth." "Youth is the heat and oil for the flame of our leaders!" declared the cover of the meeting minutes of the Shida Country Imperial Rule Assistance Association in May 1941.[97] Katō printed the "oath of food production increase" taken by the Shida Village Sōnendan in handouts:

Today food is also a weapon

We know that one grain of rice and barley, or one piece of potato, is equivalent to one airplane and one flying bullet that can determine victory or defeat in the war.

We are farmers

As we face the severe war situation and enter the harvest season, autumn is the time we farmers must all stand up. We shall do our best to reach the production goal, firmly determined to complete the hamlet's assigned obligation of agricultural donation.

Farms are our final battleground

Regarding them as our fighting field, we rely on each other and help each other to overcome hardship. We make an oath to the world that we shall absolutely achieve food production increase for the sake of victory.[98]

Katō regularly pasted articles in his scrapbooks that elevated the importance of farmers, including one from *Yomiuri hōchi shinbun* written by a leading economist, Tominaga Yoshio. This article stressed the significant role played by the farming population of fifty million people in Japan, Taiwan, and Korea, and it demanded that they sacrifice more, particularly by giving up their own food consumption to "even out the levels of hunger of all national subjects." Katō underlined these points in red pencil.[99] He also made a number of handwritten notes on Hōtokukai (Society of Repaying Virtue) lectures, perhaps in preparation for his own lectures to hamlet residents.

While Katō adopted a leadership role as an extension of his previous youth activities, others experienced a significant break from the previous period. Willingly or not, those whose social status had been considered inferior earlier—children and unmarried female farmworkers in particular—found themselves in a new race for empowerment. A children's magazine, *Weekly Junior Nation* (*Shūkan shōkokumin*), preached that children were even more responsible than adults for carrying out the war and shouldering the future of the empire. Children who grew up during wartime later wrote that they felt "happiness and pride" as they internalized this rhetoric and sought to become a "perfect imperial subject."[100] For some, reaching a decision in favor of self-mobilization was a convoluted process. A memoir written by an individual, Satō Tadao, relates a number of anecdotes in which, as a boy, he unintentionally enraged elementary schoolteachers through behavior that, in adults' eyes, represented refusal to revere the emperor. These incidents usually consisted of frivolous actions, such as tapping a ruler against a desk in rhythm when students practiced songs for the late Emperor Meiji's birthday celebration. Satō was otherwise a diligent and loyal student who had memorized imperial myths as instructed. When he received a reprimand, his personal admiration for his teachers, not his love for the nation, generated grave self-remorse. When he reached the age of eligibility (i.e., fourteen) to volunteer for the navy, shortly before the war ended, Satō applied to become a military pilot against his mother's wishes. According to his memoir, he did so primarily out of extreme resentment toward a school principal who had labeled him as unpatriotic when Satō did not immediately lower his head upon unexpectedly hearing Emperor Meiji's *tanka* poems. Becoming a soldier was a way to prove the principal's judgment wrong and gain a sense of superiority over him.[101] For Satō, wartime mobilization consisted of a series of emotional battles with adults, especially teachers.

Young female farmworkers also faced, and sometimes contributed to, a shakeup in the social hierarchy. Ōnuki village's female seinendan members established a "nonmarriage alliance" and pledged not to marry men who failed to attend military drills at youth training centers, saying, "Without military drills, they are not men!" They found a way to counter the dominance of masculinity by turning their marriage decision into a way to judge their male counterparts, at least symbolically.[102] It is beyond our ability to grasp their motivations and the effects of these acts, but it is clear that forms of nationalistic frenzy became the surest means to affirm people's social status. From the state's viewpoint, all people's individuality was supposed to blossom through their direct ties with the empire. However, it is social tensions—such as those between generations, genders, and regions—that created the seemingly symbiotic relationship between individuals and the state.

Indeed, the escalating wartime mobilization challenged some of the established social statuses. The last years of the war destabilized the long-standing social dominance of urban over rural Japan, as cities suffered critical food shortages and were targeted by daily air raids.[103] Urban populations rushed to find family connections in rural villages so that they could flee the cities. The government began arranging the evacuation of urban children in June 1944, and by September 1944, Shida county had accepted 714 schoolchildren plus 78 teachers and staff, mostly from Tokyo.[104] Scholars have argued that the nationwide phenomenon of evacuation (*sokai*) overturned the prevailing resentment toward cities among the rural population. Many urban residents suffered greatly through the sudden displacement and formed bitter memories of their sokai experience.[105] For Katō Einojō, the shift in the urban–rural relationship had a personal dimension. Two months before Japan's surrender, Katō agreed to host twenty students from Tōhoku Imperial University in Sendai, along with a professor of law, Nakagawa Zennosuke, in a community center attached to the Aratanome shrine.[106] They put up a sign that read, "The Aratanome branch of the Law and Literature Department of Tōhoku Imperial University." Katō's records do not say whether he felt any sense of superiority over the displaced urbanites, stating only his belief in the increasing responsibility of rural villages. But under the extraordinary circumstances of wartime, Katō Einojō's failed dream of seeking higher education in a city seemed to have been ironically reversed as refugees from a university sought his help in his home village of Shida.

The Collapse of the Social Mobility Complex

The social hierarchies of rural areas also were being redefined, because the "pillars of youth" had left their villages, causing the demise of the social mobility complex. Despite the alarm about population pressures in the 1930s, the agricultural population sharply declined in the late 1930s and early 1940s. The number of soldiers in the Japanese military increased exponentially, from 278,000 in 1931 to 7.32 million in 1945. According to a study of postwar survey statistics, more than 45% of the entire age cohort of males who were born between 1916 and 1920 were drafted.[107] The continuing governmental efforts to send farmers to Manchuria and war-related heavy industries also absorbed young people. Nangō village, which eagerly promoted emigration to Manchuria, saw a rapid shrinkage of its tenant population, to the extent that landlords suffered shortages of workers in 1941 and 1942.[108] The diminishing numbers of village youth are shown in simple demographic statistics. In 1930, the dominant demographic group in the agricultural sector was young men between fifteen and twenty years of age. This was particularly true in Tōhoku, where these teenagers were presumably responsible for the overpopulation that needed to be eased through migration.[109] In comparison, a 1948 study of Shida village pointed out that "the size of the male population in their twenties and thirties dropped precipitously" and argued that "this speaks vividly of the demographic change during wartime."[110]

The loss of manpower in Shida village came mainly from military casualties. From 1944 to 1945, the number of registered deaths almost doubled from 125 to 220 (causes unspecified).[111] A village history of 1950 lists 240 soldiers who died in Manchuria, on islands in the Pacific, in Okinawa, and elsewhere between 1937 and 1946—approximately 8% of all male residents. Many others came home maimed. The numbers convey the gravity of wartime loss, especially when compared with the twenty soldiers who died during the sixty years of the Meiji and Taishō periods combined.[112] Katō Einojō's hamlet newsletters tell of Aratanome's struggles in dealing with declining manpower as well as the deaths of its young soldiers. Katō often reported news of Shida village's group funerals held at the elementary school, requesting that hamlet residents raise a mourning flag.[113] He also asked every remaining male resident between twenty-one and fifty years old to attend the inauguration of the Patriotic Labor Corps in September 1943, organized to compensate for the declining number of available workers.[114] In 1944, the village organized several "Military Assistance Emphasis Weeks." Schoolteachers and village officials, including Katō, visited the families of conscripts to hear the details of their circumstances.

With very few young men remaining in rural villages, older men and women moved to the forefront of village management. The sōnendan (adult associations), consisting of those who had passed conscription age, took over the roles formerly played by the seinendan and provided volunteer labor and leadership in farming.[115] Katō Einojō took positions in the Shida Village Sōnendan and became a manager of Shida County Sōnendan in May 1943. Young women also played an increasingly large role in the labor force. In 1939, when women of age seventeen and eighteen formed a "young ladies' corps" (otome butai) to go to villages in Fukushima and helped their silk production, a newspaper featured a large photo of young women lining up at Furukawa station as a striking piece of news.[116] But within a few years, female labor mobilization became the norm in Japan, as in other countries, and "reinforcement corps" (engun) for agricultural production became a synonym for young women's labor units.[117] Young women formed the teishintai (female volunteer corps) and took the place of the seinendan in the final stage of the war.[118] Women authored most of the memoirs that recounted the sufferings of everyday life on the home front—surviving serious shortages of food and basic materials, working in fields and factories in abysmal conditions, teaching students war slogans, panicking in air raids, and finding the burned bodies of their children in the shelters.[119] By contrast, after they returned home, young men often had difficulty sharing their experiences outside the circle of their peers, a phenomenon we will examine in the Epilogue.

The Japanese countryside underwent an era of youth mobilization that stretched from the Russo-Japanese War in 1905 to the peak of the Asia-Pacific War. As seen in chapter 2, many factors leading up to the 1920s produced the social mobility complex, through which young men in the countryside enthusiastically promoted their own versions of the Japanese national–imperial ideology. In the 1930s, the symbolic value of rural youth continued to rise. State and army officials managed to integrate rural youth training into their nationalization efforts while heavily depending on seinendan networks and activities to create grass-roots supporters of the imperial and militaristic cause. Throughout this process, the discursive emphasis on rural youth as true pillars of the nation-empire continued to accelerate until the end of the war. Paradoxically, however, the intensive mobilization had been causing young people to leave their home villages since the late 1930s, emptying the social mobility complex of its protagonists. The grassroots mechanism of youth's self-mobilization was long gone when the war ended in August 1945.

The wartime experiences of village youth in Miyagi were closely tied to the empire. Many of them became conquerors on Japan's behalf, committing aggression on the Chinese continent, in Southeast Asia, and on islands in the Asia-Pacific region. Agrarianism helped rural residents to imagine imperial expansion as primarily *their* project, developing rural imperialism. Japanese village youth also became main targets of totalitarian Japanization, the homeland equivalent of *kōminka* for colonial populations. In consolidating both nation and empire—which shared almost the same boundaries in the assimilationist vision of the Japanese Empire—village youth across the imperial domains were disciplined and mobilized simultaneously.

Under such empire-wide mobilization, the phase of totalitarian Japanization greatly altered the equation of the social mobility complex. From the beginning, the complex stood upon a peculiar balance between social opportunities and submission to the state. That balance tilted during this period, affecting people in different ways. For those who participated in the rise of rural youth in the 1920s, like Katō Einojō, war mobilization validated their earlier assertion of agrarianism and youthful leadership. By contrast, younger generations, who had no chance to avoid military or labor deployment, had to prove their self-worth through ostensibly nationalistic acts. Some young female farmworkers started to experience greater social leverage, though it also was propped on a fragile balance between opportunities and submission. Through this peek into people's everyday lives, another aspect of totalitarian mobilization becomes apparent. In an environment where the label of "unpatriotic" was so quickly used to denounce others, interpersonal tensions inevitably intensified, creating a highly charged atmosphere. Contrary to the state's attempt to reprogram individuals as national beings, wartime mobilization roused local-level emotions, rather than overwriting them with a national–imperial identity.

INTERLUDE

Okinawa's Place in the Nation-Empire

Before we move on to local cases in Taiwan and Korea, some reflections on rural youth mobilization in Okinawa may help to illuminate the nature of assimilation in different parts of the Japanese Empire.

Many scholars of the modern history of Okinawa use the term *colonization* to describe the nationalization and marginalization that occurred there. The term fits for multiple reasons. After the establishment of Okinawa prefecture in 1879 in place of the former Ryūkyū Kingdom, Okinawans remained in a state of limbo of integration under the Preservation of Old Customs Policy for about two decades. Despite the policy's name, this period saw the previous ways of Ryūkyū governance quickly removed by a foreign ethnic group, the Yamato people (as those from Japan's main islands were called), who instituted policies that served the interests of the main islands of Japan. One such policy was to replace rice-centered agriculture for local consumption with sugarcane cultivation.[1] The Japanese school system was introduced and run by Yamato teachers, although most of the Okinawan population remained outside it and sons of the Ryūkyū gentry class continued to study Confucius classics.[2] Political representation or citizenship rights were extended extremely slowly to include Okinawa. After these two decades, Yamato officials attempted to rapidly convert Okinawan populations into loyal, hardworking, Japanese-speaking imperial subjects, which historians aptly call *kōminka* (Japanization), borrowing the term from the history of wartime Taiwan and Korea. As in the formal colonies, students were punished if they used the *uchinānchu*, the native Okinawan language, in school. Racial and

ethnic discrimination against Okinawan people persisted throughout the prewar and postwar periods. In effect, Okinawa suffered the longest colonial-like
period in Japanese history, stretching at least into the 1970s.[3] It is not surprising
that a postcolonial intellectual outcry has occurred in the writings of Okinawan
history. These historians fight, rather fruitlessly, against the public forgetting of
the Okinawan experience in today's Japanese politics much as historians of Algeria have raised their voice against French policymakers regarding the myth of
decolonization.

Despite such uniqueness of Okinawa, its Japanization process during the prewar years shares many elements with that of other peripheries of the main islands
of Japan. The most decisive element that made Okinawa closer to the metropole
rather than to the colonies was the relatively early initiation of military service. In
1885, it became mandatory for students in the normal school to participate in six
weeks of active service; in 1898, military conscription was applied to Okinawan
men. If Okinawa's economic conditions had been similar to Miyagi's, the presence of the army and the national goal to improve the conscription success rate
through youth training centers could have affected the social position of youth in
the countryside. Another element that distinguished Okinawans from Taiwanese
and Koreans was Okinawans' stronger drive for national assimilation, influenced
by the labor market of the 1920s. Although both Korean and Okinawan laborers
constituted the cheap labor used to support industrial production in Japan, Okinawans faced a relatively more flexible structure of ethnic discrimination. The
historian Tomiyama Ichirō has discussed the process of Okinawans' "self-loss"
because the labor markets incentivized Okinawan laborers to actively hide their
Okinawan background and act as ideal Japanese workers to elude discrimination.[4] Notwithstanding the cruelty and insensitivity that characterized this process, it offered a path to self-assimilation that was not available to the Taiwanese
and Korean working classes in Japan.

Thus Okinawa embodied a blurring of metropole and colonial positions.
But Okinawa's perceived status was not exactly midway between Japan and its
colonies or "semi-colonial." Rather, it often suffered an even more subaltern status than colonial Taiwan and Korea. The imperial government invested more
resources in ruling and establishing large-scale industries in Taiwan and Korea.
Whereas spectacles of urban modernity in Taipei and Seoul impressed visitors,
Okinawa's capital, Naha, suffered the notoriety of having massive red-light dis-
tricts, a manifestation of "barbaric" old customs from the viewpoint of social
reformers.[5] In 1908, a serious debate took place among Japanese politicians as to
whether Okinawa should be ruled by the colonial governor of Taiwan. The idea
generated an angry response in Okinawan newspapers, but it also led to a realization that being in the inner territories on the official map was the sole source of

self-esteem for Okinawan leaders relative to the colonial populations.[6] In essence, Okinawa found itself at an extreme margin of both the Japanese inner and outer territories throughout the prewar period. Along with the Ainu in Hokkaidō and the aborigines (*seiban*) in Taiwan, Okinawans provoked an image of savagery in the national–imperial public imaginations.

In this social, economic, and political position specific to Okinawa, how did the discourse of youth and the movement to produce model rural youth through the seinendan function? How did village youth in Okinawa—youth at the triple peripheries of the nation, empire, and prefecture—react to the discursive rise of youth? In Okinawa too, the idea of *seinen* became a focal point of contestation between the state and various sectors of local society. The question of who defined the meaning of youth became analogous to that of who could determine the future of local communities, thereby triggering the widening of not just a generational divide but also class, regional, ethnic, and ideological cleavages. Recently, Wendy Matsumura has related the history of Okinawan peasants in the light of their active anti-capitalist struggle.[7] The division among the state, local leaders, and peasantry, which occupies a central place in her work, is manifested in our story as well.

One notable consideration is that although some conditions in Okinawan rural society were favorable to promoting the category of ideal and modern rural youth, they did not lead to the formation of a social mobility complex for village youth. In other words, young people could not pursue career developments while remaining in rural villages or share pride in being model rural youth with peers in other regions. The most decisive factor hindering this opportunity was the economic devastation of the 1920s, which occurred on a scale rarely seen elsewhere in the empire. Young Okinawan villagers were encouraged to relocate to major industrial areas, unlike their counterparts in Tōhoku, who were prevented from migrating to cities.

This Interlude briefly examines characteristics of youth mobilization that unfolded in the Okinawan setting. The Okinawan case shows that the existence of premodern communal age groups did not always help the seinendan to penetrate the countryside. It also demonstrates that state programs to assimilate and mobilize village youth did not automatically lead to the rise of rural youth. Many social conditions had to be aligned to allow a social mechanism of youth empowerment and mobilization to emerge and develop. In other words, state policy in pursuit of nation-empire building was heavily conditioned by local social dynamics.

The institutional trajectory of the seinendan in Okinawa reflected the trend seen on the main islands of Japan. Around the beginning of the twentieth century, newspapers and education journals began reporting the formation of local "youth groups" (*seinenkai*) that aimed to "reform customs."[8] The Russo-Japanese War (1904–1905) encouraged more night study groups and youth groups to emerge. In 1912, Kunigami county, the large rural district in the north, reorganized its county youth group by referring, for the first time, to the Boshin Rescript (1908), which offered an ideological principle to village youth associations around the country. In 1916, a prefecture-level federation of seinendan was established in response to the 1915 national decree that called for nationalizing and standardizing village youth associations.

Despite this linear institutional development, the seinendan did not easily establish the image of modern rural youth in Okinawan villages. In Miyagi and elsewhere in Japan at large, the seinendan came to dominate the discourse and activities of village youth by overriding two rival groups: the youth groups popular among more educated, urban young people in the 1890s and traditional hamlet youth groups that preserved old rural customs. In Okinawa, however, the term *youth* continued to represent both the most modern, urban, educated group of Okinawans and the robust continuity of the traditional social order of rural communities through the first few decades of the twentieth century. Advocates for the development of model rural youth through the seinendan had a harder time bridging these conflicting images.

There are several reasons for the continuing strength of these opposing images of youth. The modern image of youth in Okinawa did not just emerge from the national discourse on the rise of seinen inspired by Tokutomi Soho in the 1890s (see chapter 1). Rather, young leaders, mostly from families of the gentry in the Ryūkyū Kingdom, who had obtained modern education in Tokyo formed a political faction during the transitional phase under the Preservation of Old Customs Policy. Confronting the older generations of Okinawans who resisted Japanese rule and tried to align with Qing China, the "youth faction" (*seinenha*) advocated rapid assimilation to Japan. The core members of this faction established the main newspaper in Okinawa, *Ryūkyū shinpō*, which promoted Japanization as the only means of survival. They accepted that assimilation implied political subordination, arguing, "Assimilation of our people, regardless of whether it occurs in tangible forms or in intangible ways, and without debating whether it is good or bad, means becoming similar to other prefectures of the inner territory in every aspect."[9] Their evidently cynical tone notwithstanding, this determination to achieve assimilation bears a resemblance to that of colonial intellectuals. This faction became a dominant force particularly during the Qing-Japanese War in 1894–1895. Thus youth as a representation of the pro-Japanese force had a larger political presence in Okinawa than student groups in other parts of Japan.

The youth groups established by Okinawans in the Meiji period were outlets of these highly educated youth and embodied the specific position that they occupied in Okinawan society. On the one hand, they served as spokespeople for Okinawa and fought prejudice. They propagated the great potential for assimilation of Okinawans to Japan in and outside the prefecture. The Okinawa Seinenkai, established by Okinawan students studying in Tokyo in 1890 in order to "present the status of Okinawa prefecture to the world," performed this role most saliently.[10] It claimed that "the history of our prefecture in relation to the mother nation is not like Taiwan's, Karafuto's, or Korea's, but teaches us that we have familial kinship with the Yamato race." It simultaneously encouraged people in Okinawa to quickly adopt Japanese national consciousness and sought to dispel the image of Okinawan savagery often held by outsiders.[11]

On the other hand, these youth groups' modernization effort was often ignored in local (particularly rural) societies, which operated according to traditional communal rules and ties. Through night study groups and youth gatherings, these youth attempted to teach villagers the standard Japanese language and alter old living customs, particularly the premarital sexual conduct that was common in youth gatherings called *mōashibi*.[12] A teacher in Ōgimi village reported in 1912, however, that night study groups in villages "appear and disappear, appear and disappear, like bubbles and illusions."[13] These young men were confronted by the absolute power of the older generations in villages. Some night study groups had to dissolve, according to *Ryūkyū shinpō*, because of the conflict between old and young villagers.[14] Iha Fuyū, one of the most influential public intellectuals in Okinawa, pointed out the modern youth's lack of leverage as late as 1921: "No matter how loudly youth speak [to villagers], unless those in their fifties become willing, no reform is possible," and those in their fifties "do not understand standard Japanese."[15]

The efforts of these educated youth met a major challenge because the second kind of youth, who remained protectors of traditional communal organizations, prevailed in rural villages. Okinawan rural communities had generally organized cooperation and adopted regulations through age- and gender-based groups in a similar way to Miyagi and other parts of Japan. Groups of working-age men (often called *nisēzuri*) took charge of fire control, labor sharing, patrolling, festivals, and so on. One element that distinguished the Okinawan nisēzuri from traditional hamlet youth groups on the Japanese main islands was their continuing power to execute communal laws even after the turn of the century. As late as 1919, when the seinendan had replaced hamlet youth groups and largely detached young men from the means of village governance and violence in other parts of Japan, many Okinawan communities still depended on the nisēzuri to punish outlaws.[16] Moreover, the age range of the nisēzuri was too wide (fifteen to sixty) to correspond to the official regulations governing the seinendan (twelve to twenty or twenty-five). In 1915, when the government issued a decree to standardize village youth associations, those in Okinawa still included men in their sixties.[17] This situation rendered the image of youth not youthful at all, as these associations still contained the most powerful layer of villagers, mostly old men. But even among younger people, the custom of mōashibi gatherings remained popular despite the frantic attempt to ban it by modernizing reformers, and many young villagers still could not hold a simple conversation in standard Japanese even in the 1930s. Another sign of the strong continuity of traditions is that small children and youth embraced a more authoritarian age hierarchy, as assumed in traditional Okinawan villages, than the seinendan usually witnessed in other prefectures.[18]

These conflicting representations of youth overshadowed the seinendan's effort to create hardworking, nationalistic, and modern cadres of rural youth, composed of pre-conscripted young male villagers. The promotion of the seinendan became a pressing agenda for prefectural officials, however, when they faced the difficulty of turning Okinawans into functional Japanese soldiers. Since the inception of military conscription in Okinawa in 1898, the army had complained incessantly about the inability of Okinawan men to communicate in Japanese. The standing army in Okinawa depicted Okinawans as "incomplete in the understanding of the imperial national polity," "slow and sluggish, not agile," "poor in military ethos and disliking being soldiers."[19] Local officials viewed the education of future conscripts through the seinendan as a solution to this problem.

In fact, the militarization of Okinawan youth in general had been a distinct area of collaboration and contestation among different representations of youth. In some areas of militarization, all forces came together. Most typically, sports events (undōkai) held by schools and youth groups became popular in villages across Okinawa as a source of entertainment before universal military service began.[20] The physical strength, discipline, soldier-like masculinity, and communal bonding exhibited in these events were intended to impress the audience. All competing forces—modern reformist youth, traditional communal pillars of youth, and seinendan advocates—encouraged the spread of sports festivals to promote their own goals.

At the same time, military conscription was an issue that divided these forces, and conscription exam sites (particularly in Kunigami county) often exhibited volatile tensions. Many local residents, including the examinees' families, gathered at the sites in an inebriated state and watched as the police and army conducted the examination. This environment readily produced violent clashes between the authorities and the crowd. The Motobu Incident of 1910 was one of such instances. Officials viewed the "riot" by local residents at Motobu's conscription exam site, perhaps accurately, as an expression of resistance to the "Yamato" state's intervention in the life cycles of young villagers.[21] In this confrontation between Japanese officials and local communities, modern educated youth found an opportunity to separate themselves from state authorities. Criticizing the decision by prefecture officials to tighten control over local youth groups and strengthen the seinendan network immediately after the Motobu Incident, they argued that state control was an infringement of youth's autonomy. "Youth groups are supposed to respect each other's freedom," and "they should be family-like groups spontaneously established based on the accumulation of individual desires," a letter to *Ryūkyū shinpō* argued. Using the vocabulary commonly employed by youth leaders of the autonomy movement, the letter criticized the "supremacy of bureaucracy" (*kanken bannō shugi*).[22]

Experiences in military service, by contrast, were often a turning point of nationalization for individual Okinawan men. They encountered more direct and harsher discrimination in army units composed mostly of people from other prefectures.[23] A few Okinawan soldiers who knew Japanese had to work as interpreters to relay commands from their superiors to other Okinawans.[24] To prove their level of nationalization to army members from other prefectures, many Okinawan conscripts reportedly became fervently loyal to the emperor, volunteering for the most dangerous missions.[25] Regardless of the accuracy of such reports, military service exposed many Okinawan farm youth to the outside world and forced them to recognize Okinawa's position in the structure of the empire. As the number of army ex-conscripts increased, so did support for the seinendan, particularly for their function of teaching young men military discipline and Japanese.

To expand the army's presence in very young villagers' everyday lives, military exercises offered a spectacle of military drills and performances, much like those in Miyagi. In 1914, *Ryūkyū shinpō* reported the reactions of schoolchildren after they observed a military performance at their school, noting that "118 [boys] wish to become soldiers, 15 wish to become generals, 130 wish to become cavalrymen, 48 wish to do a military exercise as soldiers," while 48 boys concluded, "I'm lucky to have been born as a man." Many girls also said they would want to become cavalrymen and army generals had they been men, and 68 girls "regretted having been born as women," some of whom even blamed their parents for this misfortune.[26]

Over the course of the 1910s, supported by the ongoing militarization of the younger population, prefectural officials attempted to turn local youth groups into more metropole-style seinendan and promoted their goals of creating nationalistic and hardworking model rural youth. They introduced a set of concepts designed to enable the state to inspire young villagers and influence their social relationships, including self-cultivation (*shūyō*), love for one's native place (*aikyōshin*), and hardworkism (*kinrōshugi*) of individuals, for example.[27] Through youth training, prefectural officials linked Okinawa to the larger nation-empire. "Youth education is directly connected to the matter of national survival," they emphasized, requesting that educators "reflect upon the mission of the empire," which had become "the leader of Asia."[28]

The divergence in the rise of rural youth in Okinawa, despite the accelerating efforts by the prefectural government, was caused by chronic, widespread famine in the 1920s. This famine was called "the sotetsu palm hell" because many people resorted to eating the fruits of sotetsu (sago) palms, despite the accompanying risk of death by liver failure. The devastating poverty resulted from Okinawa's economic vulnerability in the fluctuating global sugar market. To make things even worse, after the price of sugar plunged in the 1920s, the imperial government concentrated its effort on expanding the sugar industry in Taiwan and deprived Okinawa of a means to develop a sustainable economy. Under these circumstances, Okinawan village youth had no choice but to emigrate in search of jobs as laborers. The economic historian Tomiyama Ichirō has shown that Okinawan village populations moved mainly from the countryside to urban areas inside the prefecture during the 1910s, but the economic devastation following World War I triggered mass migration, both male and female, to cities in the Japanese metropole. The average age of migrants also shifted from the thirties to the late teens and early twenties.[29] The Naha police counted about six to seven hundred young people leaving the countryside of Okinawa to find paid jobs outside the prefecture in the month of January 1925.[30] In 1926, nearly 12% of the total population registered in Kunigami county lived outside the prefecture.[31]

The need to migrate for sheer survival diminished the appeal of the common seinendan rhetoric of agrarian supremacy. Nonetheless, some seinendan advocates condemned the urban migration of young villagers. In an essay titled "Detest the Meaningless Migration" in a seinendan newsletter of Nago district, the author depicted young people's intention to migrate as "dreaming of an effortless life."[32] Such anti-migration rhetoric only widened the distance between the reality of Okinawan village lives and the empty slogans of the national seinendan movement.

By the 1930s, it was clear that the attempt to expand the seinendan among average farm and working youth had failed. The long period of economic depression worsened the class gap in the Okinawan countryside, and the category of those who could remain in the village and attend the seinendan narrowed to a relatively affluent class. The village seinendan still took charge of seasonal festivals and sports competitions, but the Kunigami county seinendan became a study group among select farmers on the topic of agricultural management, attended by only one or two men per school district.[33] In this environment, average farm youth did not establish a sphere of communication or cultivate a traveling identity as modern rural youth. Instead, their social ties developed in the location where they landed as migrants, typically urban slums and factories in Osaka.[34]

The careerization of rural youth, which took place through the expansion of youth training institutions in Tōhoku, did not happen in Okinawa, either. In 1926, following government policy, a youth training center (*seinen kunrenjo*, later turned into the youth school, *seinen gakkō*) was established in each elementary school. Of ninety to one hundred instructors in the entire Kunigami county, twelve to twenty-five were hired from among army reservists, and the rest were elementary schoolteachers.[35] These figures were too small to inspire youth to regard teaching as a realistic career option. The lack of opportunity to build a career as an agricultural professional further diminished the possibility of turning "rural youth" into a career path.

In essence, unlike the villages of Miyagi during the 1920s and early 1930s, Okinawa did not see an improvement in social status or an increase in the social leverage of village youth. Rather, in the early 1930s, some of the village seinendan in Okinawa became more detached from the mainstream seinendan of the metropole. Influenced by leftist activism, they became the central force organizing political protests against state and prefectural policies. One example was the Arashiyama Incident of 1931–1932, in which a coalition of village seinendan members protested against the government's plan to build a leprosy sanatorium in Arashiyama, Haneji village.[36] Another well-known incident was the Ōgimi Village Administration Reform Movement, which started during the same years. Young men in Kijoka hamlet in Ōgimi village established a self-proclaimed "soviet commune" and demanded tax reduction, welfare improvement, and increased accountability by village administrators.[37] Both movements involved thousands of villagers and outside supporters and obtained major concessions from the authorities. Wendy Matsumura frames these events in the context of peasants' struggle to maintain means of survival and "full participation in political and economic life."[38] Indeed, they seem to represent young villagers' stronger attachments to peasant communities, rather than the rise of a separate generational identity.

The extent of military mobilization in the 1940s and Okinawa's tragedy of becoming a combat zone once American troops landed in April 1945 are well known. In the late 1930s, military drills became the sole activity in the seinendan and youth schools. The local historian Fukuchi Hiroaki has published detailed accounts of many kinds of mobilization that targeted Okinawan children and youth. Recruitment for the Young Volunteer Corps for the Development of Manchuria-Mongolia started in Okinawa in 1938, albeit on a relatively small scale. Of those who received training to go to Manchuria at the famous Uchihara training center in Ibaraki prefecture, many came home and formed the Patriotic

Agricultural Corps (Hōkoku Nōheitai), recruiting many more Okinawan children to support food production. In October 1944, after a massive air raid, the army recruited Okinawan youth school students between twelve and seventeen years old to form the home village defense corps (gokyōtai) and expand guerrilla warfare.[39] Between January and March 1945, every man and woman was called to join the defense force as a soldier or a nurse. More than twenty-five thousand people were conscripted between the summer of 1944 and the end of the war, according to official records, and more than half of them died during the Battle of Okinawa.[40]

The memoirs of people in Okinawa reveal that, during this intense mobilization, the perceptual divide between Yamato people and Okinawans widened. Many Okinawans continued to have difficulty communicating in Japanese. Because of persistent discrimination, conscripted Okinawan laborers and soldiers were frequent targets of violence by people from the metropole. During the Battle of Okinawa and in its immediate aftermath, surviving Japanese soldiers, who hid in the mountains and lived as desperate bandits, committed several massacres of Okinawan villagers, claiming that the locals were "spying on behalf of the enemy."[41] Ironically, however, once Americans occupied the villages, the former linguistic disadvantage became a ticket to survival. Ability to speak the Okinawan uchinānchu proved that the speakers were noncombatants and distinguished them from "Japanese spies" disguised as Okinawan residents, preventing them from being seized as prisoners of war.[42]

This brief look at how ideas about youth developed and were contested in villages of Okinawa serves as a prelude to our forthcoming examination of the complexity of colonial situations. As in Miyagi, the role of youth had dual faces of modernization and historical continuity, but in Okinawa the duality was situated at two ends of a far wider spectrum between pro-Japanese assimilating forces and robust resistance against it. Therefore, attempts to define the role of youth stirred unbridgeable social and political tensions to a degree unfamiliar to mainland seinendan advocates. As an early experience of colonization, the Okinawan case also suggests the importance of recognizing rural–urban differences in colonial dynamics. Although forces of Japanization were felt more imminently and visually in the cities, rural regions experienced colonial politics in the form of severe social tensions. Competing concepts of youth triggered heated social battles in the countryside, though they did not necessarily become explicitly ethnic confrontations.

The Okinawan case also illuminates how, in the 1910s, military recruitment and the presence of the army served as a catalyst in the spread of the seinendan, even in the villages filled with social tensions. But those factors alone could not replicate the social mechanism of producing a local basis of nationalistic enthu-siasts. In the 1920s, the series of youth training programs failed to bring about a social revolution in young farmers' lives, either in career prospects or in shared self-esteem as rural youth, because of Okinawa's marginalized position in Japan's imperial economic policy. Without a mechanism that allowed state policies to interact with the social dynamics of village youth, the state's use of young human resources during wartime, especially in light of Okinawa's deadly battles, was largely exploitative and without redeeming benefits.

Through the lens of youth mobilization, Okinawa's position in Japan's nation-empire becomes clearer. It was not the exemplary big brother to the other colo-nies as it often claimed. It was rather an extreme periphery in the unfortunate position of being a part of the inner territories. It neither enjoyed the autonomy of territories untouched by the imperial state nor received attention from inter-national eyes concerned with monitoring colonial practice. From an early point, the majority of Okinawan youth sought survival by migrating to various parts of the Japanese Empire and beyond, experiencing the empire from angles very dif-ferent from those of farm youth who, albeit against their will, remained in their native villages through the 1920s and 1930s.

Part 2

THE SO-CALLED OUTER TERRITORIES

4

COLONIAL INTELLECTUALS

The rise of youth in discourse was a global phenomenon. In Asia, the metaphor of the human lifespan gave colonial intellectuals a vocabulary that explained their society's status in a social Darwinian world. Childhood, youth, and old age represented the nation's vulnerability, vitality, and weakness, respectively. Liang Qichao, a leading reformer in late Qing China, famously applied this metaphor in his 1900 work *Young China*. Liang argued that as a dynastic empire, China was old and weak, but as a nation-state, it was young and had hope for the future. "If youth of the entire nation act youthfully, China will become a country of the future, its progress without bounds," he wrote, "but if youth of the entire nation act like the aged, China will become a country of the past and will soon meet its demise. Therefore, the responsibility for the day rests completely upon our youth alone."[1]

The concept of rural youth—the stronghold of imperial nationalism in Japanese public discourse—took on symbolic meanings for anticolonial intellectuals in Japan's own colonies as well. But for them it represented a powerful counterforce against imperial aggression. Highly educated Korean and Taiwanese students studying in Japan and China, influenced by Tokutomi Sohō's argument that the Meiji Restoration was a youthful achievement, saw youthfulness as the secret to national strength. They were also inspired by political ideologies popular in the early twentieth century, mainly socialism and communism. These students joined in the global wave of youth activism, interacting with reformers in Japan, China, and sometimes the Soviet Union. This internationalism, however, split the anticolonial movements. On the one hand, so-called nationalist youth advocating for nation building through modernization and social reform viewed the recent expansion of the seinendan in Japan as a model to emulate. Socialist youth, on the other hand, criticized these "bourgeois" enlighteners for romanticizing the countryside and highlighted the exploitation of colonial peasants. Despite their rivalry, these colonial intellectuals developed a large discursive consensus on the importance of mobilizing rural youth to restore national sovereignty.

As in Okinawa, these intellectuals encountered insurmountable challenges in pursuing their political goals. Besides their ideological beliefs, their generational identity as youth forced them to struggle on multiple fronts. They battled against Japanese colonizers, older generations, traditional landlords, and other anticolonial groups in a battle over issues of legitimacy and leadership. For them, more than the crackdown by colonial police, the widening gap between students and farmers constituted a major obstacle. As they intensified their attempt to align with young peasants in the countryside, they discovered to their dismay that urban students and impoverished, illiterate tenant farmers had little in common. Even those who joined the youth group movements in larger provincial towns were stuck in their own politics in the local social contexts, instead of operating as agents of youth leaders in Taipei or Seoul.

In retrospect, this chasm between the two widely discrepant social worlds of intellectuals and peasant youth, respectively, provided an opening for Japanese activists to pursue seinendan mobilization. Despite the confrontations and crackdowns, the colonial authorities never sought to suppress the youth-centered discourse and agrarianism spread by anticolonial youth. Instead, by investing more resources and deploying familiar methods of seinendan mobilization, colonial officials further propelled the trend. In other words, imperial youth mobilization in the 1930s to some degree built upon the conceptual foundation established by anticolonial intellectuals of the 1920s.

Korean Students and Modern Youth

Just as the seinendan movement in Japan was part of a global trend of youth mobilization, so too were youth movements on the Korean peninsula. Japan constituted a large component of the international context that affected Korea. Since the mid-nineteenth century, Japan had been the focus of profound interest among Korean leaders as it simultaneously represented the possibility of an independent Asia and a serious threat to Korea's own independence. Japan rapidly transformed itself from an old feudal system into a modern Western-style polity, aggressively absorbed Western knowledge, and intervened in Chinese and Korean politics. It turned Korea into a protectorate by 1905 and formally annexed it in 1910. Yet despite the heightening political tension, the pressing threat of Western imperialism and the proximity of Tokyo led many Korean leaders to look to Meiji Japan as a model.

The concept of youth (*ch'ŏngnyŏn*) as an engine of modernity was introduced to Seoul by Korean students studying in Japan. Ch'oe Nam-sŏn is an illustrative example. Having been sent to Japan by the Chosŏn government in 1904 at age fourteen, Ch'oe avidly read Japanese and Western magazines in Tokyo. Upon his return, he started a mass magazine, *Sonyŏn* (Youth, 1908–1911), as a pioneer of the genre in Korea. Inspired by *Taiyō* (The sun), a popular Japanese magazine in the 1900s, *Sonyŏn* published literary and social commentary aimed at urban youth. In some ways, it possessed a novelty similar to that of Tokutomi Sohō's *Kokumin no tomo* (The nation's friend), a famous youth magazine and catalyst of youth movements in 1890s Japan. After working on a number of youth and children's publications, Ch'oe started another youth magazine, *Ch'ŏngch'un* (Youth, 1914–1918).[2] Through these magazines, writers like Ch'oe Nam-sŏn and Yi Kwang-su, both of whom would become influential cultural leaders of Korea in the subsequent decades, sought to inspire youth to become the protagonists of a modern society.[3] Korean-language newspapers embraced the youthful forces of the time. In both of Korea's main newspapers, *Hwangsŏng sinmun* (Capital gazette) and *Taehan maeil sinbo* (The Korea daily news), the number of articles that discussed *ch'ŏngnyŏn* increased rapidly during the course of the first decades of the twentieth century.[4]

In contrast to most other colonial societies, where the image of immature and innocent infants was often used to describe indigenous populations, publications in Korea at the turn of the century defined Korea as an old, debilitated nation: "Our nation Korea is more than four thousand years old—politics is old, the bureaucracy is old, people are old, like a man of seventy or eighty years."[5] Its age was also associated with corruption and laziness, which the present day's strong and healthy youth were "responsible for cleaning up" to "realize the world of reform and civilization."[6] The authors making these comments were well aware that the new attention to youth was a worldwide phenomenon, not unique to Japan. In a 1905 article called, "Advice to Youth," in the *Capital Gazette*, the author divided human life into four stages, in the same way that the American scholar Stanley Hall and others conceptualized it at the time, and argued that the second stage, youth, was the key period for education. He explained that "civilized and educated men in the Western powers studied youth education and designed youth groups," and that "this wave has reached Japan, China, and also our Korean capital."[7] To these Korean authors, youth education was a new global standard of civilization to which Korea should be ready to adjust.

These authors established the category of youth by contrasting the progressive nature of young people to the incompetent older generations. In June 1910, Yi Kwang-su, then an eighteen-year-old student studying in Japan, captured the feelings of intellectual youth in an article, "Circumstances of Korean Youth Today," published in *Sonyŏn*. "We youth do not have predecessors who can teach and lead us as older generations did," he argued, continuing, "It is a fact that nine out of ten schools are clearly not qualified to teach us." His unfavorable view of earlier generations was probably attributable to the failure of a series of modernization attempts: the Kapsin Palace Coup (1884), the Kabo reforms (1894–1896), and the Independence Club Movement (1896–1899). These attempts did not succeed either in their original purposes or in preventing Korea from losing its national sovereignty. In a country surrounded by multiple imperial forces and on the verge of annexation by Japan, Korean youth, "compared to those in other countries or other times, need to make tens or hundreds times more effort" to construct a new nation. Yi added that "whether we youth are aware of our own situation determines the line between the prosperity and decline of the Korean nation." This was surely a time of crisis, but also an opportunity for youth to achieve greatness because "it is a time like this that made Napoleon a Napoleon, and Washington a Washington."[8]

The drive to educate themselves was common among these educated youth. Yi Kwang-su advocated "self-training and self-cultivation" (*chasu chayang*), both individually and in groups. Yun Chi-ho, an American-educated Christian leader, established a youth group among students in 1909—which the participants called "one large spiritual circle of committed youth"—to exchange knowledge and become leaders of society.[9] Similar kinds of intellectual youth groups had existed among Korean students studying in Tokyo since the 1890s.[10] Although they were not as numerous as the youth groups formed across Japan in the 1890s, reports of voluntary gatherings and lecture events involving "motivated youth" in the Korean homeland often appeared in newspapers in the 1900s and 1910s.[11]

Some of these youth groups embraced the idea that young generational force was more important to successful nation building than national roots or tradition. Meiji Japan, in their view, presented a strong case study of the linkage between youth initiatives and national independence. Despite Japan's colonial rule over Korea, fascination with the Meiji leaders' success in repelling Western imperialism persisted in the writings of Korean students. "The day when the American fleet arrived in Urawa Port was, indeed, a crisis that challenged Japan's national survival . . . and the Japanese nation analyzed this enormous problem and brought about a breakthrough. . . . No one but the Japanese nation—[or rather] Japanese youth—solved their own problem. We have to be like Japanese youth of forty or fifty years ago, rather than like those of today," a student study-ing in Japan wrote in a 1918 essay.[12]

Many of these students engaged in anticolonial movements, but they also believed that Korea should deal with its crisis by emulating Japanese youth who had faced a similar challenge half a century earlier. Korean nationalist youth regarded the modern nation-state as a product of generational achievements in the world of social-Darwinian competition.[13] They turned for inspiration to the youthful figures in Japan's recent history or to Europe's empire builders rather than to their ancestors in the long allegedly continuous history of Korea.[14] Embracing a strong generational identity and a strictly modern temporal percep-tion, these youth believed that the value of youthfulness transcended geographic, ethnic, and racial divides and would be critical to their anticolonial activities, which culminated in the March First Independence Movement of 1919.

Local Youth Groups after the March First Movement

The March First Movement sparked changes in colonial rule and triggered a new form of youth activism in Korean society. Urban youth—mostly students—played the leading role in the movement. Inspired by Woodrow Wilson's speech on self-determination, Korean students in Seoul (also in Tokyo) drafted declara-tions of independence, conducted school strikes, and led street demonstrations that spread across the peninsula within a couple of weeks.[15] The official record states that nearly thirteen thousand students enrolled in both public and private schools participated in the movement.[16] The literary leaders who created Korea's youth discourse were actively involved in organizing the nationwide mobiliza-tion. They included Ch'oe Nam-sŏn, whom the colonial authorities described as "the person most trusted by youth and students."[17]

After these demonstrations were quelled, Korea saw a surge of youth groups at the county level. "At least ten youth groups are being created around the country every day, and there are more than seventy groups just in Seoul right now," the newspaper *Tonga ilbo* reported in June 1920.[18] Both Korean reporters and colonial officials described the rapid growth of youth groups as "sprouting like bamboo shoots after a rain."[19] The government counted 251 youth groups (*ch'ŏngnyŏnhoe*) in 1920, 446 in 1921, and 488 in 1922.[20] It was not an exaggera-tion when *Tonga ilbo* wrote in December 1922 that "purely social youth groups flourish and have reached more than five hundred in number. Every county is witnessing an expansion of youth groups, and including religious youth groups, there are more than a thousand such organizations."[21]

The rise of youth groups in county capitals reflected a number of changes underway in Korean society in the post–March First period. One was the formation of new alliances between traditional landlord families and younger elites outside Seoul. During the demonstrations, the student generation began to collaborate with local landholding leaders. Many sons of the landed class were attending schools in urban areas, and through their student networks, the landed class also mobilized rallies in rural areas. In fact, 56% of arrests during the movement were of people in the agricultural sector, whereas students and teachers composed only 13% of those arrested.[22] The eventual failure of the independence movement caused the student leaders to realize that they needed to expand their popular support in the countryside so as to achieve their goal of recovering sovereignty.[23]

At the same time, the explosion of youth groups also reflected the denser ties developing between local leaders and colonial authorities under a new colonial policy called "cultural rule," which was intended to expand education and promote the cultural assimilation of the Korean population. This policy attempted to placate anti-Japanese forces by allowing Korean-language publications and giving Korean leaders greater access to capital and governance. It made possible the launch of two new national newspapers in April 1920, *Tonga ilbo* and *Chosŏn ilbo*. These publications created a new social medium for Korean provincial leaders and served as a catalyst for the spread of local youth groups, which gleaned information from the newspaper reports and copied each other's approach. Typically, the landholding class, who had donated a significant sum of money for organizing a youth group formed a preparatory committee. For an association's inauguration ceremony, they organized events such as sports festivals and public lectures. Their attitude toward colonial authorities was ambivalent, if not overtly friendly. They invited colonial officials to participate—the county head, the president of the financial union, the chief of police, school principals, and other powerful figures in the county.[24] Combining slogans equally popular to the Japanese seinendan and the YMCA, they stated that their goals were "to improve mind, spirit, and body of the youth," "to expand modern education," and "to improve social morals." They pledged to engage in lectures, debates, amateur plays, tennis competitions, and night schools for uneducated villagers.[25] In short, these groups represented a shared sphere for colonial officials and local notables.

These youth groups not only mediated between colonial officials and Korean leaders but also bridged generations of local leadership. The example of Chaenyŏng county in Hwanghae province shows that through the new county youth groups, the traditional local (landed) leaders sought modernization while maintaining the previous social hierarchy. In Chaenyŏng, a small number of landlords initiated a youth group movement in May 1920. These leaders worked as *Tonga ilbo* representatives in the region and formed the Chaenyŏng landlord association at the same time. They advocated for modern education, arguing that "we should alter the previous use of the *hyanggyo* (local Confucian academy)" and "establish a school that could teach new customs and new thinking, sometimes provide lectures and debates, and spread new knowledge."[26] Rather than challenging the old Confucian social order, the scholar Tsuji Hironori argues, this youth group facilitated collaboration between old and new forces in the local community.[27] Perhaps these groups also provided a way to reabsorb highly educated but jobless youth back into the local social order.[28] These youth groups, led by multiple generations and supported by both Korean and Japanese leaders, played a mediating role among many parties in county politics.

Young intellectuals in Seoul who were more overtly anticolonial did not overlook the opportunity to network with these local youth groups. They established the Korea Youth Group Association (Chosŏn Ch'ŏngnyŏnhoe Yŏnhaphoe) in December 1920. Soon one-fifth of the local youth groups on the peninsula had joined this national association.[29] The core organizers of the association were well-known anticolonial activists, such as Chang Tŏk-su, Kim Myŏng-sik, O Sang-gŭn, Kim Sa-guk, and Yi Yŏng, some of whom were also known as writers for *Tonga ilbo*.[30] They had come to embrace a Korean national consciousness, socialist ideas, or both while studying in Japan and became vocal negotiators with the colonial authorities upon returning to Korea. O Sang-gŭn, the association's president, pointed out the need for such a national organization that could "unite the spirit, principles, and activities" of important local forces.[31] To improve cooperation among youth groups, the association planned to support publications, lectures, workshops, night schools, and sports festivals. It placed the strongest emphasis on the reform of old customs and on supporting youth's schooling.[32] Although the organization recruited fewer members than the leaders were aiming for, their connection with *Tonga ilbo* allowed them to exercise considerable influence over other groups that paid close attention to their voices and activities.

One would easily notice that the activities and structure of both individual youth groups and the national Korea Youth Group Association resembled those of the Japanese seinendan. These young nationalists had witnessed the expansion of the seinendan institutions and their agrarian nationalism in Japan and so the seinendan served as their clearest reference point. "European countries, following Germany, are all trying to organize youth groups. Especially in a country like Japan, they ally with people who have prominent social stature to organize youth groups everywhere and train youth," wrote O Sang-gŭn a few months after launching the association.[33] "In Japan and other countries, youth groups developed in each and every village, spreading like a cobweb. Considering that, our current status may not be a cause for pride, yet as a newcomer, the growth [of youth groups] in such a short period is a world record," wrote *Tonga ilbo* on the association's second anniversary.[34] Despite their empire–colony relationship—or perhaps because of it—the seinendan format was attractive to young Korean intellectuals who hoped to nurture national consciousness among the wider population, just as it had been to state officials and social reformers in Japan.

Taiwanese Students between Japan and China

While county youth groups were spreading on the Korean peninsula, similar ideas regarding the social role of youth also circulated among intellectual youth in another Japanese colony, Taiwan. Taiwanese students studying in Tokyo started a journal, *Taiwan qingnian* (spelled as *Tâi oân chheng liân*; Taiwan youth), in 1920. Like the rapidly growing youth groups in Korea, this journal reflected the post–World War I global slogan of self-determination as well as Japan's new cultural rule, which was also introduced in Taiwan. As the first organized voice advocating self-determination and Taiwanese nationalism, *Taiwan qingnian* occupies a unique place in the modern history of Taiwan. The publication's editors explicitly described both its writers and its target audience as youth.

The term "youth," or *qingnian*, first appeared in Taiwan earlier than the journal itself and represented the generation educated in Japanese and Chinese institutions. The "youth sector" became a common phrase in *Taiwan nichinichi shinpō*, a bilingual newspaper of the colonial Government-General of Taiwan (GGT), in 1905. It referred to a group of city youth who had obtained a modern school education and Japanese language skills in addition to training in the Chinese classics. Since the acquisition of Taiwan in 1895, the GGT had been attempting to subvert the prestige of the civil service exam previously offered by Qing China and supply a new status symbol with its own institutions. Toward this end, the GGT established an elite Japanese language school and gave titles of honor to local leading figures. By 1905, a decade of colonial rule and Japan's recent victory in the Russo-Japanese War had encouraged the development of a small group of bilingual youth among the upper classes. Taiwan's traditional elite classes expected those in the youth sector to more effectively negotiate with the colonial authorities.

The new focus on youth, however, had the effect of disturbing the traditional age-based hierarchy common among the Taiwanese upper class. The new generation envisioned a transition from the privilege of seniority to youth-centered nation building. Chen Boyu, for example, wrote in an article titled "Taiwan's Youth Sector" in October 1905, "There are old people (*lao*), youth (*zhuang*), and children (*you*)." He explained the division of ages in classical Chinese terms, but then claimed that "those who represent the nation (*guomin*)" and "take on the great responsibility" are the youth—expressed in the new term *qingnian*. Chen did not extol the masculine, militant characteristic of youth that the Japanese public was celebrating at the time. Rather, he warned readers against the danger of reckless acts that had characterized Taiwanese youth's resistance against the Japanese, as well as the meaningless deaths of many Japanese soldiers fighting the Russians. Youth should observe the "large forces of the world" and "become citizens of the greater nation"; to achieve the nation's goal, they should "never give up, but study."[35]

The youth sector worked more closely with Japanese colonizers than the older leaders expected. They formed youth groups in the 1910s under the auspices of colonial authorities. These groups compensated for a shortage of schools rather than nurturing anticolonial alliances. Around this time, new Taiwanese leaders like Lin Xiantang, supported by Japanese social activists, called for a movement to "reform the old customs" and "learn the Japanese language." To become part of this trend, an increasing number of local elites created groups for highly educated youth.[36] This initiative expanded the scale of the youth sector and generated among these youth a more collaborative attitude toward the GGT.

To this steady expansion of GGT-sanctioned youth education, the journal *Taiwan qingnian* delivered a powerful blow. Contrary to the pro-colonial character of these youth groups, the Taiwanese students in Tokyo tied the category of youth specifically to Taiwan's national consciousness. More than the Taiwanese writers, the Japanese contributors, including the famous Taishō democracy activist Yoshino Sakuzō and Meiji University professor Izumi Akira, exhibited a greater anti-government attitude and advocated for the value of Taiwanese ethnic identity. "Taiwan is not the GGT's Taiwan. I demand that Taiwanese people be self-aware of being Taiwanese," Izumi argued, and in the inaugural issue of the journal, he defined their goal as a "self-ruled Taiwan."[37]

In reality, the task of building an ethnic consciousness was anything but straightforward. Nationalist activists allied with the students abroad established the Taiwan Cultural Association as their operational base in Taiwan in October 1921. Very quickly, this association became the largest body of anticolonial activists. But the students in Tokyo and activists in Taiwan faced a challenge unknown to their Korean counterparts. Their conception of Taiwan started from a bitter realization that it was a tiny island located at the periphery of the world.[38] To make up for this sense of inferiority, they naturally traced their heritage back to China, priding themselves on the magnificent history and culture of the Han Chinese. "The 3.5 million current Taiwanese residents are part of Han ethnicity, which enjoys a long history of more than four thousand years," Lin Chenglu claimed in an article on the self-awareness of Taiwanese youth, continuing, "Needless to say, we are totally different from the eighty thousand uncivilized barbarians inhabiting the Central Mountains and Taidong mountainous region."[39] Even Cai Peihuo, who was more reflective about Taiwanese discrimination against the aborigines in his advocacy for equal treatment of the Taiwanese, proudly presented the "Han group's distinctive features" as "loving peace, admiring ancestors, valuing substance, and forbearing."[40]

These Taiwanese youth were drawn to the anticolonial revolutionary movements of early 1920s China. A pioneering magazine for these Chinese movements, *Xin qingnian* (New youth), first published in Shanghai in 1915 as *Youth Magazine*, was an obvious source of inspiration. The journal of the Taiwan Cultural Association reprinted a copy of the article "Call to Youth," which the leading revolutionary Chen Duxiu published when he founded *Youth Magazine*. It included this passage:

> Youth is like early spring, like the rising sun, like trees and grass in bud, like a newly sharpened blade. It is the most valuable period of life. The function of youth in society is the same as that of a fresh and vital cell in a human body . . . I only, with tears, place my plea before the young and vital youth, in the hope that they will achieve self-awareness, and begin to struggle. What is this self-awareness? It is to be conscious of the value and responsibility of one's young life and vitality, to maintain one's self-respect, which should not be lowered. What is the struggle? It is to exert one's intellect, discard resolutely the old and the rotten, regard them as enemies and as the flood or savage beasts, keep away from their neighborhood and refuse to be contaminated by their poisonous germs.[41]

The connection with Chinese youth activists, however, posed an ironic challenge to the Taiwanese elite youth who valued the heritage of Han culture. Chen Duxiu and other Chinese authors were waging a war against the Confucian system of knowledge and governance. Attracted to their revolutionary attitude, *Taiwan minbao*, the main newspaper of the Cultural Association, also adopted vernacular Mandarin Chinese as the main language of publication in 1923. But Taiwanese intellectual youth still quoted ancient sages and warriors in the original literary Chinese.[42] They hesitated to deny Confucianism at large, fearing that it would undercut their self-definition as great Han descendants. Simultaneously, they offered a passionate voice in favor of liberating women and reforming the oppressive family system, conceptually separating this aspect of modernization from their longing for national roots. But in these areas of social reform, Japanese activists and even the colonial government were a step ahead of the Chinese reformists.

The most notable characteristic of the vision of these young Taiwanese intellectuals was their rejection of a social-Darwinian world. Their diasporic identity crisis, split between their embrace of China's great historical heritage and an
urge for modern reforms that often justified Japanese dominance, drove them
to value their very in-between-ness. "Taiwan's new youth are equipped with the
unique character and capacity to become the middleman for realizing Japan–
China friendship," Zhou Taoyuan argued in the third issue of *Taiwan qingnian*.
He deplored the neglect of Taiwanese youth by these two nations, questioning
whether "it is because the government authorities are afraid of too much potential" of Taiwanese youth, or because "Taiwanese youth have not sought development abroad owing to a lack of discipline and energy."[43] The ideal of perpetual
world peace that circulated globally after World War I was not mere utopian
rhetoric for Taiwanese youth. Their self-worth rested in pursuing cooperation
between nations—particularly Japan and China—and not in the severe competition assumed in the social-Darwinian framework. The editors saw "justice,
humanity, freedom, and peace" as characterizing the coming new era, and they
called for Taiwanese youth to realize this ideal.[44] This vision stood in stark contrast with the concept of survival of the fittest, which their Korean counterparts
embraced.

The attachment of Taiwanese youth to mainland China also shaped their
critique of older people, which was significantly milder than that expressed
by Korean, Chinese, and Japanese youth of the same period or even the Taiwanese youth sector prevalent earlier. The articles published in *Taiwan qingnian* and *Taiwan minbao* called on youth to attain' self-awareness, defining
them as the most important agent of social reform. But they rarely expressed
antagonism toward older generations. The youthful characteristics praised
by activists in Japan and Korea may have been vague and inconsistent, but
Taiwanese youth's respect for the old constituted a significant obstacle to
demarcating their generational category, however eagerly they appropriated
the word *qingnian*.

Japan as a colonial oppressor was the only clear "Other" for these Taiwanese
youth. Instead of opposing the old, they worked against "conservative" forces,
which referred to the oppression of the colonial government and the Taiwanese elite who curried favor with it.[45] *Goyō shinshi* (government-hired gentlemen) were their nemesis. The confrontation centered on two policy areas: equal
access to education for Taiwanese and Japanese students and the establishment
of a Taiwanese parliament, modeled after Irish home rule. Adding legitimacy to
their anticolonial identity construction were the crackdowns conducted by the
GGT. Once branches of the Cultural Association began spreading around 1924,
reports on violence, arrests, and oppression by the GGT filled the pages of *Taiwan*

minbao. These reports and experiences, in turn, nurtured a common identity as Taiwanese youth.

At the same time, Japan was an obvious modernizing model. The leaders of the Meiji Restoration appeared just as heroic in Taiwanese eyes as they did to Korean youth. "Look at the era of the Meiji Restoration. Itō, Ōkubo, Saigō, Itagaki, Niijima [*sic*] were steadfast among the youth," Wu Keji argued, contrasting them to those "lacking patriotism and group spirit" in the new Republic of China.[46] Along with the Meiji Restoration, establishing constitutional politics and winning the Russo-Japanese War "all depended on youthful enthusiasm and struggle," another author claimed in 1924.[47]

The Japanese seinendan drew the attention of Taiwanese youth in the same way as they had attracted the notice of O Sang-gǔn in Korea. Xu Qingxiang published an article titled "Encouraging Local Seinendan," which expressed his admiration of the wide network and activities of Japan's seinendan. Their volunteer labor during the construction of the Meiji Shrine particularly impressed him. "Dear wise youth, please look at how actively youth in every city, town, and village [in Japan] work and how earnestly society gives guidance and support to them," he begged the reader. Xu did not even modify the state-centric organization of the seinendan when advocating for it in Taiwan; he stated that the members should be "elementary school graduates," and the head of each seinendan should be "the village head or school principal whenever possible." This was the first time that Taiwanese youth discussed the importance of enhancing *local* culture and enlightenment. In other words, attention to the countryside was generated through a discussion of the seinendan.[48]

Accompanying the rising popularity of the Taiwan Cultural Association, youth groups spread across Taiwan during the 1920s. But the association had difficulty in counting the exact number of affiliated youth groups. Since many local groups of the youth sector established in the previous decade were also endorsed by colonial officials, they frequently maintained a sort of dual allegiance. The historian Chen Wen Sung details the activities of the Yanfeng youth group in Caotun, Taizhong, which the Cultural Association described as the most "solid" youth group. Even in this case, the Japanese village head Atsumi Kanzō endorsed the Yanfeng group and gave speeches at its ceremonies until it officially became a branch of the leftist Taiwanese People's Party in 1927.[49] It embraced a Chinese revolutionary spirit, as expressed in its 1924 statement of purpose, which quoted the first half of Chen Duxiu's "Call to Youth." The founding members erected a Yanfeng youth group building directly in front of the village office, as if to embody the group's simultaneous association and confrontation with colonial authorities.[50]

The leaders of the Taiwan Cultural Association tried to differentiate their youth groups from the previous GGT-led ones in various ways. Since both waved the banner of modernization—abolition of old customs of funerals, marriage, family hierarchies, and so on—they competed to claim that they truly represented the Taiwanese population. *Taiwan minbao* put the slogan "The only organ of public opinion of the Taiwanese" before its name. By 1926, "study group" (*dushuhui*) had become a popular name for youth groups, mirroring many similar groups formed in mainland China.[51] Backers of study groups claimed that most of the other youth groups (*qingnianhui*) advanced interests of colonial officials, whereas study groups were independent and would "conduct real measures to respond to society's needs."[52] These assertions paradoxically reflected the difficulty involved in obtaining recognition among wider populations and legitimizing the struggle against colonial authorities. As in Korea, the central body of the Cultural Association stood clearly against the colonial authorities, but the local branches often remained ambivalent and more subject to politics among local leaders.

Socialist Youth Groups and the Question of Age

In both Korea and Taiwan, colonial officials, anticolonial leaders, local notables, and youth all had a stake in shaping youth groups to meet their needs. As a result, competition for influence was not limited to that between colonial and anticolonial forces. Youth mobilization was complicated by various factors, but one of the greatest sources of chaos was the split in the anticolonial camp at the national level. This division became evident when socialist youth loudly asserted a position separate from the enlightenment movement and self-strengthening programs advocated by so-called nationalist youth leaders.

In Taiwan, this split was symbolized by a change in leadership of the Taiwan Cultural Association in 1927. In the early 1920s, a number of Taiwanese students, including Lian Wenxing and Jiang Weishui, came into contact with Japanese socialist figures like Yamakawa Hitoshi and Sakai Toshihiko. Others decided to devote themselves to communism while studying in China. For example, Chen Duxiu met a Taiwanese student, Xu Naichang, in Shanghai and helped him travel to Moscow as a Chinese citizen.[53] "Every year since the establishment of the Cultural Association, influences from the Chinese Revolution, the Bolshevik Revolution in Russia, Comintern activities, and anarchism and communism in Japan steadily grew in the enlightenment activities conducted by the Cultural Association," the colonial police recorded.[54] After an internal power struggle between Lian Wenxiang, Jiang Weishui, and Cai Peihuo in 1927, Lian came to represent the Cultural Association and established the implementation of communism as its goal. Jiang, Cai, and other previous leaders who did not embrace communist class struggle left the association and formed the more moderate (but still left-leaning) Taiwanese People's Party.[55] The previous leaders denounced the communist forces for their inflexible political orientation, referring again to the Meiji Restoration, in which "merchants and masterless samurai allied with the nobles . . . these facts provide a good lesson for Taiwan's liberation activists to learn from."[56]

In Korea, the split within the elite circles transpired even earlier than in Taiwan. A leadership battle arose due to mounting frustration about stagnant youth activism at the local levels. In March 1921, an editorial in *Tonga ilbo* stated that "observing the current status of each youth group, we see almost no activities or development, because of (1) the difficulties in maintaining the group owing to the trouble in collecting membership fees and (2) the lack of projects and activities."[57] The national association also lost steam in the second year. Yi Kang explained in retrospect, "To write down activities between the first anniversary [of the Korea Youth Group Association] and the third general meeting in April 1922, I tried hard to dig up the material I have, and I asked my friends who were committee members, but pitifully, I did not find anything worth noting. If I have to write something, it would only be an increase in member youth groups and the four issues of the journal *Asŏng* . . . I cannot help but feel sad at how stagnant the youth movement in Korea was during this time."[58]

The harshest criticisms came from the socialist youth who collaborated with nationalist leaders in establishing the Korea Youth Group Association. From the very beginning, they fought what they considered the "bourgeois" forces led by the *Tonga ilbo* group. Accusing them of corruption and lack of activism, the socialist youth attempted to oust their founding leaders, O Sang-gǔn, Kim Myŏng-sik, and Chang Tŏk-su, at their third regular meeting in April 1922. After this no-confidence motion was voted down, the leading leftist group, Seoul Youth Group, and those pursuing a vision of class struggle quit the Korea Youth Group Association altogether. Instead, they held an All Korea Youth Party Convention (Chŏn Chosŏn Ch'ŏngnyŏndang Taehoe) with seventy-four youth groups in March 1923. This drastically changed the climate of youth politics. Those remaining in the Korea Youth Group Association tried to address the increasingly heated issues of peasants and workers, but they could not stem the socialist tide created by the Seoul Youth Group. In February 1924, the association decided to rejoin the Seoul Youth Group, and together they formed the Korea Youth General Alliance (Chosŏn Ch'ŏngnyŏn Ch'ongdongmaeng).[59] This time the leadership of the Seoul Youth Group, as well as the main goal of class struggle, became clear to everyone.

Korean youth, in comparison with their Taiwanese counterparts, had already shown a strong generational identity and antagonism toward the old. When the socialist youth groups gained momentum, they pushed the concerns about age to another level by introducing a new question: what is the age limit that defines youth? In Japan, the age-based politics that unfolded in the autonomy movement developed from the army's intervention in setting an age limit for the seinen-dan. Youth in places like Nagano generated a new consciousness about age and demanded that people over twenty-five years old not intervene. In Korea, on the other hand, the question of age came from a greater distance. It reflected a debate developing among international Communist leaders about whether youth should be in leadership positions as the vanguard of social revolution or subordinate to the Communist Party. When the theory of youth as vanguard sub-sided and the party set a clear age limit for Komsomol membership at fourteen to twenty-three years old, leftist youth groups in Korea rushed to establish age limits as well.[60] The Korea Youth General Alliance also introduced an age limit of thirty, later changing it to twenty-seven.[61]

The strict age limit did not strengthen the power of youth leadership but instead became another tactical weapon in the competition among them. From the beginning, the Communist Party in the Soviet Union had set an age limit for Komsomol membership in order to contain the power of youth. Leftist leaders in Seoul, in turn, used the age constraint as a tool in their power struggles for recognition by international Communist authorities. On some occasions, they attacked the Seoul Youth Group as promoting vanguard-like youth groups that assumed too much leadership in all sectors, such as workers, peasants, and women, against the decision of the Communist International;[62] at other times, they criticized it as insufficiently progressive or young. Pak Hyŏng-byŏng, a thirty-year-old leader of the Korea Youth General Alliance, was condemned as "the old president" by other committee members.[63] In short, when socialist leaders brought in the question of age from the outside world to strengthen their legitimacy, they simultaneously imported the volatile climate of global youth discourse, which did not help the situation in Korea.

At the county level, the strict age limit affected the politics of youth groups in a different way. In county capitals, conflicts between leftist youth and traditional notables were erupting everywhere. Socialist youth raised the question of age—insisting that youth group members ought to be young—as the first measure of progressive reform (hyŏksin). Since youth groups were collaborative forums that linked the worlds of local officials, the traditional upper class, and the newly educated, many groups allowed membership up to age forty, and even people older than forty had a say in the groups' activities.[64] Leftist youth saw this situation as a problem and deployed the age argument to eliminate interventions by unwelcome forces. Around 1925, one youth group after another adopted a new age limit, usually thirty years old, to replace the original committee members.[65] Through such progressive reforms, they attempted to shift the priority of their activities. In Chaenyŏng, for example, landed leaders preferred to invest resources in industry-stimulating projects, whereas socialist youth wanted to operate night study groups for illiterate peasants and women. Illiteracy remained a serious problem in rural life and the biggest obstacle to mass mobilization.[66] Although the question of age was a double-edged sword for leadership circles in Seoul, setting an age limit allowed country-level leftist youth to distinguish themselves from the older, more powerful, traditional upper class that did not share the goal of mobilizing the wider masses.

The Agrarian View of Nationalist and Socialist Youth

In Korea's intense youth politics, local youth groups were valued not only as branches of their movements. At the beginning of the 1930s, the countryside began to hold ideological importance in efforts to preserve national purity. Korean nationalists eagerly adopted and promoted the global discourse of agrarian romanticism through the 1920s. Korean agrarians, like their Japanese counterparts, deepened an anti-capitalist and anti-urban ideology, imagining the rural villages as the basis for a new Korea.[67] A student in the 1930s, Young Hook Kang, recalled the popular belief among nationalist leaders: "In those days, we were fond of reading novels such as Yi Kwang-su's *Hŭk*, Yi Ki-yŏng's *Kohyang*, and Sim Hun's *Sangnoksu*, etc. The major theme of these novels was the enlightenment movement in the countryside. The nationalist leaders in these days appeared to have believed in the possibility of maintaining our national identity and national spirit in the Korean farmers, whose lives had deep roots in Korean soil."[68]

Many leftist leaders fought the idealized view of the countryside and shed light on the cruelty of colonial–capitalist exploitation of Korean peasants. Starting in the late 1920s, left-leaning literary authors and critics, such as Yi Sŏng-hwan, Kim To-hyŏn, Paek Chŏl, and Hong Hyo-min, repeatedly called for engaging the countryside in new literature. The debate developed in several theoretical directions; some asserted the enlightening role of literary works in guiding peasants, whereas others defined peasant literature as part of proletarian literature. Confronted by the lack of literacy, they debated the challenge and mission of intellectual authors and attempted to counter the romanticized image of the countryside. Yet they shared with nationalist-agrarians the assumption that the future of Korean independence rested in the hands of peasant masses and in the rural countryside.[69]

The growing attention to rural areas stimulated other forces, particularly religious groups, to strengthen their rural programs. The historian Albert L. Park has shown that, between 1925 and 1937, the YMCA, the Presbyterians, and the Ch'ŏndogyo (Religion of the Heavenly Way) all pursued the reconstruction of rural Korea into "a heavenly kingdom on earth" through community building.[70] Particularly active was the Korea Farmers Company (Chosŏn Nongminsa), operating under the Chŏndogyo Youth Party, which was also a member of the leftist Korea Youth Group General Alliance. They formed cooperatives and provided night classes in rural villages.[71] Articles to inspire youth in the countryside appeared in the 1920s in their periodicals, *Farmers* (*Nongmin*) and *Korean Farmers* (*Chosŏn nongmin*), as well as in *Tonga ilbo* and other newspapers.

These publications, although they provided a means for intellectuals to convey their messages to village youth, never became a forum for the uneducated agrarian youth themselves. For instance, "A Letter Sent to Rural Youth," which appeared in *Kaebyŏk*, another journal published by young Chŏndogyo activists, betrayed a vast discrepancy between urban and rural contexts. The author explained, "I am *not* writing this letter in a desolate field or a boring rural village in which all you find is collapsing old houses like where the reader might live. . . . The city I currently live in is the capital of Korea, and the center of modern culture in Korea." After showing an understanding of the hardship of life in rural villages and excitement of urban centers, it argued, "cities flourish and develop by exploiting rural villages . . . [Becoming city people] means becoming an exploitative class . . . If you still want [to come to the city], I would rather like to discuss whether turning from an exploited class to an exploiting class really means the improvement of personality."[72] This author assumed the moral superiority of rural life, but his moral argument denied rural populations a way out of their poverty.

Many articles on rural education targeted students who would visit their home villages over summer vacations. "Experience farming," "observe the lives of lower-class people," and "try real labor" constituted the advice given to those students.[73] They were also encouraged to fight rural illiteracy by teaching youngsters the Korean alphabets, even though summer was the busiest farming time of the year. Overall, these suggestions were meant to help students achieve a better understanding of rural life and develop wholesome personalities, not necessarily to empower farm youth. These articles could not conceal the gap between elite activists and the most youth in rural villages, who were uneducated, poor, caught in family farming, and left outside the national youth movement.

In Taiwan too, attraction to the countryside grew in the rhetoric of nationalist and leftist activism. The post-1927 Cultural Association identified the development of "culture in farm villages" as the top priority in its activities.[74] As in Korea, the most powerful images of the countryside among young intellectuals came from literary works. The new proletarian literature that described rural backwardness and colonial exploitation dominated the scene, with superstitious old people, opium-addicted youth, corrupt policemen, and exploitative landlords among the common themes.[75] The nativist literature movement widely shared the perception that the majority of the Taiwanese population were miserable farmers.

Despite various authors' serious engagement, the nativist literature in Taiwan produced more confusion than agreement on what constituted Taiwanese national origin, however. The matter of language was particularly complex, raising such questions as whether vernacular Mandarin was appropriate for Taiwanese readers and whether the use of the Holo (today called Taiwanese or Minnan) language would separate Taiwan from mainland China.[76] These questions never disappeared from intellectual discourse and later, particularly in the 1970s, became central in the second nativist literature debate. In addition to this issue of defining Taiwanese ethnic nationality, leftist authors, like their Korean counterparts, faced difficulty in filling the gap between themselves and the majority of rural farmers. A representative leftist writer in Taiwan, Yang Kui, deplored that "[our works] cannot go beyond the circles of literature-loving youth. This proves that today's New Literature and proletarian literature lack mass-ness. They exist merely as an ivory tower."[77]

In short, although the concept of rural youth became critical for both nationalist and socialist youth leaders in Korea and Taiwan, it neither mitigated ideological differences nor bridged the gap between national leaders and youth in the countryside. The local youth groups spread widely in provincial capitals and towns, but very little in remote villages. Despite the efforts of intellectual youth, they did not establish a mutual communication sphere with youth in the countryside, most of whom were illiterate and did not have access even to local youth groups or youth journals. Unable to align with village youth, students started to blame farmers as immoral and irrational. Young Hook Kang, the Korean student who had embraced nationalist-agrarian ideals earlier, expressed this alienation in his memoir: "As time passed, we had to acknowledge the crude fact that farmers and the countryside were not a repository of national spirit and conscience as some national leaders had hoped. As long as their lives were not threatened and the social order maintained, they seemed rather indifferent to the nature of their leadership. In my observation, the Korean farmers were so amenable that they had no difficulty in adapting themselves to Japanese rule. Thus, I was driven to despair by thoughts of the possibility of losing our national identity forever."[78] To students like him, the indifference of the peasants to the anticolonial effort appeared as a grave betrayal.

Attempts of Colonial Governments

The colonial governments in Taiwan and Korea did not remain silent as agrarian ideas and youth groups sprouted in their territory. In fact, colonial authorities actively participated in shaping youth discourse and agrarianism among urban intellectuals. With regard to the goal of formulating an image of rural youth as pillars of modern society, anticolonial forces and colonial officials were in an unintended collaborative relationship, and their political rivalry accelerated rural youth mobilization. But the rural youth programs of colonial bureaucracies, with greater institutional resources, aimed to step more directly into the social dynamics of rural populations.

The experiences of the Japanese seinendan naturally determined the directions of youth-centered agrarian ideals advocated by colonial officials. In October 1926, the Government-General of Taiwan established a bureau of education (Bukyōkyoku), a new office dedicated to the education and kyōka of Taiwanese youth; "social education," a recent trend in Japan, was named the central task of the bureau.[79] The new head of civil affairs, Gotō Fumio, designed many of the bureau's programs. In Japan, Gotō was known as a top leader of seinendan associations. Holding an executive position in the national seinendan bureaucracy, he emphasized the importance of centralizing youth education.[80] Under his leadership, the years 1926 and 1927 saw many government surveys and studies on Taiwan's local youth groups, women's groups, and other community organizations that encouraged agricultural and neighborhood cooperation.[81] Gotō also increased the number of local officials specializing in educational affairs, invited Japanese seinendan leaders like Tazawa Yoshiharu to Taiwan, and suppressed activities of the Taiwan Cultural Association and *Taiwan minbao*.[82]

Together with the bureau, the Taiwan Education Association, as well as various kyōka groups and Shūyōdan groups that spread at the provincial and county levels, played a large role in promoting the emphasis on rural youth. They published teaching materials that highlighted the power of youth and the countryside, importing the ideas publicized by seinendan leaders in Tokyo. A common saying from Japanese agrarianism—"If nature is our god, those who are embraced, cared for, and given the most benefits by that god are people in rural villages"— was often repeated in "youth readings" distributed by these offices.[83] The colonial effort to standardize agrarian youth groups steadily progressed over the course of the 1920s and 1930s. In 1930, when kyōka reached its peak of importance in the governance of Taiwan, the GGT officially issued an act to standardize youth groups throughout the island.[84]

In Korea, parallel to the agrarian discourse developed by nationalist, socialist, and religious activists, the Government-General of Korea (GGK) also adopted agrarianism as the core ideology of its operations. In the 1920s, colonial officials produced a series of studies on Korean rural lives. In 1922, for example, Kon Wajirō, an architect and folklorist then specializing in Japanese rural houses and a student of Yanagita Kunio, traveled through Korea to study living conditions. With his trademark detailed sketches, he offered a fresh look at Korean housing in both urban and rural settings. Throughout his study, he stressed the rationality and natural beauty of Korean houses, and sometimes their superiority to those of the Japanese. In the introduction to his report he wrote, "I saw slums. I saw that they were unexpectedly beautiful . . . not like the filthy ones we see in Japan."[85] In the countryside, he was fascinated by the *ondol* (floor heating): "In Korea, no matter how primitive the house is, there is *ondol*. Japanese primitive houses do not even have *tatami* mats."[86] Other scholars studied different aspects of Korean rural life.[87] Most famously, Zenshō Eisuke, the GGK's leading researcher on Korean affairs, compiled massive volumes on various *kye* (community agreements), hamlet organizations, social customs, and clan-based communities, as well as Korean economy and industry in the 1920s.[88] These studies gave the GGK a basis for its attempt to revive traditional communal organizations in the rural campaigns of the 1930s. Colonial officials viewed them as basic units for implementing Japanese kyōka campaigns at the grassroots level. From a larger historical point of view, the praise of colonial local cultures was typical in empires of the time, but unlike others, Japanese colonialists celebrated them to further facilitate their assimilationist goal.[89]

The GGK also began reining in youth groups in provincial towns in the 1920s. The clear continuity from the March First Movement to local youth groups alarmed colonial officials, who were concerned about their political intentions. Almost simultaneously with Japan, the colonial government in Korea planned workshops and programs of social education, targeting local youth group members in the early 1920s.[90] In 1922, for instance, when the Ministry of Education conducted a survey on "the situation of social education centering on schools" in thirteen prefectures in Japan, the GGK collected the same surveys from local offices in Korea.[91] Many government programs emphasized building a sense of community spirit to keep youth away from political opposition. In South Chŏlla province, officials invited forty-six youth group leaders to a five-day "Youth Self-Cultivation Lecture Series" in November 1921, offering such lectures as "The Basic Principles of Cultural Rule," "Current Affairs of Youth Groups in Japan,"

"Finances in Rural Villages," and "Responsibilities of Local Youth" and show-ing motion pictures on the local improvement activities in the province.[92] The GGK also paid for trips by about thirty selected youth group leaders across Korea to visit model youth groups in Japan. The officials reported with satisfaction that many of the participants were impressed by the passionate lecturers and the achievements of the Japanese seinendan.[93]

The emphasis on agrarianism intensified when the GGK promoted a program called "graduate guidance" in the late 1920s and the early 1930s. Each elemen-tary school chose "training-worthy" graduates from farming families and made them the visible symbol of rural youth.[94] Throughout the 1930s, as the colonial measures to counter rural poverty increased in number and intensity during the depression, the GGK further integrated model rural youth into agricultural cooperatives and kyōka campaigns.

In these programs, colonial governments in both Taiwan and Korea further propelled the conceptual emphases on youth and agrarianism that had been developed by anticolonial intellectuals. They had the upper hand because they monopolized the resources, means of violence, and experiences of the Japanese seinendan. But as we will see in the coming chapters, permeating village societies was equally as challenging, if not more so, for Japanese colonialists as for intellec-tuals. Their incessant efforts did not bring immediate results. Not until well into the 1930s did colonial programs start to synchronize with local social conditions and trigger the social mechanisms of empowerment.

In colonial Taiwan and Korea as in Japan, rural youth became a powerful social construct by the late 1920s. Colonial intellectuals attempted to create a rural basis for their own nation building by aligning with young peasants in the country-side. Japan's seinendan network offered a model for these leaders to emulate. In generating their youth and agrarian discourses, however, they found them-selves subject to an intense interplay of transnational influences. Japan, China, the Soviet Union, and the Western powers inspired them with political ideologies and sometimes provided them with institutional support. These transnational forces in turn produced splits and confrontations within anticolonial leadership in Taipei and Seoul. Unlike the situation in the Japanese seinendan, which grew by absorbing conflicting interests as they defined the role of rural youth, here the similar goal of creating ideal rural youth did not help youth leaders to overcome the differences between their visions.

The biggest challenge for anticolonial youth activism was the gap between highly educated youth and illiterate rural farmers. Students increasingly felt frus-trated by farm youth, while farm youth remained neglected in youth politics in Taipei and Seoul. The fact of colonialism exacerbated this situation. Under arbitrary and inherently exploitative foreign rule, social conditions varied tremendously across the territory. This discrepancy made it more difficult for urban intellectual youth to engage with the social dynamics of rural societies. The temptation for youth leaders to blame village youth's ignorance did not help to bridge the gap, either. As we will see, village youth lived in more intricate webs of social relations and emotions than central leaders ever imagined. In fact, their envy of and grudges toward urban elites constituted some of the main motivations for farm youth to eventually join colonial programs. The anticolonial youth leaders' failed attempts demonstrate that an ideological movement alone, even one with a strong instinctive appeal of national independence or emancipation of impoverished peasants, cannot produce viable mass mobilization. That goal required a variety of social elements to emerge together, which was beyond the ability of any single mobilizing force to generate on its own.

5

FINDING RURAL YOUTH IN TAIWAN

The largest obstacle for Taiwanese anticolonial intellectuals, as seen in the previous chapter, was the difficulty of integrating village youth into their movements. Their repeated emphases on *youth* and *rural* did not resonate in the social environments of remote villages. To the colonial government, the chasm between the urban and rural social spheres did not offer an advantage for the colonizing enterprise. On the contrary, the need to manage unfamiliar and diverse social relationships posed a similar or greater challenge to the Japanese. After all, they were foreign occupiers.

In fact, the Government-General of Taiwan (GGT) faced a puzzling phenomenon in its pursuit of assimilationist policies. In Taiwan, basic infrastructure to implement nationalization—elementary schools, moral suasion groups, and youth groups—spread relatively smoothly in comparison with Korea.[1] But these institutions were slow in transforming previous social values and people's ways of life. Colonial directives seemed to be easily accepted at first, only to be ignored later. The facade of quick acceptance meant, as colonial officials soon realized, nothing but people's indifference toward colonial authorities, particularly in the countryside. Making Taiwanese people conscious that they belonged to the empire, and ultimately making them care about it, became the primary goal of assimilationist programs, especially in rural youth mobilization. This goal of turning indifference into emotional commitment was not achievable by merely preaching to villagers. It required colonial agencies to find ways for their ideology to seep into grassroots social relationships. The first few decades of trial and error in colonial youth mobilization, starting around the Russo-Japanese War of 1904–1905, were about figuring out the ever-changing local dynamics of rural villages, and then influencing them through young pillars of nation-empire building.

Such a process of assimilation was not necessarily dissimilar to the nationalization process in the countryside in Japan, except for one element inherent in colonialism: the lack of state legitimacy. There was, literally and perceptually, a great distance between the imperial center and people at the colonial periphery. But the challenge of understanding and shaping colonial society did not arise simply from the fact that the Japanese were foreign intruders; it also derived from Taiwan's unique social conditions. Because Chinese migrants had arrived in Taiwan and colonized coastal towns and remote mountainous villages at different times over the centuries, when Japan invaded Taiwan in 1895 it confronted a great variety of social dynamics based on class and racial relationships. On the one hand, the coastal capital of Xinzhu province, Xinzhu city, resembled a town in mainland China, in terms of its deep-seated stratification according to social class. In these provincial cities, anticolonial intellectual youth established local youth groups, as discussed in chapter 4, and tried to reach the rural population from there in the 1920s. By contrast, a newly conquered mountain village, Beipu, in the same province had not established a stable social order by the late nineteenth century. Village life revolved around ongoing racial tensions between the Chinese Hakka and the indigenous Saisiyat. After 1895, Hakka leaders used the presence of the Japanese to secure their control over the mountains, which were still a source of wealth and adventure. In these villages, where youthful leadership had been the norm in previous armed conquests, the phrase *rural youth* did not provoke the same marginalized image as in Japan or Korea at the turn of the century. This diversity in social environments produced difficulties in implementing uniform programs across the island.

In these efforts to build bridges linking the local society and the colonial government, Japanese elementary schoolteachers played an indispensable role. They had taken root in remote villages since the earliest stage of colonization and became a prime source of direct contact between villagers and the Japanese people. It is through their eyes that we can obtain a glimpse of colonial village societies of that time, albeit tainted by their biases. In Xinzhu province, schoolteachers became major advocates of seinendan-style youth groups. They taught Japanese agrarian nationalism and tried to develop model rural youth as pillars of villages and the empire. At the same time, their leadership also revealed the weakness of rural youth groups in Taiwan up to the early 1930s. Despite the premise of the "locally driven" seinendan, village youth groups were "led" by teachers or landlords, rather than representing an autonomous space for participants themselves.

Since they did not create job opportunities, their activities alone did not produce a social mobility complex like the one seen in Miyagi either. Nonetheless, teacher-led rural youth mobilization up to the mid-1930s succeeded in spreading hard-workism, frugality, and the ideal image of rural youth in Taiwanese villages—desirable traits of Japanese subjects from the perspective of GGT officials.

In a nutshell, until the Second Sino-Japanese War started in 1937, rural youth mobilization in Taiwan experienced only an incremental development without a major breakthrough. The series of failures of colonial programs during this period reflect a typical struggle of a "weak" colonial state seeking to carry out social engineering. But colonial attempts did begin synchronizing with local social dynamics by the 1930s—namely, the combination of the increasingly stratified social hierarchy in mountain villages, now void of the previous frontier character, and the relatively high schooling and literacy rate that helped to transmit the idea of model rural youth. Paying attention to how local dynamics consumed top-down youth mobilization efforts, whether anticolonial or impe-rial, will help us to make sense of Taiwanese responses to colonial rule, which exhibited considerable diversity that eludes simple classification on the spectrum from resistance to collaboration.

Youth in Xinzhu City and Beipu at the Turn of the Twentieth Century

Once Japan's colonial rule over Taiwan started in 1895, establishing the authority of the imperial state among local leaders and restructuring social values accord-ingly became a leading policy priority. In Xinzhu city on the northwest coast of Taiwan, society was regulated mainly by class divisions. Chinese settlement in this area had begun in the late seventeenth century. By the late nineteenth cen-tury, wealth generated from trade, the mastery of Chinese classics, and the privi-lege of passing the Qing civil servant examination defined the upper class—in other words, their social status depended on the Qing sources of prestige. After 1895, the GGT sought to find a way to replace the authority of Qing civil ser-vice and neo-Confucian education with new institutions. Along with elementary schools, early youth groups in Xinzhu city functioned as one of the institutions that enhanced the upper-class status of the wealthy and the educated.

Japanese elementary and language schools were the first colonial institutions that aimed to provide a new source of status and privilege. Modern schools spread relatively quickly, and by 1904 their popularity equaled that of the *shufang*, pri-vate Chinese schools run by local literati.[2] However, schools did not immediately function as a status signifier. In 1903, a Japanese elementary schoolteacher in

Xinzhu city, Hayashi Genzaburō, observed that the new school system had disrupted the previous avenues of generating social status in a way that Japanese officials did not expect. Families of Chinese descent had not abandoned the idea that the Chinese classics were the most authentic body of knowledge, so they sent their sons to *shufang* rather than to the Japanese school.[3] Only after their children grew up and recognized the need for Japanese language education did they enter the elementary school. As a consequence, students over age fifteen constituted more than 44% of the total of 255 students in Hayashi's school, and they were increasing in number every year. But because the supply of elementary schools was far smaller than the demand, the Japanese introduced an age limit for admission. Hayashi raised concerns about what would happen to these youth who were willing to study in school but were deprived of the opportunity. In his eyes, many had already lost discipline and hope, falling into a nihilistic and hedonistic lifestyle. Hayashi contended that "it is the fault of the Japanese that they strayed from the right path," because previously, when the Qing-style elite course was still in place for urban students, they had no free time for drinking, playing, or wasting money. The Japanese had destroyed the life cycle for middle- and upper-class youth without providing alternative pathways.[4]

Instead of elementary school diplomas, the term "youth sector" defined the new privileged class of the transitional period (as seen in chapter 4). The youth sector of Xinzhu began appearing in the government bilingual newspaper *Taiwan nichinichi shinpō* (Mandarin Chinese: *Taiwan riri xinbao*) in 1906. The term referred to a new generation that had acquired both Chinese- and Japanese-style education. *Youth* connoted modern attitudes distinct from those of previous eras, and it specifically challenged the seniority assumed in the Confucian value system. It also signified a new group formation, defined loosely by similar educational backgrounds and business (or academic) relationships with both Japan and China.[5] To enhance their privileged class identity, these young people organized youth groups in Xinzhu city. A number of "motivated youth" set up a youth group to "pursue learning and advocate civilization" in a temple in Xinzhu city in 1911, for example. They gathered every Sunday to "exchange knowledge," particularly of Confucian scholarship, and to learn Japanese, Chinese, and mathematics.[6]

Whereas the word youth symbolized the new bilingual class emerging under Japanese rule in Xinzhu city, in the small mountain village of Beipu the Japanese presence affected racial and ethnic relationships more than class divisions. Beipu, though only thirteen miles southeast of Xinzhu city, had developed community dynamics and social values notably different from those of coastal areas.[7] The social dynamics in Beipu were defined primarily racial tensions between Chinese Hakka residents and the Saisiyat aboriginal groups living in the neighboring

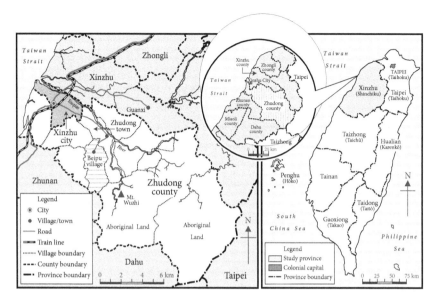

MAP 3.   The locations of Xinzhu city and Beipu village

mountains. The Hakka colonizers, the Jiang family, had conquered the area for agricultural settlement only half a century before Japanese rule.[8] Hakka migrants arrived in Taiwan much later than the Chinese Holo (or Minnan) people from the Fujian region, whose presence drove the newer Hakka migrants inland to form "belt-like residential areas at the foot of mountains, comprised of self-defensive hamlets, between the Fujianese Holo in the open land and the aborigines in the mountains."[9] Jiang Xiuluan and his armed men seized Beipu and established the Jinguangfu land development company in the 1830s.[10] Jinguangfu operated like a small government mostly independent of Qing China—deploying anti-aboriginal patrols, building irrigation systems, facilitating land cultivation, keeping track of tenancy, and collecting rents. During this process, many aboriginal men waged bloody battles against the Chinese colonizers and were forced deeper into the mountains.[11]

Perhaps because they were facing more imminent threats from the Saisiyat, Beipu leaders relatively quickly accepted the Japanese colonizers. The Jiang family offered valiant resistance at first. When Japan acquired Taiwan after the Sino-Japanese War in 1895, Jiang Shaozu, a twenty-year-old great-grandson of the family founder, gathered hundreds of armed men to fight the Japanese army.[12] But after his death, Beipu villagers found the presence of Japanese police force useful in maintaining security against the Saisiyat. The number of permanent Japanese settlers was small; even in the 1930s, the village had only ten to twelve Japanese households with a total of fifty to sixty residents.[13] Despite this small number of Japanese residents, the Jiang family promptly incorporated a Japanese-style administration and worked closely with the GGT.[14] In 1896, they reorganized their patrol headquarters into colonial police stations and invited the Japanese to set up an administrative office in Beipu. In 1899, the Xinzhu police established a civil defense system (*baojia*) at the direction of Gotō Shinpei, head of civil affairs in the GGT.[15] As early as May 1898, local elites and colonial officials set up a Japanese language school in the village temple Citiangong, which was renamed Hoppo Kōgakkō (Beipu Elementary School) five months later.[16] To build a new school facility, the Jiang family and other local leaders contributed a considerable amount of money.[17]

Social status in Beipu and other mountain villages in Taiwan had been determined mostly by the ability to suppress aboriginal forces. The Japanese helped the Jiang family to consolidate the wealth and status they had achieved through battles against aboriginal groups. In contrast to their social class remaining intact, however, racial and ethnic tensions increased in complexity after the Japanese arrived. In 1907, Saisiyat tribesmen and Chinese rebels attacked Beipu and killed fifty-seven Japanese residents, including schoolchildren, in the "Beipu Incident."[18] Interethnic mistrust escalated further among the Saisiyat, the Japanese, and the Hakka after the police executed at least a hundred Hakka residents for their alleged involvement in the uprising. At the same time, the incident demonstrated dominance of Japanese armed power. The Japanese police quickly quelled the uprising and restored order, subduing the rebel forces in less than a day and reestablishing the aboriginal border patrols in four days.[19] In later years, the Jiang family and Japanese village authorities used the anniversary of the Beipu Incident to perpetuate the violent image of neighboring aboriginal men and emphasize the security offered by colonial authorities. Even in the 1930s, children living on Beipu's outskirts were fearful of the sight of Saisiyat people.[20]

Without realizing it, the Japanese intervened in the hierarchy and tensions involving different Chinese descendant groups as well. Dai Guohui, a Taiwanese Hakka who grew up in Zhongli, Xinzhu province (and who later became a historian in Japan), argues that before Japanese rule, Taiwanese society had been characterized as a "frontier equivalent to the wild West" and that "grudges and hostilities between [Holo and Hakka] people that had grown in the frontier history flowed at the bottom of Taiwanese society" during colonial rule.[21] The Japanese used the blanket label of "Han Chinese," consequently enabling Hakka people to seek new opportunities in Holo-dominated communities.[22]

Compared to the coastal areas of Taiwan, mountain villages like Beipu had placed less emphasis on the Confucian sense of seniority. Because of the recent history of armed settlement, the social meanings of old and young differed from those in Miyagi, Okinawa, Korea, or even Xinzhu city. Young men had been central in founding and protecting the village, as is apparent from records of the Jiang family, which reveal a high generational turnover in leadership.[23] Moreover, *rural*, indicating mountain regions, signified adventure and wealth, not stagnation or poverty. Contemporary Japanese ideas of rural youth would have had no appeal to villagers in Beipu. There was no mass migration of youth from villages to the cities, expressions of a desire for *risshin shusse* (rising in the world) by emphasizing youthful characters, or outpouring of grudges against urban intellectual youth, all features that dominated the writings of young people in the Japanese countryside around this time. The social environment was simply very different.

The two separate social worlds—particularly with regard to the different meanings accorded to the concept of youth—of Xinzhu city and Beipu generated two very different responses to the early colonial attempt to establish youth groups. In 1915, when Japan issued the first decree to establish a national federation of the seinendan in the metropole, the colonial Xinzhu governor Mimura Sanpei planned to create a similar network in the province. In the name of celebrating the twentieth anniversary of Japan's rule over Taiwan, Mimura established the Xinzhu Youth Group (Japanese: Shinchiku Seinenkai, Mandarin Chinese: Xinzhu qingnianhui). By expanding the network across the province, he aimed to "organize youth groups that include three thousand elementary school graduates, public servants, graduates of *shufang*, and three thousand dropouts of elementary schools to improve youthful morals and to have them practice the Japanese language."[24] His plan cast a wide net over both urban and rural residents.

In Xinzhu city, this attempt appeared to achieve initial success before it faltered. The Xinzhu Youth Group started providing night study sessions, mainly offering Japanese language instruction. *Taiwan nichinichi shinpō* described these sessions' popularity: "Since its establishment, the membership has increased every day. . . . The first session had 40 people. The second session had 156, of whom 60 had absolutely no previous knowledge in Japanese."[25] After a few months, however, these gatherings ceased to function.[26] In the 1910s, the youth sector continued to view youth groups as a status-producing institution. As a result, Mimura's attempt to establish an inclusive network, integrating thousands of dropouts from elementary schools, did not align with the youth sector's aspirations. Elite youth in Xinzhu city still sought exclusive groups as late as September 1919, when they discussed reviving the Xinzhu Youth Group. They decided to begin anew with a "gentleman's group" and another group that consisted of only middle school graduates and above.[27] As Xinzhu province did not have a single middle school until 1922, the membership was necessarily restricted to members of wealthy families, educated in Taipei or Japan.

In Beipu, Governor Mimura's initiative failed for a different reason. The idea of youth groups did not attract local people even as a status symbol. The villagers did not oppose Mimura's proposal; on the contrary, they established the first Beipu Youth Group as one of the earliest such entities among Taiwanese rural villages. The celebration of Japanese rule accompanied another campaign—cutting off the Qing-style queue (long braided hair) of all students in the Beipu Elementary School.[28] Despite these attempts to facilitate the colonial campaign, the youth group existed in name only and disappeared quickly.[29] Little is known about this short-lived youth group, but the village leaders' eagerness to follow the colonial order—without any intention of changing the substance of their ways of life, as colonial authorities had envisioned—was Beipu's typical response to colonial rule.

Xinzhu City Youth Groups in the 1920s

In the 1920s, the Taiwan Cultural Association, the first island-wide organization that advocated for self-determination for the Taiwanese people, began organizing local youth groups in provincial cities. The groups' activities appear to have had considerable influence over youth in Xinzhu city, driving them to become involved in battles between colonial and anticolonial forces. Yet a closer look at the reports about them reveals that status marking remained the central function of these youth groups.

In 1921, a Taiwanese elementary schoolteacher, Zhang Shigu, and four other men in Xinzhu city established a new youth group (once again named Xinzhu Youth Group).[30] Initially, Zhang's group exhibited a strong pro-Japanese character, saying that it would "promote a community spirit, exchange knowledge, and study Japanese."[31] It gained official support from Japanese school principals and local officials and provided lectures on aspects of modern social life, such as "Tax Duties" and "Hygiene for Children."[32] In 1925, which the police authorities described as "the crazy time of public speeches by the Taiwan Cultural Association," the Xinzhu Youth Group scrapped its ties with the colonial authorities and joined a branch of the Cultural Association.[33] While reforming the youth group, its leaders also started a "Xinzhu Study Group."[34] *Taiwan minbao*, the newspaper published by the Cultural Association, promoted study groups as supportive of progressive self-rule, as distinguished from the other youth groups that were associated with pro-colonial figures.[35] Both the Xinzhu Youth Group and the Xinzhu Study Group declared their support for the Cultural Association, leading to some arrests and even violence during their lecture events.[36]

In reality, regardless of their institutional affiliation, both groups still functioned as elite youth clubs. The Xinzhu Youth Group did not bother to update
its list of activities, which had involved mainly the reform of the old customs, as
if they were of little importance.[37] The group's main concern, *Taiwan minbao*
critically reported, was networking. The newspaper warned of the continuing
ties between leaders of the Xinzhu Youth Group and colonial authorities, stating that "some of the leading members with ambitious minds actively visit the
pro-colonial figures and help them criticize the youth group."[38] Once these youth
achieved their goal of networking through the youth group, according to *Taiwan minbao*, "they all turned inactive."[39] The newspaper further reported that
the Xinzhu Study Group had turned into a party after meeting four or five times.
"The organizer uses various excuses to turn a simple dinner into a drinking
party in order to show his hospitality," one member complained; "this happened
mostly without the members noticing, but it changed an occasion for academic
studies into one for evaluating menus."[40] Despite efforts to restore these groups,
they continued to suffer from a "lack of passion among the executive leaders"
and the presence of "one or two conceited members," and they ended up being
dissolved soon afterward.[41]

After the demise of these groups, a few dozen of their members formed a
brand-new Shinchiku Seinendan in 1929, this time with support from Japanese officials, school principals, and local elites. When the Shinchiku Seinendan
turned to the colonial authorities for assistance, it claimed to be getting rid of
old forces and making a "purely young" organization composed of people of
seventeen to twenty-five years old.[42] Now "youthfulness" meant being aligned
with colonial authorities, after a short period during which the Cultural Association had emphasized youthfulness as a force *against* the colonial establishment.

The Emergence of "Modern Youth" in Beipu

In contrast to what was occurring in cities, the Taiwan Cultural Association's
anticolonial activism did not exert much influence on young people's lives in
rural areas. But new colonial policies of the 1920s, particularly the strengthening
of kyōka campaigns under the Japanese policy of cultural rule, shifted the locus
of youth mobilization from provincial cities to the more remote countryside.
The 1920s, with colonial rule long consolidated, also witnessed a different social
dynamic in the Taiwanese mountain villages from previously.

It is to counter anticolonial movements that assimilationism through
kyōka campaigns became a serious colonial goal in the 1920s and 1930s. The
term *kyōka* had been widely used in Japan for ideological education to spread

emperor-centered nationalism, the spirit of hard work, frugality, and modern living customs. In the Taiwanese context, kyōka campaigns encompassed a wide range of programs designed to enhance people's acceptance of the Japanese Empire with a similarly strong emphasis on the reform of daily customs. In the 1920s and 1930s, all administrative levels had an institution that supervised kyōka programs. At the national level, the Association of Social Work was established in 1920 and the Taiwan Kyōka Association in 1933; Dōkōkai at the Xinzhu provincial level and Jinshinkai at Zhudong county and village levels were created in 1929.

Beipu in the 1920s seems to have embraced kyōka campaigns. For the Jiang family, taking charge of colonial programs allowed them to claim their role as local modernizers, influence villagers' everyday lives, and monopolize government funding. In 1919, for example, the Jiang family established an industrial credit union under the supervision of the village administrative office.[43] They organized various kyōka programs under the auspices of a reform association, Zhenduohui, created in 1924.[44] As one of its many reform projects, for example, Zhenduohui introduced a money offering box in the central temple, Citiangong, so that people would not "spend money wastefully" by buying paper offerings to deities and spirits that were burned during prayers.[45] A village branch of Jinshinkai also came to Beipu in 1929. In the village chronicle, written in 1934, Jinshinkai provided a long list of "points of improvement in daily life." Beginning with suggestions on clothing ("Do not buy new clothes or garments frequently") and marriage ("Use your own home or a religious facility for weddings and avoid restaurants"), the seventy-six points covered customs regarding funerals, parties, celebrations, gifts, invitations of guests, meals, houses, public manners, and so on.[46]

These kyōka programs not only enabled the Jiang family to extend their dominance, but also ushered in the leadership of a new generation who had never experienced the conquest of aboriginal territories. Like Katō Einojō, the son of a landlord in Miyagi who grew up in a series of kyōka campaigns after the Russo-Japanese War of 1904–1905, the new generation who grew up under Japanese assimilationist rule emerged in the governing circle of Beipu. Jiang Ruichang, a symbol of the Japanese colonial generation—one of the first Taiwanese teachers hired by the Beipu Elementary School who had graduated from the elite normal school—became the village head in 1920. Under his governance, the Beipu Youth Group, with sixty members, was founded on October 5, 1923, in response to an initiative by the head of civil affairs, Gotō Fumio. The youth group leaders also came from the new generation: Peng Qingqin, a young public translator; Liu Muzai, a secretary to the Beipu village head; and Jiang Axin, a young business leader from the Jiang family who had graduated from

Meiji University in Tokyo.[47] The youth group worked closely with both the dominant Jiang family and colonial authorities. In events like the celebration of the completion of a new Beipu credit union building in 1930, the youth group played "the industrial union song," visually and audibly symbolizing the presence of the new generation.[48]

Again, little is known about how villagers perceived the leadership of the new generation and the Beipu Youth Group, but these youth appear to have shared many features of "modern youth" embraced by their Japanese contemporary counterparts. Officially, the youth group operated as another kyōka institution under the supervision of Jinshinkai, but its role was not limited to activities within the village. Through the colonial network, the Beipu Youth Group connected the village to the larger world. Its members practiced sports and formed a musical band—activities popular as symbols of modern youth across the empire.[49] The colonial bureau of education promoted interactions among youth groups across Taiwan. As a part of such efforts, Xinzhu province organized large-scale joint sports festivals that brought together four thousand schoolchildren, youth group members, and schoolteachers.[50] News from other parts of the empire reached Beipu through the youth group. In 1927, the group collected funds for the victims of the earthquake in Kyoto by organizing a charity concert.[51] Through these activities, youth group members symbolized the rise of the new generation and its connection to the larger empire.

In sum, although their political orientations appeared to differ and although they operated within separate social dynamics, the youth groups in both Xinzhu city and Beipu village developed in ways consistent with the 1920s discourse of the rise of youth. In both places, the social position of "modern youth" was monopolized by relatively wealthy and well-educated youth. In Xinzhu city, this was a continuation from the elite youth sector, marked by both generational and class divides. But in Beipu, the emergence of modern youth meant a significant departure from prior practices. The village was now characterized by a solidified social class hierarchy, not by volatile ethnic tensions. Power and wealth derived not directly from the mountains, but from modern education and from business successes attained through collaboration with the empire. In this environment, youthful leadership no longer suggested an image of masculine armed conquerors, but modernizers and social reformers. In other words, Beipu's social configuration began to resemble that of Miyagi villages in the 1910s and early 1920s, where the role of modernizers was transferred from traditional village notables to the younger generation who embraced a new generational identity, just as in the case of Katō Einojō. This change also meant that average farmers had little access to upward mobility. To them, opportunities in the urban areas began to look like an attractive way out.

The Turn to Elementary School Graduates in the 1930s

Against this background of class stratification, Japanese educators started to apply the model of the Japanese seinendan to Taiwanese youth groups. Elementary schoolteachers were the single most important agents of colonial youth mobilization in Taiwanese villages. As local residents, they analyzed Taiwanese rural society with confidence, criticized government policies, and condemned local upper classes for leading hardworking village youth astray by importing urban culture. Their writings reveal how eagerly and blindly they applied the Japanese experience of seinendan mobilization to the Taiwanese context.

The year 1930 marked a new phase in the development of village youth groups in Taiwan. Over the prior decade, colonial policies on youth education had developed incrementally. But the 1930 decree to standardize group names (using the term *seinendan*) and establish common rules, including stricter age limits, reflected the urgency of mass mobilization after the onset of the economic depression. The Beipu Youth Group, now the Beipu Seinendan, incorporated the new standard, adopting stricter age limits (fifteen to twenty-five), reducing its membership to forty, and attaching itself to the local elementary school in 1931. It also had a new set of written rules, which stipulated the group's main goal as nurturing youth to become "loyal members of the nation."[52] Like Xinzhu city's Shinchiku Seinendan, which sported new uniforms and a new flag at the inauguration ceremony, the Beipu seinendan began to appear more uniformed and disciplined.[53]

The 1930 decree also brought about a significant shift in the institutional landscape among youth groups. It produced both phenomenal growth in the number of youth groups and a dramatic shrinkage in the total number of participants— from around fifty groups with seven to nine thousand members in 1925–1926 to nearly one hundred groups but only two thousand members in 1934.[54] The overall number of participants declined by 42% between 1930 and 1931 alone.[55] The scholar Miyazaki Seiko argues that the precipitous membership decline was intentional and aimed at suppressing anti-Japanese youth activities—or, in the language of Japanese colonial authorities, activities of "bad youth."[56]

Japanese educators in the countryside of Xinzhu province did not, however, regard cutting the size of youth groups as a means of social control. They genuinely felt a need for institutional reform because the groups had not been developing into motivated, active associations composed of average farm youth. Miyajima Yutaka, an elementary school principal in Guanxi village, initiated his discussion of "The Reality of Rural Youth Groups in This Island" in 1932 by stating, "Youth groups in local rural villages in Taiwan are extremely inactive.

Currently, most of them exist in name only, showing no activity or development, and are rather useless things."[57] Each youth group covered too broad an area, had too many members, and thus lacked community cohesion; the age range (fifteen to thirty-five) was too large; the groups were not well funded; and people expected the youth groups to produce results in the form of projects rather than encouraging shūyō.[58]

Another educator from Zhudong county, Matsuo Shōji, argued ironically that the *lack* of a visible passion for anarchism, communism, and nihilism among Taiwanese youth was actually more difficult to handle than the presence of anti-government activism. "The damage of the economic depression is not being felt [in Taiwan] as severely as in Japan," he wrote, and consequently, "we do not really see among Taiwanese youth group members those, like the ones in Japan, who pretend to be dangerous thinkers by talking big and who are infected by trendy ideas."[59] In official records, the unemployment rate remained low in the early 1930s, especially in remote villages like Beipu.[60] But the worsening living conditions of tenant farmers had become an issue, and Taiwan saw a rise in the number of tenant disputes during the late 1920s.[61] Still, what colonial educators feared most was not "dangerous thoughts" like socialism, but the individualistic tendencies of Taiwanese youth. Matsuo continued, "From now on (or it may be already so), if we start to find in youth groups those who do not talk big, recruit others, or engage in demonstrations, but just quietly read and contemplate, then they would really be threatening as they are extremely difficult to deal with and beyond the control of simple-minded youth group leaders. They would leave the youth groups before we knew it."[62]

The Japanese teachers thought that the problem lay in Taiwanese society, not in their plan for creating the seinendan. Miyajima attributed the inactive nature of youth groups partially to the absence of similar kinds of groups in Taiwanese society prior to Japanese rule, whose history as an immigrant society was marked by "sheer battles with hardship" and made up of "defensive lives constrained within conquered territories." Such struggles left the Taiwanese no alternative but to operate in "defense-oriented, independent, and extremely kinship-centric groups."[63] Miyajima went on to identify two characteristics of Taiwanese social relations as the largest obstacles. First, youth were "under the strict control of their parents," who did not understand the merit of youth groups. Since the parents' generation had not experienced youth groups themselves, they were not at all supportive. Second, he claimed, "youth lack admiration for older leaders [outside their families]. It might be a result of their history in which they only sought wealth and power, but this is one reason why the youth group leaders have difficulty in directing the members."[64] While puzzled by this observation, these teachers did not consider other possible explanations, such as that youth perhaps had previously enjoyed greater stature than the teachers assumed. Neither did they seem to realize that strong kinship-based ties already provided a social organization that was more solid than horizontally structured youth groups. Overly focused on the success of the seinendan network in Japan, these colonial teachers never seemed to ask why Xinzhu villagers would want a seinendan-like youth group in the first place.[65]

These teachers thought they represented a higher ideal of empire than did colonial officials, whom they saw as too mired in compromises with the powerful Taiwanese upper classes. They expressed their dissatisfaction with the sons of the landlord class, who were the primary members of the youth groups in the 1920s. Miyajima described the children of landlords as the source of almost every problem in village youth groups:

> Most of the landlord youth who make a living by renting out farmland to tenant farmers never handle a shovel or a plow by themselves, but they proceed into higher schooling even after middle school. Even those without academic ability or talent go to private schools, studying academic theories that have no practical application, and once they come back to the villages, they turn arrogant and do not understand agriculture, showing little sympathy for the hardship of tenants. They are often affected by urban culture, become accustomed to luxurious living, despise rural villages, and do not enjoy associating with rural youth. Many second and third sons leave the village as salaried workers, and they sometimes become village celebrities after improving their social status, but usually they are not helpful to the village as a whole. Instead, some harm the spirit of simplicity and fortitude by becoming objects of aspiration among village youth in deleterious ways.[66]

Miyajima's frustration with wealthy youth convinced him of the need to recruit a different type of village youth.

The ideal recruits for the local seinendan, Miyajima and other Japanese educators in Xinzhu argued, were graduates of elementary schools who helped in family farming on their own or rented land. The middle school graduates "are arrogant and disdain their fathers' occupations," and "their brains alone have grown, but they lack practical ability." By contrast, elementary school graduates were generally loyal and trustworthy. They were "in the greatest need of guidance and most worth guiding."[67] Even if they could not afford to go to elementary school, those who demonstrated admirable character in Japanese language centers should be regarded as model youth as well.[68] The Japanese educators preferred youth engaged in agriculture over those working as office clerks or in their own business, saying that "agriculture is an occupation that Taiwanese people look down upon. First of all, we need to inspire the pride of farmers."[69]

Emphasizing discontinuity in 1930 was important to these educators as they sought to put a fresh face on the youth group. Since they were still establishing a foundation for local youth groups that had no historical roots, "selecting members requires tremendous attention," Miyajima argued. "First and foremost, we should weigh only the quality of the members, and not be concerned about the number.... Ten or so would be enough. Increasing the number is impractical and would not be accompanied by good results. Making it a group of high-quality youth would also make the label of youth groups valuable to youth and villagers."[70] Exclusivity was an important characteristic of elite youth groups (especially prevalent in provincial cities) in the 1920s. The new goal was to transform the previously upper-class-dominated youth group into one that was still limited in membership but based on commitment to the community and ability as farmers, not on class status.

These teachers obviously had in mind the model of Japanese seinendan, which had formed rapidly in Meiji Japan on the basis of premodern hamlet youth associations. In Taiwan, however, they could not create a facade of spontaneously formed youth groups. Their attempt to transplant the Japanese model created a dilemma: how could the youth groups represent the villagers, not the colonizer, when all the initiative came from Japanese teachers? Hashinabe Kazuyoshi, another school principal in Xinzhu, feared that personal biases in the selection process would make the youth group appear to represent a particular interest group.[71] The educators themselves had to be wary of the thin line between their own favoritism and constructing a definition of model youth that villagers could appreciate. Here again, they viewed the absence of "dangerous youth" inspired by socialism as making their task more difficult, not easier. In Japan and Korea, many youth group members promoted the legitimacy of their groups by positioning themselves against leftist youth. Without the visible presence of such "politicized" youth, educators in the countryside of Xinzhu province faced a more complex challenge in identifying local demands and creating an attractive picture of model rural youth.

The Japanese teachers' decision to make elementary school education a key membership criterion arose from their confidence in the extent to which Japanese schools transformed Taiwanese children. An increasing number of children attended at least to elementary school during the 1920s and 1930s. The Beipu elementary school principal recorded that, in the central part of Beipu, the schooling rate in 1934 was 77% for male children and 35% for female children. Starting in the early 1920s, the school saw 50 to 70 students graduating every year; by 1934, it produced 1,195 graduates (1,017 male and 178 female), of whom 404 (all male) worked in agriculture upon graduating.[72] A villager who attended the school between 1933 and 1939 noted, "Almost every boy, regardless of whether they were poor peasants or wealthy landlords, could go to school."[73] The school became a space where Beipu residents had close daily interactions with Japanese teachers, for the first and perhaps the only time. Their personal connections turned into nostalgic memories later, and many of the graduates remained in contact with their Japanese teachers even after they left Taiwan. The deep roots established by the elementary school in the local community put the Japanese teachers in the best position to influence Taiwanese children.

At the school, Taiwanese pupils internalized a new social order, embracing the authority of their teachers and an age hierarchy among students, which the educators in Xinzhu thought had been traditionally lacking among villagers. The most obvious achievement of school graduates was ability in the Japanese language. The spread of Japanese did not come naturally but had to be enforced through various means, and the topic of Japanese-language pedagogy generated heated debates throughout the five decades of colonial rule. When early youth groups started to appear in the 1900s, colonial authorities expected them to promote Japanese language instruction much as village youth groups in Japan promoted "accent-free" standard Japanese pronunciation. But elementary schoolteachers were the only people equipped with the skill and willingness to provide Japanese classes either in or outside the school.[74]

Various institutions for Japanese language education, and consequently other assimilation programs, revolved around elementary schools and schoolteachers. The school became the most reliable institution for seinendan advocates, and the most familiar site of modern learning for village youth. The elementary school had already been associated with the earlier Beipu Youth Group. Its members marched in a musical band and distributed pamphlets to encourage children in the village to attend the school.[75] Both the public learning center (kōmin kōshūjo) for graduates of the elementary school and the Japanese language center (kokugo kōshūjo) for school-age (mostly female) children and youth who did not enroll in the school were created within the Beipu Elementary School in 1931 and 1933, respectively.[76] The centrality of the elementary school in the wide range of educational programs kept both Japanese and Taiwanese teachers extremely busy and even feeling "exploited," as village heads observed.[77] "Everywhere I go, I witness with my own eyes that teachers today have no time to spare in their lives, and personally I cannot help but truly sympathize with them," observed an education official who visited a number of vibrant seinendan and language centers in the Xinzhu countryside.[78]

Creating Model Rural Youth

These Xinzhu educators, with their respected presence in local society, deployed the long-tested rhetoric of Japanese agrarian nationalism in their battle against the social-class hierarchy embodied in the youth groups of the 1920s. They identified the promotion of shūyō—through lectures, reading, and character-building activities—as a particularly important battleground. From their writings, they appear to have firmly believed that only through shūyō would village youth learn agrarian nationalism and take charge of larger kyōka campaigns. The emphasis on shūyō also reflected their desire to detach kyōka programs from dominant landlords and bestow moral authority on average farm youth.

Shūyō was surely not at the top of the agenda for village youth groups that operated under landlords' supervision. Matsuo believed that they engaged in too many volunteer public projects instead.[79] This was partly the fault of the colonial government. Because of the absence of a centralized seinendan network and a military conscription exam, the GGT had assessed group achievement based on the numbers of events, gatherings, and participants.[80] Matsuo pointed out that "it was a bad idea that government authorities considered only the results of events and gatherings in selecting the best youth groups."[81] When the Shinchiku Seinendan was designated a model group in 1932, for example, the committee praised its wide array of activities:

> The first day of every month, they have the day of public service and an early-morning study gathering. Every Saturday they have a military drill supervised by an assigned officer. . . . They held various events celebrating the emperor's visit, a cinema showing for citizens, a harmonica band performance, a singing and dancing party, and a table tennis tournament in April. They opened a new youth building and created a group song in May, and they held a record concert and a debate roundtable in June, a music festival and early-rising events in July, and a mobile camping and baseball games in August.[82]

From Matsuo's point of view, organizing this extensive series of events did not necessarily mean successful training of youth. "'Home guidance' (*katei shidō*) should be the criterion for a youth group's success" because the goal of shūyō was to influence their everyday lives.[83]

Now teachers could advance the shift toward shūyō more assertively, because the metropole was embarked on major kyōka campaigns in the 1930s. They promoted "sociable interactions, leisure, and learning" as three necessary core elements in youth training.[84] Among their favored training methods, night camping and mountain climbing were widely implemented. Beipu's southern wall, Mount

Wuzhi, was a popular destination for mountain excursions by Xinzhu youth. In teachers' eyes, a mountain-climbing trip was full of shūyō opportunities, as the youth switched positions frequently according to individuals' strengths so that the team would reach the destination as a coherent group without spreading out, learned to appreciate the beauty and mystery of nature, and did not leave the slightest bit of litter after stopping for lunch. As the teachers described it, "Climbing in this way would bring about not merely physical exercise, but high-quality self-cultivation."[85]

Contrary to such emphasis on shūyō, during the transitional period from landlord-led groups to those composed of model farmers, the seinendan were widely advertised as a modernizing force by both upper-class village notables and schoolteachers, as well as by colonial authorities. The seinendan increased their social presence in the early 1930s by organizing popular public events. It was a newsworthy event, for example, when forty-five members of the Shinchiku Seinendan went on a cycling tour of northern Taiwan from Xinzhu to Taipei, showing off their bicycle-riding skill while strengthening their bodies.[86] On another occasion, the Xinzhu police deployed a musical band composed of seinendan members at the front of their automobile parade, distributing twenty thousand brochures to promote awareness of traffic rules.[87] Seinendan members from various regions demonstrated their mastery of Japanese on the radio show *Kokugo fukyū no yūbe* (Evening of the promotion of national language, 1930–1933) twice a week. They presented a dozen different performances, including Japanese folk songs, marching songs with a Manchurian theme, conversational skits, and essays composed by the youth themselves.[88]

As a tool of kyōka assimilation campaigns, the educators also promoted "youth amateur plays."[89] In these dramatic performances, participants literally played model rural youth in front of villagers: they were "artists of soil" who created vegetables and rice, helped their younger family members to complete elementary school education even in dire poverty, and encouraged their parents to abandon superstitious beliefs and trust modern medicine. These plays almost always included a subplot of young people's opposition to arranged marriages, which traditionally involved the transfer of a large amount of money from the bridegroom to the parents of the bride.[90] By performing these plays, the seinendan not only spread kyōka messages as a modernizing force but also challenged traditional elitist norms that frowned on dramatic acting.[91]

Helped by the relatively high literacy rate among younger generations, Japanese educators attempted to create a space for communication among Taiwanese village youth. The new magazine *Kunpū* (Summer Breeze, 1932–) presented the colonizer's messages in the form of essays written by Taiwanese rural youth. This created a semblance of the seinendan newsletters that Japanese youth circulated on their own. Many of the essays in *Kunpū* highlighted the youthful authors' desire to rise in the world and argued that success was possible for rural residents without higher education. One youth group member, Cai Qingzi, asserted that youth should start saving money as soon as possible, declaring, "Saving is difficult at the beginning, but the first principle of youth is patience. Those who work very hard with no distraction would always bloom one day."[92]

Xinzhu's seinendan raised its profile most powerfully in the context of a natural disaster, just as the Japanese seinendan did by responding to rural famines. On April 21, 1935, Xinzhu and Taizhong were hit by large-scale earthquakes, which killed more than thirty-two hundred people and destroyed more than 38,500 buildings.[93] In response, 623 members from forty seinendan in Xinzhu province rushed to the severely affected villages in Zhunang and Miaoli counties to rescue survivors, dig up bodies, clear rubble, and set up emergency shelters. They provided food, distributed medicine, and secured lifelines by working alongside police to rebuild roads and bridges.[94] Newspapers and *Kunpū* emphasized the sacrifices of these youth who committed themselves to the public rescue mission despite the damage that their own families had suffered. These youth served as excellent boosters of the kyōka campaign more broadly. One youth play published in *Kunpū* a year later was staged in a post-earthquake rural village in Xinzhu. The protagonist was a young man who participated in the rescue mission. In the play, he remained humble about his sacrifice and donated the entire award money given to him by the Xinzhu governor to earthquake victims. A typical touch of kyōka appeared in the end when he decided to marry a woman with the same family name, rebelling against the customary taboo of marrying within one's own clan.[95] Through these media, in Xinzhu as in Tōhoku, the seinendan's roles in natural disasters were described as heroic and increased public recognition of the value of rural youth and their masculinity.

Did the rise of rural youth and the establishment of the seinendan for elementary school graduates create social mobility for average young farmers in Taiwan? The seinendan alone did not systematically produce job opportunities as youth training centers did in the countryside of Miyagi. Yet according to the anthropologist Miyazaki Seiko, the seinendan in not-so-remote provincial towns began providing social mobility to youth outside the upper class in the early 1930s. In the transition from landlord-centered youth groups to the seinendan of model rural youth, the youth situated between these classes found a window of opportunities. In the town of Xinzhuang in Taipei province, where Miyazaki conducted oral history research, the seinendan had members who were elementary school graduates, but they generally came from relatively well-off families and few of them engaged in agriculture. Through group gatherings, they established connections with local notables and officials. The affiliation with the seinendan allowed them to access jobs in administrative offices that had normally been occupied by middle school graduates.[96] This example suggests that, although limited in scale and dependent on an elitist method of networking, the seinendan in Taiwan began to produce a mechanism of social mobility for less privileged youth in outside urban areas by the mid-1930s.

Tracing the development of youth groups in Xinzhu city and Beipu shows how uneven a terrain Taiwan was and how difficult it was for Japanese colonizers to implement policies applicable to all parts of this small territory. Japanese officials incessantly applied assimilationist programs, ranging from building new schools and co-opting the upper classes to standardizing local youth groups. But the colonial government was essentially a weak state that could not depend on local enthusiasm to adopt and promote national–imperial ways of life. In Taiwan, finding rural youth—the reliable pillars of nation-empire building—was unexpectedly challenging for Japanese colonial authorities.

Over time, however, the social meanings of *rural* and *youth* changed substantially, reflecting shifts in Taiwan's social dynamics. At the beginning of the twentieth century, the concept of youth—a signifier of a new privileged class educated in Japanese and Chinese in Xinzhu city—did not resonate in the remote mountain village of Beipu. Nor did the image of rural youth that was developing in Japan seem attractive to Beipu's upper-class or peasant youth. Their indifference was not due to any absence of youth mobilization efforts by colonial officials; on the contrary, it existed despite Governor Mimura's initiative in 1915. It derived from social dynamics conditioned by the recent settlement of Hakka migrants in the region, whereby the statuses of both rural and youth had already been highly valued. The example of Beipu shows that establishing youth groups and preaching agrarian ideologies did not automatically result in successful mobilization of village youth. It was crucial for seinendan advocates to grasp local social relationships that defined the rural population's desires and aspirations. In the early 1930s, Japanese educators in Xinzhu, although with a lens tainted by the model of the Japanese seinendan, analyzed the dynamics of Xinzhu's rural society. By then, even mountain villages had assumed a rigid social hierarchy that centered on large landed families—a social structure familiar to Japanese eyes. The teachers believed that in Taiwan too, agrarianism and pillars of model rural youth would correct social grievances and generate new energy, which would consequently serve the assimilationist goal of the Japanese Empire.

Without the means to attain career advancement through youth training, however, members of the Taiwanese seinendan in remote villages in the early 1930s could not benefit form a social mobility complex—the mechanism that produced a nationalistic population in the countryside of Miyagi. But a few elements that sprouted during this period laid the groundwork for a version of such a complex to emerge shortly thereafter. Those elements included the commitment of Japanese teachers, the high rate of literacy among the younger generation, the improving reputation of the seinendan, and the communication fostered by the seinendan journal *Kunpū*. These factors allowed colonial advocates of the seinendan to gradually promote agrarian values and establish the new image of model rural youth in the remote countryside.

6

THE EMOTIONAL BASIS FOR JAPANIZATION

Seinendan training in Taiwan carried little sense of wartime urgency in the early 1930s. Kyōka instead remained the central theme. Even the government-supported youth magazine *Kunpū* contained more discussion of how to overcome traditional taboos surrounding marriage than about Japan's time of emergency. But the outbreak of the Second Sino-Japanese War on July 7, 1937 impelled Taiwan to prepare for military engagement. A flood of news reports on the fighting in China and the home front efforts in Japan had a major impact on the mood of youth training. The demand for elementary school education among the Taiwanese population increased rapidly, pushing the attendance rate of school-age children in Xinzhu city from 65% in 1938 to 73% in 1940 and 95% in 1942.[1] Youth, and rural youth in particular, were considered the engine of Taiwan's Japanization efforts. The ultimate goal of the accelerated assimilation campaign was now to produce reliable soldiers equipped with guns, plows, and Japanese language skills. The incredible statistics on the volunteer fever—with 759,276 men applying for two thousand open slots in 1944—make the Government-General of Taiwan (GGT) appear to have achieved that goal with ease.

But the process of mobilizing Taiwanese youth was far messier than the statistics on volunteer soldier applicants indicated. It relied on an alignment of various social elements that generated a social mobility complex in Taiwan's remote villages. As in Miyagi, the process was first triggered by government programs. After 1937, the GGT and its local offices expanded the seinendan and launched multiple youth training programs. As Japanese residents were conscripted, these programs created a career development ladder for Taiwanese local youth and gave them new employment opportunities. The new sense of social mobility gave ambitious Taiwanese village youth a starting point for building their version of the social mobility complex, as youth turned mobilization into opportunities and, through that process, circulated and internalized the rhetoric of Japanese agrarian nationalism. This development was accompanied by many paradoxical changes in youth's social relationships. Despite the appearance of linear, rapid, and successful top-down youth mobilization, much of the process did not go as colonial mobilizers envisioned and was instead shaped by many unpredictable social contingencies.

The personal stories of two men, Huang Yuanxing and Xu Chongfa, will serve as our lens to interpret the operating social dynamics. Both came from average rural families in poor villages of Xinzhu province and became, as they openly admitted in interviews, firm supporters of the Japanese imperial ideology. Xu, whom I introduced at the beginning of this book, preserved extensive records on Xinzhu's youth training. These two accounts, backed up by various printed documents, vividly reveal the socioeconomic conditions and gendered experiences that determined their realistic choices as well as their worldviews yet to be influenced by the final outcome of the war or postwar Guomindang rule.

The details of Huang and Xu's personal records highlight an important aspect of the ideological indoctrination of young people that is hard to flesh out in other case studies in this book: the formation of an emotional basis for Japanization.[2] Studies of youth mobilization, unlike studies of children and childhood, have rarely discussed the emotional component of the process, even though many extant anecdotes and memoirs describe the emotional experiences in major youth groups.[3] This is perhaps because state bureaucrats, social experts, and young people themselves defined the category of (particularly male) youth in terms of the target of discipline—the opposite of emotional beings. In the case of Japan's colonial history, the entire Japanization campaigns are seen as a methodical oppression of indigenous ways of life. For historians, the forceful conversion of ethnic identity (even ethnic cleansing) had become common analytical parlance.[4] But, as the stories of Xu and Huang show, it was the development of shared emotions in youth training that ensured young people's ideological commitment, self-discipline, and allegiance to the empire. Prewar Japanese nationalism extolled agrarianism, viewed youth as pillars of the nation, and elevated the value of soldier-like male bodies. These components of the Japanese national–imperial ideology delivered an emotional emancipation to colonial village youth, who had developed a deep grudge against the urban, the educated, and sometimes older generations in local social contexts. At their youth training sites, which provided intense bonding experiences, the participants acquired a

sense of moral superiority and confidence to challenge the social hierarchy. Viewing the mobilization in this way frees us from an undue fixation on mutually
exclusive ethnic identities. The social and emotional mechanism of creating ideal
Japanese nationals among colonial village youth was, it turns out, not fundamentally different from that in the Japanese countryside.

The War and the Seinendan

With the outbreak of the Second Sino-Japanese War, the Taiwanese seinendan
quickly supported Japan's cause. In Xinzhu province, 350 leaders of youth groups
and the governor gathered in Xinzhu city on September 17, 1937, to pray at the
Shinchiku Shrine for a Japanese military victory. After their shrine visit, they held
a convention to discuss seinendan activities to support the war effort, concluding
that the seinendan needed new recruitment strategies.[5] They had been targeting
only those who had graduated from elementary school, did not continue their
schooling, and were willing to join. Xinzhu educators in the early 1930s presented a good reason for narrowing the scope of participation, to build an organization of highly motivated youth. But for wartime mobilization, the seinendan
had to transform themselves so as to organize a much larger number of people
and train local leadership to Japanize the entire society.

Colonial officials at the provincial level had already expanded the seinendan
by establishing hamlet branches in each village in 1936. This was probably part
of carrying out the state's plan to make Taiwan the foothold for the empire's
southward expansion. In the hamlet branches, all male elementary school graduates were recruited to join the seinendan, and as a consequence, seinendan
membership increased substantially. In 1939, the membership exploded again
thanks to the policy of including those without elementary school education.
Their activities were typical of empire-wide seinendan: providing construction
and agricultural labor, offering Japanese language classes, and promoting kyōka
programs. The anthropologist Miyazaki Seiko explains that the GGT had originally planned to establish the mandatory *seinen gakkō* (youth school) system at
the same time as Japan did in 1939, but this could not be implemented because
Taiwan had not yet fully established a system of mandatory elementary school
participation. To compensate for the absence of youth schools, the GGT enforced
universal participation in village youth groups instead. Between 1938 and 1939,
the number of youth group members in Taiwan jumped from 62,906 to 269,906.[6]
The Xinzhu seinendan followed this island-wide trend.[7] In Xinzhu, the most dramatic jump occurred between 1936 and 1938—from 4,851 in 1936 to 14,554 in
1937, and then to 27,638 in 1938.[8] Xinzhu governors started using the phrase

"thirty thousand youths in the province" (*shūka sanman-nin no seinen*) as an icon that symbolized the strong Japanization movement taking place there.[9]

The new home front mobilization facilitated the nationalization of the seinendan. In June 1938, for the first time in Taiwan, seinendan institutions created a central body, the Taiwan Seinendan Federation, to oversee island-wide activities, and it officially became a branch of the Greater Japan Seinendan Federation. At its inauguration, participating youth declared four resolutions: "We will complete the National Spiritual Mobilization Movement. We will volunteer for patriotic labor (*kinrō hōkoku*). We will establish Japanese-speaking villages and towns. We will perfect the national defense."[10] A month before this, to emphasize the role of millions of youth as an engine for the war effort, Governor-General Kobayashi Seizō had already distributed a message in the form of a gramophone record, calling on "all young people on this island" to "know the social status that you have, take charge of things passionately and pure-heartedly, and be ready, with positive state of mind, to become the salt of the earth."[11]

At the local levels, various semi-governmental groups were streamlined. The Xinzhu provincial government issued an act to reorganize the seinendan on the third anniversary of the beginning of the war in 1940. The line of communication from the provincial government to individual youth was designed to match the line of command of kyōka associations, including the moral suasion federations (*kyōka rengōkai*) and hamlet revitalization groups (*buraku shinkōkai*). The Xinzhu government expected that the seinendan would be part of the Patriotic Imperial Subjects campaign (Kōmin Hōkō Undō). At the village level, it separated young people into two groups, depending on whether they had graduated from elementary school.[12] Those who had not graduated were required to undergo two to four years of language education first before joining the seinendan. The members gathered regularly in small groups to engage in set programs of training and volunteer work, wearing the standardized uniform of the newly centralized seinendan.[13]

The institutionalization of the seinendan in wartime Taiwan both continued and destroyed the previous effort to permeate Taiwan's rural societies. On the one hand, it continued to construct the image of modern rural youth against the dominance of the landlord class. On the other hand, colonial officials ignored Taiwan's social contexts and imposed a one-size-fits-all scheme of imperial seinendan mobilization. Paradoxically, as in Japan, state officials placed a strong emphasis on localities while pushing nationalization.[14] Newspapers and journals applauded local activities. *Shinkensetsu* (New Construction), the journal of the Patriotic Imperial Subjects Association (PISA; Kōmin Hōkōkai in Japanese), for example, often publicized "unique activities" in various villages and towns. Looking back on its three years of campaign activity, the PISA headquarters staff and a group of journalists criticized the effort: "Overall the guiding principles are too abstract. Should we not suggest more concrete things in accordance with each locality?"[15] Whereas propaganda production involved a great degree of grassroots participation in Japan, PISA leaders in Taiwan felt that local initiatives were not up to par.[16]

To achieve the goal of PISA leaders, rural youth again became both a means and an end. The PISA's stress on the local characters of training programs arose from their awareness of the looping dilemma of top-down youth mobilization that trapped colonial decision makers for decades. If officials initiated the campaign on their own authority, youth would participate but would probably not be interested in the prescribed standard activities. The mobilization leaders hoped that unofficial local figures would take charge, but those who occupied managerial positions in the Japanese mobilization scheme were mostly "rich intellectuals who enjoy[ed] debating ideologies" and "lack[ed] passion in practice."[17] To solve this dilemma, Japanese officials expressed a greater determination to expand the training of rural youth who had firsthand knowledge of their villages: "Regarding youth training, we should teach how they should lead and improve their particular villages in a more concrete way, and show them individual cases, including which methods other villages used and what they achieved. . . . The future of our campaign relies to a great extent on the commitment of these youth. Youth desire excitement and inspiration. We should direct responsible work to them."[18] Rural youth were considered an alternative to unreliable local intellectuals and a solution to the problem of stagnant mobilization of the rural masses.

The Xinzhu Province Youth Training Institute

The dilemma of leadership was nothing new.[19] Before the Second Sino-Japanese War, youth leadership training remained small and slow. Colonial officials held the first Shūyōdan-style "pillars of youth" camp in Taipei for one week in February 1935, gathering sixty strong, healthy males under age twenty-five from all over Taiwan. The participants were required to have finished elementary school and been active as youth group members for more than two years.[20] Xinzhu's first attempt to provide thorough leadership training was an agricultural training center established in July 1935. The provincial government built the facility with eighty acres of land near the beach in Qiding and invited agricultural specialists to teach thirty young farmers.[21]

Thirty young people per year—this was hardly a desirable scale for leadership training, especially after 1937. In August 1938, the Xinzhu officials launched a new youth training institute (Shinchiku-shūritsu Seinen Shūrenjō), hereafter simply *shūrenjō*) as a more intense disciplining institution than other youth programs.[22] Built near the beach of Nanliao, the shūrenjō selected sixty young people from village seinendan groups in the province for thirty days of training.[23] The instructors scheduled one-month sessions almost back to back so as to train as many young people as possible. Officials were eager to compare their youth mobilization efforts to those undertaken by the Nazis. "Even the Adolf Hitler School is eight years of education, but Xinzhu province's youth training institute is going to complete it within thirty days," they bragged, emphasizing the intensity and effectiveness of the training before it even began.[24]

The shūrenjō adopted a dojo style of training—the popular method in the metropole that emphasized the bodily mastery of the Japanese national spirit through group living. The village youth who either volunteered or were selected to join first underwent a physical checkup.[25] The teachers organized the trainees into groups of six, and the youth then completed all activities, including eating, cleaning, and sleeping, with their groups.[26] They maintained a rigid daily schedule that demanded military-like punctuality, starting with waking up at 6:00 a.m. to the sound of a Japanese drum. Male trainees then ran to do *misogi*, a Shinto-style morning prayer in the ocean, wearing only a *fundoshi* (loincloth). This ritual became a symbol of the shūrenjō. After morning exercises and a simple breakfast of a bowl of miso porridge, they listened to lectures on Japanese imperial history, rural village problems, and morally inspiring stories. Before or after lunch, they performed outdoor activities, practiced martial arts, worked at the construction site near the Shinchiku Shrine, plowed new land for vegetables, and marched through the city and mountains. After an hour or two of leisure time in the evening, they practiced *seiza*, a proper sitting position that entails kneeling on the floor with the buttocks resting on the heels and the ankles stretched so that the tops of the feet are pressed flat. Seated in that position, they listened to a concluding lecture before retiring to sleep at 9:30.[27] A female participant recalled that "seiza on the hard floor was the hardest for farm youth, because their ankles were too stiffened to stretch flat."[28]

The hallmark of the shūrenjō was the intense socializing experience, intended to produce group bonds comparable to the fraternity that Japanese village seinendan members cultivated over years. Painful training was a key component, intended to nurture friendship and a feeling of mutual trust. This goal was clearly manifest in Xinzhu's biweekly newsletter on youth training, *Dōkō* (literally the same light, but figuratively after the Japanese light). The pain that the trainees endured was the main topic in their confessional reflections, published in *Dōkō* to underscore the transformative quality of shūrenjō training. In a roundtable

FIGURES 6.1. TO 6.4. Activities at the Xinzhu Province Youth Training Institute (Shinchiku-shūritsu Seinen Shūrenjō). Photos reproduced courtesy of Xu Chongfa.

FIGURE 6.1. Shūrenjō male trainees in the position of *seiza*, or formal sitting.

FIGURE 6.2. At the Shinchiku (Xinzhu) Shrine.

FIGURE 6.3. Graduation ceremony for the thirteenth-term female trainees, January 31, 1944. Behind them is the Matsugane Dōjō, constructed behind the Shinchiku Shrine in late 1943.

FIGURE 6.4. Female trainees in *yukata*, a Japanese summer garment.

interview, the twelfth group of graduates admitted their initial reactions to physical pains and discomfort:

> The seiza sitting was the most painful. The first two times I cried, but when I listened to the governor's fifty-minute lecture in seiza, it was surely painful, but I was happy that I could finally bear the pain for so long.
>
> I used a pickax for the first time during volunteer labor, and I got a lot of calluses.
>
> Doing misogi in the rain the first few times was very cold, and I shivered.
>
> I left a few pieces of *gobō* root at the first meal, but Yamada sensei told me to eat them all, so I ate them with my eyes closed. I thought I could not take it anymore.[29]

These reflections stressed that overcoming the pain together was an important part of mastering Japaneseness. In combination with photos of their activities, in which youth are shown exhibiting perfect uniformity and discipline, the vulnerability expressed in their remarks gave a personal face to the otherwise fear-provoking scenes of training and highlighted the friendship that allowed the members to share their weaknesses with one another.

Discipline was promoted not only through the strict regimen, but also through deep affective bonding. For the first time in their lives, young people received intense attention from Japanese instructors. The training site had three full-time Japanese teachers and one or two Taiwanese assistants. The teachers lived in the same building, ate the same amount of the same food, and adhered to the same schedule as the trainees. As expressed in their personal letters, published essays, and roundtable interviews in *Dōkō*, the graduates appear to have developed intimate friendships with the instructors. Some described the teachers' devotion as equivalent to parental love: "The teachers even taught us how to scoop rice and hold chopsticks. Their kindness surpassed that of our parents." The teachers' own discipline impressed the trainees: "I cannot forget that Kitamura sensei did not move even a bit during an hour-long *seiza*, saying, 'It hurts everyone in the same way, but you have to overcome that.'" Some descriptions of their physical interactions accentuated the level of intimacy: "I will not forget that when I had a pimple so badly swollen that I did not want to even touch it myself, Yamada sensei squeezed the pus out for me."[30]

Young women's training in the shūrenjō started in July 1939, after inviting a few female teachers. Although the women also underwent rigid training that emphasized physical exercise, their afternoon activities focused on learning skills and manners associated with feminine attributes of Japanese culture, including cooking, sewing, music, flower arrangement, archery, and dancing.[31] They were taught that an action as simple as washing one's face was an opportunity to develop Japanese spirituality—a misogi for women.[32] The women had minimal contact with male trainees, but like their male counterparts, they also developed close personal relationships with the teachers through living together and strove diligently to meet their expectations. Huang Chunwei from Beipu, who participated in the first group of female trainees, described the first week of her experience in her diary. Although diary writing was part of the training and Huang's writing was so exemplary that it was published in *Dōkō*, her entries nevertheless highlight the role of personal interactions in fostering self-discipline during the training:

> July 13. Finally the day of going to the shūrenjō that I long waited for . . . There was a strict physical checkup, and two people did not pass. I did not know what to say as I saw them going home disheartened. But how happy I was when I could enter the shūrenjō! . . . A teacher kindly applied medicine to my head . . . It felt like a mother doing that . . . July 16 . . . I asked Hoshi sensei to teach us dancing for the women's patriotic song. I did not memorize it well when I practiced it by just three of us, so I made a mistake and felt embarrassed. July 17 . . . We took a bath before our teachers. Since I felt sorry, I decided not to go in the water . . . July 18 . . . I have been following the teachers' words very well so far, but I think there are many things I do not notice . . . I hear that some cried when teachers scolded them, but isn't that part of our training?[33]

The teachers' hands-on instructions and trainees' respect for them were the themes permeated in her description.

The shūrenjō taught the trainees to become young pillars back in their villages, and the seinendan groups were supposed to be the first targets of their influence. *Dōkō* stressed the achievements of the shūrenjō graduates in almost every issue. An article titled "A Shining Star of the Village, a Warrior of the Soil, a Shūrenjō Graduate, Huang Kunxuan," featured a model young farmer dedicated to new agricultural technologies and promoting Japanese language education in Yangmei.[34] Another graduate, Huang Rongzhe, implemented activities from the shūrenjō at his seinendan in Zhongli—waking up at 6:00 a.m., running to perform misogi, and doing morning exercises or voluntary cleaning of the streets.[35] "He became a totally different person," noted the principal of an elementary school in Zhudong, expressing surprise at the change in a former student, Xu Yaocheng's attitude. "That introverted, passive, and quiet boy was transformed, in a short period of time, into such an active and lively young man to the extent that I could not recognize him. . . . If every single seinendan member could go to the training center, how lively and worthy the Xinzhu seinendan groups would become!"[36]

But even if these graduates intended to play the expected role of invigorating the local seinendan as *Dōkō* advertised, in reality their experience at the shūrenjō often had a reverse effect. Certainly, the training there did transform the trainees, removing their indifference and making them more committed—but also, consequently, more frustrated. The graduates were increasingly dismayed at their inability to transfer their enthusiasm to the still largely indifferent village youth back home. In a letter to one instructor, a female graduate of the shūrenjō wrote that she and another institute graduate were "working hard for the seinendan, but the participation rate is not great. The members are not united, and they are individualistic and insincere."[37] She regarded a shūrenjō graduation certificate from the institute as certain evidence of a transformed mind. When she discovered otherwise, she felt betrayed: "There are some shūrenjō graduates whose minds are so wicked that I cannot believe they also went to the shūrenjō."[38] Meanwhile, many graduates had a hard time transitioning from their intense bonding experience back into the circles of village youth, let alone being able to exercise leadership. Another graduate wrote, "When I clean up [the school] with the school principal in the morning, other people say behind my back, 'She's showing off because she went to the training institute.' I don't do it to be praised. I felt really lonely."[39]

The graduates also experienced social alienation in their family relationships. They were expected to influence their family members, but as a consequence of their efforts, families became a site of colonial confrontation and negotiation. Their most important task was to encourage their parents to learn Japanese. *Dōkō* published a message from one trainee: "Mother, I thank you and Auntie for traveling so far from home to visit me at the shūrenjō. When Mother visited me in the office, we talked a little in Taiwanese. I felt really terrible at the time. Since I had decided that I would speak no Taiwanese during the one-month training period, I felt embarrassed in front of those outside the room. Mother, please go to the Japanese language center and study hard. I want you to be able to speak in Japanese at any time with anyone as soon as possible."[40]

Such articles pressured *Dōkō*'s young readers to tell their mothers the same message. One of their goals was to enable their family to receive a certificate as a "Japanese-speaking household" by educating their older family members.[41] For the older generations in many rural families, who had been able to avoid any serious interactions with Japanese colonialists, their children suddenly became the unfamiliar colonial and foreign element in the household. For female trainees, acquiring a level of learning above that of their parents meant overturning the generational and gender hierarchy altogether. The subversive role of young women was highlighted in the September 1939 issues of *Dōkō*, which featured a series on the female trainee Zheng Liangmei, who had fallen seriously ill and died during the second term of women's training. On her deathbed, *Dōkō* reported, she talked in Japanese to her mother, who could not understand the language, and sang the Japanese national anthem, "Kimi ga yo." *Dōkō* depicted the tragically alienating scene, fictional or not, as a heroic achievement by Zheng Liangmei.[42]

The reports in *Dōkō* tell us that the goal of the shūrenjō was to transform individual young people into ideal Japanese subjects through ideological indoctrination and then let them become the source of change in their villages and families. To be sure, the trainees' time at the shūrenjō seems to have had a great impact on them. However, their personal letters reveal that their most intense experience were social and emotional rather than ideological. Being chosen to go to the shūrenjō became the mark of a new social status. At the same time, the training at the institute not only generated a sense of bonding; it also reconfigured social relationships back home in their villages and families and consequently produced a sense of alienation that neither the trainees nor the instructors had anticipated. It thereby forced the graduates to shape new self-images that distinguished them from other village youth.

The Taiwan Patriotic Labor Youth Corps

How did young people view the rapid change in their social relationships? A series of interviews that I conducted with Huang Yuanxing and Xu Chongfa in 2011 helped me to situate the experiences of youth training in the context of their personal lives and social surroundings. In essence, they framed their experiences in terms of climbing up the ladder of youth training, viewing their shifting social relationships as a sign that they were successfully overturning social hierarchies.

Huang Yuanxing was born in Beipu on August 24, 1925, the second son in a farming family of Hakka origin. After his father died, his elder brother became the main source of family labor. He explained that although his family owned some land (unlike most of the farmers in Beipu, who rented land from the Jiang family), "We did not have money, and [that is why] none of my seven sisters went to school. Instead, five of them were adopted by other families in exchange for cash." Huang entered an upper-level curriculum after finishing the six-year elementary school in March 1939.[43] But he quit soon afterward because of a "personal clash" with a son of the Jiang family in the same class, whom he considered a bully. Moreover, because his family could not pay for him to continue into middle school anyway, he preferred to help the family by farming. He performed well in the village seinendan, which he joined immediately after dropping out of school. When he became the branch leader, the head of the village seinendan (the Beipu Elementary School principal) selected him to go to the shūrenjō.

"Everything was determined based on the schoolmaster's recommendation letter," Huang reflected. He endured a painful time there: "The training was militaristic and strict—they had a very unique training called misogi. . . . There was a
teacher called Nemoto Kenji, who I did not know was Taiwanese at the time, and
he was particularly strict. He often shouted loudly at us."[44]

When Huang met Nemoto Kenji at the shūrenjō, Nemoto spoke a sophisticated Japanese, exhibited Japanese mannerisms, and had gained the full trust
of the other Japanese teachers. Only after the end of Japanese colonial rule did
Huang Yuanxing find out that Nemoto had a Chinese name, Xu Chongfa. The
third son of a carpenter in Guanxi village, also in Xinzhu province, Xu was only
three years older than Huang. He was not Hakka, but he grew up speaking both
Hakka and Holo. He too had to give up middle-level education because his family
could not pay for it, but he ordered lectures from Japan by mail and completed
the entire curriculum of the middle school of Waseda University independently
while working as a carpenter. Even when we met more than seventy years later,
he treated the completion certificate that Waseda University mailed to him, on
April 1, 1939, as a personal treasure. Xu became the branch leader of the local
seinendan, and went to the shūrenjō in 1941, at age nineteen. Because of his outstanding grades on academic exams, Xu immediately became the representative
of the sixty trainees and delivered a speech at the graduation ceremony.

It was the Taiwan Patriotic Labor Youth Corps (Taiwan Kingyō Hōkoku
Seinentai; hereafter Labor Corps) that turned youth training into a ladder leading toward honor and prestige for Huang and Xu. The GGT started the Labor
Corps program in March 1940, gathering two hundred to three hundred men of
around twenty years old, to have them engage mainly in construction labor work
for three months at a time. They went to one of three sites—Taipei, Hualian, or
Taizhong—either to construct shrines, or to work on the highway between Hualian and Taizhong.[45] The program emphasized mastering Japaneseness through
physical labor: "Through labor-volunteer life and training, let them physically
understand the essence of the Japanese spirit, 'selfless patriotic service' (*messhi
hōkō*), and complete their character as imperial subjects by training their minds
and bodies."[46]

To attach prestige to the Labor Corps program, colonial officials cast it in the
image of military service, which was not implemented in Taiwan until 1942: "In
Korea, they started the volunteer soldier program and achieved a good result. We
should not forget that the result of our Patriotic Labor Youth Corps has a special
meaning. It is a good opportunity to measure the progress of youth in Taiwan."[47]
Xinzhu officials repeatedly discussed the similarity between the Labor Corps and
conscription in *Dōkō*: "Unfortunately, there is no duty of military service for
youth in Taiwan. The fact that you cannot participate in military service means,

FIGURE 6.5. Xu Chongfa (Nemoto Kenji) at age nineteen. Photo reproduced courtesy of Xu Chongfa.

FIGURES 6.6–6.7. The Taiwan Patriotic Labor Youth Corps (Taiwan Kingyō Hōkoku Seinentai) in Hualian, September 30, 1941. Photos reproduced courtesy of Xu Chongfa.

not only that you cannot directly stand at the frontier of national defense during these grave times, but also that you do not have an opportunity for the most serious group education where you obtain training in the real Japanese soul.... The Patriotic Labor Youth Corps recently initiated by the GGT is the most appropriate facility for group education."[48] The Labor Corps, like army conscription, was supposed to provide the socializing effect of creating national subjects.

Around this time, the image of the Japanese army became a notable source of hegemonic social value even in the colonial countryside. It was already common to evoke the image of military service in Xinzhu's shūrenjō and seinendan activities. "When I was going to join the dojo [shūrenjō]—I hear that Japanese youth are struck by solemn inspiration when they enter military service—I had a similar feeling," one of the first trainees stated on a radio show.[49] The shūrenjō instructors themselves also used military images to enhance their program's reputation: "Citizens were all surprised by the vigorous marching of the shūrenjō trainees, singing military songs in a proud manner in and out of town, [they told us that] 'they look exactly like soldiers.'"[50]

Youth had already come to realize that prestige and social alienation were two sides of the same coin. The Labor Corps program aroused a sense of being select rural youth among the participants. When they came back from service, they were called "reservist corps members" (*zaigō taiin*), echoing the title of respect given to military reservists (*zaigō gunjin*) in Japan.[51] At the same time, the term reservist also meant further detachment from their native home and society. Anticipating another frustrating encounter back home, Xu Chongfa, who joined the Labor Corps in Hualian, wrote in his diary five days prior to the end of his service, "When I return to the village, I will have to act differently as a reservist member.... Training will become useless if I get assimilated back in the village."[52]

Career Opportunities and the Sense of Rivalry

This ladder of youth programs were not the only reason why the participants perceived themselves as a select group. After completing these programs, the graduates gained new job opportunities. Job prospects had a strong psychological effect in improving self-esteem, especially by allowing the graduates to gain a status comparable to that of urban, educated youth, who had had better access to salaried jobs.

After returning to Beipu from Labor Corps service near Wushe in Taizhong, Huang found his career prospects suddenly improved. He immediately signed up for the four-month teacher training program and became an elementary school assistant teacher in September 1943. In an interview nearly seventy years later,

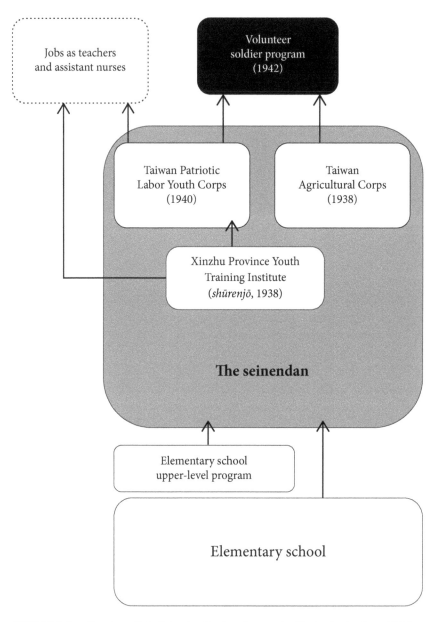

FIGURE 6.8. Rural youth training institutional setup in Xinzhu in the late 1930s. After the expansion of the seinendan in 1936–1937, most of the elementary school graduates participated in the village-level seinendan. Of the seinendan members, select youth went on to join other youth programs.

he justified his participation in colonial youth training, saying, "I was able to get a job only because I went to the Labor Corps, but only the graduates of the shūrenjō were qualified to get into the Labor Corps. . . . To go to the shūrenjō, they had to do well in the local seinendan. . . . I felt lucky that, even though I could not pursue formal education, I was able to become a teacher just like those who went to middle school or normal school." As Japan's war continued, an increasing number of Japanese teachers and officials were conscripted, leaving positions open to local youth. Teaching was a popular occupation among the young people in the village, partly because teachers had a large presence in their everyday lives, and also because teachers, like policemen, could move on to other governmental positions.[53] Although he retained bitter memories about the son of the Jiang family who had bullied him at school, Huang reflected that he had made the right decision in pursuing a career through youth training because "I did well in the end." He continued as a schoolteacher until his retirement fifty-seven years later.[54]

Although Huang Yuanxing's career development path was more typical, Xu Chongfa excelled as a model rural youth. After returning from the Labor Corps in Hualian in 1942, Xu was recruited to become an assistant instructor at the shūrenjō. The Japanese teachers gave him his Japanese name, Nemoto Kenji, under which he played the role of the strict, sometimes intimidating, and spirited teacher until the end of the war. Although he continued to believe in the excellence of Japanese-style youth training, Xu Chongfa also admitted the importance of job prospects it afforded: "The shūrenjō was popular because the graduates could become schoolteachers without going to normal school. Women could also become assistant nurses." Another Xinzhu resident who did not even join the seinendan, let alone the shūrenjō, also remembered that "the Shinchiku shūrenjō was famous because the graduates could become teachers."[55] In the tightly controlled wartime economy, many people in both Japan and its colonies lost their jobs. Despite the wartime slogan of "eight corners under one roof" (i.e., a world united under the Japanese emperor), ethnic discrimination was rife in the job market across the empire. When "getting a job was extremely hard for Taiwanese people, and it felt like rising to heaven if you could find a salaried job," four months of intense training away from home—one month at the training center and three months at the Labor Corps—offered a golden opportunity to broaden one's horizon.[56]

The fact that these men were seeking practical benefits does not mean that they viewed the Japanization campaign only instrumentally. Ideological conviction and pragmatism were mutually reinforcing. On many occasions, Taiwanese youth defined their value and competed with each other according to the metric of Japanese nationalism. The ranking system of the Labor Corps, for example, fanned competitive feelings among youth from different provinces. As in the military, they all started as second-rank trainees, but received two chances to move into the first rank and then to a separate upper rank. Xinzhu youth felt most competitive with those from Taipei province, where the colonial capital was. A participant in the first-term Labor Corps program wrote to the shūrenjō teachers, "It seems that many are getting sick among the Taipei team, but we on the Xinzhu team are fortunately all doing well without any accidents. . . . There was an announcement of our grades on April 23, and nineteen of twenty-four Xinzhu members passed to the upper rank, whereas eleven of forty Taipei people did."[57] Newspapers frequently reported the number of upper-rank trainees from Xinzhu, and the Xinzhu governor also pressured the prospective participants to achieve even better results.[58] Xu Chongfa's diary from his time in the Labor Corps is filled with nervous feelings about the rankings: "I have to voluntarily engage in difficult work and go home as an upper-rank trainee by any means!"[59] Huang Yuanxing had similar recollections: "Because the previous draftees from Xinzhu had achieved a good reputation and outstanding grades, I thought, as a Hakka youth from Xinzhu, I would do everything to become an upper-rank trainee."[60] He also narrated the history of youth programs backward, saying that the purpose of the shūrenjō was specifically to train Hakka youth to outperform other Taiwanese in their achievements at the Labor Corps.[61]

Provinces and ethnicities were not the only boundaries recognized by the competitors. They also harbored animosity toward urban youth from both within and outside Xinzhu. "I thought those from urban areas talk a good game, but their practice does not live up to their words," one Labor Corps reservist complained.[62] By contrast, aboriginal youth, once the formidable Other in Hakka residents' collective memory, were highly respected at youth training. Labor Corps members often wrote that the Takasago zoku (aborigines) were "innocent" and "wonderful."[63] During his Labor Corps service, Xu Chongfa felt ashamed that his skin was not suntanned, because the instructors often asked him to build furniture while others engaged in outdoor labor. Tanned skin became a masculine symbol of hardworking rural youth, thereby further elevating the image of dark-skinned aboriginal youth.[64]

In the same way, the sense of rivalry with intellectual youth grew stronger. Urban youth who possessed higher academic degrees made Xu and many seinen-dan youth defensive about their lack of formal schooling. Xu, who was confident in his academic ability, felt hurt when someone with more education beat him in youth training: "Qiu Renzhang became the top student among three hundred of us. Alas, it should not be surprising because he is a middle school graduate."[65] When Xu later became the representative of all the upgraded trainees during the Labor Corps program, it meant more to him than just doing well as a Xinzhu youth; it was also a mark of achievement by someone with only very basic school-ing. Back in their villages, youth with only elementary education continued to harbor the same feelings toward the well-educated. Huang Xiuying, a female graduate of the shūrenjō, wrote to Xu in July 1945, frustrated by the intense competition for positions in the village office. "What is it about a graduate of the women's school that makes her superior to me? I believe I am by no means inferior to her. Seeing the person who wasted three years studying [in school], I felt really miserable, but society is on their side. Facing this issue, I felt that society is so pointless."[66]

The formation of village youth participants' social identities and self-esteem as rural, less-educated, hardworking Xinzhu youth evolved as part of a tightly bonded community that developed in the shūrenjō. In other words, the shūrenjō became a sphere where personal feelings and political (or ideological) beliefs became inseparable in the face of various social battles. The graduates called it "the home of our hearts" (kokoro no furusato), a place where they often came back and shared the frustrations and excitement they encountered in the Labor Corps and in their villages. The solemn melody of "Umi yukaba"—an imperial martial song about being ready to die for one's lord—represented the bond that developed among the teachers and trainees, who remained in contact with each other long after graduation.[67] In their letters, they often said that they would work as hard as possible in volunteer labor and at local seinendan inspections because they did not want to embarrass their teachers.[68] It seems that Xu Chongfa seems to have revealed his Taiwanese background more openly to female train-ees and kept in close touch with them, perhaps in hopes of finding a marriage partner.[69] These women called him "my elder brother" (anisama) in return and continued to seek advice from him.

These youth training institutions triggered a mechanism that functioned in the same way as the social mobility complex we have seen in Miyagi. Although the institutional setup, the means of providing job opportunities, and the ways in which youth shared the identity of rural youth differed, Taiwanese village youth gained a chance to "rise in the world" and challenge the dominance of urban youth and the landlord class. They received no résumé-writing experience as in Miyagi (or at least the remaining records give no such indication), but they saw each training institution as a rung on a career ladder. This opportunity power-fully transformed young people from perpetual farmers to career seekers.

Seinendan- and shūrenjō-based career opportunities were not available to all village youth, however. On the one hand, when participation in local seinen-dan groups became mandatory in 1937, it lost its appeal for upper-class youth who had appreciated the elitist nature of the earlier youth groups.[70] Those who aspired to higher education were not interested in seinendan activities even if they resided in the countryside.[71] The class gap is apparent in many later autobio-graphical novels written by Taiwanese intellectuals, which often cynically depict the village seinendan as composed of a group of ignorant peasants brainwashed by the Japanese colonizers.[72] On the other hand, it remained difficult for the poorest stratum of farmers, those who struggled to survive, to participate fully in seinendan activities. They could not afford to leave for four months to attend the shūrenjō and the Labor Corps program. During wartime, a new social sphere opened up mainly for the second and third sons of middling-class families, espe-cially those who owned a small farm or shop.[73] Their families could spare their labor temporarily, but (as was the case for Xu and Huang) they could not afford higher education. Those who were recognized as model rural youth through the series of training programs had a good chance to fill the positions that became vacant when Japanese teachers and low-ranking officials were conscripted and left Taiwan, even when they were competing against more educated youth.

The Onset of Fully Militaristic Training

In the late 1930s, military drills became central to seinendan activities. The GGT had been reluctant to promote overtly militaristic training until Kobayashi Seizō became governor-general in 1936.[74] Kobayashi did not immediately plan to enlist Taiwanese youth in the army, but he regarded military training as the most effec-tive method of Japanizing the population. Upon his inauguration, he asked the army to become involved with Taiwanese youth, saying that "it would be doubly beneficial if we train the finest Taiwanese youth and those who demand mili-tary service in our army—the smelting furnace of the Japanese spirit—and the GGT takes charge of those who finish the training and lets them supervise local youth."[75] The army rejected his plan, but at the local level, simple military drills such as marching and basic commands had already been incorporated in the training of youth groups.[76] At the national level, the outbreak of war in 1937 gave a go-ahead to seinendan supervisors.

As the war situation worsened, military service commenced in Korea and Taiwan. When the Japanese cabinet passed the Army Special Volunteer Soldier Program Act for the colonies in 1938, it was not implemented immediately in Taiwan, mainly because of concerns about Taiwanese ethnic kinship with the enemy state, China. In 1941, when the GGT finally decided to implement the act, army officials planned to initiate conscription ten years later after examining the results of the voluntary soldier program, but they subsequently accelerated the timetable, beginning to draft Koreans in 1944 and Taiwanese in 1945.[77]

This delay of recruitment, compared with the earlier start in Korea, stimulated Taiwanese leaders and led to an overheating of the *kōminka* (Japanization) campaigns.[78] The movement to implement the volunteer soldier program was popular not only among pro-Japanese elites in Taiwan, but also among home rule activists who had viewed military service as a way to achieve equality between Japan and Taiwan since the late 1920s. The historian Kondō Masami argues that the most decisive voice was an editorial in *Taiwan shinminpō*, formerly the loudest anticolonial organ in Taiwan, that appeared on August 10, 1940.[79] The article demanded that Taiwanese people "display their passion and sincerity in their desire for military service."[80] Youth were viewed as being responsible for making military service possible in Taiwan.

To show that they were prepared, local seinendan groups began working closely with Japanese army officers and practicing army drills. In December 1938, the Xinzhu province seinendan conducted city- and county-level inspections. Army Lieutenant Colonel Iwasa Hiroshi, later an instructor at the shūrenjō, evaluated every move made by the youth in these inspections. "Regarding the straight-standing posture: 1. It is a pity that many move their eyeballs. Stare at one point and stand still. 2. Stretch the arms out fully. There are some whose mouths are open." *Dōkō* reported the details of Iwasa's evaluations so that "the supervisors and leaders of seinendan would read carefully and learn for future training."[81]

Females also experienced basic army drills. *Dōkō* reported that female students "used to be shy, and even avoided meeting teachers on the street, but now female seinendan members do training and troop marching confidently, emulating their male counterparts . . . During the inspections, they followed Lieutenant Colonel Iwasa's orders and commanded the troops in a very impressive way."[82] Even though these women would not become fighting soldiers, the officials saw military drills as an opportunity to teach Japanese discipline and a way to demonstrate that the entire society was ready for military service. The army's top official, Tanaka Kiyoshi, lectured on the radio in 1941 that the coming volunteer soldier program required the entire population of six million in Taiwan—"the young, old, male or female" —to be trained properly "as in Germany." To become mothers of high-quality soldiers, female bodies were particularly important.[83]

The Warrior of Language and the Warrior of the Plow

In the midst of the fever for yet-to-come military service, actual participation in the battlefields began in the form of civilian military employment (often called *gunpu* or porters; officially they were a part of *gunzoku* or auxiliaries). A far larger number of young Taiwanese men became civilian military employees than soldiers by the end of the war.[84] Gunpu held the lowest rank in the Japanese military, even below conscripted horses and dogs. Their death rate was ten times higher than that of Taiwanese soldiers.[85] Officials regarded them as voluntary participants, but in reality many of them were forcibly drafted, especially at the beginning, and the military learned of many attempts to escape the draft through residence registration fraud. Japanese officials consequently turned to the seinendan in an attempt to recruit those who were somewhat Japanized already. The army also provided draftees with compensation of one yen a day, equivalent to the starting pay of a regular salaried job for young people in Taiwan.[86] This strategy presumably worked, as it yielded a sudden jump in voluntary participation from 103 participants in September 1937 to 1,953 volunteers in October.[87]

Among civilian military employees, the vast majority, or tens of thousands of Taiwanese youth, were hired as translators.[88] Since the Japanese confused Hakka with Cantonese, the Japanese army recruited many educated Hakka youth in Xinzhu province as translators of Cantonese or as schoolteachers to work in the Japanese-occupied region of Guangdong in southern China. Pan Jinhe, who later became Xinpu village head, recalled that a group of young members of prominent families, including himself and Jiang Axin, a business leader from the Jiang family of Beipu, worked for the army in Guangzhou to produce propaganda. "Cantonese people do not speak Hakka although we encountered a number of Hakka people and we could communicate with them," he said. "Because of the military's needs, they made us learn Cantonese and become translators. . . . We Hakka learned it a lot more quickly than the Japanese did."[89] Once Japanese forces occupied Southeast Asian territories in the early 1940s, the scope of recruitment expanded massively to include less-educated youth. According to the Japanese government, the total number of recruits dispatched to China and Southeast Asia numbered 126,750 by the end of the war, although the number of translators remains unknown.[90] Xu Chongfa's second elder brother, Xu Chongyi, was serving the Japanese military as an interpreter when he died on a battlefield in Burma.

In contrast to those interpreters—who were large in number but whose recruitment was an ad hoc process—the Taiwan Agricultural Corps (Taiwan Nōgyō Giyūdan) was more well-organized and functioned as a formal training program.[91] Upon request from the army fighting in mainland China, officials in Taiwan recruited one thousand Taiwanese farmers who were around twenty years old to form the Agricultural Corps in April 1938. Their mission was to till the abandoned land and provide Japanese soldiers with fresh vegetables. They were stationed in Shanghai, Nanjing, Wuchang, Wuhan, Anqing, or Hankou, for one year at a time and were also paid one yen a day.[92] Their everyday life emulated life in the army: They had no freedom from 6:00 a.m. to 9:00 p.m., and when not doing agricultural work, they learned how to stand up straight, respond to orders, march, raise their hands straight, and look like real soldiers. The program contained a noteworthy educational aspect, as the military officers not only gave lectures on the cause of Japan's war in China but also took the youth to the destroyed villages to show them the devastation suffered by the "losing side" of the war.[93]

The stories of these youths were similarly symbolic and heroic to those of the Labor Corps participants retold in the articles of Dōkō. The editors had already been stressing that farmers were equivalent to soldiers fighting on a battle-field.[94] The Agricultural Corps was the ultimate embodiment of this "warrior of the plow."[95] Many pages of Dōkō printed letters from the Labor Corps and the Agricultural Corps participants side by side to report frontier experience. Membership in the Agricultural Corps was not restricted to the seinendan, but many from Xinzhu province were seinendan members. They found the agricul-tural techniques in Chinese villages so primitive that "invigorating production requires the use of Taiwanese-style agriculture, and clearing and cultivating the land properly requires the hard labor of Taiwanese youth."[96] While developing their self-image as Taiwanese farmers superior to their Chinese counterparts, the Agricultural Corps, typical of youth training programs at the time, also provoked rivalry between provinces. The Xinzhu youth participants proudly reported to Dōkō that "we from Xinzhu are leading the other provinces and, with very few sick people, achieving good results. We enjoy a good reputation. I am so happy that we are doing better than those from the other provinces."[97]

The Agricultural Corps not only provided the first exposure to the battle-field for many Taiwanese youth, but also introduced them to a new destination of conquest. Many Xinzhu youth participated in the Agricultural Corps with the intention of remaining in mainland China after the one-year program and becoming long-term agricultural colonizers.[98] Despite the difficult nature of the work, the Agricultural Corps presented a new frontier to conquer and colonize as Taiwan's mountains were exchanged for with the Chinese mainland, and later for the jungles of Southeast Asia.

Volunteer Fever

When the volunteer soldier program was launched in Taiwan in 1942, young men in the countryside viewed it as the new top rung on the ladder of youth training programs. Its arrival produced volunteer fever across the island, with hundreds of thousands of men submitting applications each year. Becoming a volunteer soldier, especially because of the intense competition for openings, represented the most prestigious achievement for Taiwanese men who pursued seinendan-based youth training. In terms of both job prospects and social recognition, the volunteer soldier program promised to remedy the marginalized position of farm youth overnight.

In this environment, many young men could not separate their personal urge to apply from the social pressure on them to do so. The seinendan were positioned at the heart of social enthusiasm. Members received the most direct orders and group pressure to apply. After a Japanese school principal encouraged the seinendan members of Xiangshan village in Xinzhu to apply, for example, every single member signed the form—male applying for the volunteer soldier, female for the volunteer assistant nurse.[99] Other seinendan units submitted their members' applications in groups, hundreds and thousands at a time. The hype about military service created in the various youth training programs eliminated any real chance for graduates to decide for themselves whether to apply. Xinzhu's official newsletter reported that youth rushed to the counter as soon as the city hall started accepting applications; it was "almost like a battle scene." The number of applicants in Xinzhu reached 20,586 in the first two weeks.[100] Being a proud imperial youth, Xu Chongfa not only felt the need to apply but also desired to pass the examination, as noted in the introduction to this book.

The seinendan had an amplifying effect on mobilization, in that the participants' volunteer fever motivated other people to join the war effort, thereby further increasing the social pressure on seinendan members. The female gaze played a powerful role. In an essay in an official colonial journal, a young woman named Yang Qinghe expressed her excitement about watching a youth play, *Kokumin kaihei* (All national people are soldiers), presented in perfect Japanese by a seinendan group: "I was moved so deeply . . . It was as if they had shown me a dazzling thing by suddenly opening a box . . . A feeling of intense surprise ran through my body. Taiwanese youth have matured so much!" She portrayed her excitement about seeing and hearing volunteer soldiers as an almost sensual experience: "Late at night, when I hear military songs sung by those coming back from military drills, I immediately recognize 'that is a soldier,' and 'that is a volunteer soldier!'" Yang was even more surprised to hear a Japanese friend expressing similar excitement about the Taiwanese volunteers.[101] Young women pressured their male counterparts in different ways. Like those in the countryside of Miyagi who formed a no-marriage alliance against men who had not attended military drills, 140 female seinendan members in Zhudong county vowed not to marry anyone who had failed to apply to the volunteer soldier program.[102] Similar stories were reported all over Taiwan.

The prestige that came with being a volunteer soldier transcended the boundaries between social groups, elevated the status of rural youth, and exerted pressure on intellectuals as well. Literature supporting the Japanization campaign (*kōmin bungaku*) directly connected the image of model rural youth to the volunteer soldier. In a famous short novel from 1941, *Shinganhei* (The volunteer soldier), the young author, Zhou Jinpo, treats the act of applying to join the volunteer soldier program as the final test in the internalization of Japanese ideology.[103] Although the novel narrates the dilemma of Taiwanese intellectual youth with deep sympathy, it ends by depicting the triumph of the acts of village youth (submitting blood applications) over the logic of intellectuals (rationalizing Japanese dominance). Whether or not this idea resonated among readers, the novel demonstrates that the superiority of rural youth had penetrated the discourse of intellectuals.

Total Mobilization and Social Change

Compared with previous youth training programs, the volunteer soldier program more deliberately promoted changes in social relationships. It provided average farm youth with the quickest way to escape their peripheral position. But once total war mobilization started, labor and mandatory army conscription destabilized the social hierarchy in unexpected ways. As the imperial machine's dependence on colonial youth deepened, the relationships between colonizer and colonized and between the young and the old exhibited new dynamics.

The devastation became apparent in the final years of the war. One clear sign was the recruitment of factory boys (*shōnenkō*), which began in 1943. Thousands of young teens—mostly age thirteen and fourteen—were mobilized to build aircraft in Japanese navy factories. Boys responded to the earnest and forceful recruitment calls by their elementary schoolteachers in the Taiwanese countryside. Promised attractive pay and an engineering diploma within five years, approximately eight thousand Taiwanese boys headed to the Navy C Factory in Yamato city, Kanagawa, in Japan. Once trained there, they were sent to factories across the country. These teenagers found harsh living conditions, severe air raids, and frequent corporal punishment.[104]

The onset of military conscription, although it was not planned when the volunteer soldier program started, did not surprise the Taiwanese. The government put it into effect in September 1944 and started drafting young men in April 1945, a mere four months before the end of the war. Taiwan had already experienced severe air raids starting in October 1944. When conscription exams began on January 16, 1945, Taiwan had just experienced another round of massive air raids that made their methodical, enormous nature plain to all.[105] Xinzhu was among the hardest-hit areas.[106] Beipu residents remember hearing air raid alarms almost daily, and children had neither the time nor the inclination to sit in a classroom or to study.[107]

Despite Japan's lagging fortunes in a war that led to more forceful mobilization, official publications advertised conscription and labor recruitment as the final stage of Japanization. But in propelling such rhetoric, the imperial hierarchy separating Taiwanese and Japanese populations was being redefined. The author Ōsawa Sadakichi argued that the inevitable next step after mandatory conscription was to encourage Taiwanese-Japanese intermarriage. He advocated it to "improve the genes of our offspring by mixing blood" and give the Taiwanese "experiences with truly Japanese feelings and environments."[108] Ōsawa and other Japanese writers continued to exhibit the colonizers' chauvinistic attitudes. But as their burdens increased, the Taiwanese began to realize—as their burdens increased—that they had gained the moral upper hand. In response to a Taiwanese commentator who argued that perfecting the Taiwanese people's Japanese required more cooperation from Japanese residents, a Self-Defense Group (*sōteidan*) leader, Li Meishu, complained in a roundtable discussion in *Shinkensetsu*, "I really want Japanese people to stop using sloppy Taiwanese language. Rather than speaking Taiwanese with weird accents, it is more important to speak Japanese all the way."[109] His condescension toward Japanese settlers slipped out in his comment on their inadequate acquisition of the local language. The devotion of Taiwanese to the imperial cause was feeding a sense of moral superiority over their colonizers.

Universal conscription was something entirely different from the volunteer soldier program, or even the recruitment of factory boys with the promise of a school diploma. The mandatory aspect was the opposite of the exclusivity accorded to the volunteer soldier, which had been a crucial element in stirring volunteer fever. Still, the celebration of masculinity and the excitement of war influenced many rural conscripts. Huang Yuanxing, for instance, readily accepted his conscription notification, which he received while working as an assistant teacher at the Beipu Elementary School.[110] But many Taiwanese youth tried to escape the call to duty. Even in Beipu, where no clear anti-Japanese feeling had existed since 1907, it was reported that two of thirteen young conscripts swallowed a bottle of soy sauce at their own send-off party and had to go to the hospital. The angry Japanese village head allegedly grabbed two middle-aged men in the crowd, a barber and a doctor of Chinese medicine, and pushed them into a car as replacements.[111] Huang did not remember this incident, but he agreed that some people tried to escape conscription.[112] Whatever the truth of these rumors, they convey the frustration and fear aroused by the fanatical mobilization of the villagers, who were already subjected to food rationing, the forced donation of anything made of metal, and mandatory monetary savings in postal accounts, not to mention the daily air raid alarms.

Ironically, the best way to escape conscription duty was to become a cog in the production line of soldiers. A well-known postwar author from Xinzhu, Zhong Zhaozheng, a Hakka born in the same year as Huang Yuanxing, intentionally escaped conscription by entering a youth teachers school. This new program trained students specifically to become teachers at militaristic youth schools, of which there was a great need in wartime. Zhong was the Other kind of youth to whom Huang Yuanxing had contrasted himself—one of those educated in middle school who grudgingly became an elementary schoolteacher in the countryside of Xinzhu. Typical of educated youth, he maintained a cynical view toward wartime mobilization. In his autobiographical novels and memoirs, he describes the youth teachers school as "a crappy school," because it was full of Japanese students whose only goal, like his, was to avoid conscription.[113]

During these last few years of the war, as the military increased its reliance on youth across the imperial domains and yet faced a rising degree of skepticism in colonial society, colonial officials embraced a strategy of exploiting the gap between the younger and older generations more markedly. They attempted to maintain the pretense that youth and officials were pursuing the same social agenda, calling on the "pure" youth to persuade those "ignorant old parents" who opposed their children's desire to apply for the volunteer soldier program.[114] Schoolchildren were presented as a model for the rest of society in Japanization campaigns. Nagata Tomiki, a teacher at the Beipu Elementary School, noted that students frequently called each other by their Japanese names, even in personal letters. Contrasting this situation with adults whom he heard saying, "Even if we adopt Japanese names, we do not get any rights or one *sen* of profit," the teacher lamented, "Why would they not be able to join the children and try harder?"[115]

Some Hakka parents viewed this generational divide-and-conquer strategy as a threat to their ethnic heritage and attempted to counter their children's rapid Japanization by teaching them about the Hakka's historical roots. Yet this effort did not close their generation gap. Dai Guohui recalls that he developed hostility toward his father, who preached to him about the proud historical origins of the Hakka in the Central Plain of the Yellow River. "I thought, 'My father is uneducated and ignorant, is very conceited, likes empty talk, and gives me all kinds of bullshit orders,' and began to despise him."[116] He even took out a Japanese scholar's book that his brother brought back from Tokyo and showed his father that his stories were nothing more than myths or legends.[117] Wartime mobilization made both a scientific mind and an unconditional faith in the empire markers of Japanized youth. By exacerbating the generational divide, state officials attempted to maintain the social ground for mutual co-optation with young people in their effort to extend Japanese nationalism.

During the short period between 1937 and 1945, rural youth mobilization in Taiwan, situated at the core of a mass mobilization scheme, produced a large number of volunteers and laborers to assist the Japanese Empire's war effort as well as enthusiastic local promoters of Japanization campaigns. From colonial officials' point of view, youth mobilization was an unmistakable success. But the outburst of emotions exhibited in the volunteer fever phenomenon and other social reactions to wartime mobilization could not possibly have been manufactured by governmental preaching. The personal experiences of young participants—like those of Huang Yuanxing and Xu Chongfa examined in detail in this chapter—are essential in analyzing the puzzle of the sudden, rapid, and large-scale mobilization of Taiwanese society. Their stories make it clear that local dynamics—whether through village youth's relationships with landlord youth, their family finances and occupations, rivalries with urban intellectual youth, comparative education levels and ambitions for personal success, or sexual interests—attached social values to colonial youth training programs.

In the case of the Xinzhu countryside, the ladder of programs—from the village seinendan, the shūrenjō, the Labor Corps, and the Agricultural Corps to the volunteer soldier program—helped to transform the self-image of village youth from a perpetual underclass peasants to highly capable, select, career-oriented rural youth. This was a Taiwanese version of the social mobility complex, like the one formed in Tōhoku Japan a decade earlier. Like Miyagi youth, Xu and Huang shared a strong identity as proud rural youth and harbored a sense of moral superiority over urban youth and intellectuals. They employed the rhetoric of Japanese nationalism in their emotional and personal expressions. The social mobility complex explains the highly emotional nature of public responses to imperial mobilization.

There is no denying that much of the local social conditions were products of state policies. This was especially so in the colonial setting. The colonial economy was designed to support the metropole, and educational and employment opportunities directly reflected state priorities. Still, the colonial state had at best a tenuous influence on the values shared in each family, village, generation, and ethnic group. At the early stages, colonial officials experienced a long period of trial and error in youth training programs because they had little knowledge of how a combination of various state policies would affect local dynamics. Even with the unprecedented amount of energy put into social engineering during wartime, the shūrenjō in Xinzhu unexpectedly produced a sense of social alienation among its graduates, which paradoxically strengthened their loyalty to the empire.

During wartime, what aligned the interests of the state and the social dynamics of Taiwanese villages was, again, the versatile and capacious quality of the concept of rural youth. Young villagers did not aspire to become ideal Japanese subjects as such, but to become model rural youth. The image of disciplined, respected, and modern rural youth eventually permeated colonial villages, created a social mobility complex, and allowed state officials to engage local societies. It was not a mere surrogate of Japanese nationalism, however. Rather, the idea of rural youth had an immeasurable ideological potential of its own. To ambitious young men, it provoked dreams of youthful leadership in an agrarian utopia, a future that seemed more attractive and relevant than the propaganda of the Greater East Asia Co-Prosperity Sphere or any of the emperor-centered slogans cited by youth themselves. Volunteer fever could be considered one expression of such an expansive imagining of the future shared by colonial youth.

Recognizing the utopian vision embraced by Taiwanese youth may compel us to question the utility of the familiar lenses of colonialism, wartime exploitation, or even Japanization as means of interpreting their subjective experiences. Behind their emotional commitment to the imperial state's ideology, the final destination of Taiwanese youth's self-mobilization diverged from imperial goals. This suggests that, although it functioned as a conveyer of agrarian ideals, the state did not omnipotently define their subjectivity—on the contrary, youth defined the value of the Japanese Empire within the framework of realizing their agrarian dream.

7

MODEL RURAL YOUTH IN KOREAN VILLAGES

Korea is often regarded as having been an industrialized colony, in contrast to predominantly agricultural Taiwan. Yet most of its people lived in farm villages even in the late 1930s, when the colonial government was investing in heavy industry in northern cities. Since the 1920s, the agriculture-centered southern provinces had played an important role in meeting the empire's needs for food. As in the governmental campaigns in the metropole, agrarianism became a core ideology for the Government-General of Korea (GGK), especially in the Rural Revitalization Campaign, launched in 1932. As with the earlier Local Improvement Movement (1906–1918) and the concurrent Economic Revitalization Campaign in Japan, military ethos, agrarian ideals, and Japanese nationalism converged in the youth mobilization that occurred in the Korean countryside during the 1930s.

Until this agrarian campaign, however, young residents in rural villages were largely untouched by the urban discourse on the rise of youth, which developed in the first three decades of the twentieth century (see chapter 4). Although colonial governors and local Korean notables attempted during the 1910s to modernize ways of farming and living in the countryside, neither of them leveraged the youth discourse in their projects. The youth activism for Korean independence that was popular in county capitals in the 1920s did not spread to influence farm youth either. The story of Korean village youth until the 1930s was one of isolation from national movements (with the important exception of the March First Independence Movement of 1919), from state and county capitals, from the idealized image of rural youth, and from opportunities for social mobility. In the 1930s, with the onset of the Rural Revitalization Campaign, the center of gravity of youth mobilization finally shifted from county capitals to small villages. The image of model rural youth being the pillars of the village and the empire was established, consequently affecting social values and relationships as well as the consciousness of young villagers.

As in the Japanese and Taiwanese cases, an examination of this process requires sensitive treatments of location-related, generational, and class-based factors, as well as changes over time. Kwangsŏk village, in South Ch'ungch'ŏng province, offers us a site with such specificities. Through the lens of Kim Yŏng-han, a young villager who grew up in Kwangsŏk, we can grasp how young men of a certain class background became protagonists in the development of a social mobility complex in the 1930s. This mechanism of upward mobility and modern youth consciousness emerged very differently from the one in the Xinzhu countryside of Taiwan, however. The Korean countryside was plagued by the slow pace of elementary education expansion and a low literacy rate under colonial rule, as well as by the rigid and fine stratification of social classes that had developed through the centuries of Chosŏn rule (1397–1897). Because of these elements, only sons of relatively well-off families could graduate from elementary school, and the social mobility complex was also small in scale compared with its Japanese or Taiwanese equivalents.

Nonetheless, the emergence of model rural youth in Kwangsŏk shows how, albeit in relatively limited ways, state programs and rural society began to align more closely, to an extent that affected the psychology of village youth. I faced a greater challenge in collecting firsthand accounts of colonial youth programs in the Korean countryside than in Taiwan, likely because of the widespread fear of being labeled as pro-Japanese in contemporary South Korea. But the story of Kim Yŏng-han, told in his carefully chosen words, reveals how the new generation and class had the chance to restructure the prevailing social system in the early to mid-1930s. Like Xu Chongfa and Huang Yuanxing in Taiwan, Kim associated colonial youth training institutions with career opportunities. Kim also adopted Japanese agrarian nationalism to assert his superiority over older generations and characterized his career in local offices as a success story.

Many historians of colonial Korean villages have highlighted the colonial government's suppression of Korean ethnicity, the capitalist exploitation of tenant farmers, and the everyday resistance by villagers. Without denying the importance of such aspects of village life, this chapter presents the more fluid nature of social interactions, particularly from the perspective of changing generational relationships. The GGK could not mobilize the rural population for war as it did without effectively permeating their local societies. Such permeation does not mean that there was no resistance, or that all policies were successful or justifiable. A social history of rural youth mobilization in Kwangsŏk reveals multiple experiences even in a single village while also indicating similarity across the empire with regard to how young men in certain social positions turned state mobilization into social opportunities in their local contexts.

Kwangsŏk Village in South Ch'ungch'ong

Japanese intervention in Korean politics and the Korean economy began before the formal annexation in 1910. Kwangsŏk village in the Nonsan region, in the central part of what is now South Korea, saw a sudden influx of Japanese settlers at the beginning of the twentieth century. Villagers resisted these settlers' inroads, sometimes violently. Despite the colonial tensions, Kwangsŏk society had many commonalities with Shida in Miyagi, rather than with Beipu in Xinzhu.

The Nonsan region was a prominent agricultural producer, known for its massive fertile plain, created by the Nonsan River and the larger Kŭm River.[1] The Nonsan Plain was part of the Sannam (the southern three) provinces,

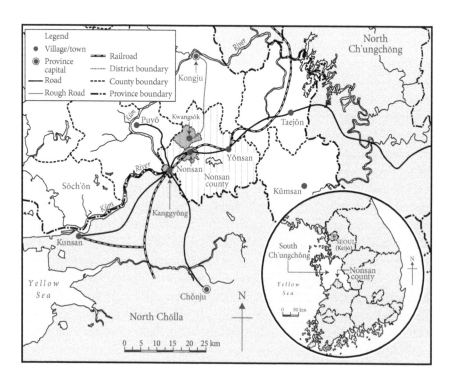

MAP 4.   The locations of Kwangsŏk village, Nonsan town, and Kangyŏng town

which reportedly produced 70% of all rice consumed in premodern Korea.[2] The plain yielded nearly forty-five thousand tons of rice annually during the 1930s.[3] The Kŭm River, which runs to the Yellow Sea, had long been an artery for goods and people. From the seventeenth century until the 1910s, when new railroad systems replaced water transportation, the commercial hub of the Nonsan region was a river port town, Kanggyŏng, the last port large ships traveling the Kŭm River could reach.[4] From there, goods were redistributed further inland on small boats. Because Kanggyŏng was also located on the inland route between Seoul and Chŏlla, it became a hub of regional circulation. Rice, grain, cotton cloth, tobacco, fish, and a variety of other products were traded there, and rice and grain from the region were sold as far away as Seoul and Cheju Island.[5]

After the Chosŏn government was forced to open its ports to foreign powers in the 1870s and 1880s, the commercial opportunities in Kanggyŏng attracted dozens of Japanese settlers. Once the Sino-Japanese War in 1895 gave Japan privileged status in Korea, more Japanese merchants came and formed a settler community protected by Japanese troops. The mixed residence of Korean locals and Japanese settlers became common in provincial port cities, but the settlers built their schools and shrines and ran commercial unions separate from the Korean community. These merchants often ignored the agreements between the Korean and Japanese governments, illegally acquiring real estate, expanding their businesses, and virtually creating a foreign concession in Kanggyŏng.[6] When Japan formally annexed Korea in 1910, the number of Japanese residents in the town already exceeded one thousand, and it continued to increase until the 1940s.[7]

In contrast to the urban settlement in Kanggyŏng, which generally resembled the foreign settlements in Chinese port cities, the Japanese inhabiting the Nonsan Plain viewed their migration more as pioneering open land.[8] They held this view despite the fact that the southern provinces of the Korean peninsula were densely populated, making Nonsan by no means open territory.[9] The first Japanese settler in Nonsan, Miyake Suejirō, a native of Okayama, moved to Nonsan village from Kanggyŏng in 1899. He sold Japanese farming instruments to Korean farmers. Other immigrants followed, and around 1910 the number of Japanese households surpassed one hundred.[10] Nonsan was attractive because the introduction of railroads gave it easy access to major cities; the travel time by rail was less than twenty-five minutes to Kanggyŏng and two hours to Taejŏn and Kunsan.[11]

The early settlers emphasized the violence and danger they faced on a daily basis in a chronicle they wrote in 1914. The pioneer Miyake had to "avoid fiendish insurgents" to conduct his business.[12] Nonsan was the frequent target of bandits who torched houses and stole valuables. The Righteous Army (composed of anti-foreign local volunteer troops) attacked the Japanese residents in Nonsan in 1907.[13] The chronicle argued that security was a serious problem for Korean as well as Japanese residents. In 1906, although there were only eleven Japanese households, they requested that the provincial government establish a police post. Episodes in the chronicle, however, reveal the enormous distrust between Korean and Japanese residents rather than the actual threats posed by outlaws. In one episode, Korean vendors panicked at the alarm bells rung by the Japanese to warn of approaching bandits, believing that the Japanese were going to enslave them as laborers.[14] By not engaging closely with the preexisting Korean community and by stressing lawlessness of some natives, the Japanese settlers maintained a perception of Nonsan as a new frontier to conquer.

This image of an uncivilized land that framed the Japanese settlers' narrative was not the self-image long held by local notables in South Ch'ungchŏng. The area along the Kŭm River was once the political and strategic center of Paekche, one of the ancient Three Kingdoms (52–668). Chinese culture, religion, and technology were transmitted from this region to Japan.[15] Yŏnsan in the Nonsan region was considered a candidate for the capital of the Chosŏn dynasty. The region was famous for its tradition of neo-Confucian scholarship (the Kiho school), and a many *yangban* (landlord literati) families lived in the Ch'ungch'ŏng provinces—nearly 41% of the entire yangban class in the peninsula.[16] Even Kwangsŏk village had twenty-nine yangban families in 1909.[17] At the turn of the twentieth century, these scholarly families viewed themselves as a bastion against modernization programs promoted by new generations in Seoul.[18] They often looked down on Japanese settlers—many of whom came from lower social strata—as uneducated, materialistic barbarians.[19]

How did the environment of villages in Nonsan compare with that of villages in Taiwan and Japan? Kwangsŏk, a typical farm village on the northern edge of Nonsan county, was starkly different from Beipu, Taiwan with regard to the nature of the local community before colonization. Beipu was a frontier for Hakka immigrants where youthful leadership and physical courage were highly valued. The presence of conflicts between the Hakka and the aboriginal peoples afforded Japanese colonizers an opportunity to mediate between them, while Hakka residents took advantage of the colonial partnership to expand their dominance and business. By contrast, rural areas in Korea had solid class and generational hierarchies with landlord-literati families standing between the central state and peasant communities.[20] The Japanese settlement in Kwangsŏk, which was four times larger than that in Beipu, caused a sudden disruption of the long-established social dynamic.[21]

Japanese schools and schoolteachers in Korean villages did not take root as quickly as those in Beipu, and the Japanese teachers had very limited interactions with their Korean neighbors even in the 1920s. In Korea, the education system had long been monopolized by the yangban literati class. Distinguished scholars of the Nonsan region studied at the Nogang Academy and ran their own small private schools (sŏdang) in their local towns.[22] Their emphasis on the Chinese classics remained strong. At the same time, Nonsan also saw a quiet movement for modern education among some literati, especially after the Japanese victory in the Russo-Japanese War of 1904–1905. For example, the largest landholder (about 350 hectares) in Kwangsŏk, prominent yangban Yun Chi-byŏng, established a new private school, the Usin School, in 1911.[23] The Usin School provided six years of education to relatively well-off residents, both male and female, including training in the Japanese language and agricultural skills. Yun Chi-byŏng's son, Yun Hŭi-jung, continued to develop its curriculum. But unlike the school in Beipu in Xinzhu, which was quickly turned into a public elementary school, the Usin School remained a private institution until 1929.[24]

Japanese police, not Japanese elementary schools, maintained a powerful presence in Korean villages, especially during the uprisings of the Righteous Army before the 1910 annexation and then during the March First Independence Movement in 1919. In Kwangsŏk, two hundred people gathered to demonstrate in Ch'ŏndong hamlet on April 4, 1919. The Japanese police cracked down on them, shooting and killing one of the villagers.[25] The police presence remained strong through the 1920s. In the late 1920s, a contemporary scholar, Edmund de Schweinitz Brunner, wrote in a report on rural conditions in Korea: "Japan's greatest social influence on the local community is exerted through the police." Brunner observed that the police took charge of a wide range of regulations, from burial permits to passport applications.[26] Although the police had similar functions in Taiwan, at least the Hakka residents in Xinzhu perceived them as playing a mediating role between them and aboriginal groups, whereas in Korea the police reinforced the clear gulf between the colonial authorities and local residents.

The social environment of Kwangsŏk, including the role of young people, had more in common with that of Shida village in Miyagi than with Beipu. Both Kwangsŏk and Shida were predominantly rice-growing farm villages, adjacent to the county centers, Nonsan and Furukawa, respectively. Kwangsŏk's access to provincial cities (Kanggyŏng, Taejŏn, and Kongju) was similar to Shida's access to Sendai. Both villages had patriarchal family institutions, the yangban in Kwangsŏk and landlord families in Shida, which had maintained local labor relationships and provided certain services to the community.[27] Korean and Japanese hamlets also enjoyed horizontal ties that allowed peasants to preserve space somewhat autonomously from the ruling family. Indeed, the Korean social associations, kye, closely resembled the community agreements (keiyakukō) in

Miyagi. In addition to the kye, each hamlet (*maŭl*) formed a labor-sharing group or *ture*. The ture had a function similar to Japan's pre-Meiji youth associations, or Okinawa's *yui* or *nisēzuri*, as they were often loosely age-based associations whose activities were not limited to agricultural labor but included entertaining, dancing, drinking, and other kinds of peer bonding.[28] Although extent records on the role of ture are limited, scholars suspect that ture groups in multiple hamlets cooperated with one another, even coordinating peasant and political uprisings in the nineteenth century, in a similar way to political activism of the Japanese hamlet youth groups in the very early Meiji period.[29]

Early Attempts at Rural Modernization: Shinkōkai

It is based on these traditional forms of village organization that early attempts at rural modernization took place. Major initiatives came from colonial provincial governors. Transferring the Meiji experience of reorganizing hamlet communities, Ohara Shinzō, a Japanese bureaucrat and governor of South Ch'ungch'ŏng, advocated for the establishment of the *shinkōkai* (Korean: *chinhŭnghoe*, or revitalization groups) in 1916—around the same time that the Xinzhu governor Mimura Sanpei attempted to build youth groups in Taiwan.[30] Ohara transformed the kye into groups to promote the reform of old customs, modernization of agricultural production, self-cultivation, public hygiene, and so on.[31] Through the kye, he tried to spread the agrarian ideology of Ninomiya Sontoku in the Korean countryside. At the same time, he valued the traditional form of authorities. Ohara visited yangban families, proffering government policies in the form of a written prayer at Confucian shrines to gain support from powerful local elites. His attempt at rural reform soon slowed, but in 1920 another governor, Tokizane Akiho, again advocated for the establishment of hamlet shinkōkai. By 1923, the provincial government was boasting about the rapid development of shinkōkai, reporting that the number of such groups had increased from 761 (67,482 members) to 1,415 (104,345 members) between 1917 and 1922.[32]

The foremost agenda of shinkōkai groups was to introduce the modern and rational lifestyle envisioned by Japanese social activists. Under the auspices of provincial, county, and village officials, these groups produced a long and detailed list of rules for daily life, such as "Do not forget to clean the toilets," "Save some money every month and one-third of supplementary incomes," "Return borrowed things as quickly as possible," "Shoo sparrows away when you walk along rice paddies," and the like.[33] The list resembles those of kyōka groups in the villages of Xinzhu, Taiwan during the 1920s and 1930s. The imperial effort to transform rural subjects through grassroots kyōka groups—the Hōtokukai in the Japanese countryside, the Jinshinkai in Xinzhu, or the shinkōkai in South Ch'ungch'ŏng—took place almost simultaneously across the territory. Unlike their counterparts, however, the shinkōkai at this stage did not place a strong emphasis on youth. Instead, the colonial governors seem to have relied on senior leaders who maintained patriarchal power over entire communities.

Youth Groups in Nonsan in the 1920s

Attention to rural youth as a new social category thus did not accompany rural modernization attempts of the 1910s and 1920s, and the concept remained limited to urban intellectual thinking. As discussed in chapter 4, anticolonial nationalist and socialist activism beginning in the 1920s produced a symbolic image of Korean rural youth. These activist leaders viewed the spread of local youth groups in county capitals as a means of expanding their influence and a step toward integrating the rural masses. The intensifying youth politics of the 1920s, however, rarely reached remote rural hamlets, let alone mobilized peasant youth.

In fact, rural youth mobilization was not among the main goals of youth groups in provincial towns. These groups did not manifest brand-new forces, as anticolonial leaders in Seoul or the *Tonga ilbo* and *Chosŏn ilbo* publications assumed. Certainly, the experience of the March First Movement triggered the formation of these groups, and their missions were cast in the language of new political ideologies—self-strengthening, Korean nationalism, class struggle, and *hyŏksin* (progressive reform). Urban centers of the Nonsan region participated in this peninsula-wide trend, with the formation of the Kanggyŏng Youth Group, the Nonsan Youth Club, the Taejŏn Youth Club, and many others. However, a closer look shows that these groups reflected a strong continuity with, not a break from, local leadership of earlier years. They were organized by local leaders already in their fifties and even sixties. Before 1919, the established local notables, colonial bureaucrats, schoolteachers, and county officials had already begun forming "youth associations." Many post-1919 youth groups were simply renewed from these previous groups.[34] A good example of this was the first such group in South Ch'ungch'ŏng, Nonsan Youth Group, created in 1917. Its leader, Ch'oe Tal-sun, was a land survey technician working for the GGK. Ch'oe continued to preside over the Nonsan Youth Club when it was "reestablished" in 1920.[35] Its goals echoed the familiar phrases of the Japanese seinendan, such as "self-cultivation (*suyang*) of the spirit," rather than promoting social change or Korean nationalism.[36] The historian Ji Soo-gol (Chi Su-gŏl) calls these groups "advisory institutions for county governance"[37] because the members tended to be employed in local offices, including village advisory councils and credit unions. Most likely the youth groups functioned as networking clubs for these local elites, rather than as stepping-stones to the remote countryside.

The ambivalent political color of the post-1919 youth groups displayed the unclear boundary between colonial and anticolonial movements in provincial towns, as in 1920s Taiwan. They did integrate newer forces, such as students and leftist activists. The close association of older leaders with the colonial administration did not necessarily hinder them from supporting the cultural movement advocated by *Tonga ilbo* and nationalist leaders either. They emphasized the importance of modern knowledge, self-cultivation, and physical health. They invited students from Seoul to deliver public speeches and organized amateur plays to spread enlightenment ideas in opposition to "feudal" customs. In fact, they did not have to choose between a pro-GGK or pro-nationalist position as long as they adhered to the enlightenment and modernization goals advocated by both sides. Potentially, night school courses might have embodied political leanings, but the youth groups in Nonsan did not provide many night classes.[38] Local youth groups often showed their active support for nationalists' efforts to establish a private university and promote domestic production.[39] But these goals reflected an urban, upper-class vision of national sovereignty and soon foundered without gaining much support from the wider population.

At the same time, being inclusive of all ages, ideologies, and social positions led to mounting frustrations among youth group members in negotiating their goals, and battles over leadership quickly became severe. Corresponding to the discursive rise of youth, age became a major point of confrontation in leadership battles within and among youth groups. The hyŏksin movement in 1925 sparked generational conflicts in Nonsan. Younger members viewed the generation in power as an obstacle to a new Korea. In their eyes, the older members lacked the will to change the old social order. The young members in Nonsan youth groups thus advocated new age limits of sixteen to thirty, but they could not expel the older members. In most cases, older generations remained in power, forcing the younger forces to break away from the group. By 1927, Nonsan had eight conservative youth groups, two proletariat youth groups, two labor youth groups, and two "equality" (*hyŏngp'yŏng*) youth groups.[40] This newly formed collection of youth groups competed against one another, sometimes resulting in violence.[41] The leftist youth groups in regional towns rose and fell until they were crushed by police forces by the end of the 1920s.

While generational conflicts, cloaked in ideological rhetoric, divided local leaders in county capitals, in Kwangsŏk village the only recognizable event that indicated the influence of the rise of youth was Yun Hŭi-jung's activity. In 1923, Yun, the son of the largest landlord in the village, converted his house to a night school classroom to teach Japanese, Korean, math, and the Chinese classics. More than eighty children and working youth gathered to study. Not much is known about Yun's intentions, but like Katō Einojō's youth group in Miyagi, Yun's initiative reveals his sensitivity to the larger changes in urban politics. His focus on nonprivileged children and youth was certainly revolutionary in the village context. His brother-in-law, Cho Tong-sun, served as the main teacher.[42] A local historian argues that both sympathized with leftist thought to the extent that Cho himself and Yun's family members later migrated to North Korea during the Korean War.[43] Perhaps they hoped to practice leftist ideals through engaging the poor. Perhaps it was their way of asserting their youthful leadership, as Yun and Cho were both in their twenties. In any case, Yun and Cho still operated within the confines of the social system of Kwangsŏk village instead of breaking it. There is no sign that they advocated for inspiring and mobilizing average village youth to resist colonial rule. In the end, the discursive emphasis on rural youth among intellectuals in Seoul had little impact on how youth groups in provincial towns operated or on the consciousness of average village youth in the countryside.

Rural Centrism in the Assimilationist Policies of the 1920s

While the rural sphere grew in ideological value in the imaginations of nationalist and socialist activism (although not accompanied by effective programs), the GGK also began conceiving of it as central to its assimilationist goals. Elsewhere, I have discussed how colonial officials in Korea came to adopt the "ruralist paradigm" by the late 1920s, viewing Korean society as consisting mainly of rural peasants and understanding Korean social problems as primarily rural problems. With a ruralist mindset, they placed Japan and Korea on the same continuum of predominantly agrarian societies, and yet they simultaneously characterized Korea as more rural and thus more important in the ideals of Japanese agrarian nationalism, *and* as more primitive and backward as represented by the negative image of uneducated and impoverished peasants.[44]

As the GGK pursued assimilationist goals under the cultural rule of the early 1920s, the distinction between urban and rural became salient in the eyes of colonial officials. In their understanding, the nature of Japanese–Korean interactions differed significantly between the two spheres. Japanese settlers in urban areas, whom the historian Jun Uchida calls the "brokers of empire," posed a great obstacle to the assimilationist effort. Many of them opposed the assimilation programs advocated by the colonial government since the 1910s. Their attitudes often intensified public hatred for the Japanese.[45] Although the shock of the March First Movement led some settler organizations to promote ethnic harmony, everyday encounters between Japanese and Koreans in the cities were characterized by ethnic tensions.[46]

The GGK perceived the situation in the countryside differently. Although earlier settlers had adopted an attitude of conquerors, Japanese people who settled as tenant farmers had been cooperating closely with Korean farmers. Colonial officials applauded these Japanese for building friendships with the locals. One settler in Kwangsŏk village, Aoki Kihachi, received a page of praise in the government journal *Chōsen* (Korea) for his assimilation into the community. He settled in Kwangsŏk in 1911 and became a tenant on the sixteen thousand square kilometers owned by the Kunitake Farm Company. The journal stated, "Mr. Aoki learned Korean as soon as he arrived in Korea, associates with Korean people with politeness, and does not engage in discrimination. . . . He always does manual labor together with Koreans, does his best to attend their gatherings, never opposes community activities, invites hamlet residents for drinks and cakes on New Year's Day, and never changes his attitude."[47]

The ongoing local-based shinkōkai movement also strengthened the GGK's confidence in its ability to work with Korean rural communities. After the movement became a national one, the GGK provided funding for establishing county- and provincial-level networks and gave awards to model hamlets. Kwangsŏk village had one of the most famous groups in Korea, the Kalsan Shinkōkai. It was recognized fourteen times for its activities between 1918 and 1930, featured in journal and newspaper articles, and even made the subject of a documentary film. Kalsan hamlet differed from the rest of Kwangsŏk in that Japanese companies owned most of its land. The large presence of Japanese companies transformed the community and gave rise to a new category of local leaders, Korean middlemen (*marŭm*). Kalsan's middlemen, Pang Chong-ku and O Yi-sŏn, established a community reform group in 1915, which was renamed a shinkōkai when Governor Ohara issued his decree in 1916. They created a new kye to regulate customs and finances for funerals, established a private school for children, banned alcohol, and offered free guidance on new agricultural methods. Kalsan was highly regarded because neither Pang nor O exploited the tenants, a behavior widespread among the majority of middlemen in similar positions. Reportedly, they even redistributed land among small tenants at their own loss.[48]

Kalsan exemplified a new form of Korean-led, GGK-sanctioned, locally driven modernization of a hamlet community. Instead of developing out of a traditional landlord-centered social system, Kalsan's community structure was built anew. But other cases in which traditional landlords led the shinkōkai also appear to have displayed an eagerness to take up the government's approach rather than an anticolonial line of modernization. These local notables stayed clear of the nationalist and socialist movements that were prevalent in urban areas, while absorbing both the resources of colonial authorities and the inspiration for modernization derived from all corners in the 1920s.

Observing the shinkōkai movement while maintaining an idealized image of Japanese tenant settlers, the GGK conceived of the rural sphere as the frontier of its assimilationist rule. Rural youth training was envisioned in this context, as a means of strengthening colonial rule through programs in rural areas. Youth, thus far considered as playing a lesser role in the patriarchal rural communities, became an important target in the new drive for rural mobilization. While cracking down on the leftist and *Tonga ilbo*–led youth groups in provincial towns, colonial officials sought to establish the concept of model rural youth as pillars of the empire through educational programs offered to village leaders in more remote areas.[49]

One critical problem hampered the promotion of seinendan-style gatherings in Korea, however. The spread of elementary schools, which had been a prerequisite for youth training in Japan and Taiwan, was very slow in Korea. Because colonial officials did not readily approve the establishment of public elementary schools, and also because the precolonial tradition linked education to upper-class male culture, access to elementary education remained extremely limited in the countryside. Colonial officials even turned their attention to private schools run by local literati, or *sŏdang*, as an alternative basis for developing village youth groups. In their report on youth group guidance, South Chŏlla officials argued, "The *sŏdang* is already the place of learning for youth in hamlets and villages between farming seasons . . . Although the students of *sŏdang* do not identify themselves as youth groups yet, we think that, in the future, they might offer the most appropriate conditions should we want to form successful [youth] groups."[50]

In Kwangsŏk village, the colonial attempt to bolster kyōka programs and establish a basis for rural youth training in the late 1920s bestowed a new status on the landlord Yun Hŭi-jung. His Usin School suddenly came to be recognized as a facilitator of rural assimilation. The school obtained the status of a public elementary school in 1929, and it served as a home for youth training institutions that developed over the course of the 1930s. With increasing government support, the ambivalent political character of Yun Hŭi-jung became even more iridescent. Yun also established a shinkōkai, but he combined it with the hyŏksin movement, promoting both socialist and government goals at the same time. Arguing that "the first and critical task of our society is to reform women's society," he established a shinkōkai specifically for female villagers.[51] Yun's brother-in-law, Cho Tong-sun, was recognized as a "model shinkōkai leader" by colonial officials in 1929, despite Cho's leftist orientation. Their acceptance of government support shows another example of synchronization between state policies and individual interests, however paradoxical and ironic this alignment might appear. They established a typical relationship of "two dreams in one bed," if expressed in a common Asian phrase. But instead of weakening their position, such a relationship aided the colonial authorities in consolidating their presence in rural societies.

The Rural Revitalization Campaign

In early 1930s Korea, the double urgency of the economic depression and war was felt much more strongly than in Taiwan. Korean villages became increasingly impoverished each day, and the GGK demanded greater cooperation from Korean rural labor forces.[52] In 1932, Governor-General Ugaki Kazushige launched the Korean version of the Rural Revitalization Campaign. Like the previous and simultaneous rural campaigns in Japan, it emphasized the ideological transformation of rural populations into people who would work hard, spend less, and worship the emperor. Kyōka and social education programs were at the heart of such ideological indoctrination, and to strengthen these programs the GGK established an organization called Kyōka Dantai Rengōkai (the Federation of Moral Suasion Groups) in 1935.[53]

For the GGK, the Revitalization Campaign was not merely an extension of the Japanese campaigns. Rather, it was a chance to place Korea at a position of utmost importance in the empire and advertise its effective administration. In an article in their journal, *Chōsen*, officials situated the campaign amid the increasing international tensions:

> The full development of Korea, which is filled with potential, will be a great contribution toward the goals of securing the empire's glorious position and continuing to expand it in the face of the difficult international situation. If the empire's authority stays firm and rock-steady, the peace of East Asia will be maintained, and the uncertainties of the world will be naturally lessened. Pursuing this grave international mission of the empire requires the energetic industry of Korea and the souls of twenty million well-trained masses. Indeed, it must be the case that "light comes from Korea." This is the international basis of the Rural Revitalization Campaign.[54]

Defined in this grand language, the campaign did indeed mobilize the population on an unprecedented scale. The hamlet shinkōkai promoted reform programs and the micromanagement of household economies. By 1934, 7,861 hamlets had established shinkōkai, which then organized women's groups and (male) youth groups (*shinkō seinendan*). As in Japan, the campaign in Korea assumed that Japanese nationalism coupled with Ninomiya Sontoku agrarianism would make people more productive and self-reliant. Ninomiya's hardworkism appeared everywhere in articles in *Jiriki kōsei ihō* (Self-revitalization news, 1933–1941), an official newsletter of the campaign published by the GGK. In addition to farming methods and techniques, a belief in efficient use of resources, time, and labor constituted the core of the message.[55] By the mid-1930s, Governor-General Ugaki had definitively announced that the countryside, not the cities, was the champion of assimilation efforts. He complained that cities "tend to lag far behind farm and fishing villages in promoting national spirit and self-reliance."[56] These repeated remarks by top officials sought to foster a new awareness of rural leaders and to shake the supremacy of urban intellectuals and culture.

At the same time, the Rural Revitalization Campaign forced the GGK to squarely face rural conditions. The economic system that enforced the impoverishment and exploitation of Korean farmers was deeply rooted.[57] Since the beginning of the 1920s—reflecting the policy of exporting Korean rice to the metropole in the wake of the 1918 rice riots in Japan—the GGK had conducted various research on the practices of tenancy around the peninsula, and its reports had already uncovered the slave-like conditions of tenant farmers. South Ch'ungch'ŏng province published a report on tenant practices in 1930, confirming once again the problems that had been well documented since the 1910s, such as the dominance of landlords and the exploitation of tenants by Korean middlemen to the extent that they were called "government-generals of the countryside" and "evil demons."[58] When the depression struck and the price of rice fell in 1931 to only 39% of what it had been in 1925, rural economies completely collapsed. Although middle-class peasants had already conducted protests in the mid-1920s to demand tenancy rights, tenant disputes became smaller in scale, more focused on tenants' basic survival, more frequent, and more widespread in the 1930s.[59] *Tonga ilbo* described the rural devastation as "a starving hell."[60] No rural campaign during this period could have avoided taking measures to alter tenant exploitation. The GGK set up official arbiters in provinces and enacted a tenancy law in 1933, before a similar law was introduced in Japan, in the hope of spreading long-term, stable tenancy.[61]

A Generational Shift in Rural Villages

The measures, goals, and processes of the Rural Revitalization Campaign resembled much of Japan's nationalization effort right after the Russo-Japanese War. In Korea, too, the creation of young pillars became a means and a goal in the campaign. As of 1932, however, the GGK believed that many Korean youth groups were still too left-leaning to implement its plan for the comprehensive mobilization of Korean youth.[62] In the same year, the GGK notified the provincial governors of "the basic principle" of youth group guidance: "The fundamental mission of youth groups is to improve personal character and increase physical strength through the forces of mutual shūyō of youth."[63] As is apparent from experiences in Japan, the use of the term *shūyō* by state officials was a code for depoliticization and developing discipline through seinendan-like associations.

To achieve this goal, the government established two programs for young men in the countryside during the late 1920s and 1930s: the guidance for elementary school graduates (*sotsugyōsei shidō*) and the revitalization of youth groups (shinkō seinendan) under shinkōkai supervision. In 1935 alone, the guidance program worked with 12,736 model graduates, and by 1938, 156,761 Korean youth had become members of 3,056 shinkō seinendan.[64] If the reported numbers of participants reflected reality, these programs easily surpassed the reach of nationalist and socialist youth groups that had grown "like bamboo sprouts" in the early 1920s. This was perhaps because the target population was not the most privileged (often urban) youth but elementary school graduates. Although still limited in scope to young men who could afford elementary education, these groups under the Rural Revitalization Campaign began influencing village dynamics and the consciousness of young participants, eventually allowing a social mobility complex to emerge.

The story of Kim Yŏng-han, a villager born in Kwangsŏk's Ch'ŏndong hamlet, illustrates the experience of a young man living in the new dynamic. Although he was not wealthy enough to pursue education beyond elementary school, Kim Yŏng-han came from a relatively prominent family. His great-grandfather had been a lower-rank bureaucrat (*muban*) who took the position of village head in 1900, and his grandfather was a sŏdang teacher.[65] Although most of their land was lost during the grandfather's generation, Kim Yŏng-han's father attended the Usin School. Its modern-style education usually positioned its graduates for promising careers, such as schoolteachers and village officials. But because his brother-in-law was an imprisoned independence activist, Kim Yŏng-han's father was blocked from obtaining an official job and instead worked at exchange markets in port towns. Born in 1920, Kim Yŏng-han faced the combined pressure of financial difficulty and a proud family lineage. In 1928, he entered the Usin School, as his father had done before him. When it became a public elementary school the following year, he passed the exam to become a second-grader. Since the Kwangsŏk Elementary School had only a four-year program, he entered the fifth grade of the Nonsan Elementary School in 1932 and walked three miles every day to attend until he graduated two years later.[66]

Kim received his first official title when he finished the four-year program as one of the two model graduates of the elementary school. The guidance of graduates began in ten schools (serving 102 graduates) in Kyŏnggi province in 1927 as a pilot program.[67] After the pilot's success, the program expanded to forty-one schools and nine hundred graduates, and the other provinces adopted the same program between 1930 and 1932.[68] Kim Yŏng-han belonged to the first generation of model graduates in South Ch'ungch'ŏng province.

As a model graduate, Kim became a walking advertisement for the Revitalization Campaign. He had to attend ceremonies as a new pillar of the village. "It was quite troublesome because every time the school had an event, they called up model graduates," he recalled; "no matter how busy you were, you could not refuse to go." But he also remembered that "there were many benefits" of his status. One of them was easy access to fertilizer and livestock.[69] The model graduate program encouraged new agricultural methods, characterized by the heavy use of fertilizer.[70] With these techniques and knowledge, the model graduates were supposed to challenge the advantages of wealthier farmers, including the Japanese, and raise the morale of average Korean farmers.[71]

The guidance given to these graduates was the first step toward creating pillars of youth in the Rural Revitalization Campaign, and colonial bureaucrat Masuda Shūsaku called it an outstanding program unique to Korea.[72] This guidance, of course, emphasized self-cultivation in addition to productivity and scientific farming. Yahiro Ikuo, a leading bureaucrat in Korean rural social work, summarized its intended purpose as "to foster good farmers, good villagers, useful people, and people who contribute to the village." The greatest importance was placed on the spirit of hard work. "Never spare a moment but work" was the core principle.[73] In the ideal scenario, the young graduates would transmit their high morale to their families and communities. Yahiro argued that these graduates had already had a great impact:

> [Among the model graduates' families] there are many who fell into financial difficulties because the fathers did not work diligently and wasted money. Once a model graduate made a serious effort to restore the family business and showed good results, his father began to work together with him. So did his mother and younger siblings, leading the entire family participate in hard work. In another family, even a blind brother was led to operate a rope-weaving machine and make straw storage bags with his wife. . . . In many places, graduates teach writing and math to uneducated children in the neighborhood at night classes. Others teach how to make compost. This is a spark of the youth's resolution to do something [for their communities].[74]

The graduates were considered the most authentic grassroots agents in the eyes of these officials.

The program marked a new phase of village politics in which model rural youth gained the opportunity to challenge one particularly stubborn sort of social hierarchy: that based on age. Japanese bureaucrats repeatedly noted that the rigid age and class hierarchies remained unchanged in the villages. "It is truly not an easy thing for young people around twenty years old to stand above older leaders and lead the hamlet," Masuda argued as late as 1936.[75] A government report claimed that because Korean society "despise[d] young people," youth organizations had been hampered in their development.[76] The graduate guidance program was therefore designed to create new horizontal ties by "recruiting those who share a same age-cohort feeling."[77] Kim Yǒng-han explained that, as a model graduate, he did receive unusual respect from villagers. Although he admitted that the "model graduates did not have the power to guide others" as the Japanese bureaucrats claimed, the experience planted in him a new identity as a leader of a new generation.[78] The program also subtly impacted the class hierarchy. Most model graduates came from relatively well-off farming families, but not from the yangban class.[79] The schooling rate for Korean male children in the countryside in South Ch'ungch'ǒng remained as low as 30% in the early 1930s, and 80% of the villagers were unable to read either Korean or Japanese.[80] School graduates in rural villages were thus not average farmers, but members of a newly emerging "middling class"—those who could attend an elementary program but who were not wealthy enough to pursue higher education in the city and a position in the colonial bureaucracy.[81]

Being more privileged than average farmers, however, these model graduates tended to aspire to a nonfarming, more academically oriented career than the GGK had anticipated. Kim Yǒng-han wanted to pursue further education at an engineering school in Japan. He went to a couple of private schools to prepare for the exam while working part-time as an agricultural instructor hired by the village administration. At the local Yungjǒng School, village youth preparing for various exams assisted one another without a formal teacher. Kim used mail-order lectures from the middle school program of Waseda University in Tokyo, as Xu Chongfa in Taiwan did. He tested his progress by sending his sample exam answers to the Japanese journal *Shikenkai* (Exam world), which then mailed his score to him.[82]

Regardless of his aspiration to leave the village, Kim's profile as a local leader expanded when he joined the shinkō seinendan. While preparing for the exam and working as an agricultural instructor, he was selected to become, at the age of sixteen, a member of the shinkō seinendan. Kim explained that every village shinkōkai chose about twenty of one hundred village youth and formed the shinkōkai seinendan to promote modernization of living customs and agricultural improvement. A Korean schoolteacher became the leader of the Kwangsŏk Shinkō Seinendan, and its members experimented with modern agricultural techniques in the school-owned collective farms.[83] They were also hired by large landholders for farm work, by which means they earned collective savings. Like the model graduates, the shinkō seinendan members were given preference in the land redistribution sponsored by the GGK and in livestock loan programs. Despite the similarity of these activities to those of Japanese seinendan during the 1900s and 1910s, Kim Yŏng-han described the agriculture-centered shinkō seinendan in Korea as quite different from the Japanese seinendan, which had adopted military training early on. In our interviews, he corrected me repeatedly when I omitted the word *shinkō* in front of *seinendan*.[84]

In Kim's view, the shinkō seinendan occupied a leadership position in village affairs and offered him a higher status than the model graduate program had done. Membership in the shinkō seinendan was restricted to those who were widely recognized as accomplished farm youth. They wore new uniforms and caps, increasing their sense of being an elite group. Kim recalled, "Wearing the uniform made us feel very different. People whispered, 'He is a model youth.'" Members regularly provided "hamlet guidance," explaining current affairs and war situations to the villagers, most of whom were illiterate. Another responsibility of shinkō seinendan members was to teach farming techniques to female villagers. Women were rarely involved in agricultural production before the Revitalization Campaign, and many villagers remembered this change as one of the most revolutionary aspects of the period.[85] After two years of working in the village shinkō seinendan, Kim Yŏng-han found a job in Taejŏn, but because he was also a former model graduate, he returned to Kwangsŏk village frequently to help with youth activities.[86]

Improving the status of young people without disrupting the local order was a carefully designed goal. Local officials recognized that, in the process of introducing new lifestyles and a new work ethic, younger generations might encounter opposition from older, traditional forces. When they were reorganizing hamlet shinkōkai groups, officials tried to include both generations in leadership positions to mitigate the tension. Organizing youth in a separate group was one way to increase the space for youthful leadership without directly confronting the older generation.[87] In Kwangsŏk, the shinkō seinendan developed without disrupting the status of the powerful landlords. Kim Yŏng-han recalled, "There was no opposition to the seinendan's activities. Our work—mostly instruction in agriculture—did not provoke any resistance."[88] Defining the role of the shinkō seinendan strictly within the agricultural production campaign may have helped to avoid the generational conflicts that were prevalent in urban youth groups of the 1920s.

As in the Japanese and Taiwanese villages, the elementary school and school-teachers were the center of both the rural campaign and youth organizations in Korea. Colonial officials expected schoolteachers to raise the schooling rate and influence the entire community. The official Yahiro Ikuo explained the "grave mission" of teachers: "Teachers go around to the model graduates' homes in their leisure time, after finishing work on weekdays and on Saturday afternoons and Sundays. Even on boiling hot or severely cold days, they show up, get a plow, and take some compost to work alongside the model youth. In fact, they do not 'guide' them but 'work together.'"[89] An official in Kyŏnggi province, Cho Wŏn-hwan, argued that rural seinendan should develop based on the trust established between teachers and students. "Only schools can serve as the source of youth guidance," he argued; "youth guidance is about unconditionally influencing youth through the virtue and feeling of the teachers."[90] Thus, in the 1930s, the responsibility of teachers extended far beyond teaching the school curriculum. In some cases, social education was emphasized more than academic subjects. In the mid-1930s, when the GGK started to support shortened elementary courses—which consisted of one teacher offering two years of literacy, math, and vocational education in remote hamlets—local officials described the appropriate attitude of teachers: "You have to be ready to be a father, not only a teacher, to children from underprivileged families" and "Your entire family should be ready to be teachers to the whole hamlet."[91] Teachers were considered the approximate equivalent of religious missionaries of assimilation during the Rural Revitalization Campaign.

The Post-1920 Generation

Horizontal networks already existed among village youth in labor-sharing associations (ture) before Japanese rule. In a way, the colonial rural programs attempted artificially to reinstall old ture groups among graduates of the elementary school under colonial supervision. At the same time, the generation of Kim Yŏng-han represented a new type of villagers who grew up in a different social environment. Born after the March First Movement of 1919, these young people had no firsthand memory of youth politics, socialist mobilization, or government crackdowns in the towns during the 1920s. For them, colonial rule was an established fact and Japanese settlers were their neighbors. Their future prospects depended on how well they managed within the existing system.

For this generation, the Japanese were no longer a monolithic colonial ruler—or the "Other," as perceived by anticolonial intellectuals of the 1920s—but a group with a variety of characteristics. In Kwangsŏk, Kim Yŏng-han developed amicable relationships with most of the Japanese residents. He indicated in our interview that they had shared community life with Korean farmers, such as by organizing seasonal festivals together. "The rent charged by the Japanese landlords and the Oriental Development Company was half of what the Korean landlords charged," he repeatedly claimed. Overall, "the Japanese lived well with us," he recalled.[92] This perception stands in stark contrast to the confrontations between Koreans and Japanese in the early 1900s and during and after the March First Movement. Kim's interactions with the Japanese as a pillar of youth and a local official allowed him to observe the dynamics in the Japanese community: "They still labeled themselves as the 'former samurai' class or 'new citizens' [former outcasts]," he remembered, and "those from Tokyo were arrogant," often making fun of those from Okinawa.[93] His observations of Japanese residents were sensitive to class, origin, occupation, and personal traits rather than casting a categorical image of colonial ruler.

In fact, class became the primary source of frustration for Kim, and ethnicity became a subordinate category to class. Kim Yŏng-han was not only a member of the post-1920 generation, but also in the new middling class. They were better off than average farmers but resented the distinction between themselves and those who could pursue higher education toward a bureaucratic career. Kim Yŏng-han's situation was typical of the sons of formerly wealthy but declining families. As the first son, he was under pressure to recover the family name and support the household financially. For many like him, the crackdown on nationalist and socialist activists—mostly college-educated and from the upper class—in the 1920s opened space for upward mobility. From his perspective, the Kwangju Student Movement from 1929 to 1931 seemed to belong to a different class because most of the activist youth came from the upper strata. Once they were blacklisted, their family members and relatives were blocked from official positions in the same way as Kim Yŏng-han's father had been.[94] With the harsh colonial crackdown and the youth training programs that started in the 1930s, class hierarchy was shuffled, providing new opportunities to young men of his background.

Overcoming class differences was a goal of other villagers as well. In the course of the 1930s, average male villagers competed to join this newly emerging middling class. Many families sought elementary school education despite the financial burden involved. The schooling rate expanded especially in the average to lower strata of farmers. Between 1922 and 1932 in South Chŏlla, for example, the schooling rate of owner-tenants increased from 1.5% to 38.8%, and that of tenant farmers increased from 1.8% to 22.3%, while that of landholding farmers remained the same (68% for landlords, 45% for owner-cultivators). The historian Kim Puja argues that the boost in the national schooling rate in the 1930s—from 30% to 47.4% between 1930 and 1937—came from the "schooling fever" of average- to lower-class farmers in the countryside; it would continue until the end of the war.[95]

The identity of model rural youth, separate from that of activist youth, was also shaped by the cognitive distance from Seoul. In Kwangsŏk, only the school and hamlet heads subscribed to one national (*Asahi shinbun*) and one local newspaper (*Chūsen nippō*), and most villagers did not read them. Kim Yŏng-han did not even know that there were other newspapers, like *Tonga ilbo* and *Maeil sinbo*, until he was in the fifth grade and the names appeared in a school play. The shinkō seinendan served as an important source of information, teaching him such things as the achievements of Korean athletes in the 1936 Olympics, news that he relayed to other villagers through hamlet guidance. Apart from this, Kim had to depend on relatives in Seoul to send him newspapers. He particularly liked reading serialized novels in these papers, but he did not know nationally famous authors, including Yi Kwang-su.[96]

The limited exposure to news sources not only isolated these youth from anticolonial activism; it also posed a challenge to colonial authorities as they sought to promote a sense of belonging to a wider network of rural youth. South Ch'ungchŏng province published monthly newsletters, *Kinnan geppō* (Kinnan Monthly) from 1925 and *Chūnan shinkō geppō* (South Ch'ungch'ŏng Revitalization Monthly) from 1934, to encourage kyōka programs in rural villages.[97] But these publications did not create a shared discursive sphere as the seinendan newsletters did in Japan.

Nonetheless, this generation of the middling class suited the GGK's policy of social reorganization and its new emphasis on the pillars of youth. The colonial official Masuda Shūsaku divided central village figures into two groups: the older, wealthier, well-established leaders and the pillars of youth from ordinary families. He warned that since family reputation and age hierarchy formed the heart of local leadership, youth should not try to take the place of older leaders. Nevertheless, his article clearly emphasized how to cultivate pillars of youth. Indeed, it was an observable fact that the Rural Revitalization Campaign gradually turned middling-class farm youth into leading figures in village affairs. In the 1928 government list of central figures in the shinkōkai, almost all were government officials or from the landlord classes; in the 1936 list, only 29% came from these strata.[98] Both the GGK and the youth were engaged in a conscious effort to shift local leadership from traditional figures to younger, less wealthy farmers.

Through elementary schools, the model graduate program, and the shinkō seinendan, Kim Yŏng-han's desire for local reputation and access to education grew. Kim represented a new generation and a new class who regarded these colonial institutions as a major part of social reality, rather than as a threat to their ethnic autonomy as intellectual activists had done in the 1920s. He even conceived of the colonial programs as a means to recover his family prestige. In short, the post-1920 generation of children from middling-class rural families began to discover a social mobility complex. They harbored a new consciousness as modern youth and sought to build a career out of government youth programs. Although they did not seem to share a communication space with other village youth, their pride as model rural youth grew separately from the youth discourse that circulated in urban areas.

Kim's example shows how colonial programs in the 1930s opened a small yet substantial crack in the rigid social system of rural villages. But at the same time, it also reveals contradictions inherent in state policies. Most decisively, the low rate of schooling and literacy in Korea, a result of overall colonial rule, prevented colonial officials from establishing the category of model rural youth among average-class farmers. The competition for admission to elementary school became fierce among villagers. In South Ch'ungch'ŏng, schools could accommodate only sixty thousand students from among 190,000 school-age children in 1936. The newspaper *Chosŏn chungang ilbo* argued that the remaining children were in "an illiteracy hell."[99] In this environment, graduates thought of themselves as a select group and pursued further education opportunities outside their home villages. Consequently, the meaning of model rural youth in Korean villages was quite different from how the term was understood in Miyagi or Xinzhu. In the former, it connoted the possibility for attaining further academic advancement, whereas in the latter it signified career development outside the school system, although both were considered alternative routes to higher education, which was available to only the upper class.

Kim's experience also illuminates how young men in remote villages mapped their worlds. On the one hand, Japan was close. Kim subscribed to a Japanese journal, studied a curriculum from Waseda University, and planned to go to an engineering school in Japan. On the other hand, Seoul and the discursive world of Korean intellectuals felt far away. The two leading Korean-language newspapers of the time, *Tonga ilbo* and *Chosŏn ilbo*, were unknown even to Kim, who was an eager reader. At the same time, his association with the shinkō seinendan did not seem to generate a sense of belonging to the larger seinendan cohort of the empire. Even retrospectively, Kim believed that the two had been completely separate entities.

The complicated combination of geographic connections and isolation is another sign of the power of local contexts. Kim's worldview was colored by his ambition for education and economic advancement, as well as his family background and his confidence as a model rural youth. This perspective differed significantly from what Korean nationalist (and socialist) leaders had imagined earlier or the vision that colonial officials promoted. Again, social contexts determined the meanings of rural, youth, and government programs, despite the intense political battles that unfolded in urban areas.

8

OPPORTUNITIES AND LOOPHOLES

At first glance, rural youth mobilization in the Korean peninsula, which started with the model graduate guidance program and the shinkō seinendan, expanded step by step, leading to the recruitment of volunteer soldiers in 1938 and culminating with army conscription in 1943. One might interpret this series of steps as a process of steadily intensifying imperial power over Korean native society. But as we saw in the Japanese and Taiwanese cases, the expansion of youth programs did not produce a linear, gradual change in youth's consciousness. Rather, the process was full of unpredictable results, hidden conflicts, and sudden watersheds. The worldviews of village youth were more multifaceted than can be captured by a colonizer–colonized divide. Even in seemingly clear instances of resistance or collaboration, assessing what people really sought requires careful consideration of their social circumstances.

Identifying the presence of a social mobility complex, once again, helps us make sense of the messy picture of identities, emotions, and motivations in the Korean countryside. In the previous chapter, through Kim Yŏng-han's story, we saw how a social mobility complex began to form in Kwangsŏk village in the early 1930s. An elementary school diploma already gave graduates a sense of elitism, and the two subsequent youth programs provided the equivalent of a career ladder. Model youth had an authoritative voice when they relayed national news to illiterate villagers, and they revolutionized the role of women by teaching agricultural methods to females. The emergence of model rural youth also triggered a shift in the age hierarchy in local leadership.

In the mid-to-late 1930s, with the establishment of youth training institutions at the provincial and peninsular levels, officials tried to turn model rural youth into nationalistic pillars of the empire. These youth did adopt, often eagerly, the prose of Japanese agrarian nationalism. But the emotional and social tensions underlying their embrace of the image of model rural youth were shaped by Korea- and village-specific social conditions.

We should also note the stark difference, in the Korean case as in Taiwan, between the volunteer soldier program and mandatory conscription. Village youth regarded the volunteer soldier program as the most prestigious achievement available to them. It guaranteed access to salaried jobs, opened doors to higher education, and garnered absolute respect from villagers. By contrast, the universal character of army and labor conscription at the height of the Asia-Pacific War produced an opposite effect devoid of prestige. As the propaganda calling on rural youth to support total mobilization became louder, it ironically diminished the social value attached to select model rural youth, driving away ambitious young men. They instead used their ability to find loopholes in the system to maintain control over their own destinies. In 1943 and 1944, while Xu Chongfa and Huang Yuanxing in Taiwan were moving up the ladder of youth training institutions and developing new careers, Kim Yŏng-han was maneuvering to escape labor conscription. This evasive action clearly manifested the collapse of the social mobility complex in the Korean countryside.

Recently, scholars such as Takashi Fujitani and Brandon Palmer have detailed the recruitment of Korean soldiers and laborers, which involved the use of literary and cinematic propaganda along with state programs that forcibly integrated the Korean population into the wartime empire.[1] Here we invert the perspective from the state to the recruits. Our focus remains on the social relationships of young men living in the countryside under total war.

The Expansion of Rural Youth Training Programs in the 1930s

Following the launch of the Rural Revitalization Campaign in 1932, establishing youth training institutions beyond village-level programs in the Korean countryside became a political imperative even before the outbreak of the Second Sino-Japanese War. An examination of the institutions suggests that the expansion of youth training progressed seamlessly over the course of the 1930s. The strong emphasis on agrarianism offered a smooth ideological transition to militarism without any apparent rupture.

Besides the graduate guidance program and the shinkō seinendan, the Government-General of Korea (GGK) and provincial governments promoted several training institutions that specifically targeted young men in the countryside. Starting in 1931, the GGK organized the All Korea Local Pillars of Youth Training Session for seven to ten days every year.[2] In 1933, Kyŏnggi province established the first agricultural training center in Korea.[3] In South Ch'ungch'ŏng, the opening of an institution for female youth preceded one for male youth by two months. At the Rural Women's Training Center, founded in April 1934 in Yusŏng, thirty women age seventeen to twenty-two who had elementary school degrees spent nice months learning the basics of agriculture, sericulture, apiculture, stockbreeding, and housekeeping techniques.[4] Yusŏng's facility for young men, the Rural Youth Training Center, served a larger group, sixty men between the ages of twenty and thirty, also for nine months.[5] It adopted the popular camp training method advocated by the Japanese Shūyōdan, dividing the trainees into twelve households consisting of five family members each and forming two mock hamlets of six households each. Through this self-rule exercise, the participants were supposed to learn methods of collective farming, agricultural renovation, effective financing, and a disciplined farmering life.[6] Within two years, South Ch'ŭngch'ŏng had built two more rural youth training centers in Sŏch'ŏn and Yesan, each training thirty young men at a time.[7]

The main purposes of the training at these institutions were to spread agronomic knowledge and nurture agrarian patriotism. The Yusŏng Rural Youth Training Center stated that it would not become a school but would remain a "training dojo" to teach the "Way of Imperial Farmers."[8] The trainees started each day at 4:00 a.m. with a prayer for the prosperity of the nation ruled by the emperor.[9] These institutions displayed Ugaki Kazushige's famous slogan *shinden kaihatsu* ("spiritual field cultivation," a pun on the "virgin field cultivation" policy of Tokugawa-era Japan), which stressed mastering the Japanese spirit. According to Ugaki, success in agricultural production depended on self-cultivation through rituals at Shinto shrines and an embrace of religious faith, as well as learning the virtues of frugality and hard work.[10]

The emphasis on the spiritual education of village youth through these institutions developed into wartime mobilization after 1937. In September 1937, 241 participants at the All Korea Pillars of Youth Convention gathered at the Chōsen Shrine to pray for the Japanese army's success. The convention consisted of a series of lectures on rural youth's responsibility in the time of war.[11] Policymakers advocated establishing more "farmers' dojo" (*nōmin dōjō*) because "farmers are the foundation of the nation and the source of people's fresh blood." Referring to German and Italian policies of dispatching urban youth to work in rural cultivation, an official of South Kyŏngsang province, Ōno Ken'ichi, equated the strength of rural youth with that of the national defense. Ōno cited the words of a famous ideologue of the time, General Ishiwara Kanji, that "the basis of the military rests in the rural village, and the rural problem centers on the issue of morality," so as to emphasize the importance of moral education of agrarian youth.[12]

The Consolidation of the Social Mobility Complex

Did these youth training institutions in Korea affect young people's lives as powerfully as those in Taiwan? At the Xinzhu youth training institute, the trainees developed an emotional bond, on the basis of which they cultivated firm identities as "Xinzhu youth" and "little-educated rural youth." While enrolled there, Taiwanese youth learned to embrace and voice Japanese nationalism as a faith and a means of competing effectively with urban youth. Some of these characteristics can be seen in the Korean youth institutions as well. They constituted a similar ladder of career development—from graduate guidance to the shinkō seinendan, and then to the rural youth training center. After graduating from these institutions, most men obtained jobs as village office secretaries.[13]

Unfortunately, there are few accounts of what Korean youth experienced and how they felt at the training centers of South Ch'ungch'ŏng or anywhere else.[14] The Japanese instructors claimed to have developed emotional ties with the Korean trainees. The head of the Yusŏng training center stated, "It is my principle that, as an instructor, my attitude toward trainees is based on sincerity and a warm heart as well as a relationship resembling that between fathers and sons."[15] Their training periods were significantly longer (nine months) than that in Xinzhu (thirty days). Theoretically, the Korean trainees could have developed a tight sense of community with one another and with their instructors.

Even if they did form personal bonds, however, a distinct identity as uneducated rural youth probably did not develop. One main reason was that these trainees were in fact relatively well-educated. Just as model graduates and shinkō seinendan members came from a pool of relatively well-off families in the village, the trainees at the rural youth training centers were of a new middling class. Even in 1938, the seinendan represented the "intellectual class" in many villages.[16] The training centers for rural young women, in particular, were regarded as upperclass institutions. They required an elementary school diploma, the possession of which was still rare among Korean women in the countryside.[17] "[The Rural Women's Training Center] was the fashion center of the village. These women, with the clicking of their high heels on the way to classes, appeared beautiful to me as a child," one witness recalled.[18]

These youth attending various training programs did not criticize urban youth as morally inferior, but they did envy their urban peers' educational opportunities. "For seinendan members, graduates of middle schools and other higher education were the object of admiration," Kim Yŏng-han remembered, "but it was unimaginable to go to middle school when graduating from elementary school was already so difficult."[19] Despite the hurdles, Korean youth could hardly abandon the hope of educational advancement, which was the most common path for wealthy youth. This desire ran counter to the intention of Governor-General Ugaki and Japanese instructors, who deemphasized careers based on higher education.

Yet the colonial state and ambitious youth continued to share an interest in creating (or being) model rural youth. Kim Yŏng-han maintained a strong desire to pursue further education, and when this option proved to be not feasible, his career path turned to local administration. At each step, his association with the graduate guidance program and the shinkō seinendan was an asset. Facing increasing financial pressure after his father's death in 1939 and needing to support eleven members of his household, Kim first worked in a silk spinning factory in Taejŏn. After a few months, a Japanese official in the county office found out that Kim was a former model youth and referred him to a Japanese coal retail company, Mikuni Shōkai, where he nearly quadrupled his salary. Kim Yŏng-han adopted a Japanese name before the official policy of name changes was implemented. He picked Kanayama as his surname because his relatives in Japan had been already using it, and the storeowner, Nakashima Tōchi, added the given name Eiichi after the famous Japanese industrialist Shibusawa Eiichi. Kim left his job at Mikuni Shōkai after two years because he wanted to take the entrance exam for an engineering school in Osaka. In the meantime, the Nonsan county administrative office hired him and persuaded him to stay there and postpone going to Japan. "I really wanted to start studying, since I was already twenty-one," he said, showing me the school brochures that he had requested from Japan. But his mother fell ill, and the war against the United States started soon afterward. Kim Yŏng-han realized that "there was no way I could go to Japan any more."[20]

Becoming a village secretary was a popular option for ambitious young men in the countryside in the early 1930s. In the course of the decade, elementary school graduates became competitive against people with higher educational diplomas, outnumbering those with middle schools or equivalent degrees in village and town administrative posts. By 1937, 86% of village secretaries were either elementary school or sŏdang (private school) graduates.[21] This seemingly subtle change in the local employment pattern brought with it an enormous psychological effect on the newly employed youth. A large number of village officials came from families, like Kim's, with financial difficulties but prominent backgrounds. The pressure to recover their family's lost status heavily influenced their life decisions and ambitions.[22]

These young men were extremely eager to pursue higher positions and further education. They commonly studied mail-order lectures from Japanese universities, discussed different types of examinations, and often submitted opinions to the journal *Chōsen chihō gyōsei* (Korean local administration), instead of sharing essays and poems with village youth as their Japanese counterparts did. Reflecting their desire for upward mobility, annual turnover in these positions was high, reaching 20% in 1937.[23]

Career savviness characterized Kim Yŏng-han's youthful days. At each turning point in his life, he contemplated multiple career options. He had also tried to become a village secretary directly upon completing his schooling but the regulations required him to wait until he reached age twenty. At one point, he considered becoming a police officer because, although the salary was lower than that of village office positions, police officers appeared to be influential in local affairs. As it turned out, the background check and physical examination were too strict for Kim. He then investigated the elaborate requirements to become a teacher. Unlike in Taiwan, however, in Korea certificates from youth training institutions did not offer any preferential treatment for those seeking a teaching career. It was nearly impossible for those without middle school or normal school training to meet the requirement of passing exams in sixteen subjects within three years.[24] Kim also looked up career paths available for middle school students out of curiosity. Becoming a military officer trainee, for example, was "such an accomplishment" for them.[25] In the 1940s, when there were more kyōka training programs for local officials and teachers, Kim viewed them mainly as a tool for promotion.[26] This career-oriented attitude among people of his class and generation turned colonial youth institutions into an attractive route to success and consolidated the social mobility complex. But their primary aspiration was still to enter a school in the city or in Japan. Thriving in villages was neither the only nor the most desirable option for them.

Nonetheless, through their pursuit of educational and career development, many Korean youth adopted the rhetoric of Japanese agrarian nationalism in their public and private writings. In the journal *Korean Local Administration*, young village officials emphasized a love for their home villages, showing their determination, as one young official put it, to "remain in a periphery and devote myself to agricultural development," "bring benefits and happiness to the village," and "be ready to bury my body here."[27] The diary of O Chŏn-bok, a young man who grudgingly became a farmer in South Chŏlla after quitting an upper-level elementary program, shows his embrace of Japanese agrarian teachings. While waiting to be hired by the village office, he repeatedly reminded himself of the sanctity of hard work to overcome his everyday misery.[28] The popular ideas of love for one's native place and a dedication to agriculture thus provided a powerful moral justification for their life situations. They derived pride from the fact that they had overcome adversity by studying hard, echoing the typical story of Meiji Japan's *risshin shusse* (rising in the world).[29] But many appeared to believe that they deserved better, and their expressed determination to remain in their village often carried a tone of self-sacrifice rather than representing their embrace of a dream occupation.

Although they did not share an identity as the little-educated, these youth's generational identity seems to have grown significantly over the course of the 1930s. Just as the youth groups in county capitals in the 1920s contained a major element of generational power politics, one could observe a generational divide in village administration in the 1930s, with village advisers from the old landlord class on one side and an increasing number of young village secretaries on the other. As seen in the dynamic of shinkōkai leadership, members of the young generation struggled to expand their power. Despite their advancement in local offices, they reacted bitterly to the persistence of a strict age hierarchy in village society, which had driven many youth into clerical positions instead of toward implementing innovative farming practices in the first place.[30] Their official positions gave them a sanctuary from which they could voice their rebelliousness; for example, they used *Korean Local Administration* to assert the superiority of youth. They advocated, "Set up a youth group of village officials!" and "Hire secretaries directly from model youth of the village," arguing that the youth could serve better as liaisons between the administration and villagers.[31]

In short, the social mobility complex in Korean villages was not just a career-producing mechanism through which many young men attained positions in local offices. It was also filled with intense emotions generated by specific social relationships in which middling-class village youth participated—the pressure to restore the family fame, a desire for higher education, self-justification using Japanese agrarian nationalism, hopes for career advancement, and an urge to challenge the older establishment in village society—based on what we can detect from scattered sources. The impact of youth programs on their lives was undoubtedly significant, but colonial officials had very little control over how their policies would interact with these social and emotional dynamics of the participants. Village societies gave meaning and value to colonial programs, not vice versa.

Militarizing Rural Youth

As was apparent from Kim Yŏng-han's clear distinction between the Korean shinkō seinendan and the Japanese seinendan, the former functioned mostly at the hamlet and village levels. Even rural youth training centers brought young men only into provincial-level associations. In 1937, to strengthen the horizontal and vertical networks of village youth and establish a direct and deep tie with the imperial state, GGK officials established a national association of the seinendan.

In 1937, the GGK Departments of Education, Agriculture, Police, and Home repeatedly issued notices to provincial governors to expand seinendan institutions, urging them to transfer their affiliation from the shinkōkai to county and provincial administrative offices. The outbreak of all-out war with China added a sense of urgency to these notices: "Since the Northern China Incident . . . the gravity of the mission of the seinendan has increased day by day . . . The seinendan is the most powerful organization to respond to national crises and conduct disciplined activities to fulfill social duties. Particularly in Korea, as we reflect upon the surrounding situation, this need is felt even more deeply."[32] Such notices emphasized the shared destiny of Japan and Korea in the war. At the same time, colonial officials hesitated to recruit all village youth, perhaps out of fear of spawning anticolonial youth movements. They still recommended limiting membership to "those with solid principles among graduates of public elementary schools" while also seeking to expand elementary schools.[33]

The gatherings of the new seinendan associations were thoroughly militaristic, aiming to transform young farmers into national soldiers. The inauguration ceremony of the Chōsen Seinendan Federation took place on September 24, 1938. More than four thousand seinendan members in their khaki uniforms marched and sang the Japanese anthem as well as "Umi yukaba," a song about preparing to die for one's lord also sung by Japanese and Taiwanese youth of the same period. They recited the "Oath as Subjects of the Imperial Nation" (kōkoku shinmin no seishi), prayed at the Chōsen Shrine, and gave three shouts of banzai (long live) to celebrate the solidarity of 150,000 Korean youth. They also visited the brand-new volunteer soldier training center and met the first Korean recruits. One member from North Kyŏngsang expressed his emotional response to the volunteer soldier trainees: "[When I heard their words,] so many emotions overwhelmed my heart, and I could only shed tears. We could not help but pray for their advancement and cry out from the bottom of our hearts, 'Volunteer soldiers! Please represent the youth of the peninsula and pursue the mission of an imperial subject.' I also deeply understood the degree of seriousness the authorities are giving to the seinendan movement."[34] Of course, essays in official journals such as Korean Local Administration indicate what the youth were expected to say and not necessarily their personal feelings, but seinendan members clearly perceived that their ultimate goal was to become soldiers and that their endeavors toward this end should be filled with emotion and enthusiasm.

The names of the rising European fascist nations often appeared to promote a sense of a global youth network. North Kyŏngsang provincial seinendan associations, for example, announced that they had adopted the German Arbeitsdienst (labor service) as a "groundbreaking" program to train Korean youth.[35] The new German phrase gave a fresh image to the old slogan of hardworkism, even though volunteer labor programs had already been widely practiced in the shinkō seinendan all over the peninsula and in other parts of the Japanese Empire.[36] A gathering of the Chōsen Seinendan Federation in April 1939 reminded a newspaper reporter of "the flourishing of the Fascist group led by Mussolini, as well as the endeavors of young national heroes who contributed to our nation's [Meiji] Restoration." The article went on to argue that "our Japanese seinendan is based on the Yamato spirit and is a unique organization which should be separated from the Italian Blackshirts, but there is no difference in the purpose of nurturing solid thoughts."[37]

Anticipation of the coming military recruitment began to color the local-level seinendan as well. Kim Yŏng-han, who continued to participate in seinendan activities in Kwangsŏk village while living in Taejŏn until about 1940, explained that the membership had a strict age limit of twenty years "because the officials assumed that members would join the military afterward."[38] He also emphasized that the seinendan "cultivated loyalty to the state" to support war mobilization.[39] Furthermore, their activities also began to have military elements. At the village level, they largely focused on agricultural production, but at the county and provincial levels, the seinendan conducted military drills. Once a year, village seinendan members gathered in the country's capital, Nonsan, for a week to practice military drills. At the provincial level, an army officer who usually taught middle school students offered group training in the cities of Kongju and Kapsa.[40] These training camps created opportunities to interact with other seinendan members. The instructors gave prizes based on performance, fostering a sense of rivalry between groups or counties. These camps were too short to nurture a collective identity as "rural youth" or "South Ch'ungch'ŏng youth," however, unlike the symbolic identification as "Xinzhu youth" in Taiwan.

Military features were even more central in another major institution promoted by the GGK, youth training centers (*seinen kurenjo*). This was a parallel institution to the one initiated by Ugaki Kazushige in Japan in 1926, which coexisted or merged with supplementary vocational schools in rural Japan. These youth training centers (separate from the rural youth training centers in Korea, which were established by provincial governments) were introduced to Korea in 1927 to allow Japanese reservist associations to provide military training privately to Japanese settler youth.[41] In 1929, the GGK started building youth training centers as attachments to elementary schools. Although these centers focused on Japanese settler youth, a portion (one-seventh to one-third) of the trainees were Korean men.[42] The total number of youth training centers remained low (around fifty to sixty) in the first half of the 1930s, but in 1938 the GGK planned a rapid expansion. The youth training center became "the only institution" to prepare for war a large number of Korean youth, who did not have conscription duty.[43] The GGK had built more than two thousand such centers by the end of the war, and from 1940 on, every elementary school was supposed to have one youth training center attached to it.[44] Its purpose was also rewritten to target Korean youth: "The purpose of the youth training center is to provide working

FIGURE 8.1. Kim Yŏng-han at seinendan training in Kapsa, August 5, 1938. Photo reproduced courtesy of Kim Yŏng-han.

FIGURE 8.2.   Kim Yŏng-han at seinendan training in Kapsa, August 5, 1938. Photo reproduced courtesy of Kim Yŏng-han.

youth who did not continue into upper school after elementary school, and who are engaged in some occupation, with teaching and training when they are not at work, to enhance their quality as imperial subjects, and share their occupational skills, as well as to conduct basic military training, and increase the nation's defensive ability. On this point, it is the equivalent of the youth school in Japan."[45]

The emphasis on localities as the flip side of nationalization, widely seen in Japanese and Taiwanese wartime mobilization, became a trend in 1930s Korea as well. The compilation of local histories and chronicles by schools and provincial governments became a widespread phenomenon around this time. Writings on South Ch'ungch'ŏng province often emphasized the tie between the ancient kingdom of Paekche and Japan. Governor-General Minami Jirō contended that Paekche's princes had come to Japan and become top-rank bureaucrats in the Asuka period (592–710), and that Japanese generals had served the Paekche kingdom. He described these exchanges as the foundation of *naisen ittai* (Japan–Korea Unified Body).[46] The unique historical background of South Ch'ungch'ŏng, often emphasized in youth training activities in the province, served to undergird an empire-wide national consciousness.

The nationalization of the seinendan, the expansion of youth training centers, and the local chronicles all aimed to nurture an identity as Japanese national–imperial subjects. Youth, particularly the model rural youth targeted by these movements, incorporated the increasingly nationalistic and militaristic tone into their expressions, but they still viewed these mobilizing effort within the framework of their own career development. As the GGK and the Japanese army increased their dependence on youthful manpower, young men realized that both their social opportunities and the risks of submitting themselves to the state were expanding. The volunteer soldier program in Korea, launched as an experimental pilot in 1938, was thus characterized by various kinds of expectations, hopes, fears, and tensions among all parties involved.

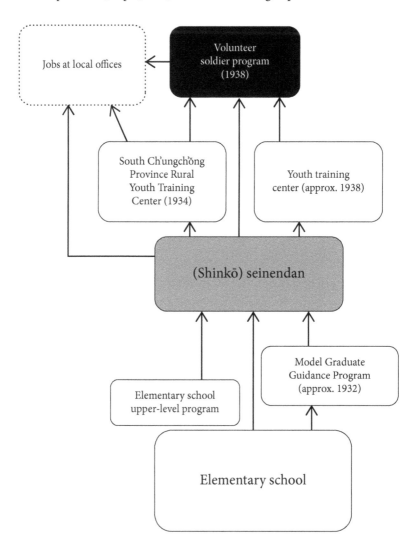

FIGURE 8.3.   Rural youth training institutional setup in Nonsan in the mid-to-late 1930s. The shinkō seinendan became prevalent between 1932 and 1934, and it was detached from the shinkōkai and became the seinendan in 1937. Those who went through these series of youth training were a select few in each village. The seinendan became an all-in organization in 1941 on paper.

The Elite Volunteer Soldier Program

The Korean Special Volunteer Soldier System was introduced in February 1938, three years before its analogue in Taiwan. As noted in the introductory chapter of this book, the first year of recruitment saw nearly 3,000 Korean youths applying for 400 open slots; the numbers of applicants and slots increased to 303,394 and 6,300, respectively, in 1943.[47] Although the applicant–slot ratio did not rise as high as that in Taiwan, many Korean applicants, either voluntarily or forcibly, submitted applications signed in blood as well. In August 1944, the volunteer soldier program was absorbed into the conscription system and the first group of Korean conscripts entered the Japanese army in December 1944.[48]

The introduction of military service in Korea arose more from the need for a boost in kyōka campaigns than from a shortage of military manpower.[49] Consideration of the military recruitment of Korean youth began even before the war itself, but no early plans set the goal as to improve combat capacity.[50] In fact, the number of slots the Chōsengun (the standing army in Korea and a part of the Japanese army) prepared in the program's early years was too small—four hundred in 1938 and six hundred in 1939—to be considered a serious expansion. *Opinions Concerning the Korean Volunteer System*, a thirty-five-page report submitted to the Ministry of the Army in Tokyo by Chōsengun officials in June 1937, also stated that "it is absurd opportunism to regard the volunteer program as a sheer means to increase manpower."[51] Instead, the primary goal was the socialization effect of training select Korean youth in the Japanese army, as both governors-general Ugaki Kazushige and Minami Jirō had believed since much earlier in their careers. These young men were expected to enhance the morale of society and propel forward further Japanization of the population. Another Chōsengun report expressed confidence in the role that the Korean volunteer soldiers would play in their home villages: "Including Koreans in the army and making them directly experience and foster the imperial spirit will not only train and develop the volunteers' own spirit, but will also have a tremendous impact on society after they are discharged and will help them start to play the role of pillars of Korean youth back their home."[52] Rather than an analysis based on observations, this was a statement of faith commonly held by officials around the empire, as seen in Japan and Taiwan alike.

The timing of introducing military service appeared optimal to GGK officials with the beginning of the Sino-Japanese War.[53] After all, Japanese officials had to be cautious about handing weapons to Korean youth, who had exhibited more active anticolonial engagement than their Taiwanese counterparts; they had not forgotten the March First Movement two decades earlier or the more recent Kwangju student movement. The GGK and the Chōsengun carefully assessed the Korean people's reaction to the new war situation. On the one hand, many Korean intellectuals had been demanding that the GGK open a path for military service for Korean youth and, subsequently, suffrage for the Korean population.[54] On the other hand, there were "those who consider that the Japanese would strip them of their rights and exploit them as cannon fodder on the battlefield."[55]

Colonial officials aimed to fend off both reactions. At the same time, some of the demonstrations in support of military service opportunities for Koreans struck colonial officials as sincere and genuine. The colonial police department reported on a meeting attended by thirty-three renowned Korean intellectuals in Seoul in November 1937 to launch a movement to introduce military service in Korea. The report described that the participants as saying that "considering the international situation in East Asia, Koreans would remain an inferior race in East Asia if they missed this opportunity to stand up and serve in the military as Japanese citizens."[56] Although the police and Chōsengun decided to disallow the movement, "looking at the way they began the meeting with the Oath as Subjects of the Imperial Nation and 'Long Live the Emperor,' as well as the sincere attitude of the presenters, the atmosphere of the place seemed more serious than at any time previously."[57] This optimistic and celebratory tone prevailed as the empire entered the war, which provided a favorable environment for initiating the recruitment of Korean youth.

As primarily a kyōka institution, the volunteer soldier training center also adopted dojo-style training. During six months of group living, the select trainees endured a rigid schedule from 5:30 a.m. to 9:45 p.m.[58] They prayed for the emperor, recited the Oath as Subjects of the Imperial Nation, and sang "Umi yukaba." Every morning and every afternoon contained three to four hours of training, which consisted of spiritual lectures, academic subjects such as history and economics, military drills, and volunteer (construction) labor. They finished each day with *seiza* formal sitting to "reflect upon the day's instructions" and pray "for the safety and repose of their parents."[59] The training center implemented "comprehensive lifestyle guidance," which viewed even mealtime as an opportunity to acquire Japanese mannerisms ("Do not make noise while eating," "Do not waste a drop or a grain of food"), learn hygiene and health ("Wash your hands," "Chew thirty times before you swallow"), gain scientific knowledge (of nutrition, digestion, and parasites), and contemplate about larger national issues (agricultural renovation, the science of fertilizer, national food security), and so on.[60] As such, physical training was only a small part of the trainees' daily life. The main focus was to instill a solid identity as Japanese subjects through conforming to an idealized Japanese regimen.

As was repeatedly emphasized in army officials' reports, the graduates of the volunteer soldier program were expected to exercise leadership roles in village society. In August 1939, provincial governments set up "promotion corps" (*suishintai*), consisting of the discharged volunteer soldiers, graduates of the volunteer training center who were waiting to serve in the army, and youth who had attended other youth training institutions. They received special treatment as local leaders, and the emblem on their shirts symbolized their elite status in the countryside. By November 1940, fifteen hundred young men worked in promotion corps to facilitate wartime mobilization. Many of these youth also became the heads of patriotic units (*aikokuhan*) that connected each household to the mass mobilization machine throughout Korea.[61]

At the same time, relative to youth trained in local institutions, the volunteer soldier enjoyed unparalleled prestige and obtained a clearly different status. Even though many participants in the "volunteer fever" had been more or less coerced to apply, once selected as volunteer soldiers they were treated as national heroes.[62] This was by far the most admirable achievement available to village youth, to the extent that every time Kim Yŏng-han mentioned anything about the volunteer soldier program in interviews, he could not help but repeat that "volunteer soldiers boasted of their status so much!"[63] Newspapers devoted their entire front pages and more to reporting on the inauguration of the volunteer soldier training center, calling it "a historic first step" and "an epoch-making event in the history of the rule of Korea."[64] The deployment of such propaganda by the GGK and Korean intellectuals alike contributed to the volunteer program's renown and bestowed peninsula-wide attention on the select trainees. The trainees also received cash from the "special volunteer soldiers support associations" and wealthy notables in their home counties. One trainee was reportedly sent off at the train station by a crowd of more than four thousand people, and another received more than eight hundred yen in gifts.[65]

The establishment of the volunteer soldier program and the nationalization of the seinendan and youth training centers were closely linked to each other. Most of the volunteer soldiers were from the agricultural sector and had graduated from six-year elementary schools. This pool of youth overlapped with members of the seinendan.[66] The GGK described the seinendan as the "central force" of national mobilization that would make the volunteer soldier program and universal education possible.[67] Applicants to the volunteer program were also encouraged to go to youth training centers beforehand because then the training at the volunteer soldier training center was "like a review."[68] The seinendan also took advantage of the volunteer program's prestige as a way to attract public attention. It was not coincidental that the inauguration of the Chōsen Seinendan Federation took place only three months after the nationwide celebration of the volunteer soldier training center, where the seinendan members had an arranged meeting with the brand-new volunteer soldier trainees.

Through these institutions, the GGK sought to align itself closely with the young men of Korea. "The old leaders long grounded in the Chinese classics are deeply affected by the thought that 'soldiers should be despised.' They could not understand the volunteer soldier program," said Governor-General Minami.[69] Emphasizing the generational divide, the GGK attempted to establish direct ties with Korean rural youth. Resembling the ways in which being "young" conferred a superior status in the wartime Taiwanese and Japanese countryside, the masculine body of the volunteer soldier was viewed as symbolizing a dramatic change in status for young rural Korean men.

A unique feature of the reception of the Korean volunteer soldier program, however, was that youth viewed it in the context of their aspirations for educational achievement. From the beginning, flashes of academic prestige associated with the program inspired the participants. The first group of trainees lived on the campus of the Imperial University of Keijō, Korea's only national university, for three months until the training center's facility was completed. The instructors noticed that the trainees were awed by the academic setting and felt deeply proud of this experience.[70] Many of the trainees planned to continue their schooling, especially in the military establishment, after their service. In an interview, trainees stated with regard to their prospects after serving that "I am not sure about the situation yet, but would like to go to the upper school in the army," and "many of us want to go to military officers' school in Tokyo or other army-related schools."[71] *Chosŏn ilbo* reported that some of them, indeed, were later admitted to the army's engineering school.[72]

The trainees' desire for school-based careers was not what the GGK originally intended. Colonial officials had expected to recruit youth from upper-class and educated families and turn them into pillars in their local areas, because they were the main military service proponents.[73] The result was the opposite. They ended up recruiting mostly rural agrarian youth and turning them into youth who wanted more schooling. GGK officials adjusted their expectations and soon took advantage of these men's ambitions, but without hiding their contempt for the wealthy class: "The fact that sons of those with high status, academic degrees, or wealth are extremely few [among applicants] shows that Korea still has a tendency to look down upon military service. People of the wealthy and leading classes enthusiastically welcomed the proclamation of the [volunteer soldier] program. But when it comes to volunteering, do they not commit a contradiction by recommending others but not allowing their own sons [to apply]?"[74]

The GGK's disappointment at upper-class youth only increased the value of rural elementary school graduates. Comparing them with most middle school graduates—the vast majority of whom did not even apply—an editor of *Maeil sinbo* declared, "I express respect for the pure patriotism of elementary school graduates" who rushed to apply.[75] At the local level, too, middle school graduates were notorious for their laziness and low productivity when hired by village offices.[76] Their poor reputation convinced the GGK even more firmly of the reliability of model rural youth.

In addition to being as a step toward educational advancement, the volunteer program brought improved job prospects, especially for the early trainees. Like their Taiwanese and Japanese counterparts, they were promised a special advantage in obtaining employment in the police force or local administration upon their discharge.[77] "Early applicants encouraged one another to apply, saying that they could become village secretaries afterward," Kim Yŏng-han, who also applied but did not pass the examination, recalled.[78] For the first few years, not all volunteer soldiers entered the military after their training. If they returned to their home villages as the First Reserve and became village secretaries or police officers, they were exempted from further military service.[79] In other words, seen better in retrospect, one way to avoid military service, which would soon become mandatory, was—ironically enough—to graduate from the volunteer soldier training center early on and become settled as a local official.

Youth under Total Mobilization

As we have seen, the various youth training programs focused on elementary school graduates to cultivate a reliable layer of national pillars during the 1930s. But the war drove the GGK to build a more inclusive network for total mobilization. Soon the youth programs were transformed into institutions that would reach every young male villager, with a series of new regulations and programs in the 1940s moving toward total inclusion.

Although historical scholarship has tended to depict the state as steadily intensifying its control over the population through the 1930s and until the end of the war in 1945, from the viewpoint of Korean youth, total mobilization was not a continuation of previous programs. In fact, it reversed many social opportunities that they had acquired, forcing them to seek new strategies for self-advancement, or at least self-preservation. Model rural youth like Kim Yŏng-han maneuvered to avoid military and labor conscription by choosing which cog of the war machine they would become.

Total mobilization on the Korean peninsula was largely managed by the Korean League for National Spiritual Total Mobilization (Kokumin Seishin Sōdōin Chōsen Renmei).[80] Established as a peninsula-wide governmental organization in 1938, it built a network of aikokuhan (patriotic units) to reach every household in Korea. The aikokuhan, similar to the *tonarigumi* in Japan or the *baojia* strengthened in Taiwan, facilitated mutual cooperation and policing among ten or so households to fulfill the mandatory contributions of rice and metal, reform daily customs, and reinforce thought control.[81] Compared with the shinkōkai under the Rural Revitalization Campaign, which were voluntary organizations, aikokuhan groups were compulsory and left little space for individual villagers' initiative.

In actual programs and goals, the spiritual mobilization did not depart much from what former governor-general Ugaki Kazushige founded in the 1930s. His famous slogan of shinden kaihatsu (spiritual field cultivation) functioned as the moral basis of the new movement.[82] In 1939, Korean agriculture was damaged by a severe drought, and more than half the farming population harvested less than 30% of their average annual yield. Even the drinking water in wells dried up.[83] To recover from the famine and turn Korea into a "military base for the continent," increasing agricultural production became an even more urgent task assigned to the villages. Journalists echoed the importance of "the reorganization of agriculture" to accelerate the programs initiated by the Ugaki administration.[84] Although industrial production expanded in the northern part of Korea to meet military needs, agrarianism and the "farmers' spirit" did not decrease in importance in the campaign. Agrarian ideals and militarism were still twins. "The farmer's dojo is a military camp for farmers," argued Watanabe Toyohiko, who happened to be a former director of education in Miyagi and who became an expert in agricultural development in the GGK bureaucracy.[85]

The seinendan were also transformed from institutions focused on the middling class into an all-inclusive network. In January 1941, the director-general of administration, Ōno Rokuichirō, issued a decree to reorganize the seinendan. Now called the Chōsen Seinendan, it included all male youth between the ages of fourteen and thirty who were not attending school and also, for the first time, unmarried female youth age fourteen to twenty-five.[86] As a departure from the earlier seinendan, now the central goal became teaching uneducated children and youth the Japanese language and military discipline.[87] This instruction was intended to compensate for the lack of universal schooling, which was widely proposed by both Korean and Japanese leaders as a prerequisite for military service and total mobilization. Even with a rapid increase in school facilities, the enrollment rate for Korean children barely reached 50% in the 1940s.[88] The previous seinendan for elementary school graduates were renamed *seinentai* (youth corps) and functioned as branch units of the Chōsen Seinendan. The new regulation encompassed the earlier emphases on emperor-centered nationalism, unity between Japan and Korea, group discipline, and improvement of agricultural production. It also stated that the main feature of the new organization was a commitment to nurturing "the ideologies of national defense."[89] To achieve this goal, the youth corps and youth training centers were expected to closely coordinate their military training programs.

On paper, with the help of the network of aikokuhan, the expansion of the seinendan led to a rapid increase in participants. At the same time, the departure from the pre-1941 seinendan was so significant that it widened the gap between reality and the fantasy of official statistics. Kim Yŏng-han argued that the years when he participated (1936–1940) were the most active for the village (shinkō) seinendan, but as war mobilization progressed, many youth had to leave their villages for military or industrial service. Based on his experience, Kim did not believe that the village seinendan functioned as a mandatory institution, although he knew it had started to recruit youth with no schooling.[90] For him, the term *village youth groups* continued to refer to the former, exclusive groups of model youth until the end of the war. Consistent with Kim's recollection, other evidence suggests that the expansion of the seinendan met with difficulty. Newspapers of the time reported that many Koreans mistrusted the intentions behind the mandatory seinendan participation, worrying whether it would result in young men sent away for forced labor and young women being deported to Manchuria for forced marriages.[91] Overall, the establishment of a universal seinendan system to train uneducated youth seems to have failed entirely.

The peak of total mobilization for the young male population was mandatory military conscription, which began in Korea at the request of the Tokyo government in 1944.[92] The conscription program differed fundamentally from the volunteer soldier program in a way that resembled the Taiwanese case. Minami Jirō had already expressed his desire to implement universal conscription in Korea when he became governor-general of Korea in 1936.[93] The announcement of the conscription program in 1942 was thus not a surprise, but it triggered a mixture of reactions throughout the peninsula. For Korean intellectuals, the conscription decree provided leverage for negotiation when they pressed for suffrage and universal education. In fact, they gained approval from Tokyo on both issues near the end of the war.[94] For young men themselves, the decree gave little incentive other than the hope that they might be better fed in the army than in their villages should another famines like those of 1939 and 1942 occur.

Despite more than a decade of intensifying effort, the kyōka campaigns had not prepared impoverished Korean farmers for mandatory conscription. The increase in elementary schooling in the 1930s came too late. In the 1940s, more than 70% of the male population of conscription age did not understand Japanese.[95] If recruited, they would need basic training in the Japanese language. Because the new seinendan made so little progress in addressing this problem, the GGK hurried to find a solution on the eve of the start of conscription. In Japan and Taiwan, this was not a significant problem, since elementary schools were widespread and because night schools and the seinendan helped to maintain the graduates' academic level. Lacking a similar capacity, the GGK had to start a new program in 1942, the *renseijo* (training facility), for youth with little schooling. At the renseijo, working youth received Japanese language training for twelve hours a week, or six hundred hours a year.[96] But this makeshift program had little effect. In 1944, 68% of conscription-age youth still did not understand Japanese and the government had to administer the conscription exam in Korean.[97]

Since the government also intended to use Korean human resources for industrial labor, the scope of army enlistment was much narrower in Korea than in Japan.[98] Still, the loopholes in the system had the effect of filtering out those with sufficient means to maneuver through it. As a result, the majority of conscripts came from the poor strata of farm families, who then lost manpower in the already desperate rural conditions. Korean conscripts were deployed mostly in administrative roles and as rear support troops, and many anecdotes indicate that Korean youth frequently evaded the conscription exam or deserted from the army.[99] Japanese officials issued a statement describing this situation as normal, pointing out that Japan encountered similar resistance even in its homeland when it first implemented universal military service in the Meiji era.[100] But this admission only underscored the difficulty of recruiting Korean youth from poor families and transforming them into reliable soldiers.

The mobilization of civilian military employees (*gunzoku*) and forced labor that absorbed young men from rural villages took place on a larger scale. As in Taiwan, many people hired as civilian military employees between 1937 and 1941 had relatively high educational background or technical skills. They served as interpreters, technicians, sailors, and drivers.[101] After 1941, the scale of recruitment expanded. Some Koreans became prison guards monitoring prisoners of war in Southeast Asia and were convicted as Class B or C war criminals by the Allies in trials after the war. Others became construction laborers and built military bases on newly occupied islands in the South Pacific.[102] Between 1937 and 1945, Japan employed 4.1 to 7 million Koreans as laborers, either in private companies or in government agencies, and then later as conscript laborers, who were essentially subject to conditions of labor slavery. Millions were relocated to Japan, China, Manchuria, Southeast Asia, and the Pacific. Since the families of labor conscripts were not allowed to talk about the draft, villagers did not know exactly how many men served as laborers or where, but Kim recalled that "most of my seinendan friends either went into the military or were recruited as laborers."[103]

The result of this labor mobilization—with nearly 10% of the Korean population being forced to relocate—was a rapid disappearance of people from the countryside.[104] Combined with voluntary migration, it left almost no young people of around twenty years of age remained in the southern parts of Korea by 1943, according to a mobilization officer. The age makeup in a village in South Chŏlla in 1944 reflected the disappearance of both male and female laborers, mostly age between twenty and forty.[105] The likelihood of leaving the village deprived new institutions like the all-in seinendan and renseijo of having any real effect on village life. In this situation, the social mobility complex had evaporated, reflecting the end of village youth leadership both in ideological terms and as available manpower.

The Last Dream of a New Frontier

As wartime mobilization engulfed the lives of a great number of Koreans, middling-class youth found themselves in a difficult position. The emphasis on youth, which had earlier helped them to counter (at least psychologically) the age hierarchy in village society, continued in slogans and propaganda. But in this time of "national emergency," it had a new meaning—a demand that youth submit to state control.

Ironically, those trained as model rural youth became the individuals most capable of finding and exploiting the loopholes in the mobilization system. Becoming a village secretary, for example, provided young people with some protection from mobilization. Another option, especially if they clung to a dream of educational success, was to join a prestigious program like the volunteer soldier. The GGK created a few new programs with the promise of academic advancement to co-opt their sense of elitism.

Kim Yŏng-han found himself in a rapidly changing social environment. He had jumped successfully from one position to another during the 1930s. When the Pacific front of the war began in late 1941, he was working at the Non-san county office. He was content with his work, recalling that "many villagers envied me because I was only twenty years old or so and had already become a local official."[106] As the war progressed, he noticed that the "Japanese were disappearing" from his workplace as they were conscripted into the military.[107] In 1944, he was surprised to hear the news that even the son of his Japanese superior, who was studying at the Imperial University of Tokyo, had become a volunteer student soldier.[108] When military conscription was about to start in Korea, Kim missed the mandatory conscription age by one year. A common fate for someone in his situation was labor conscription. Like many other youth in his position, Kim studied the exemption rules carefully. "Village and town secretaries, police officers, and higher-ranking officials were exempted." He recalled. "Many middle school graduates suddenly rushed to apply for positions of village secretary for this reason."[109] His official job in Nonsan county, however, would not exempt him.

Kim found a way around the rules by securing a new position managed by the county office. He explained, "The county office needed me to stay, so it sent me to a local unit of the Air Defense Guards. It did that with many good employees." He first had to pass an exam on the identification of different models of aircraft, but once he joined the Air Defense Guards, it had guaranteed him an exemption from labor conscription. His life as a guard involved three-hour shifts around the clock, alternating between training, watching, and resting. He considered it "exactly the same as the military, with uniforms and caps all provided, like the seinendan." Some former seinendan members also joined local units, which consisted of seventy to one hundred guards each.

Joining the Air Defense Guards not only helped Kim to remain in Nonsan county but also offered the possibility of promotion. "The supervisor told us that, if Japan won, the guards who worked hard would receive the Eighth Order of Merit," said Kim, noting how honorable that would have been. In the end, there were no serious air raids in Korea, but only a few minor bombings near Nonsan, which destroyed a bridge and construction materials. Kim Yŏng-han was still serving in his unit when he heard the news of the Japanese surrender in August 1945.[110]

Besides seeking to escape army and labor conscription, many middling-class youth chose to join other programs outside Korea that would potentially bring them better social status and job prospects.[111] Manchuria, which appeared to many as a solution to the domestic problems troubling both Japan and Korea—lack of resources, interethnic tensions, and persistent rural poverty—was depicted as a new frontier for model rural youth. The imperial government initially set up the Young Volunteer Corps for the Development of Manchuria-Mongolia for Japanese young men, but the corps also started recruiting Koreans in 1940. The GGK described this program as laying the foundation for the development of Manchurian agriculture and the realization of Manchukuo ideals of racial harmony. Admission was highly competitive; elementary school graduates age fifteen to twenty were eligible. Those selected spent eight months of training in Kangwon province and three more months in the famous Uchihara training center in Ibaraki, Japan, followed by eighteen months at training facilities in

Manchuria. The program provided only three yen in salary per month in addition to basic daily needs. The greatest benefit of participation emphasized by the GGK was that Korean youth would share the experience with Japanese youth, embodying racial harmony.[112] The stress on the power of youth on the new frontier and the strict qualification requirements boosted the program's repute in the eyes of middling-class youth, quite unlike the mass migration of poorer peasants to Manchuria that the GGK promoted simultaneously.[113]

Another frontier advertised by the GGK to ambitious village youth was the Japanese countryside. Especially after the beginning of the Pacific War, traveling to Japan for an academic or career goal became something unimaginable, forcing Kim Yŏng-han to abandon his plan to study in Japan. Unless people had significant capital of their own, study trips through the seinendan or local village offices were the only way to visit Japan. Seventy years later, Kim still wished that he could have gone on a study trip to Japan as a model seinendan member; no such program existed in Kwangsŏk village. What did help to increase the morale of youth like Kim was the Korea Agricultural Patriotic Service Youth Corps, founded in 1940, which dispatched farm youth to Japan to learn Japanese agricultural practices. Fifteen times between 1940 and 1944, groups of between twenty and three hundred men were sent to rural Japanese villages and lived for one month, most of them living with families whose sons or fathers were away or had died in the military. The participants were selected from among the graduates of rural youth training centers.

A journalist, Kagawa Tomomi, called these youth corps members the "troops of the sacred plow" because they marched in an orderly fashion in their military-like uniforms, sporting a seinendan-style flag.[114] In addition to capitalizing on Korean youth's desire to travel to Japan, the program produced many so-called beautiful anecdotes, depicting the harmony between Japan and Korea for propaganda purposes. GGK officials reported such comments from the participants: "I was so moved because the families welcomed us in the rain as if we were returning soldiers"; and "Japanese elderly people work very hard. They work nearly three times harder than Korean youth. I wonder how they can work so much."[115] Women's labor and the centrality of ancestral worship intrigued these youth.[116] Japanese families also offered enthusiastic comments about the sincerity and diligence of the Korean youth they hosted. They were often amazed by the young Koreans' mastery of the Japanese language and their politeness. Many villages were initially uncertain about accepting Korean farmers, but after they lived with the trainees, "their doubt turned to gratitude. . . . The villagers understood the real Korean people." Other typical reports stated, "An aged grandmother was exhilarated to have a Korean young man as if her grandson had come back," and "Our bonds deepened over the short period of one month.

We grew close to each other, and it felt as if I was sending my own son off at his tearful departure."[117]

Despite these concerted efforts to maintain the morale of ambitious village youth, the contradictory reality of intensifying total mobilization diminished their enthusiasm. At the county office, Kim Yŏng-han witnessed the sabotage of mobilization efforts by government agencies and villagers alike: the provincial government rarely provided the full amount of food stipulated under rationing guidelines to county or village offices, and villagers often tried to escape the mandatory contribution of food and other materials. In this widening gap between the state and villagers, the model rural youth who had earlier managed to bridge both worlds as pillars of the empire lost their leverage in village society. State efforts to align with model rural youth were at an end.

Did the social mobility complex in South Ch'ungch'ŏng, which flourished for a short period of time in the 1930s and very early 1940s, instill an identity as Japanese subjects in village youth? This is a difficult question to answer today because, unlike Xu Chongfa and Huang Yuanxing in Taiwan, their Korean counterparts generally avoid the topic to protect themselves from being branded as colonial collaborators. Yet descriptions of Kim Yŏng-han's everyday life indicate that they usually did not react against the rhetoric of Japanese nationalism. Kim's favorite reading was battlefield reports written by a popular Japanese author, Hino Ashihei. He also enjoyed a lecture by Japan's leading agrarian activist and scholar, Yamazaki Nobuyoshi. *Kokumin sōryoku* (Total strength of the nation), the GGK's wartime magazine, was Kim's primary source of news. He remembered being greatly inspired by a story in that magazine about an entire class of female students at Maizuru (Muhak) Woman's High School in Seoul who applied to join the women's volunteer corps (*teishintai*).[118] Like Taiwanese and Japanese village youth in the early 1940s, Korean youth like Kim incorporated the prose used by the state into their lives, finding even entertainment and inspiration in them. But youth programs lost traction as a source of social opportunities for Kim, and he did not feel the same pressure to become a volunteer soldier as Xu Chongfa did. Nonetheless, in his youth training and his pursuit of a successful career, he came to accept the rhetoric and ideology of Japanese nationalism through a psychological mechanism similar to that produced a nationalistic population in other parts of the Japanese Empire. It was *despite* the brutality of total mobilization—not *because* of it—that a group of ambitious youth internalized a sense of Japanese agrarian nationalism based on their aspirations and emotions that they experienced within their immediate social surroundings.

As in Taiwan, the ladder of career development and a shared identity of model rural youth in Korea emerged out of a series of youth programs designed by state officials. In Korean society as well, the prestige of the volunteer soldier program gave widespread recognition to the category of rural youth and solidly confirmed their route to success. Although the participating youth's ambitions did not diverge much from urban, school-based career development, *rural youth* became a highly respected label in assimilation programs. Again, as in the Taiwanese and Japanese cases, state policies constituted only half of the mechanism; it was social contexts specific to each particular class, generation, and location that attached certain value to the state programs. State officials' inability to predict reliably what social dynamics would result became apparent in the actions of model rural youth as the war situation became more demanding. The total nature of the mobilization, including civilian military employment, labor conscription, and patriotic unit networks, had turned ambitious youth away from the imperial cause of war rather than leading them to embrace it. More crucially, in this period, a large number of Korean young men relocated outside their villages. Despite the intensifying institutional effort, mobilization did not lead to an expansion of the social mobility complex but, instead, to its demise.

Behind the appearance of strong pragmatism in the Korean case lay important psychological and emotional aspects of mobilization. Much of these young men's emotion had little to do with their perceived connection to the imperial state. But they used the rhetoric of Japanese agrarianism to express their grievances and aspirations generated in their local contexts, making their association with the state ideology more and more emotionally charged. I contend that the Japanese nationalism expressed by Korean youth during the 1930s and the early 1940s was no less real than that of their Japanese and Taiwanese counterparts. The combination of a desire to pursue success and a feeling of moral superiority was at the heart of their internalization of the Japanese ideology.

Before concluding, I should make a brief albeit perhaps obvious observation on the postwar political label of "pro-Japanese collaborators." The issue of collaborators and traitors has been a sensitive political topic especially since the democratization of South Korea in the 1990s. The presidential truth-finding committee identified thousands of "pro-Japanese collaborators" in 2005, based on the assumption that the upper strata of Koreans exploited the lower strata by selling their ethnic identity for personal benefit.[119] But evidence shows that class dynamics were much more complex. In the 1930s, all classes tried to achieve better lives through government mobilization, and among them, the new middling class, to which Kim Yŏng-han belonged, was particularly successful. More important, Korean ethnic identity, however strongly embraced, did not bring with it as a moral obligation to resist colonial mobilization for most people. Kim did not think that he had pursued his career at the expense of the Korean ethnic community. Until the war was over, he did not see Koreanness and Japaneseness as mutually exclusive. The social mobility and dynamics of rural villages, as seen from the viewpoint of agrarian youth, cannot be captured by the retrospective definition of "collaborators" and "betrayal against the Korean nation." Rather, they reveal the fluid and amorphous nature of identity in the actual lives of village youth.[120]

Part 3

CONSEQUENCES

9

AS YOUNG PILLARS OF THE NATION-EMPIRE

Most of the village youth in the seinendan across the Japanese Empire were trained locally and did not have the chance to meet their counterparts from other parts of the empire. Yet even without physical encounters, many of them shared an idealized self-image of rural youth and used similar rhetoric of national–imperial agrarianism. Through their institutional connection to the larger youth network, some of these youth satisfied their desire to prove their self-worth and their curiosity about the larger world. In many ways, the local process of creating model rural youth served the empire's pursuit of assimilationist goals, or nation-empire building. In short, the phrase "young pillars of the empire" denoted a very vaguely imagined community that enhanced a sense of empire-wide coherence and unity.

Seinendan leaders and state officials sought more than grassroots production of model rural youth, however. Hundreds of thousands of disciplined young men in uniform provided a picture of great symbolic value when the empire was undertaking frantic efforts of mass mobilization. In the late 1930s and early 1940s, model rural youth from various localities were brought together at seinendan conventions to visually embody pan-imperial solidarity. Top seinendan officials went further by establishing trans-ethnic youth leadership encompassing Japan, China, Manchuria, Burma, and other parts of Asia in 1943 to realize the imperial goal of the Greater East Asia Co-Prosperity Sphere.[1]

Another major propaganda resource was the colonial volunteer soldier programs. The multiethnic sections of the military helped to advertise the strength and ideal of an integrated empire. These programs in turn offered a small group of village youth a chance to visit another part of the empire and interact with their counterparts. Such programs and events became opportunities to turn an imagined community into an actual one, composed of rural youth from the empire. How did they experience these encounters with each other? Did their emotional bonds transcend ethnic, cultural, and colonial boundaries? Ultimately, was the project of constructing a nation-empire materialized in these programs?

This chapter examines the reactions of the participants in the pan-imperial programs and their experience as young pillars of the empire. Most of them arrived at the programs with high hopes, regarding themselves as select, capable, exemplary rural youth. But their experiences did not straightforwardly enhance their imperial identity as officials claimed. As they found themselves regulated by new social dynamics in these programs, they constantly remapped their positions in new structures. Such subtle changes in their self-perceptions are not easy for historians to detect. The voices of those undergoing change, though not totally muffled, are partial and scattered. The available sources present obvious difficulties. For example, the youth's "diaries" were not the hidden voices of inner selves, but took the form of essays being developed for possible publication. As Aaron William Moore has shown, diary writing was an educational tool that promoted self-discipline and enforced the internalization of the narratives that surrounded the diarists.[2] As a medium that connected public discourse, ideological teaching, and personal experiences, their diaries are evidence of the thorough intermixing of these elements and do not allow us to isolate the writers' individual feelings, if they were separable at all. It is even harder to analyze their diaries here than in previous chapters because we have so little information about the family, village, and social contexts of these individuals. That leaves us without a grasp of their personal stakes. Besides, pan-imperial seinendan events were designed to temporarily ignite the pride of rural youth and produce imperial bonding, and their long-term impact was a separate issue. Any passion emanating from the diary entries would not necessarily indicate a long-lasting embrace of youth's mission as the pillars of the nation-empire.

"Memory" has other issues. A number of survivors wrote memoirs and retrospective essays, or were interviewed by scholars decades later about their experiences as (colonial) soldiers. With regard to our goal of tracing the consequences of national–imperial identity construction, the problem here is not about the factual accuracy of their accounts, but the layers of interpretations that individuals attached to their experiences so as to maintain coherent life narratives. All aspects of soldiering—living in harsh conditions with Japanese cohorts, killing enemies, witnessing the death of friends, learning about the empire's defeat, and returning home—and the drastic regime changes of the postwar period required repeated adjustment of their narratives. Most of the retrospective writings are somewhat confessional in nature, as the writers sought salvation through addressing irreconcilable chapters of their life. Yet, by piecing together the frag-ments of their experiences, they formed a narrative arch stretching from the cause of their actions (why they applied to the volunteer soldier program) to the consequences (how they survived the postwar period). One discovers that the reasons for volunteering stated retrospectively in their memoirs, having been reframed over and over, exhibit a slight difference from those constructed based on the pre-1945 sources or from the personal stories of Xu Chongfa and Kim Yŏng-han. Most noticeably, in these memoirs, volunteering is detached from the ladder of youth training. Such a difference should not discredit either narrative as incorrect, but it highlights how central and troubling their military experiences became in the writers' retrospective life narratives.

At the same time, these interpretative issues make their diaries and memoirs rich sources that reveal the writers' deep relationships with ever-changing social contexts. Rather than dismissing their accounts as untrustworthy or unrepresen-tative, I invite you to imagine the twists and turns in the youth's surroundings and their consciousness. This chapter does not intend to thoroughly examine the many things that happened during and after the war to hundreds of thousands of youth deployed abroad; that task deserves its own separate investigation. Here, with a few examples of firsthand accounts, we remain focused on young people's fluid and confusing self-perceptions and the social tensions that affected them.

Both policymakers of the empire and the former model rural youth of the colonies soon realized that bringing people together from colonizing and colo-nized societies had an ironic, reverse effect on the construction of the nation-empire. The personal accounts show how fragile the concepts of "model rural youth" and "pillars of the empire" became once colonial youth were integrated into a genuinely Japanese-dominated social structure outside their home villages. The rhetoric of Japanese nationalism and self-sacrifice dictated the public dis-course during wartime. Amid the seemingly continuous use of the same rhetoric, colonial youth bitterly realized that they had hit the limit of assimilation. At that point, the divide between colonizer and colonized emerged as the central social tension in their lives. In response, colonial youth replaced their former emphasis on becoming model rural youth with an aspiration to "become truer Japanese." Contrary to the literal meaning of the term, the new expression signified their awareness of unbridgeable ethnic divides, not a success of nation-empire building.

Visiting across the Empire

In the 1930s, as the empire was consolidated, the leaders of the seinendan aimed at impressing young people with the expansive imperial sphere and the diversity of its populations. Those who had become model rural youth in various localities were expected to imagine a new community, that of the young pillars of the nation-empire. To facilitate this understanding, the seinendan scaled up their exchange programs. A select few seinendan members from Taiwan and Korea visited the *naichi* (inner territories), and those in Japan often toured in Korea and Manchuria. As envoys from rural villages, the participants recorded and published their observations in official journals and newsletters back home.

Seinendan conventions were the most symbolic of such occasions. In November 1928, the Greater Japan Seinendan Federation held its fourth convention in Kyoto, in order to officially celebrate the enthronement of Emperor Hirohito. This became the first opportunity for a small number of seinendan members from major colonial branches to gather with their Japanese counterparts at a single venue. The ceremony had 842 participants, including four from Karafuto, two from the Kantō (Kwantung) region in northern China, six (and two teachers) from Taiwan, and fifteen from Korea. These representatives from colonized territories shared accommodations with eleven Japanese seinendan members (from Gunma and Iwate) in the Myōshin Temple. The Taiwanese delegates consisted of two Japanese settlers, three men of Chinese-descent, and one aboriginal man. The Korean team was composed of eight Koreans and seven Japanese.[3] In a report published in the journal *Korean Social Work*, Suzuki Yoshiaki, a young Japanese settler in South Hamgyŏng province in Korea, claimed that the youth delegates from various places built warm friendships with one another: "Because many of us were from the colonies, we shared characteristics of living in the colonies, hit it off immediately, and had lively conversations as if we had known each other for a decade." He was impressed by the Taiwanese members' mastery of Japanese, their rich knowledge, and their quality as model rural youth, in no way inferior to that of other participants. By contrast, Suzuki was dismayed to hear of the politicization of village youth that prevailed in late-1920s Japan. He emphasized the apolitical and "pure" nature of the colonial seinendan to make a contrast: "In Gunma prefecture, where political competitions are severe, [seinendan activities] strongly reflect that character. They said [seinendan members] had acted as running dogs of political parties at the time of the election," wrote Suzuki, "but it is reassuring that in Korea, Taiwan, and other [outer territories], the seinendan would not become the prey of politicians."[4]

Official seinendan conventions always placed a strong emphasis on the role of youth in establishing a new kind of empire. Suzuki summarized the speeches of twenty-three seinendan members: "In memory of the accomplishments of the Meiji Restoration, three million young people across the empire must unite and start a national movement for the establishment of the Showa Restoration." Suzuki, in his own speech, raised the issue of the ethnic assimilation of the empire. Although settler youth did not necessarily share the same experiences as native Korean village youth, he felt compelled to represent Korea to the crowd of seinendan youth. He described "the sadness and misery of losing the mother nation held by Korean young people" and declared that "we [seinendan] youth must form a one and inseparable body with [Korean youth] under the newly [constructed] Japanese ethnicity and circulate young bloodstreams." The reports indicated that Japanese seinendan members responded to his words with enthusiastic applause.[5]

The best-advertised instance of an empire-wide seinendan gathering was the fifteenth convention held in September 1939. For the first and last time, a city of the outer territories, Seoul, was chosen as the venue, symbolizing the official integration of Korean and Taiwanese seinendan federations into the Japanese network during the previous year. Four thousand Korean seinendan members welcomed 952 members and leaders from Japan, thirty from Taiwan, thirty from Manchuria, and twenty-five from five parts of China. The convention stressed the solidarity of seinendan members across the empire in preparation for the intensifying war.[6] The members declared, "We shall further strengthen the unity of imperial youth [through the principle of] the Japan–Korea Unified Body, and we will consolidate the bond of a thriving Asia (kōa) widely with youth of fellow East Asian nations. . . . The completion of the establishment of the East Asia New Order is on our shoulders."[7] The program was filled with usual rituals: bowing in the direction of the imperial household and the Imperial Ise Shrine, singing the Japanese national anthem, delivering speeches, conducting joint marches and exercises, and visiting the Chōsen Shrine. Reflecting its emphasis on Asian solidarity, the convention organized a reception of the "Japan-Manchuria-China youth representatives" as a centerpiece of the event.[8]

The intended goal of developing the idea of a united cohort of imperial youth and boosting the morale of young people in support of war appears to have been successfully achieved to some degree. We have very few personal accounts that indicate the participants' impressions of these programs. But those that do exist show signs of excitement and the embrace of a trans-ethnic youth identity. According to a handful of official diaries written by a few participants from Nagano, Japan, the Japan-Manchuria-China reception did make a deep impression. One diarist wrote that the youth representatives "roared" their determination to deliver the ideals of friendship and peace and that their enthusiasm "filled the convention hall." The same diarist was most touched by a visit to Korea's new volunteer soldier training center. He observed that the Korean trainees "had an extremely strong consciousness of being Japanese," and "there was no sense of being ethnically different. No distorted emotion could be found; I could see only the determined expressions of youth who are truly fired up with mutual love as imperial sons." These scenes, in his account, brought tears to the visitors' eyes and stirred "feelings of respect and awe."[9]

Another participant from Nagano emphasized the special role of seinendan members from both Japan and Korea vis-à-vis the general population of colonial Korea. He regarded the main purpose of the seinendan convention as to inspire residents of Seoul through spectacles. He wrote, "The large musical band performed by the Korean seinendan attracted the attention of passersby, and the spirit-stirring march of the Japanese seinendan must have inspired intense feelings in Korean and Japanese residents."[10] In his narrative, youthful leadership distinguished Korean seinendan members from ordinary residents of Seoul. The experience affected Taiwanese members similarly. Decades later, for example, one participant from Taipei province, a graduate of the Taiwan Patriotic Labor Youth Corps, proudly shared his memory of being selected to attend the fifteenth convention, showing his photos and memorabilia to his interviewer, anthropologist Miyazaki Seiko.[11]

The large-scale seinendan conventions and events, where hundreds of members got together for several days, provided a typical "eventful" moment of identity production.[12] The youth were urged to, and were often eager to, demonstrate their identity as the empire's model youth. Even on such occasions when their seinendan identity was actively being performed, however, the extent to which it eliminated ethnic cleavages is questionable. On the contrary, the mutual encounters often had the effect of hardening regional and ethnic boundaries. Traveling to the metropole, although it kindled excitement, also placed colonial youth in an alien environment, which could disrupt their image of a shared community. The trips from Taiwan, in particular, were designed to impress the participants with the gap between the metropole and the colony. Taiwan's colonial journal, *The Friend of Social Work*, in its report on the 1928 seinendan convention, focused on the participants' reactions to Japan's advanced technology and culture—the majesty of the Kobe port, the miracle of new machinery exhibited at the Yahata steel mill and the Osaka Expo, and the heartfelt politeness of a female elevator operator—while mentioning the seinendan event only briefly.[13]

The recollections of visiting Japan provided by Xu Chongfa, a shūrenjō instructor analyzed in chapter 6, offer further evidence that the central goal of these visits remained that of clarifying the metropole's dominant position, even in later years. In 1942, Xu was one of the sixteen graduates of the Taiwan Patriotic Labor Youth Corps who participated in the volunteer service of planting rushes (to be used for the roofs of the Imperial Ise Shrine). Xu crossed the ocean in the midst of war, sailing through the darkness to avoid air raids by the Allies. He remembered working with participants from Korea and Manchuria. Aside from describing Japanese and Korean youth as "hardworking brothers," however, he had no substantial interactions with them.[14] Instead of deepening a shared identity as rural youth with his counterparts as the officials emphasized, the event made him view the participants along ethnic lines, defining himself as representing a backward Taiwan. In his report published in Xinzhu province's *Dōkō*, the boundaries between Japan and Taiwan—the developed and the under-developed—occupied his attention, replacing his usual emphasis on the "rural," "little-educated," Xinzhu youth. The dichotomy led him to write of his return to Taiwan that "It felt like coming to China." His expression aroused an uncomfortable feeling in his friendly readers. One of his former students wrote to him, "Calling our native home 'like China'! That is mean, teacher."[15]

Aside from the large events and annual conventions, colonial seinendan youth also made longer-term visits to the metropole, which were supposed to further transform these young people into Japanese-style model rural youth. In Korea, a handful of farmers (three to seven) with elementary school diplomas received a scholarship from the Korea Education Association (Chōsen Kyōikukai) each year and worked for "model landlords" in Japan for one year. This immersion program started in 1931, primarily to transfer agricultural management skills, long before the larger but shorter-term Korea Agricultural Patriotic Service Youth Corps began in 1940 (see chapter 8).[16] Other village youth also joined locally arranged study visits to Japanese villages on an ad hoc basis. Their diaries and reports appeared in almost every issue of the journal *Bunkyō no Chōsen* between 1933 and 1938. Writing reports was an important part of the training, as they learned how to use the vocabulary of agrarianism that tied together the Japanese and Korean countryside. They described many detailed measures of Hōtoku agrarian morality that regulated Japanese villages, pointing out traits of Japan's rural communities. One frequently highlighted characteristic was the physical strength of Japanese farm women. One participant from South Kyŏngsang province related an anecdote in a roundtable discussion: "No matter how fast I reaped rice, the [host mother] caught up with me. . . . In the end, with my back hurting, arms about to fall off, and eyes not functioning, I lost to her in our competition."[17] The youth noted the importance of religion, in the form of worshipping ancestors and neighborhood deities, in promoting diligence and frugality. Some observed that religious customs protected rural virtue from the influence of urban decadence. The high literacy rate and common practice of reading newspapers in ordinary farm families also surprised them.[18] By elaborating on these characteristics, as expected by the program, the participants narrated themselves as missionaries of imperial agrarian morality from the metropole back to Korea.

These long-term interactions, however, did not necessarily create bonds that transcended ethnic lines any better than the annual conventions did. Suddenly transplanted into a village of strangers, the colonial youth inevitably felt a sense of isolation, along with the pressure of the social and imperial hierarchy that was imposed upon them. Their published reports, showing only their positive impressions of Japanese families and criticizing their home villages as underdeveloped, betray the stressful nature of highly monitored (and self-monitored) daily life. Above all, a mixed community of model rural youth does not appear to have been constructed. No report contains any mention of participating in or mingling with the local seinendan despite the writers' observations about that institution. That fact alone shows how limited the integration of the Korean trainees into Japanese village society actually was. In fact, two Korean trainees fled their assigned village in August 1933, claiming that "there was nothing to learn about, the master was irrational, and his attitude was extremely discriminatory and abusive." In *Bunkyō no Chōsen*, their escape was discussed by another trainee, who condemned the escapees as an "awful failure, an embarrassment to Korean youth."[19] As late as 1940, officials in charge continued to fear that the Korean participants might flee. They taught the Korean youth to "never use the Korean language," so as not to generate suspicion among Japanese hosts, and to "never raise trivial ideas of dissatisfaction and complaints just because the language and customs are different."[20] Such admonitions reveal the frequency with which discrimination and even abuse awaited the Korean participants.

In Manchuria

The preceding programs, as well as most of the local seinendan activities of this period, involved careful monitoring of the participating youth, for both disciplinary and protective purposes. To achieve the overarching goals of raising the morale of farm youth, fostering their loyalty to the empire, and preparing them for mass mobilization, seinendan members had to be reasonably well fed, well dressed, and well behaved. Once they went outside the protective shell of such "training" and became real cogs of the land-grabbing, empire-sustaining machine, however, they encountered conditions that shook the fundamentals of the ideological and religious beliefs they had absorbed in the seinendan system.

One occasion where the line between training and active deployment disappeared, especially for Japanese members, was the armed agricultural settlement in northeast China through the three-year program of the Youth Colonization Volunteer Corps for Manchuria-Mongolia. Although this was nominally a training program, the participants, mostly between the ages of fourteen and twenty-two, often fell outside governmental protection in the demanding environment of training camps. Their lives as armed agricultural settlers rarely led to the realization of ethnic harmony or participation in an imperial brotherhood of East Asia, as officials claimed.

For many boys in the economically devastated Japanese countryside, the frontiers of Manchukuo, a symbol of Japan-led pan-Asian solidarity and the long-standing "lifeline" of the empire, stimulated their desire for adventure. Manchukuo itself was a young nation, and youthfulness appeared to be the most crucial quality for a new kind of state building. In fact, the main far-right organization advocating for revolutionary state building in northeast China in the late 1920s had been called the Manchurian Youth League (Manshū Seinen Renmei). Its founders considered themselves analogous to the "youth in the Meiji Restoration" and regarded their political activities primarily as a youth movement. The youthful Meiji Restoration had been a popular image in the publications of Tokutomi Sohō during the 1880s, but in the late 1920s it gained new momentum among right-wing activists.[21] The centralized, large-scale youth training of the population under the Concordia Association (Kyōwakai), the dictatorial party of Manchukuo that had evolved out of the Manchurian Youth League, gave Manchukuo's mass mobilization a fascist character.[22]

Once the Sino-Japanese War began in 1937, youth training centers were established across Manchukuo, offering dojo-style group living programs. Within a few years, 140 youth training centers housed twenty-five thousand trainees of Japanese, Korean, Chinese, and Mongolian origin. Other mass organizations developed around these centers: the boys' groups (*shōnendan*) for those between ten and fifteen years of age and the youth groups (seinendan) for those between sixteen and nineteen. Once they turned twenty years old, they were supposed to become regular members of the Concordia Association. In 1939, about seven hundred thousand young people in the boys' and youth groups, as well as in private and local youth groups, officially formed one national federation under the control of the Concordia Association.[23] Manchukuo's political leaders envisaged producing three hundred thousand youth leaders (graduates of youth training centers), five hundred thousand seinendan members, and thirteen million members of the Concordia Association by 1947 as a mass base of Concordia rule.[24]

The village youth from the Japanese countryside in the Youth Colonization Volunteer Corps for Manchuria-Mongolia, who amounted to over eighty-six thousand young men trained across ninety-four camps by 1945, were also integrated into the structure of Manchukuo's youth organization.[25] Despite the celebration of multiethnicity as the corps' underlying ideological premise, however, their exchanges with Manchukuo's other groups of young people were extremely limited. Nor did they have regular interactions with local Chinese residents, aside from their dependence on Chinese labor to build their barracks and acquire daily necessities.

Unfortunately for the youth corps, even before the camps were set up, the way in which the Japanese had forcibly acquired the land and houses from their former Chinese owners at well below market value had aroused widespread resentment among the locals.[26] The youth corps members themselves, who had no knowledge of the long-standing tension over the land and property, immediately understood how naive the slogan of ethnic harmony sounded in reality. "When I first arrived in Manchuria, Manchurian peasants gave us a peculiar look as if we had come to bully Manchurians," one member from Ibaraki prefecture wrote in his report. He did not hide his own antipathy toward them: "I was surprised at how extremely filthy they appeared and thought that the realization of 'Five Races under One Union' wouldn't be easy."[27] Many corps members continued to dislike the local peasants, and their lack of respect was sometimes reflected in criminal behavior, such as theft and assaults against their Chinese neighbors.[28] With such widespread hostility, even *Shin Manshū* (New Manchuria, later *Kaitaku*), the official journal of the youth corps, failed to create a facade of interethnic friendship. Occasional mentions of other ethnic groups only exacerbated stereotypes. Even in an essay titled "Friends in Manchuria," the author warned the reader that "I should perhaps rewrite the title as 'friends in Manchuria who could not become friends.'"[29]

Living as part of a military-like group in an alien, harsh environment surely affected the psychology and interpersonal dynamics of the youth corps. Manchuria's climate, particularly in the north, and the material conditions at the camps were far more severe than the youth had initially anticipated. One graduate recalled, "At thirty degrees below zero [Celsius], the body parts exposed to the air got instantly frozen and suffered from frostbite. ... Underneath the snowsuits were massively infested by lice." Food shortages were the most serious threat for teenage boys. "Those who did not steal food died of malnutrition. . . . We sometimes killed and ate dogs and cats." The youth's health deteriorated as they experienced dysentery and pneumonia. Depression caused by homesickness, which they called *tonkonbyō* (colonization sickness), disabled many younger members so severely that they could not work or even communicate with others. Bullying based on seniority was pervasive. Trainees questioned the official intention of teaching agricultural colonization. In one interview, a former participant recalled, "Teachers had no experience in large-scale farming . . . There was no one who could improve productivity . . . Five instructors for three hundred trainees cannot, from the beginning, provide monitoring and guidance. In short, such a plan was a total farce."[30]

These living conditions triggered participants' defensive instinct and led to the formation of small communities based on their home villages as vital survival units. "There was a certain wall even between villages [among the trainees]," one youth said later. "If there was some distance [between home villages], it produced conflict."[31] Not until the youth returned home did their experiences foster a group identity as graduates of the corps. While in the barracks, they had few interactions with other Japanese corps members in different locations, let alone their late-arriving Korean counterparts. There was no chance to nurture a shared sense of imperial brotherhood in this program. Ironically for the ideals of Manchukuo, their group consciousness was directed toward their home villages instead.

Life as Soldiers

Becoming a soldier in the Japanese military was a decisive moment when mobilized young men moved beyond the training stage and experienced the end result of pursuing a career as model rural youth. The military experience crucially altered their life narratives. For colonial youth in remote villages, as discussed in chapters 6 and 8, becoming a volunteer soldier was the most prestigious achievement possible. But what awaited these select youth were the cruel and often irrational treatments of soldiers, routinized violence based on seniority, day-to-day ethnic discrimination, disease, fatigue, starvation, and death at battlefronts in extreme climates. Joining the Japanese army as volunteer soldiers landed these youth in a massive paradox of self-achievement and exploitation.

In a large and complex organization like the military, with its operations spread throughout Asia and the Pacific, the personal experiences and memories of individual soldiers varied significantly. According to the Japanese government's records, 4,525 Taiwanese and 19,830 Koreans had become volunteer soldiers by the end of the war.[32] When the many other forms of mobilization are included, an estimated 207,183 Taiwanese men and 377,404 Korean men were deployed (as soldiers and civilian military employees in the army and navy) by the war's end. Among the 257,404 Korean men in the army, 58.7% remained in Japan and Korea, 30% were deployed in China and Manchuria, and about 6.7% joined the Japanese forces in Southeast Asia and on islands in the Pacific.[33] We do not have a rich pool of detailed accounts from colonial soldiers, despite the extensive efforts by scholars to capture individual memories. Nonetheless, those available confirm that soldiers faced a very different life from the dynamic of youth training.

Many of their reflections start with the question of why they had applied to become volunteer soldiers. This is in fact one of the most challenging areas of memory, destabilized by the problem of determining in retrospect the degree of their own decision-making agency.[34] After their experiences in the army, ex-soldiers generally concluded that volunteering had not been an ideal option. Many attempted to explain the external factors that inhibited their capacity to make the right decision. The most commonly mentioned factor but also the most difficult one to articulate was the social atmosphere, including ideological indoctrination. One interviewee stated, "I was willing to do many things without questioning because I had received Japanization education since I was small. Because I was born after the annexation of Korea, I had no understanding that the Japanese were forcibly ruling our nation. . . . I thought only that we would fight for the peace of Asian peoples. I intended to fight in accordance with the slogan of the 'Japan–Korea Unified Body.'" As another described it, "There was no reason not to follow the instruction because I was repeatedly told that joining and dying in the Greater East Asia War would bring peace to Asia since before I turned twenty."[35] Yet another reflected, "It is natural for those [born in the late 1930s onward] to say 'Japan is an enemy,' but we, who lived through the colonial period, are different. We had completely become imperial subjects."[36]

The presence of schoolteachers was significant in creating the social pressure: "We thought teachers were like gods. We said 'yes, yes' to everything [they said]."[37] At the same time, their descriptions of the social atmosphere included the positive image attached to volunteer soldiers. Volunteer soldiers were celebrated as "like heroes of the village" and received special treatment from the village office and the police. Children often dreamed of becoming one someday when they saw volunteer soldiers playing a trumpet at the top of a hill.[38] These aspects made it difficult for them to separate their own desires from the social pressure. The ex-soldiers' memoirs and interviews reflect bitter postwar judgments, but their descriptions of the social atmosphere tell us that the powerful dynamic was operating in wartime villages that drove young people to join volunteer soldier programs, as shown in previous chapters.

Some of the ex-soldiers recognized their decision to volunteer as the most optimal choice among few practical alternatives. As one former soldier recalled, "The police and the village head said, 'Go to the volunteer soldier program,' and tried to persuade me almost every day. . . . They promised good arrangements for my family too, so I considered it as employment. In retrospect, I was deceived. I didn't want to go because I might die in the military. But because we were so poor, I [applied out of the feeling of] 'God damn, [I don't care] whether I live or die!'"[39] Another survivor wrote, "I graduated from elementary school in the midst of social pressure [to volunteer]. I could not continue higher education because of financial difficulty, and there was no decent employment for Koreans during the war. But it was too depressing to do totally devastated colonial agriculture. I didn't know what to do with my youthful energy, and out of desperation, I could not resist the pressure and applied."[40] Many other interviews indicate that

the associated career prospects provided a powerful material and psychological incentive. "I submitted the volunteer soldier application after I was told that
I could become a clerk at the county office, which inspired my heart.... [When my
application was accepted], I was extremely thrilled, thinking that I could finally
become a true Japanese, partly because I had been attracted to the sophisticated
look of the military uniform of Japanese soldiers."[41] Both young people and local
officials often viewed applying as a self-evident necessity for model rural youth.
The logic of persuasion—"because you are the model youth of the village, you
of all people must apply"—was used as a compliment and a form of pressure at
the same time, much as academically gifted students today are pushed to apply
to the most competitive schools.[42]

Korean and Taiwanese youth who joined the Japanese troops discovered
that ethnic discrimination was rampant. Unlike Japanese conscripts, colonial
soldiers did not form their own units according to their origins. Instead, they
were individually incorporated into Japanese-dominated platoons. For most of
the colonial volunteer soldiers, this was their first experience of living within
a genuinely Japanese social structure, and most of the Japanese soldiers had
never previously interacted with colonial youth. Violence and bullying prevailed in daily life, perpetuating the dual rule of ethnic hierarchy and seniority.
By 1943, the fear that day-to-day discrimination might turn Korean volunteer
soldiers against the empire had grown so great that top army officials circulated a detailed warning within the army. They banned the use of a derogatory phrase (*senjin*) for Koreans, raised awareness about their linguistic barriers
and cultural differences, and ordered all troops to "absolutely avoid prejudicial
hatred," and to treat Korean soldiers with "the heart of a loving father."[43] This
lengthy warning, in addition to a number of official reports on the situations
of colonial volunteer soldiers, reveals the semi-institutionalized nature of ethnic discrimination to the extent that it was threatening to military discipline.
Individual accounts also attest to its pervasiveness. The orders from above had
little impact on the well-established culture among soldiers. In place of senjin,
regular phrases such as *Chōsenjin* (Korean person) and *hantō* (the peninsula)
began to be used in derogatory fashion.[44] Similarly, the Japanese soldiers often
described the Taiwanese with a term used to despise Chinese people, *chankoro*.[45]
One Taiwanese soldier recalled that discrimination against Koreans was harsher,
although ethnic prejudice against Taiwanese soldiers was also normal.[46] Many
Korean soldiers deserted their camps; some committed suicide.[47]

The extant stories do cover the full spectrum from integration to alienation
of colonial soldiers. Two factors had a huge impact on colonial soldiers' fate:
sheer luck and his ability to speak Japanese fluently. Sometimes, especially if
they had a supportive superior, they could be confident that they would receive

fair treatment. For instance, some Taiwanese soldiers remembered the protection provided by an exceptionally generous Japanese superior.[48] Similarly, some former Korean soldiers stated that they did not personally experience ethnic prejudice. One interviewee noted, "No one could escape violence in the Japanese military. Because I was poor at home, I didn't consider [life in the Japanese army] particularly tough.... [Even when charged as a war criminal by the Allies] I didn't feel any differently [because of my Korean origin]. I never felt discrimination in the military. I worked really hard [to avoid discrimination] as well."[49]

Since the quality of the superior to which one was assigned depended on luck, mastery of the Japanese language was a more reliable predictor of a colonial soldier's future. Fluent speakers of Japanese tremendously improved their situations because they could hide their Korean or Taiwanese ethnicity under a tacit policy of "don't ask, don't tell."[50] Conversely, less-educated conscripts had greater difficulty in the Japanese army. Former Korean soldiers who grew up in the metropole observed that "those [conscripts] coming from the peninsula were particularly miserable."[51] The army eagerly integrated Koreans who willingly behaved as ideal Japanese soldiers, promoting them to higher ranks. As a consequence, the gap in experiences and perceptions between those fluent in Japanese and the majority of conscripts who remained at the lowest strata grew huge.[52] The differential treatments of Korean soldiers based on their language abilities and self-assimilation into the Japanese social order manifested the operations of what Takashi Fujitani calls "polite racism"—the kind that guided the self-reflexive subjects toward the normative choice of becoming ideal imperial subjects.[53] At the same time, however, those promoted still faced frequent incidences of "vulgar racism," a categorical and static characterization that left no possibility of assimilation, despite their proven loyalty and excellent performances.[54]

The most noticeable change in the consciousness of colonial youth, although probably not a predictable one before they joined the military, was the rapid formation of ethnic pride. During youth training, the trainees developed a self-identification based on local social divides, whether it was rural as opposed to urban, Xinzhu youth rather than Taipei youth, elementary school graduates versus highly educated youth, or young pillars in contrast to the old generations. In the army, on the other hand, they experienced a direct juxtaposition of their Korean or Taiwanese selves and Japanese others. Being part of a minority group often causes strong group bonds to develop, and daily discrimination ignited aggressive antagonism against the ethnically Japanese in many cases. This ethnic pride was expressed in a convoluted way, however. In many people's accounts, Korean and Taiwanese soldiers aspired to become "truer Japanese" and "more ideal Japanese" than regular Japanese soldiers. Not at all a sign of the ultimate success of Japanization as it sounds, it was an expression of ethnic rivalry, as the colonial youth viewed "becoming ideal Japanese" as a way to prove their superiority over their Japanese counterparts.[55] Memoirs of Korean soldiers reveal the paradoxical feeling of outdoing the Japanese by being superior Japanese. One wrote, "My motto was to be exemplary for other soldiers. I was obsessed with the idea, 'I shall not lose to Japanese people.'"[56] Another Korean survivor wrote that he felt more competitive when facing discrimination than he was treated well. "It was a strange feeling," he explained, but he was convinced that "if I have to [serve the military], I should do it extremely well," because he viewed success in the military as a weapon against those who saw him through prejudiced eyes.[57]

The development of ethnic pride through living among Japanese people, as well as the desire to excel in the imperial system to prove their superiority, was exactly what upper-class colonial youth had been experiencing since the early 1920s. In Japanese-dominated institutions of higher education and bureaucracy, they were largely detached from the social divides that village youth felt keenly; instead they faced the binary of colonized and colonizer. Compared with rural populations, educated youth had more divisive reactions to Japan's assimilationist rule, some engaging in anticolonial activism and others eagerly integrating themselves into Japanese intellectual circles as a way to overcome the ethnic boundary. Colonial volunteer soldiers repeated that experience of binary division in the military; the more interactions with the Japanese they had in their cohort, the more frustrated they became, especially knowing that they were a select few from their own society.

On the front lines, where survival was extremely difficult, Korean, Taiwanese and Japanese soldiers sometimes developed an esprit de corps out of their horrific experiences of starvation, disease, and the psychological suffering they endured due to abandoning their weakening comrades.[58] But in many instances, the lack of mutual trust between Korean soldiers and Japanese superiors was exacerbated. Memoirs of Korean soldiers who fought in the jungles of New Guinea show both the disappearance of ethnic boundaries and increasing tension, depending on the situation. In the Japanese army, the presence of Korean volunteer soldiers grew larger as the torturous war of attrition continued. Many observed that Korean soldiers survived better: "Korean volunteer soldiers were more robust and stronger, so they never collapsed. [We were all] young, around twenty years old, and could find and eat any food. . . . [Korean] volunteers survived diarrhea well, but Japanese soldiers died quickly because of their especially weak intestines."[59] Being physically fit model rural youth, as opposed to urban, well-educated, and fragile Japanese youth, reappeared as an advantage: "The first to die were intellectuals among first-year soldiers. Those who had lived a luxurious life had no immunity. . . . Korean soldiers, except by bullets of the enemy, did not die easily."[60] In one squadron, "the final survivors were only thirty people, of whom 40% were

Korean volunteers."[61] The Korean soldiers used codes to communicate with and cared for each other: "Japanese officers gave suspicious looks, saying that Koreans tend to unite, but at the final stage, we had no other choice but to unite." The increasing reliance on Korean volunteers made Japanese superiors vulnerable. "Even with the order of collective suicide, there was no reason for us to kill ourselves. Compared to Japanese soldiers, volunteer soldiers still retained physical strength and the power to fight, so [Japanese superiors] could not ignore us."[62] When the Allied troops scattered leaflets that stated, "Korean volunteer soldiers, surrender to the U.S. military. Your safety is guaranteed," many Japanese officers were shaken by the possibility that their Korean soldiers would abandon them.[63]

August 15, 1945

The war claimed an enormous number of casualties. According to the Japanese records, approximately 2.4 million Japanese soldiers and civilian military employees died in overseas battles. So did 30,304 Taiwanese and 22,345 Korean soldiers and employees.[64] Those who lived to see August 15, 1945 had various reactions to Japan's defeat, which marked not only the end of the war but also of an empire. In retrospect, it was bound to come any day. But for many colonial soldiers, the news came as a shock.

For colonial youth who had spent their formative years in Japanese youth training and the military, liberation was not a straightforward concept. Isolated from the boiling celebrations that spread immediately throughout the cities and villages of Korea and Taiwan, colonial soldiers in deployment processed the fact of Japan's defeat amid their Japanese cohort. Kim Ki-bong, a young Korean volunteer pilot in training in Ōita prefecture, considered August 15 an unforgettable turning point in his life. Listening to the emperor's announcement of Japan's unconditional surrender to the Allies on a cheap radio, he could pick up only a few words and had no clue as to what the broadcast meant. The group of Japanese students—fifteen and sixteen years old like Kim himself—still believed in Japan's eventual victory and denied the news. Kim had also "vaguely thought that there would be battles on the homeland" before the end of the war. The sudden end was hard to swallow and felt anticlimactic. In his memoir, Kim recalled that he shared with Japanese trainees a feeling of dismay at the "unpredictably early surrender," but "from there, our subjective thoughts diverged in separate directions." Kim's decision to become a pilot had been grown out of his convoluted determination to "be truer Japanese" as a means to prove his self-worth. The knot of ethnic pride and subjugation was finally untied when he could realistically imagine the future of an independent Korea: "First, I was relieved by my liberation from a sure death, and second, the joy of achieving independence, an earnest desire of the Korean people, gradually occurred to me."[65] This shift from shock and dismay to hope was common among colonial soldiers. Another Korean volunteer soldier stationed in Hokkaidō has also reflected, "I was convinced that, if Japan lost, I would not be able to go home alive. But suddenly the situation changed and [the troop was] dissolved. I was extremely lonely. I did not really understand for what I lived and I fought for. . . . The liberation of August 15 was amazing. [It brought] a hope that I could live as a true human being from then on . . . The passion to do truly worthy work for my own people occurred to me."[66]

The colonial soldiers were stuck with the Japanese troops at least for the next few days while all beliefs, assumptions, and hierarchies were turned upside down. The position of the volunteer soldier—once their proudest achievement as model rural youth—no longer had any meaning, and, in fact, the former colonizer's military was the strangest place where they could be. The Japanese who had enjoyed superiority over their colonial counterparts fell into the most vulnerable position. In Kim Ki-bong's pilot training school, sons of the Japanese settlers in the outer territories, who, "generally speaking, held a greater sense of prejudice and hatred toward us Koreans and Chinese than the boys from mainland Japan did," went into a panic. They had suddenly lost their homes, their status, and the basis of their lives.[67]

The switch between superiority and vulnerability was more dramatic for soldiers stationed in Seoul. O Rim-jun, a Korean volunteer soldier who had grown up in Japan, experienced the end of the war in Seoul as part of the forces preparing for a possible invasion by the Soviets and Americans. Compared with standard colonial volunteers who had a home in Korea and whose attention shifted from war and Japanization to Korea's independent future, O could not easily reconcile his "half-Japanese" self-identification, especially in the environment of the liberated colonial capital. During the war, his fluent Japanese had helped him merge into the Japanese cohort and launch a promising career. But on August 15, his internal coherence was shattered. He felt lost, with "a shock of being hit in the brain," when, all of a sudden, the Korean T'aegŭkki (national flag) flooded the city. While looking at Korean people overloaded on trucks and exhilaratingly shouting, "*Manse, manse!*" (Long live) to celebrate the liberation, O was still in his Japanese army uniform, holding a gun, being ready to fire on the masses if ordered to do so. His sense of guilt for being on the side of the colonizer and his lack of Korean language comprehension became a new source of his self-shame. In his memoir, he described the "collapse of a half-Japanese soul," borrowing the words of a Korean soldier charged with war crimes: "For Japanese, however much criticized and condemned, it is possible to have some consolation, or pride, about having sacrificed themselves and fought for the mother nation, but we Koreans did not even have that consolation. Rather, trying to think in that way itself triggers nothing but a burning remorse."[68]

While O's subjectivity suffered in the retreating colonizer's troops, Muramatsu Takeshi, a Japanese soldier who had grown up in Korea, also happened to be in Seoul on August 15 and experienced the overturning of social positions in the midst of the Korean celebration. As he was heading home on the train, several Korean soldiers mistook him for a compatriot and started a conversation with him. "I instinctively judged that I must hide my Japanese nationality," Muramatsu wrote in his memoir. In polite, military-style Japanese, the soldiers looked at the badges on his uniform and asked him: "You are a rank candidate, sir. Would you tell us what we should do from now on after going home? I want military superiors like you to give us directions on how to build a national military." He answered, "Although we have lost our weapons, we have our independence. We have the national flag. . . . Let's go home and meet our people in our home villages. The great elderly of our villages will guide us."[69] To survive the major reversal of his imperial position, Murakami now had to fake his ethnicity and voice the Korean ethnic pride symbolized by older generations, who had been despised as a hindrance to colonial Korea's future just a few days earlier.

The failure to build an actual community of model rural youth in pan-imperial programs clarifies what the Japanese "nation-empire" really was. It was an aspiration rather than a fact; a driving force, not an end result; an illusion and an assumption. Local dynamics that fostered youth's eagerness to embrace the national–imperial ideology notwithstanding, the empire lacked the power to realize the promise of the integration of select youth even for propaganda purposes. Perhaps some of the alienating effects of programs that brought youth to a new environment were inevitable. More critically, however, widespread ethnic prejudice failed most colonial youth. Behind the multiple slogans of the emperor-centered multiethnic nation, pan-Asian solidarity, and ethnic harmony, most of Japanese society unsympathetically rejected those who lacked perfect command of the Japanese language and customs.

But failure in one aspect hints at tremendous success in another. Considering the harsh environments of some of these programs, the fact that many of the mobilized youth still dutifully followed imperial directives demonstrates the powerful foundation that youth training had constructed. This foundation was most saliently exhibited by how Taiwanese and Korean volunteer soldiers expressed their new sense of ethnic pride. Despite their isolation from one another, so many of them aspired to "become truer Japanese" as a way to prove their ethnic group's superiority over ordinary Japanese soldiers. The metric of Japaneseness was firmly internalized by these youth through the dynamics of the social mobility complex before they joined the Japanese military. That metric continued to determine their method of surmounting obstacles even in the face of promise-breaching ethnic discrimination. Because of these complicated and convoluted perceptions of ethnic integration and segregation that appear in youth's expressions, a cursory look at their memoirs and interviews confuses the reader. Only through an investigation of how model rural youth had been produced does the psychology of volunteer soldiers become at least partially interpretable.

The issue of colonial soldiers has left some of the deepest historical scars in postwar East Asia. Japan's defeat created a tragic turn of life for many colonial soldiers and laborers. In Manchuria, thousands of Koreans, along with Japanese, were captured by the Soviet army and subjected to forced labor for years. In China and across Southeast Asia, about three hundred Taiwanese and Korean soldiers and civilian military employees were charged as Class B and C war criminals in postwar trials conducted by the Allies. Those who managed to return home suffered difficult consequences as well. Because all Koreans and Taiwanese automatically lost their Japanese nationality in the postwar international arrangement, the former colonial soldiers could not participate in the pension system that the Japanese government offered to Japanese ex-soldiers and their families. Their salary deposits in the Japanese postal system virtually vanished.[70] Even after the Japanese government passed a law to redress the issue with former Taiwanese soldiers in 1987, it offered only approximately two million yen (about eighteen thousand U.S. dollars) to those who had been severely injured and to bereaved families, a trivial amount of compensation for their grave sacrifice.[71] Another fifteen years passed before their South Korean counterparts received a similarly small amount of compensation.[72] But the inadequacy of Japan's financial and legal settlements with former "young pillars of the empire" constitutes only one dimension of the issue. These colonial youth's relationships with the empire were too complicated and intense to be articulated in legal terms. Their decolonization was greatly hindered because their postcolonial sentiments lost an outlet and an audience once postwar political turmoil set in.

EPILOGUE

Back in Villages

What happened to many village youth, and particularly the individuals featured in this book—Katō Einojō, Xu Chongfa, Huang Yuanxing, and Kim Yŏng-han— once the war was over? In the preceding decade or two, their lives had evolved around the rise of rural youth and, consequently, nation-empire building. They had obtained the ability, the opportunity, and the emotional foundation with which to challenge the establishment in their immediate social surroundings by incorporating the prose of Japanese agrarian nationalism. During the war, their careers as rural youth helped to fuel the engine of Japan's mobilization machine. Precisely because of their deep association with the imperial war effort—even though they lacked a decisively life-changing experience as soldiers deployed on the battlefield—the end of the empire brought about an equally dramatic turning point in their lives. New regimes hurriedly attempted to scrap previous beliefs and values. New nationalisms arose. Where did the Japanese Empire's model rural youth find their place?

To us, as we read their stories many decades later, the issue of continuity and rupture across the year 1945 is an intriguing one. In particular, the question of how we identify the colonial legacy in postwar Taiwan and Korea is highly political in nature. To those who lived through this period, however, continuity was a given, everyday condition—one's life can only continue on—within which political ruptures transpired. They had no choice but to bring their whole baggage of consciousness and past experiences they had acquired into the new era. Does this mean that many of their subsequent life decisions should be considered a colonial legacy? Although continuity is certainly a key factor in tracing their immediate postwar experiences, I tend to have doubts about placing a heavy emphasis on a supposed colonial legacy. Just as "imperial control" does not fully capture the nature of their youth training under Japanese rule, neither does the idea of colonial legacy suitably encapsulate their diverse thoughts and experiences in its aftermath.

Japan

Through the final stage of the war and its aftermath, the local seinendan showed astonishing resilience. The village-level seinendan suffered from the sharp decline of young populations, and many halted their activities, but the institutions themselves survived the war. This was despite the dissolution of the national body, the Greater Japan Seishōnendan, two months prior to the war's end. While receiving the government direction to expand the *gakutotai* (student corps) to further centralize youth mobilization, seinendan leaders kept the local seinendan intact. Even Japan's surrender in August 1945 had little impact on its basic format at the village level. As of the end of August 1945, Miyagi prefecture was still appointing youth school teachers and seinendan leaders.[1]

On September 25, the Japanese government, before the American Occupation bureaucrats under the Supreme Commander for the Allied Powers (SCAP) determined the policy direction of postwar education, issued a memo to encourage the regathering of village youth. "As the war ended, the gakutotai were dissolved, and male and female youth were left unorganized in their social life," it stated, adding, "New youth groups should get rid of the so-called government-manufactured and militaristic colors of the previous time and aim to develop the characteristics of local groups (*kyōdoteki dantai*)."[2] Although the memo emphasized "spontaneous development" and "youth's initiatives," it also contained a long list of articles stipulating the appropriate age range, required qualifications for group leaders, and so on. As Sheldon Garon observes, many methods of kyōka survived through the regime change of the postwar period. Social education, in which the seinendan had played a major part, reemerged as the centerpiece of efforts to promote "national morality" as early as October 1945.[3]

The SCAP attempted to minimize government involvement in civil society in postwar Japan, but American bureaucrats were not unified in their reactions to the revival of the seinendan. In the postwar constitution, drafted by SCAP staff and enacted by the Japanese parliament in 1946, Article 89 barred the government from financially assisting "charitable, educational, or benevolent enterprises not under the control of public authority." The Social Education

Law (1949) prohibited even local governments from taking a leadership role in social education.[4] In a somewhat contradictory action, however, officials in the Civil Information and Educational Section (CIE) under the SCAP earnestly supported the reemergence of local and national seinendan. CIE officials viewed the local seinendan as equivalent to recreational youth clubs that were popular in the United States. The diary of one seinendan leader in Fussa city, Tokyo, recorded how delighted CIE officials appeared to be when they saw the activities of his local seinendan, such as reading books, debating, singing songs, and practicing dance. That positive attitude of American officers relieved the youth. The diarist noted, "I shook hands with foreigners twice. Alas, how [different] are the current feelings from those at the end of the war! I had never ever imagined shaking hands with them. The antagonism that had been hiding in the bottom of my chest seems to have been blown away at once. Now it feels like I can [move toward] democratization."[5]

The CIE endorsed the prefectural and national networks, too. Russell L. Durgin, a missionary who had lived in Japan for thirty years while presiding over the Japanese YMCA, served the CIE as officer for youth organization and student activities and became a trusted adviser to the postwar Japan Youth Center.[6] Postwar seinendan leaders depicted Tazawa Yoshiharu, the "father of the seinendan," as a type of a democratic leader who had resisted the militarization of the seinendan in prewar years, and the CIE reinforced that image.[7] Durgin's successor, Donald Marsh Typer, in a speech to officials of the Japan Youth Center, called on them to "revive the Tazawa spirit!" Typer praised the continuity of the Japan Youth Center, reflecting on its history of "having been built by volunteer work and donations of more than a million members" and defining the sole reason for its existence as "to continuously serve youth in Japan even today."[8] Government involvement in organizing other civic groups also expanded. The CIE established and supervised the Boy Scouts, Girl Scouts, YMCA, YWCA, and 4-H Club. Under their auspices, in 1951, seinendan leaders established a new national body, the Japan Seinendan Convention (Nihon Seinendan Kyōgikai). In the same year, the CIE created a communication network including all youth organizations, through which it promoted recreational clubs, panel discussions, and debates, implementing American theories of "group work."[9]

American-style activities, despite the eagerness of the leaders in Tokyo to incorporate them, never became deeply rooted among young people in the countryside. Among the different types of youth organizations established in this period, the seinendan continued to be the core of youth activities in villages.[10] Rather than indicating youth's resistance to the introduction of liberal democracy, this result underscores the fact that the local seinendan reemerged out of grassroots initiatives, not in response to any instructions from Tokyo or the Occupation forces. The end of the war and the empire brought about a major shift in the social environments of villages. One immediate change was that young people who had left their homes as industrial workers, colonial settlers, and soldiers came back. In some villages, these youth gathered privately every night to share their wartime experiences, leading to the re-formation of a village seinendan. In other places, a few people took the initiative to formally resume seinendan activities.[11] Many started their seinendan as night study groups.[12] With the demobilization of the army reservist groups, gakutotai, and neighborhood associations, as well as the virtual end of youth schools and other dojos, they returned to gathering organically to heal their wartime traumas.

Indeed, young people were processing complex feelings about the new era. They reacted emotionally to the humiliation experienced by ex-soldiers in the immediate postwar society. Many of youth in the postwar seinendan had themselves been repatriated from the battlefield and were subject to a public discourse that viewed them as collaborators with those practicing militarism or as useless, unemployed, and violent criminals harming peace and democracy. "Once I came home, I received chilling looks as a returnee," one essay in a seinendan newsletter in Nagano read, "and endured the sadness of seeing my comrades falling into crimes one by one in the face of hostile treatments!"[13] The rage against people who had mobilized youth for war and then reversed their attitude after the war often came out in their writings. One returnee wrote, "While denying the dignity of those who died in battles and considering it as someone else's business, they say cheerful things like democracy and the construction of a new Japan. I cannot trust such things at all." But at the same time, as the historian Kitagawa Kenzō argues, the self-reflection and critical thinking exhibited by young people of this period went beyond bitter resentment. Another young man wrote, "More than holding a grudge against 'those who deceived me' . . . I had a stronger feeling of doubt about 'myself, who had been deceived.'"[14] One educator in Nagano stated in 1948, "Because they felt the war more deeply and closely than anyone else, [young people] trust only what they can see with their own eyes, and what they can do with their own hands."[15]

The local seinendan, restricted to a certain generation and protected from outside authorities, provided a safe haven for these young men, who desperately needed to interact with peers who shared similar experiences and feelings. While functioning as a site of confession and commiseration, many seinendan groups focused on tangible projects that kept the members away from political debates. Most notably, they devoted much effort to organizing performance events (engeikai) of music, dance, and manzai comedy shows.[16] The engeikai became a widely seen phenomenon in villages and cities across the nation. The performances, however, included songs popular during the war, as if youth

were attempting to forget about the reality of the defeat, provide a new cathar-
sis to replace wartime heroism, and express the sense of freedom acquired only
through the end of the wartime regime, all at the same time.

Seinendan youth soon returned to many other old forms of activities. They
organized volunteer work for their communities, set up study groups, gave
awards to model youth, promoted agricultural experiments, and held speech
contests, but they peppered these activities with postwar slogans of liberalism
and democracy. In the records left by Katō Einojō, whose story we examined
in chapters 2 and 3, both a big rupture and the underlying continuity between
prewar and postwar village life are apparent. Katō Einojō, as a sōnendan leader
in Shida county, experienced the hardest time of his life during this period. He
was purged from official positions. He let go of most of the land of his family's
heritage to tenant farmers and fought a government committee in court regarding his ownership of the remaining land. The Katō family no longer enjoyed the
status of major landholders in the village, and their wealth shrank further as
Katō Einojō launched new businesses that failed.[17] At the same time, the village
as a whole continued to embrace agrarianism as the main guiding principle for
the postwar period.[18] In May 1946, the Shida county seinendan started the Ōsaki
Farmers' College (Ōsaki Nōmin Daigaku), which offered training in agronomy,
farm management, and rural cultural improvement to young pillars of the Ōsaki
region (including Shida). It declared that it would "renew our culture to follow
the completely new era." And yet its slogans, such as "The culture of farm villages
leads to Japanese culture, and its progress leads to national progress," recycled the
phrases of prewar agrarianism. The continuity of agrarian ideals in society meant
that Katō did not entirely lose his political capital. He was invited to participate
in the lectures and events of the Ōsaki Farmers' College to unofficially supervise
village youth training.[19] With the end of the purge in 1951, he was elected to a
seat in the Ōsaki city council the following year and quickly rehabilitated his life
narrative of being a devoted local leader.[20]

Despite the grassroots initiatives that revived the village seinendan, official
support from government staff was still valuable to them. Sasaki Wakuri, the
head of Miyagi's social education section, received numerous requests from village seinendan groups to attend their ceremonies, dispatch a lecturer to their
night study groups, and provide official endorsement of their projects.[21] In fact,
the familiar symbiosis of the local seinendan and state authorities sometimes
grew too strong and alarmed observers. Behind their continuous search for the
appropriate relationship between village youth and the government, a concern
about remilitarization rose in many people's minds. One can observe the widespread concern in a heated debate over the issue of youth classes (seinen gakkyū),
another program initiated locally by young villagers to replace wartime youth

schools. Since their initiation in 1947 by the seinendan in Yamagata prefecture, youth classes had been adopted across the Tōhoku region. The idea spread and led to a national movement, with 13,628 classes and 892,087 students as of 1952.[22] When the Ministry of Education planned to set up legal regulations and financial aid for youth classes, however, the proposal aroused opposition among seinendan members as well as activists.[23] Miyahara Seiichi, a professor at the University of Tokyo and one of the firmest voices against the government plan, argued, "Youth classes under city, town, and village administration have become thought-guiding institutions. They have become a framework for rearmament. There remains none of the spontaneity we saw in the early youth classes."[24] The government's regulations of youth schools were nonetheless put in place in 1953.

Large-scale seinendan activities continued to stir fears of remilitarization. Some of the issues that the seinendan attempted to tackle required bureaucratic planning. The massive unemployment in rural villages was one such issue. In 1951, for example, a column in *Asahi shinbun* discussed two sets of statistics, one on the sharp increase in unemployment in villages and the other on the youth-heavy demographics of rural populations ("youth" referred to those between age fifteen and twenty-five). Calling it the "second-and-third-son problem," the author argued that "in the prewar era, [these youth] could pursue a route to be military officers, but they no longer have that option. There were so many applications to the National Police Reserve. Even if they want to, they have no opportunity outside their villages."[25] In response to the rural unemployment problem, the Japan Seinendan Convention launched the Youth Movement for Industrial Development (Sangyō Kaihatsu Seinen Undō) in the same year, obtained a substantial budget through the Ministry of Agriculture and Forestry in the following year, and encouraged youth to cultivate new land and learn new farming technologies. The Japan Seinendan Convention claimed that the movement was modeled after the Civilian Conservation Corps of the American New Deal, but it received criticisms because the program reminded the public of the volunteer labor corps and the youth corps dispatched to Manchuria during wartime.[26]

Thus the biggest challenge for both leaders and local members of the postwar seinendan was to separate themselves from the militaristic past while maintaining continuity in institutions, agrarian values, and local fraternity. Almost all news reports about the seinendan evaluated the degree to which they departed from their prewar form. Observers offered little discussion or consensus on what "prewar form" meant, however, and they inconsistently pointed to different aspects. Some newspapers criticized the apparent revival of excessive bureaucratic control over the seinendan, while characterizing village youth as a democratic force that would resist top-down control.[27] Other observers criticized the persistent "feudalistic character and customs" of seinendan instructions and village society while, again, defining young people as progressive agents of reform.[28] Still others viewed the youth themselves as "undemocratic, old-fashioned, and retrogressive." A seinendan member in Miyagi discussed how closely the village seinendan reflected the feudalistic characteristics of village society and how nostalgic seinendan leaders remained "for their lost imperialistic authority."[29] There was also a wide gap between the print media, which situated the seinendan within the postwar movement to spread the value of liberal democracy, and the local communities, which expected more continuity in youth's role. "Local people's ideas about the seinendan, generally speaking, are generated based on the seinendan activities of the old era," one seinendan member in Miyagi reported after conducting a survey in 1958. "Many people say that the previous seinendan were better" because "they were orderly and disciplined."[30]

In sum, the lack of consensus on what had gone wrong in the pre-1945 period created confusing interpretations of the characteristics of village youth, the new role of the seinendan, and the definition of "the establishment" in postwar society. Young people's initiative (*jushusei*) was loudly propagated in every possible venue, but behind that emphasis lay constant negotiations between the departure from and continuity with the past.

It was also through the seinendan that village youth erased their previous colonial links. Even though many of them had been living in Japan's previous outer territories, any reference to the former colonies was completely dropped from their printed discussions, let alone any reflection on their experiences in the colonies as imperial settlers. But as in the prewar period, the seinendan played an important role in demarcating the imagined national contours, now by excluding the outer territories and asserting Okinawa's inclusion. The seinendan stood at the forefront in the long-term movement calling for the return of Okinawa from the American Occupation forces, whereas the issue of former colonial soldiers never captured their attention. After all, youthful initiatives appeared to be conveniently compatible with Japan's new political agenda.

Taiwan

The immediate postwar period brought political turmoil to Taiwan, which was beyond the imagination of Japanese youth even if they had cared about the former colonial society. As in the Japanese countryside, Taiwanese youth organized themselves in preparation for the transition, but they were soon to be subjected to a new authoritarian rule, which also frantically attempted to mobilize young people and construct a Chinese national identity. Youth activism was split along political lines, and many young people in a suddenly chaotic social order survived by swimming through repoliticization programs. Thanks to increasingly open discussion about the 228 Incident and Guomindang (GMD) authoritarianism in the past two decades, we can obtain more information about the social upheavals created by postcolonial and neocolonial politics.

Xu Chongfa, the instructor at the Xinzhu youth training institute discussed in chapter 6, was conducting an inspection visit at a small youth training unit on the day of Japan's surrender. Since the facilities of the Xinzhu youth training institute were heavily bombed, youth training had been conducted more locally and in smaller groups since early 1945. Xu missed the broadcast of Emperor Hirohito's message but learned the news in the evening when he returned home. "The world before me turned completely dark when I thought about what on earth we should do and what Taiwan would become," he wrote three weeks later in a letter to his former students.[31] While mentally processing the end of an era during these three weeks, Xu received a few letters from his former students, who felt equally at a loss. He decided to apologize to them in his letter: "I encouraged you arrogantly, saying, 'Work hard, strenuously, powerfully, attack the Americans and British hard, and win, win over the battles in East Asia!' But it all became a lie. I am painfully ashamed. But a trivial person like me could only tell you what I read and memorize in magazines and books—I told you only what I believed and felt, yes, exactly! Please do not think 'what the hell, that teacher only told us lies.' Forgive me!!"[32]

Immersed in a sea of remorse, all Xu could do was, yet again, to repeat the announcement by the Japanese authorities, appreciating the emperor's tough decision and encouraging the Taiwanese people to calmly accept the end of the war and to become a bridge between China and Japan in the future. Before I could ask, Xu Chongfa explained to me the rationale behind the Japanese surrender, saying that "after the atomic bombs, because the emperor did not want to sacrifice more lives, he made a brave decision for us."[33] He shared the same narrative with many Japanese people of the same generation, strongly influenced by the discourse that the Japanese rulers created at the time of the defeat.

Huang Yuanxing, Xu's student, also featured in chapter 6, was more reserved in giving his impressions of Japan's surrender. He was serving his conscription duty in Taizhong and did not hear the news of the defeat immediately either. "At the army camp in Taizhong, people were talking about it in Minnan [Holo] Chinese, so I did not understand what they were talking about. I learned the news the following day."[34] Huang came back to Beipu despite the limited transportation available, "looking like a remnant of a defeated army," although he had not left Taiwan to face enemies on real battlefields.[35] With few news sources, some people in remote villages still did not realize, a month later, that the war had ended.[36]

But the war was over, and the colonizers were leaving. Aside from emotional farewells and personal dramas occurring between Taiwanese and Japanese residents, people were generally elated about the end of colonial rule. "There was no reason to worry about social order," one villager in Xinzhu remembered, "since we were so happy to go back to China."[37] Wu Zhuoliu, a well-known Taiwanese author, described people's feelings during the few months before the Chinese rulers arrived in October 1945: "They maintained the peace impeccably in the political vacuum. . . . The psychology of Taiwanese people was a sort of demonstration to Japanese people, that is to say, 'Look, our state, our nation!' . . . One can say that the Taiwanese and the Japanese competed for moral superiority for fifty years. To prove this point, one can raise an example that social order in Taiwan was never inferior to that in Japan proper, and our acts and attitudes, including not telling a lie and being faithful, were even more complete than theirs."[38]

One prevalent expression of the Taiwanese people's willingness to maintain a perfect social order and to welcome the arrival of Chinese forces was the formation of the "Three Principles of the People Youth Groups" (*sanminzhuyi qingniantuan*; hereafter *sanqingtuan*). Crowned with Sun Yat-Sen's famous doctrine (Three Principles of the People: nationalism, democracy, and the livelihood of the people), the sanqingtuan were originally established in 1938 by Chiang Kai-shek and other military officers trained in the Whampoa Military Academy as a youth division of the GMD. The GMD had launched the New Life Movement in 1934 in the hope of producing a mass revolution. Four years later, the sanqingtuan, which gathered youth between age sixteen and twenty-five, were built to help Chiang's continuous desire to mold the minds of the masses.[39] Its vision of youth mobilization, presumably copied from the Soviet Union, Germany, and Italy, was quite similar to that of Japanese leaders in its focus on transforming young minds and bodies into fighters in a political–military struggle.[40] Taiwanese independence activists, operating during these years in mainland China and fighting the Japanese to liberate both China and Taiwan, voluntarily set up a branch of the sanqingtuan within their own liberation army in 1942. This signaled the "GMD-ization" of the major Taiwanese activist group led by Li Youbang and others.[41]

Once the Japanese were gone, Taiwanese intellectuals—especially those who had previously engaged in the Cultural Association and leftist anti-Japanese activities—quickly made contact with each other to form new groups under the name of *sanqingtuan*. Zhang Shide, a former activist of Taiwan's Peasant Union who joined the Whampoa Academy afterward, came back to Taiwan and took the lead.[42] Most importantly, the Taiwanese sanqingtuan, unlike those in mainland China, developed without the GMD's direct involvement, nor was it limited to youth. The number of sanqingtuan members grew rapidly, reaching thirty thousand by March 1946 and easily exceeding the number of GMD party members, which remained at 1,215 in the same month. In fact, the two came to represent very different interests. The historian Ho I-Lin argues that the bifurcation of the upper classes during Japanese colonial rule between left-leaning activists and conservative landholders reappeared as a division between the sanqingtuan and the GMD party.[43] Wu Xinrong, a leader of the sanqingtuan, recalled that "since the organization of the sanqingtuan was made out of the [former] Cultural Association and the Peasant Union, the members naturally embraced progressive thoughts. . . . As a consequence, the organization had confrontations with the [GMD] party and had conflicts with the government."[44] This political division was further exacerbated once the Whampoa group of military officers and GMD party leaders arrived in Taiwan from China.[45]

But such distinctions in political orientation become blurry as we look at the sanqingtuan groups formed away from the center. In Xinzhu city, a branch of the sanqingtuan, established in the city hall built by the Japanese, had a slight leaning toward Cultural Association activism. A twenty-eight-year-old civil servant, Chen Cheng, joined the group because "everyone said the sanqingtuan was a good organization, and all the older generation participated."[46] For him, "everyone" consisted of a circle of friends, including his chess partner Huang Jitu, whose father, Haung Wancheng, was a former local leader of the Taiwan Cultural Association. Despite that political lineage, people gathered mainly to share information useful for day-to-day survival, rather than to engage in political activism. Chen Cheng had never heard of the Three Principles of the People until he joined the sanqingtuan. He recalled, "The youth group did not have active programs, but people gathered every once in a while to have a discussion. . . . The situation of that time was somewhat strange," so a number of young participants were "in charge of collecting information outside and reporting it back."[47]

The group's political character was even less relevant in more remote places. In the county capital, Zhudong town, local notables from the Japanese period, the Song and Liu families, collaborated to form a sanqingtuan group so as to maintain social order. Composed of the previous seinendan and *sōteidan* members, this group experienced a smoother transition from the Japanese period than groups in the urban center, which hinged their identities on their previous anti-Japanese activism.[48] In remote villages like Beipu and Guanxi, people also vaguely remembered the sanqingtuan as being "made up of former seinendan and sōteidan."[49] This is not surprising, since the village leaders and institutions from the period of Japanese rule remained in power. In Beipu, for example, Jiang Ruichang, a symbol of the Japanized generation, became village head again in August 1945.[50]

The most pressing issue for local youth at the time was to learn Mandarin Chinese, which was determined to be the new "national language." The government's Sinicization programs (*zuguohua*) included the condemnation of Japanization education as "enslaving education," the formation of a Chinese national identity, the embrace of the Three Principles of the People, and the adoption of Chinese customs and ethics. Mastery of Mandarin Chinese was the starting point.[51] Xu Chongfa did not remember joining the sanqingtuan, but his Chinese practice book shows that he attended language lessons offered by a "*sanminzhuyi* youth group" in October 1945.[52] In class, he learned Chinese phonetic symbols (*bopomofo*) by attaching the Japanese phonetics (*katakana*) next to them. Huang Yuanxing also faced the need to learn Chinese as quickly as possible. After Japan's surrender, he immediately returned to his teaching position at the Beipu elementary school only to find that "teachers' authority had been turned upside down."[53] He went to night school to learn Chinese and taught children the next morning at school the material he had just learned.[54]

The island-wide network of the sanqingtuan thus absorbed a wide variety of urban elite activists, local leaders, and people who were just beginning to learn Mandarin Chinese. Across this whole network, the celebration of Youth Day, on March 29, 1946 highlighted a still-joyous reunion between the GMD and Taiwanese locals. Students, youth group members, and the general population gathered in Taipei, Jilong, Xinzhu, Taizhong, Jiayi, Tainan, Gaoxiong, Pingdong, Hualian, and other cities to commemorate the seventy-two revolutionaries who were killed in an uprising in Guangzhou during the revolution of 1911. Xinzhu city held a Chinese speech competition among students and youth group members, and Gaoxiong city had a musical parade to distribute pamphlets that delivered a GMD message to Taiwanese youth.[55] In newspapers, Chiang Kai-shek told all "Chinese" youth to "celebrate the victory in our anti-Japanese war," and announced that "our nation has entered a new phase, and our revolution has reached a new step." Now youth's grave mission was to "protect the independent and equal national status [equal to those of other strong states], and to establish a unified, democratic, strong, and peaceful nation."[56]

The amity between the GMD and Taiwanese locals did not last long. Because the locals expected to finally obtain self-rule and gain access to political and social opportunities, the GMD's authoritarian control and monopoly over official positions enraged them. At the local level, people witnessed the messy and corrupt ways in which the GMD officers seized Japanese properties as well as their daily misconduct, from skipping to the front of the line at bus stops to requesting bribes at every opportunity.[57] Meanwhile, food production dropped dramatically, and the unemployment rate skyrocketed, and the GMD government had no effective rectifying measure for either problem. Social grievances and political tensions were growing day by day.[58]

The central leader of the sanqingtuan, Li Youbang, found himself in a difficult position when he published an essay, "A New Agenda for Taiwanese Youth" on New Year's Day in 1947. In this piece he admitted that Taiwan's youth were full of suspicion, wondering "why our national economy does not appear prosperous, but rather declining day after day; why our administrative facilities are not like what we desire, but rather looking exhausted, . . . peace is not realized, and democracy is yet to be complete."[59] Soon afterward, the 228 Incident broke out. It started when a police officer beat and injured a female black-market tobacco vendor in Taipei on February 28, 1947. People immediately went into the streets to protest against excessive policing, and when the GMD authorities fired bullets at them, it turned into large demonstrations spread across the island, gaining further momentum when protesters occupied the radio station and called for a mass uprising.[60] During the chaos, Taiwanese local leaders in all the major cities formed "committees for the settlement of the 228 Incident" and demanded a concrete set of political reforms from the GMD government. This did not put an end to the violence. Additional GMD troops landed in Taiwan on March 8, massacring and torturing members of these settlement committees and other Taiwanese, often indiscriminately. From this point, Taiwan entered the era of the "White Terror," during which GMD authorities terrorized and prosecuted political dissidents in various ways.

Ever since the tragic 228 Incident, the sanqingtuan has lost its place in Taiwanese history because it became a politically sensitive subject for both GMD supporters and anti-GMD local elites. The GMD's governor of Taiwan, Chen Yi, saw sanqingtuan leaders as the main instigators of mass uprisings and guerrilla attacks.[61] In fact, whether they were the initial instigators or not, they subsequently organized armed forces and conducted guerrilla warfare against GMD soldiers in Jiayi and Taizhong.[62] In the GMD narrative of Taiwanese history, the name *sanqingtuan* represented these dangerous radicals. On the other hand, the sanqingtuan was also a reminder for the opposing Taiwanese elites that they had welcomed the GMD and willingly adopted the term *sanminzhuyi* (Three Principles of the People) back in 1945. "In retrospect, it was an organization taken advantage of by [the GMD]," the previously cited Chen Cheng claimed in his memoir.[63] Both camps came to deny association with the sanqingtuan.

Perhaps for this reason, it was difficult to elicit comments from Huang Yuanxing and Xu Chongfa about their involvement in the sanqingtuan. Both of them told me that they stayed away from violence during the 228 chaos. Xu recalled, "Because they knew that I used to be a youth training teacher, villagers came to the door every day and asked me to lead the anti-GMD forces." At the time, he was helping at his brother's new lumber factory back in Guanxi village. "But I did not want to get involved in violence. I left home very early and came home very late, or hid inside so the villagers could not find me."[64] For Huang Yuanxing, the land reform that the GMD conducted was a more memorable experience: "They seized the Jiang family's land and properties and sold them to poor peasants at low prices." He purchased large curved panels taken from the Jiang family's mansion and decorated his bedroom with them. He continued, "The Jiang family's wealth shrank a lot, and so did other rich people's. Those who opposed the GMD were doctors and landlords, not poor people."[65] Whether it was a contemporary observation or an afterthought, Huang settled on an interpretation that explains Taiwan's political bifurcation in terms of economic classes, but not in the fashion that many of today's anti-GMD citizens would expect.

The sanqingtuan's role in the 228 Incident did not diminish the political importance of youth. Rather, it drove the party to develop a firmer grip on young populations. Officials still celebrated Youth Day on March 29, 1947, calling on Taiwanese youth to reflect upon the recent incident while giving thanks for the "generous measures" taken by the government. They preached to Taiwanese youth that "the fundamental way [to prevent such an event from happening again] is reeducation of the Taiwanese, changing the Japanese poisonous education of the past. Particularly important is to learn the language and literature, history and geography, ethnic spirits and our own ethics, transforming Taiwanese comrades into complete Chinese both in name and practice. This is the most urgent issue for Taiwan."[66] This indoctrination of youth was reminiscent of Japanese wartime mobilization, so it is little wonder that people called it the "new kōminka movement."[67]

Since the government had virtually disbanded the sanqingtuan in Taiwan after the 228 Incident, it was up to new youth organizations to carry out the new kōminka. Once the majority of GMD officials and officers had migrated to Taiwan in 1949, the party reorganized youth institutions with a new emphasis on anticommunist warfare. Youth Day in 1950 saw the establishment of the Taiwan Province Youth Volunteer Group.[68] In April, a number of college students in Taipei organized the Chinese Youth Anti-Communist Anti-Soviet League.[69] Finally, the inauguration of the China Youth Anti-Communist Corps (CYC) on Youth

Day in 1952 completed the nationalization of youth training institutions.[70] The CYC defined youth as "the pioneer of the time" and announced that "without youth, there is no revolution!" It listed three fundamental characteristics of the organization as "educational," "mass-oriented," and "war-ready."[71] Together with mandatory military drills in schools, the CYC's summer and winter military camps and daily training established a militaristic tone of youth training consistent with the GMD's continuous wartime rhetoric.[72]

Certainly, the Taiwanese people's adjustment to GMD rule—and their various sentiments that accompanied it—could not be understood separately from their experiences of the Japanese period. But it is nearly impossible for observers to fathom how their colonial memories drove them to certain decisions and emotions. Xu Chongfa did not fight the GMD, but he also declined its offer to become chief of the education department in the Xinzhu province. Maybe he regretted his deep association with the ideological mobilization conducted by the Japanese authorities and wanted to avoid stepping into the same quagmire a second time. Or maybe he still felt loyal to the Japanese and his students, and therefore he believed that becoming a GMD official would appear hypocritical. Or he might have been simply tired of politics and wanted to concentrate on family business.

Huang Yuanxing justified GMD rule by emphasizing its effective land reform, but his quick acceptance of the GMD might have been his only way to survive as a schoolteacher. Perhaps Hakka populations felt differently about the GMD, being more afraid of the political dominance by the Holo people, which the Japanese presence had restrained, and thus they aligned with the GMD more readily.[73] Regardless of how he viewed the new era of authoritarian rule, the scene felt familiar to him when he observed students' military drills conducted at school. In fact, when the government started recruiting Taiwanese soldiers in March 1950, many of the new recruits, as well as the instructors, were people trained by the Japanese institutions. Zhang Shulin, a Hakka military officer from Xinpu, another rural village in Xinzhu province, recalled that the Taiwanese soldiers were already well-trained and enjoyed singing Japanese military songs. Zhang was supposed to enforce Sinicization and condemn Japanese education, but he let his soldiers sing in Japanese.[74]

These local stories tell us that the Taiwanese were far from monolithic in their associations with the GMD, and that the grassroots experiences of their transition from Japanization to Sinicization require careful study. Individuals' reactions to the GMD were by no means predetermined. Just as under Japanese colonial rule, myriad social conditions and local contexts influenced their reactions to GMD control.

Korea

The post-1945 period, even before the tragedy of the Korean War began, turned out to be a tremendous disappointment to people in the Korean peninsula, to say the least. Their enthusiasm for an independent nation was quickly curtailed by the division of the peninsula. In South Korea, the fragmentation of Korean politics, the severe anti-leftist oppression, and the reinstatement of colonial bureaucracy by the American Occupation, which started in September 8, 1945, denied many people their hopes for a new regime.[75]

As in postwar Japan and Taiwan, youth continued to be a critically important sector of the general population in Korea. On both sides of the thirty-eighth parallel, youth represented a break from the past, and youth organizations became the core of new political and social programs. Especially in South Korea, post-1945 youth activism became intertwined with the complex web of political factions as well as with the rise of terrorist tactics in political fights. In contrast to the dominant presence of youth on the political scene, however, ordinary people's involvement in youth organizations in local towns and villages remains too sensitive a topic to discuss openly. The memory of civil violence during the Korean War and the fear of being labeled as "red" or "pro-Japanese" seem to have forced many people to actively forget the details of this period.

Kim Yǒng-han, whose story we learned in chapters 7 and 8, was also extremely hesitant to give a personal narrative of his actions and thoughts during the postliberation period. Instead, his oral history shifted to a general impression of the local town. Kim returned to the Nonsan county office immediately after the war and continued working "without a break of even a day." On these days, he presumably reflected on the implications of Japanese surrender, the overturning of previous beliefs, and his career prospects in the new era, but none of these topics came out in the interview. Instead, he emphasized the calmness and continuity that prevailed in provincial towns. The Japanese returned home in an orderly fashion, and many Koreans, including himself, hosted farewell parties for their Japanese friends. He attributed the absence of violence against Japanese people to deterrence by the still-stationed Japanese army. According to his account, once the new military government (the United States Army Military Government in Korea) replaced the local administration and the police in Nonsan in the fall, there was no longer any concern about social order. Perhaps as a conscious decision, Kim's post-1945 life was concentrated on providing higher education to his two younger brothers and cousin, all of whom went to prestigious universities. He showed me a few copies of the pamphlet *Declaration to the Korean People*, distributed in the name of George R. Hodge, the commanding general of the military government, dated

September 29, 1945. But scribbles on the back show that to his family, this historic document that marked the beginning of the new era was a source of paper for his brother's biology homework.[76]

The first few weeks of continuity that Kim witnessed were most likely preserved by local volunteers. In the same way as many Taiwanese locals voluntarily organized the sanqingtuan to preserve peace and order, many young men in Korea established security-maintaining forces across the peninsula. In Seoul alone, about thirty thousand young people joined such forces.[77] These groups had various names, some of which reflected curious similarity to the names of units of wartime Japanese mobilization, such as *haktodae* (student corps), *ch'ŏngnyŏndae* (youth corps), and *chawidae* (self-defense corps). In the meantime, central leaders of the transitional Committee for the Preparation of Korean Independence (CPKI) established the Peace Preservation Corps (*ch'iandae*) and engaged in the "peace preservation movement." The ch'iandae dispatched students to provinces for the purpose of institutionalizing the local security corps.[78] As in the case of Taiwan's sanqingtuan, local ch'iandae groups were an expression of enthusiasm for the anticipated onset of self-government. They transcended political allegiances and included both anticolonial fighters and those who had served the imperial government.[79]

Self-governance, indeed, characterized township politics in the postliberation era. Across the peninsula, in pursuit of this goal, local leaders established "people's committees," which were also eventually incorporated into the national CPKI network. In Nonsan county, the newly formed people's committee, headed by Cho Tong-sun, conducted an official ceremony to transfer county administration from the (colonial-era) county head to the people's committee.[80] Cho's profile reflected the ambivalent political complexion of the committee. Cho had been a left-leaning figure yet was actively involved in colonial shinkōkai activities. The Japanese had even given him an award as a "model shinkōkai leader." His brother-in-law Yun Hŭi-jung, a famous landlord of the region, was among the eighteen members of Nonsan's people's committee (see chapter 7). We simply cannot know what the committee's ideological goals were, if it had any, but outside observers found the organization confusing. "An Investigative Report on the Situation of South Ch'ungch'ŏng Region," compiled around this time, called the committee a group of "bad youth" who obstructed the administration. It argued that "the majority of the leaders [of Nonsan's people's committee] were a pro-Japanese faction without particular ideology, joined by a few communist members."[81] Regardless, the committee exhibited a determination among local leaders to attain self-rule. For the few short weeks until the military government reinstalled previous officials, the people's committee symbolically took over the county office.

In many places, the local ch'iandae functioned as a security force for people's committees. Bruce Cumings links the massive scale of local volunteer forces to discharged soldiers, laborers, and youth group members, as well as released prisoners after liberation. In Seoul, many of fifteen thousand former soldiers, thousands of young people, and some sixteen thousand released prisoners (in South Korea) participated in the peace preservation movement in August 1945. Others returned home, contributing to a significant increase in the population throughout the country.[82] Unfortunately, there is very little surviving information at the village and county level to tell us the precise composition of local ch'iandae members.

The political value attached to the term *youth* (*ch'ŏngnyŏn*) is hard to miss in the immediate postwar politics of South Korea. The burgeoning of political activities carried out by various student and youth leaders was more than a revival of the heated youth politics of the 1920s. Yŏ Un-hyŏng, who accepted the Japanese request to guarantee a peaceful transfer of government and established the CPKI in August 1945, had predicted that the emotional outbursts of educated youth (i.e., those with a middle school diploma or above) would pose the gravest security concern after the Japanese surrender. He observed that they had harbored the deepest resentment, fear, and animosity toward the colonial system, which discriminated against them and ended their future prospects.[83] His prediction was right, in that they filled the transitional period with an explosion of new political movements. Within a month of the end of colonial rule, members of youth groups who took part in the peace preservation movement began splitting into left- and right-leaning groups and developed into a full matrix of ideological factions. Besides their ideological commitments to communism or anticommunism, their beliefs regarding the appropriate decolonization process (especially regarding the treatment of "pro-Japanese capitalists" and former bureaucrats), and their attitudes toward the American-Russian plan of Trusteeship–based rule of Korea created a highly contested and often violent political scene among them.[84] Youth was no longer an age category, but a label that indicated militant activism in which a wide range of generations participated.

The leftist groups, in particular, garnered remarkably wide public support. Their popularity and strong advocacy corresponded with the increasingly "revolutionary" direction taken by the CPKI and local people's committees. Starting from a youth corps affiliated with the Korea Communist Party, leftist leaders continued to absorb various youth groups, forming the All-Nation Youth General Alliance (in December 1945), Korea Democratic Youth Alliance (April 1946), and Korea Democratic Patriotic Youth Alliance (June 1947). With a centralized organization, they called for the total elimination of Japanese influence, the purge of "traitors," the consolidation of united working youth, and reunification with North Korea.[85] Although the American Occupation banned the Korea Democratic Youth Alliance in May 1946 and its activities went underground, the organization still had 826,940 members as of May 1947, according to an American intelligence report. While conducting its activities mostly under the radar of the Occupation forces, a successor group, the Korea Democratic Patriotic Youth Alliance, hoped to expand its membership to two million by August 1947.[86]

Initially overwhelmed by the leftist momentum, rightist youth leaders soon developed major political power as well. They gained force through the return of right-wing nationalist leaders like Syngman Rhee and Kim Ku and by absorbing youth who had deserted from the north. In December 1945, they formed the Korea Independence Promotion All-Nation Youth General Alliance to confront the more strongly centralized leftist youth movements. Among many right-leaning youth groups that emerged, the National Society for Independence Promotion Youth Corps exhibited a significant presence. Its official membership amounted to three thousand individuals, spread across South Korea, and its members served the personal and political goals of Syngman Rhee. The military government also used rightist youth activism for its own purpose, supporting the Korea Minjok Youth Corps to strengthen security. The Northwest Youth Corps, formed by mainly those escaping Kim Il-sung's regime, quickly became famous for its thug-like violence against communist activists. Factional fights and mergers among these groups continued before they were either eliminated or unified by the Syngman Rhee regime in the early 1950s. With their terrorist tactics, many became a major part of the state's own terror-producing machine, working along with the police and the military to suppress communist activities.[87]

Living in the countryside of South Ch'ungch'ong, however, Kim Yong-han perceived youth politics of this period as nothing more than a mild confrontation.[88] "An Investigative Report on the Situation of South Ch'ungch'ong Region" listed a number of leftist youth groups but also pointed out the continuity in leadership of local notables from the colonial period. Based on this report, the historian Chi Su-gol concludes that in Nonsan county, the rightist youth groups supported by wealthy local notables remained more powerful than the opposing "revolutionary" youth.[89] Overall, Cumings's analysis also described the transition to the American Occupation in South Ch'ungch'ong was relatively orderly.[90]

Other regions did not enjoy the same calm transition. Taegu uprisings in October 1946, for instance, spread to other towns of North and South Kyongsang in the following month, causing Hodge to impose a martial law. Youth groups on both right and left exacerbated the violent nature of the confrontation.[91] During 1947, Syngman Rhee and his allies sent rightist youth groups, particularly the

Northwest Youth Corps, to suppress villages and towns that showed an inclination toward leftism. These young thugs armed the local rightist youth and
destroyed leftist elements. A similar dispatch of the Northwest Youth Corps to
Cheju Island in 1948 eventually ignited an island-wide uprising. For months,
Cheju residents suffered from mass-scale atrocities by the police and the Northwest Youth, with tens of thousands of people dying.[92]

North Korea, which more eagerly purged colonial collaborators and bureaucrats, ironically preserved more continuity from Japanese-style uniform youth
mobilization. Youth represented one of the most important mass collectives. Kim
Il-sung's regime, built upon Kim's legacy of anticolonial resistance, absorbed
local initiatives for self-rule and quickly established firm central leadership. Especially in rural peripheries, people's postliberation energy was directed toward
a ground-up social revolution. As the regime pursued building strong links
between local communities and the central government, the Sinŭiju Incident of
November 23, 1945, an event in which middle school students protested against
communist control of school authorities, made Kim Il-sung particularly keen on
connecting with youth.[93] Shortly thereafter, the government turned the Communist Youth League into the Democratic Youth League (DYL), whose membership
in official records exceeded one million by February 1948 and included 80.5% of
all eligible youth by the end of the year.[94]

Advocating the elimination of pro-Japanese elements and mass dissemina-
tion of the new ideology, the DYL nevertheless displayed a striking parallel to
the prewar Japanese seinendan. Most of its members had little education, and
DYL membership offered them upward social mobility. The DYL emphasized
dismantling the culture of seniority and bestowed a new responsibility on youth.
It celebrated the sacred nature of labor rather than higher school education.
Members not only received training but also served local needs for construction and labor mobilization. Local DYL groups instilled in young people a group
identity that transcended the political affiliation.[95] At the same time, with its local
enthusiasm and other measures that promoted the participation by the poor, the
scale and popularity of the DYL far exceeded anything that Japanese colonizers
of Korea could have imagined.

When the Korean War started in June 1950, triggering rounds of brutal massacres in local towns and villages, even Kim Yŏng-han's narrative could not ignore
the cruelty of the time. Calling it "a tragedy for our nation," Kim noted that both
leftists and rightists were killed, depending on which side was dominant side that
day.[96] Youth group members in particular became the targets of executions and
retaliatory killings. According to one study, 17,274 members of the Northeast
Youth Corps were killed or lost family members.[97] A large number of other rightist and leftist youth also fell into the spiral of retaliation. As no systematic data on

the violence exist, we know about it only through anecdotes, local research, and some photographic documentation of executions.[98]

The continuity from colonial volunteer soldiers to police and military recruits in South Korea during this period added darkness to the already tragic killings. For the families of the slaughtered, their colonial backgrounds of many of the killers evidenced the inherent evil of those in uniform. One notorious example was Kim Chong-won, a former sergeant in the Japanese army. Despite American opposition, he was appointed commander of the martial-law regime in Pusan and given other top positions by Syngman Rhee, after which he went "berserk" in executing thousands of political prisoners and anyone who showed the slightest sign of disobedience. Cumings refers to him as "Mr. Massacre."[99]

These infamous examples created an essentialized image of former colonial soldiers, and thus leaving many of them in a quagmire. For them, working for the police or the military was the only job opportunity in the midst of severe unemployment. Whether it was their own desire or not, their job entailed killing people and finding a way to survive while being targeted themselves. The memoir of O Chong-ch'ŏl, a former colonial volunteer soldier, shows how his connection with the Japanese army haunted him before and during the Korean War. On returning from New Guinea, O worked at a town office in South Chŏlla, but soon quit the job because of relentless accusations by leftists, who said, "You were a volunteer soldier for Japan! Those who betrayed the nation are not qualified to work for the town." He joined the police in Mokpo, but once the North Korean army passed the thirty-eighth parallel, the head of the provincial police department asked O to organize and command policemen to fight on the front lines because "you have Japanese army experience." While participating in the "red hunt" of the region, O attempted to acquire a fishing boat to escape to Japan, thinking that he could rely on his Japanese friends from the deployment in New Guinea, but abolished the plan when he heard that North Korean soldiers had occupied the ports. Through luck and deliberate maneuvers, O avoided being dispatched to the battlefront, and once United Nations forces landed in Inch'ŏn, he returned to South Cholla, only to find that his entire family had been slaughtered by local leftist radicals. In his memoir, he claims that because he became the appointed head of the county police at this point, he suppressed his impulse for retaliation. In the end, he concluded, "because I was a volunteer soldier, my family paid a terrible cost."[100] His record as a volunteer soldier not only lost its original honor and prestige, but turned into the gravest menace in his life.

In sum, in the Koreas the symbolic category of youth continued to weigh heavily in postwar nation building. It was North Korea that inherited the Japanese imperial style of rural youth organization. In this system, the state continued to view youth as both grassroots allies and targets of control, but for youth, a mechanism similar to the social mobility complex might have become newly available. Meanwhile, in South Korea, youth came to mean revolutionary radicals who did not hesitate to use violence. In the volatile political conditions, many who had been in the Japanese military were trapped in the vicious circle of violence in one way or another.

In this context, Kim Yŏng-han's repeated emphasis that colonial model rural youth were strictly agricultural in nature makes sense. During the Korean War, the dividing line between colonial youth training and military experience had to be consciously articulated in order to keep Kim and people like him out of the spiral of violence. Even among those who were climbing up the same ladder of career success under Japanese rule, the end results of it varied significantly depending on whether they served in the military, as shown by the differences between Kim Yŏng-han and O Chong-ch'ŏl. As in Taiwan, the postliberation experiences of former model rural youth in Korea defy easy generalization.

When I began studying the Japanese Empire, I was fascinated by the apparent continuity in the impetus to mobilize youth between Japanese rule and postwar Korean and Taiwanese societies. Digging deep into the history of seinendan mobilization and tracing how the militaristic ideology took root in colonial societies seemed a promising way to investigate the so-called colonial legacy. Doing social history was a journey of challenging every assumption I had. Many dominant analytical concepts quickly lost their usefulness while lesser-known social tensions emerged as critical. As I encountered rich human experiences shaped by intertwining historical contingencies, I grew more and more intolerant of clean typologies that describe the power of the state over society and individuals. The Japanese Empire, which once seemed so domineering and methodically controlling, now appears as an unorganized, haphazard, and fragile state that depended heavily on a variety of social forces to create and maintain its nation-like hegemony. That does not mean, however, that society was *the* secret power holder. After all, society is never a single entity; it never stops being fragmented, diverse, and fluid. Because of the uneven and amorphous nature of both state and society, various forces cut across these spheres and constantly merge and clash, not allowing us to easily identify how one element led to another.

Introducing the concept of a social mobility complex was my humble attempt to shed light on the alignment of various tangible and intangible elements that made ideological indoctrination possible. Many historians tend to assume that ideological teaching alone produced patriotic imperial subjects. But that link is not self-evident. What was the chance of success when Japanese teachers started teaching children in Taiwan and Korea that they should worship the Japanese emperor? Others think that colonial youth hid their true intentions behind a facade of obedience. But as we have seen, they were not any less sincere or opportunistic in expressing Japanese nationalism than were their Japanese counterparts. The ideology of Japanese agrarian nationalism was actively adopted and embraced by certain sectors of society at certain points in history, enabling the state's pursuit of nation-empire building from below. To understand why and how this happened, I resorted to a social-historical explanation that stresses the emotional effects produced by new opportunities for upward social mobility.

As we have seen, the social mobility complex generally emerged around youth training institutions, because they offered, sometimes accidentally, new job opportunities. The prospect of building up a career triggered the transformation of consciousness in individuals, from perpetual farmers to career-seeking modern youth. At the same time, the expansive communicative space available through the seinendan (or among local officials in the Korean case) fostered the new identity of model rural youth. This shared identity in turn nurtured a sense of moral superiority over those with higher education, urban residents, and older generations. Through such collective sharing, the ideology of Japanese imperial nationalism was reshaped, absorbed, and emotionally charged. The precise elements and emotions that constituted the social mobility complex show a great variation across localities, but identifying this microlevel mechanism allows us to view the Japanization of young villagers as the result of a wide range of historical factors, not an immediate product of state policies.

To some readers, the differences across the cases might be the most illuminating findings. As discussed in the Introduction, there was a widespread drive for assimilation across the Japanese Empire, in pursuit of the establishment of a nation-empire. Reflecting this emphasis, bureaucrats made almost simultaneous efforts to introduce similar methods of rural mobilization across the empire beginning in the mid-1910s. Total Japanization in particular, launched in the late 1930s, is best grasped as an empire-wide imperative. But within that movement, local reactions and subsequent developments varied significantly. Clearly, differences existed between Japanese and colonial villages. The prioritization of the metropole in imperial policies significantly determined the prevailing social conditions in Taiwanese, Korean, and Okinawan villages, such as the slower spread of school education, extremely scarce access to higher education, systemic poverty, and ethnic discrimination in the job market. Much of the resentment felt by colonial village youth came from deeper social institutions of seniority, urban-centrism, class hierarchy, and so on, but many imperial policies exacerbated their grievances. To state the obvious, the empire did not rescue these youth from indigenous social dynamics through assimilative rural youth mobilization, as colonial educators imagined. Rather, as seen most clearly in the Okinawan case, colonialism manifested itself in severe social, not ethnic, tensions in the countryside. Taiwanese and Korean villages saw the eventual emergence of a social mobility complex, but one with a colony-specific character. In Miyagi, the complex was relatively more inclusive because it developed based on the longstanding presence of hamlet youth associations open to most youth, whereas in Taiwan and Korea, it was more exclusive and competitive. The window of opportunities available for colonial agrarian youth was much more limited, although the exclusivity was a necessary component to create a new social status in colonial villages.

The differences between Taiwanese and Korean experiences were no less significant. The interactions of precolonial social conditions, the presence of Japanese settlers, and state policies produced different kinds of values and images of rural youth in Beipu and Kwangsŏk. In contrast to the Taiwanese mountain villages, which displayed characteristics of a frontier society, old rice-producing villages in Korea shared more similarities with their Tōhoku counterparts in many ways. But in other ways, because of the much slower spread of elementary schools and language education in Korea, the protagonists of the social mobility complex in the Korean case—more academically oriented, above-median village youth—differed from those in the Taiwanese and Japanese cases. These differences underscored diversity across the empire.

At the same time, a common pattern was present. The similarity among the Miyagi, Taiwanese, and Korean cases explains the dynamics of empire-wide mass mobilization and highlights lesser-known characteristics of Japanese imperialism, especially the importance of agrarianism. These cases revealed how central the rural areas became in Japan's assimilation and nationalization. More precisely, more than the sheer size of rural domains, the growing binary between urban and rural determined how the imperial state interacted with populations and found a way into their everyday lives. Without the widespread sense of inferiority and grievance among rural residents against urban-centered development, agrarian nationalism would never have attracted such wide support. This finding offers a new interpretation of the ideological premise of Japanese imperialism. Historians have often argued that the famous slogans of Pan-Asianism and the Greater East Asia Co-Prosperity Sphere were not mere rhetoric or propaganda, but guiding principles that determined the course of imperial policies. Perhaps that was the case among intellectuals and policymakers, but this book has shown that a more concrete image of model rural youth and agrarianism, rather than abstract images of an integrative empire, was more widely embraced by ordinary people in the countryside.

Another implication is that the connectivity across the empire came from all directions. Village youth built expansive mental geographies. Education opportunities in the metropole, particularly Waseda University's popular correspondence curriculum, were of monumental importance in the life narratives of both Xu Chongfa's and Kim Yŏnghan's. Colonial seinendan members were regularly exposed to news of the metropole, even though Taipei and Seoul were foreign to their life experience. Conversely, Japanese village youth received personalized accounts of the outer territories through seinendan newsletters, which might have more powerfully motivated some of them to join the youth corps in Manchuria than official propaganda could have done. These day-to-day links with other parts of the empire made it possible for youth to envision a sense of imperial brotherhood. In some cases, their youthful identity transcended the imperial borders. Their exchanges with the Hitler Youth, or even their readings of Tolstoy and Goethe, profoundly affected the shaping of their self-image as transnational beings. But precisely because of their imagined ties and their high self-regard as model rural youth, the Japanese army's failure to deliver the promised assimilation to colonial volunteer soldiers felt like more than a betrayal. The result was convoluted expressions of newly formed ethnic pride against the Japanese, as seen in the phrase "becoming truer Japanese."

In examining the processes of youth mobilization, we have also seen how Japanese assimilationism encompassed an emphasis on local culture and grassroots communities, rather than an elimination of them. As discussed in the Introduction, Japan's adherence to assimilationism was in a stark contrast to the global norm of associationism during the 1920s. But the tensions between local particularism and national–imperial universalism appeared in Japan and its colonies in the same way as in other colonial empires. The revival of *kye* in Korea, the development of a Xinzhu identity in Taiwan, and Miyagi's native village education closely corresponded to the global appreciation of native traditions. Again, the ideological device of agrarianism translated the localizing forces into the nationalizing effort without revealing inherent contradictions. Becoming model Taiwanese and Korean rural youth—the associationist direction from other empires' perspective—was seen as analogous to becoming ideal Japanese. In other words, agrarianism turned associationist tactics into essential tools of assimilationist policies.

From a world-historical viewpoint, however, the stories examined in this book are not merely about one version of imperialism or the question of assimilationism or associationism. Most of the everyday social tensions seen in our village cases were part of regional or global trends; the politicization of generations, rural devastation, urban migration, the critique of capitalism, and the merging of nativist and modernist orientations were all transnational phenomena. Such structural and cultural changes went hand in hand with a major political change, namely, the search for a new form of political domination beyond the familiar forms of nineteenth-century empires. Japan's attempt to establish a

nation-empire is better situated in this broader understanding of the course of
the early twentieth century. Even before they established experimental Manchukuo in 1932, Japanese leaders actively presented their empire as the embodiment
of a new kind of modernity, power, and legitimacy, much as newborn socialist
states and fascist regimes—or even old empires—made similar proclamations.
The lives of young farmers in the Japanese Empire thus went beyond typical
"colonial" experiences and became part of the global search for a new form of
mass politics. For this reason, I found it was appropriate to unchain the local
experiences from an imperial-versus-colonial framework and shift the focus to
how the state, individuals, and social forces fluidly interacted with one another.
Where the modern state seemed to historians to be extending its tentacles over
the lives and consciousness of its subjects, people themselves lived in much more
complex power relationships. Our focus on grassroots experiences has shown
how provincial the position of the state could be in people's mental worlds, even
when they stood at the forefront of state-led mobilization and embraced the
state's ideology.

As I return to the question of postcolonial continuity, I am baffled by the super-
ficiality of my original instinct. Like many abstract concepts, "colonial legacy"
became too imprecise a term to use. Obviously, colonial rule left deep imprints
in post-imperial and postcolonial polities and societies. The lack of effort by
the Japanese government to acknowledge its moral and financial responsibility
for those mobilized, exploited, and brutalized under its imperial rule and make
equitable restitution continues to hinder a meaningful reconciliation with East
Asian nations. Despite the major rupture of August 1945, the Taiwanese, South
Korean, and North Korean regimes were all consciously built upon the Japanese
systems. Historians, politicians, and people in general have good reason to pursue a resolution by redressing the lingering effects of imperialism. But at the same
time, the emphasis on a colonial legacy appears to overestimate the power of one
state to shape the overarching social values and systems. As I have argued repeatedly in this book, the social mechanism of rural youth mobilization was more
multidimensional, more diverse, and more locally grounded than anything that
state policies could possibly produce on their own. Complex webs of causes and
effects determined people's life choices, making the definitions of "traitors" and
"collaborators" impossibly amorphous. In the end, to my own surprise, rather
than adding clarity, the approach of decentering the state taken in this book further muddied the issue of colonial legacy by preventing us from separating the
guilt of the empire from other forces.

In my rounds of interviews, I touched the surface of personal postcolonial
sentiments. Thinking back on the rich array of my interlocutors' verbal and
nonverbal expressions, which were often beyond my ability to fully comprehend

or explain, I cannot help but think that there remains a critical gap between political movements to redress the colonial legacy and former colonial youth's incommunicable feelings and reflections. I do not claim that this book has filled that gap. But it has attempted to identify the long-neglected contexts—local and global, structural and contingent—that are crucial in any effort to understand former model youth's experiences. Their stories have invited us to view the paradox of opportunities and exploitation in the age of extremes from their perspectives. This book is one response to that invitation.

Notes

INTRODUCTION: NATION-EMPIRE AS GLOBAL AND LOCAL HISTORY

1. Xu Chongfa, "Seinendan o megurite," October 7, 1943 (Xu's personal archive).

2. Kondō Masami, *Sōryokusen to Taiwan* (Tokyo: Tōsui Shobō, 1996), 371–373. In the survey of the first three months of applications, 58.6% were from the agricultural sector. Those in other industries but from rural villages clearly exceeded this number.

3. Chou Wan-yao (Zhou Wanyao), "Riben zaiTai junshi dongyuan yu Taiwanren de haiwai canzhan jingyan," *Taiwanshi yanjiu* 2, no. 1 (June 1995): 97–102.

4. Naimushō, *Taiheiyō Senka no Chōsen oyobi Taiwan* (1944), cited in Miyata Setsuko, *Chōsen minshū to "kōminka" seisaku* (Tokyo: Miraisha, 1985), 62. On the military recruitment in colonial Korea, see Takashi Fujitani, *Race for Empire: Koreans as Japanese and Japanese as Americans during World War II* (Berkeley: University of California Press, 2011); Brandon Palmer, *Fighting for the Enemy: Koreans in Japan's War, 1937–1945* (Seattle: University of Washington Press, 2013).

5. "Soldiers" include volunteer soldiers, conscripts, and civilian military personnel. Palmer, *Fighting for the Enemy*; Chou Wan-yao (Zhou Wanyao), ed., *Taiji Ribenbing zuotanhui jilu bing xiangguan ziliao* (Taipei: Institute of Taiwan History Preparatory Office, Academia Sinica, 1997); Hui-yu Caroline Ts'ai (Cai Huiyu), ed., *Zouguo liangge shidai de ren: Taiji Ribenbing* (Taipei: Institute of Taiwan History, Academia Sinica, 1997). On the issue of public memory of Taiwanese soldiers in the Japanese army, see Shi-chi Mike Lan, "(Re-)Writing History of the Second World War: Forgetting and Remembering the Taiwanese-Native Japanese Soldiers in Postwar Taiwan," *Positions: Asia Critique* 21, no. 4 (2013): 801–851.

6. American intelligence analyzed the Japanese-sponsored groups. "Japanese Attempts at Indoctrination of Youth in Occupied Areas" (February 5, 1945), FOIA no. 0000709428, available at Central Intelligence Agency website, https://www.cia.gov/library/readingroom/document/0000709428.

7. Frederick Cooper and Ann Laura Stoler, eds., *Tensions of Empire: Colonial Cultures in a Bourgeois World* (Berkeley: University of California Press, 1997); Durba Ghosh and Dane Kennedy, eds., *Decentering Empire: Britain, India, and the Transcolonial World* (Hyderabad: Orient Longman, 2006); Andre Schmid, "Colonialism and the 'Korea Problem' in the Historiography of Modern Japan: A Review Article," *Journal of Asian Studies* 59, no. 4 (2000): 951–976.

8. Mark E. Caprio, *Japanese Assimilation Policies in Colonial Korea, 1910–1945* (Seattle: University of Washington Press, 2009); Oguma Eiji, *"Nihonjin" no kyōkai: Okinawa, Ainu, Taiwan, Chōsen shokuminchi shihai kara fukki undō made* (Tokyo: Shinyōsha, 1998); Komagome Takeshi, *Shokuminchi teikoku Nihon no bunka tōgō* (Tokyo: Iwanami Shoten, 1996), for example. For the effects and politics of assimilationism in colonial Seoul, see Todd A. Henry, *Assimilating Seoul: Japanese Rule and the Politics of Public Space in Colonial Korea, 1910–1945* (Berkeley: University of California Press, 2014). On wartime integration, see Fujitani, *Race for Empire*.

9. Gotō Shinpei, *Nihon shokumin seisaku ippan, Nihon bōchōron* (Tokyo: Nihon Hyōronsha, 1944), 49.

10. Ibid., 48.

11. Ibid., 50–51.

12. Yoshida Hiroji, *Katō Hiroyuki no kenkyū* (Tokyo: Ōhara Shinseisha, 1976), 71–117.

13. Limin Bai, "Children as the Youthful Hope of an Old Empire: Race, Nationalism, and Elementary Education in China, 1895–1915," *Journal of the History of Childhood and Youth* 1, no. 2 (2008): 213–214. On the ways in which Korean intellectuals and authors were influenced by social Darwinism, see Vladimir Tikhonov, *Social Darwinism and Nationalism in Korea: The Beginnings (1880s–1910s); "Survival" as an Ideology of Korean Modernity* (Boston: Brill, 2010).

14. Jennifer Pitts, *A Turn to Empire: The Rise of Imperial Liberalism in Britain and France* (Princeton, NJ: Princeton University Press, 2005), 14.

15. For eighteenth-century liberal thinkers like J. S. Mill, nationhood was "an achievement of civilization," not applicable to "barbarians." Pitts, *A Turn to Empire*, 143–144.

16. See Todd Shepard, *The Invention of Decolonization: The Algerian War and the Remaking of France* (Ithaca, NY: Cornell University Press, 2006), 19–54.

17. For discussion on external and internal conditions that drove Japan into imperialism, see Mark Peattie, introduction to *The Japanese Colonial Empire, 1895–1945*, ed. Ramon Myers and Mark Peattie (Princeton, NJ: Princeton University Press, 1984), 1–52; Peter Duus, *The Abacus and the Sword* (Berkeley: University of California Press, 1995).

18. There are a number of scholars who attempt to capture the overlap between nation-state and empire. Yamamuro Shin'ichi uses the term *kokumin teikoku*, which can be translated as "national empire" or "nation-empire." What he means by this is the prototype of modern empires that has the nation-state at home and a multiracial empire abroad. Yamamuro Shin'ichi, "Kokumin teikoku no shatei," in *Teikoku no kenkyū: Genri, ruikei, kankei*, ed. Yamamoto Yūzō (Nagoya: Nagoya Daigaku Shuppankai, 2003), 87–128; see also Tomoko Akami, "The Nation-State/Empire as a Unit of Analysis in the History of International Relations: A Case Study in Northeast Asia, 1868–1933," in *The Nation State and Beyond: Governing Globalization Processes in the Nineteenth and Early Twentieth Centuries*, ed. Isabella Löhr and Roland Wenzlhuemer (Berlin: Springer, 2013), 177–208; Gary Wilder, *The French Imperial Nation-State: Negritude and Colonial Humanism between the Two World Wars* (Chicago: Chicago University Press, 2005).

19. See Mark Peattie, "Japanese Attitudes toward Colonialism, 1895–1945," in *The Japanese Colonial Empire*, ed. Myers and Peattie, 80–127.

20. For more detail on the concepts of race and ethnicity in Japanese imperial rhetoric, see Kevin Doak, "The Concept of Ethnic Nationality and Its Role in Pan-Asianism in Imperial Japan," in *Pan-Asianism in Modern Japanese History: Colonialism, Regionalism, and Borders*, ed. Sven Saaler and J. Victor Koschmann (New York: Routledge, 2007), 168–182; Oguma Eiji, *Tan'itsu minzoku shinwa no kigen: Nihonjin no jigazō no keifu* (Tokyo: Shinyōsha, 1995).

21. See Michael Kim, "The Colonial Public Sphere and the Discursive Mechanism of *Mindo*," in *Mass Dictatorship and Modernity*, ed. Michael Kim et al. (New York: Palgrave Macmillan, 2013), 178–202.

22. Jun Uchida, *Brokers of Empire: Japanese Settler Colonialism in Korea, 1876–1945* (Cambridge, MA: Harvard University Asia Center, 2011), 9.

23. Higa Shunchō, "Nengetsu to tomoni," *Okinawa taimusu*, March 11, 1964, quoted in Ōta Masahide, *Okinawa no minshū ishiki* (Tokyo: Shinsensha, 1976), 337.

24. Government-General of Chosen, *Annual Report on Reforms and Progress in Chosen (Korea), 1910–1911* (Seoul: Government-General of Chosen), 242, trans. and quoted in Uchida, *Brokers of Empire*, 116.

25. Ōta, *Okinawa no minshū ishiki*, 341–344.

26. Okamoto Makiko, *Shokuminchi kanryō no seijishi: Chōsen, Taiwan Sōtokufu to teikoku Nihon* (Tokyo: Sangensha, 2008), 51 and 60.

27. John Cell, "Colonial Rule," in *The Oxford History of the British Empire*, vol. 4, *The Twentieth Century*, ed. Judith Brown and Wm. Roger Louis (Oxford: Oxford University Press, 1999), 232.

28. Martin Thomas, *The French Empire between the Wars: Imperialism, Politics, and Society* (Manchester: Manchester University Press, 2005), 83. Finding out the numbers of colonial civil servants in Algeria, especially after 1870 when military rule transitioned to more assimilative administration, requires elaborate work beyond my means. This is because in the system called *rattachements*, many administrative services in Algeria were directly controlled by the ministries in Paris, not by the government-general in Algeria.

29. Susan Pedersen calls it the "Lugardian moment." See Susan Pedersen, *The Guardians: The League of Nations and the Crisis of Empire* (New York: Oxford University Press, 2015), 107–111; Cell, "Colonial Rule"; Alice L. Conklin, *A Mission to Civilize: The Republican Idea of Empire in France and West Africa, 1895–1903* (Stanford, CA: Stanford University Press, 1997), 142–211; Thomas, *The French Empire*, 54–89, on associationism in the French colonies; Elizabeth Foster, *Faith in Empire: Religion, Politics, and Colonial Rule in French Senegal, 1880–1940* (Stanford, CA: Stanford University Press, 2013), 141–167.

30. On the Wilsonian moment, see Erez Manela, *The Wilsonian Moment: Self-Determination and the International Origins of Anticolonial Nationalism* (New York: Oxford University Press, 2007). On the acceleration of assimilation under cultural policy in the 1920s, see Komagome, *Shokuminchi teikoku Nihon*; Caprio, *Japanese Assimilation Policies*; Uchida, *Brokers of Empire*. On policy analysis, see also Kasuya Ken'ichi, "Chōsen Sōtokufu no bunka seiji," in *Iwanami kōza Kindai Nihon to shokuminchi 2: Teikoku tōchi no kōzō*, ed. Ōe Shinobu et al. (Tokyo: Iwanami Shoten, 1992), 121–146.

31. For an example of assimilationist operations in the interwar period, see Sayaka Chatani, "The Ruralist Paradigm: Social Work Bureaucrats in Colonial Korea and Japan's Assimilationism in the Interwar Period," *Comparative Studies in Society and History* 58, no. 4 (2016): 1004–1031.

32. Hara Takashi, *Hara Takashi nikki, VIII* (Tokyo: Kangensha, 1950–1955), 563, trans. and quoted in Peattie, "Japanese Attitudes," 107.

33. "Shiganhei kunrenjo no kaishoshiki ni atarite," *Chōsen nippō* (editorial), June 15, 1938.

34. Leo T. S. Ching, *Becoming Japanese: Colonial Taiwan and the Politics of Identity Formation* (Berkeley: University of California Press, June 2001), 6.

35. For example, see Ch'oe Yuri, *Ilche malgi singminji chibae chŏngch'aek yŏn'gu* (Seoul: Kukhak Ch'aryŏwŏn, 1997).

36. Tomiyama Ichirō, *Kindai Nihon shakai to "Okinawajin": "Nihonjin" ni naru to yū koto* (Tokyo: Nihon Keizai Hyōronsha, 1990), 236; David Howell, *Geographies of Identity in Nineteenth-Century Japan* (Berkeley: University of California Press, 2005); Mariko Asano Tamanoi, *Under the Shadow of Nationalism: Politics and Poetics of Rural Japanese Women* (Honolulu: University of Hawai'i Press, 1998), 85–114.

37. Victoria de Grazia, *The Culture of Consent: Mass Organization of Leisure in Fascist Italy* (Cambridge: Cambridge University Press, 1981); Giulia Albanese and Roberta Pergher, eds., *In the Society of Fascists: Acclamation, Acquiescence, and Agency in Mussolini's Italy* (New York: Palgrave Macmillan, 2012).

38. See Martina Steber and Bernhard Gotto, "Volksgemeinschaft: Writing the Social History of the Nazi Regime," in *Visions of Community in Nazi Germany: Social Engineering and Private Lives*, ed. Martina Steber and Bernhard Gotto (Oxford: Oxford University Press, 2015), 1–26; Geoff Eley, *Nazism as Fascism: Violence, Ideology, and the Ground of Consent in Germany, 1930–1945* (London: Routledge, 2013).

39. Stephen Kotkin, *Magnetic Mountain: Stalinism as a Civilization* (Berkeley: University of California Press, 1997).

40. Henry, *Assimilating Seoul*, 3.

41. Fujitani, *Race for Empire*. Other examples that use the Foucauldian approach (sometimes partially) to the Japanese colonization of Korea include, but are not limited to, Theodore Jun Yoo, *The Politics of Gender in Colonial Korea: Education, Labor, and Health, 1910–1945* (Berkeley: University of California Press, 2008); Hui-yu Caroline Ts'ai, *Taiwan in Japan's Empire Building: An Institutional Approach to Colonial Engineering* (New York: Routledge, 2009).

42. See, for example, Alf Lüdtke, ed., *The History of Everyday Life: Reconstructing Historical Experiences and Ways of Life*, trans. William Templer (Princeton, NJ: Princeton University Press, 1995); Sheila Fitzpatrick, *Everyday Stalinism: Ordinary Life in Extraordinary Times; Soviet Russia in the 1930s* (New York: Oxford University Press, 2000).

43. See Patrick Bernhard, "Renarrating Italian Fascism: New Directions in the Historiography of a European Dictatorship," *Contemporary European History* 23, no. 1 (2014): 151–163; Paul Corner, ed., *Popular Opinion in Totalitarian Regimes: Fascism, Nazism, Communism* (Oxford: Oxford University Press, 2009); Alf Lüdtke, ed., *Everyday Life in Mass Dictatorship: Collusion and Evasion* (New York: Palgrave Macmillan, 2016); Jeremy Brown and Matthew D. Johnson, eds., *Maoism at the Grassroots: Everyday Life in China's Era of High Socialism* (Cambridge, MA: Harvard University Press, 2015); Suzy Kim, *Everyday Life in the North Korean Revolution, 1945–1950* (Ithaca, NY: Cornell University Press, 2013); Yoshimi Yoshiaki, *Grassroots Fascism: The War Experience of the Japanese People*, trans. Ethan Mark (New York: Columbia University Press, 2016).

44. This point is inspired by Jochen Hellbeck's claim that ideology exists only in the act of individual appropriation, rejecting the view that dichotomizes "self" and "ideology" as preexisting poles. But my goal here is to analyze how social forces conditioned and caused the process of appropriation, not whether particular "selfhood" was constructed through it. Jochen Hellbeck, "Liberation from Autonomy: Mapping Self-Understanding in Stalin's Time," in Corner, *Popular Opinion in Totalitarian Regimes*, 49–63.

45. Jan Plamper, "Beyond Binaries: Popular Opinion in Stalinism," in Corner, *Popular Opinion in Totalitarian Regimes*, 75.

46. Louise Young, *Beyond the Metropolis: Second Cities and Modern Life in Interwar Japan* (Berkeley: University of California Press, 2013), 84.

47. Precise figures differ, depending on how one defines "rural" areas. According to the 1930 census, about 49 million (76%) lived in *gunbu* (villages and towns under the population size of twenty thousand) and 15.4 million (24%) lived in *shibu* (cities over the population size of twenty thousand) in 1930. In the same year in Korea, 94.4% lived in gunbu and 5.6% in *fubu* (equivalent of shibu), and 81% of the working population engaged in agriculture. In Taiwan's 1930 census, nearly 4.4 million (84%) lived in gunbu and 846 thousand (16%) lived in shibu.

48. The pioneer in the attempt to do so is Ann Waswo, "The Transformation of Rural Society, 1900–1905," in *The Cambridge History of Japan*, vol. 6, *The Twentieth Century*, ed. Peter Duus (New York: Cambridge University Press, 1988), 539–605.

49. Richard Smethurst, *A Social Basis for Prewar Japanese Militarism: The Army and the Rural Community* (Berkeley: University of California Press, 1974).

50. David Prochaska, *Making Algeria French: Colonialism in Bône* (Cambridge: Cambridge University Press, 1990), 11.

51. Todd A. Henry acknowledges the critique of a heavy emphasis on urban history. Henry, *Assimilating Seoul*, 11, esp. fn. 35. Work that has challenged the urban-centric historiography includes Albert L. Park, *Building a Heaven on Earth: Religion, Activism, and Protest in Japanese Occupied Korea* (Honolulu: University of Hawai'i Press, 2015); Yumi Moon, *Populist Collaborators: The Ilchinhoe and the Japanese Colonization of Korea, 1896–1910* (Ithaca, NY: Cornell University Press, 2013). Two chapters in Gi-Wook Shin

and Michael Robinson, eds., *Colonial Modernity in Korea* (Cambridge, MA: Harvard University Press, 1999) do discuss the rural revitalization policy and the peasant discourse, but they both focus on the intellectuals and policymakers: Gi-Wook Shin and Do-Hyun Han, "Colonial Corporatism: The Rural Revitalization Campaign, 1932–1940," 70–96; Clark Sorensen, "National Identity and the Construction of the Category 'Peasant' in Colonial Korea," 288–310.

52. See, for example, Pang Kie-chung and Michael D. Shin, *Landlords, Peasants, and Intellectuals in Modern Korea* (Honolulu: University of Hawai'i Press, 2010). For a more systematic analysis, refer to Gi-Wook Shin, *Peasant Protest and Social Change in Colonial Korea* (Seattle: University of Washington Press, 1996).

53. "Children" and "childhood" had been recognized as a more separate category than "youth" had been in neo-Confucian societies. Kee-hun Lee (Yi Ki-hun), "Ilcheha ch'ŏngnyŏn tamnon yŏn'gu" (PhD diss., Seoul National University, 2005), 15–28; Ping-chen Hsiung, *A Tender Voyage: Children and Childhood in Late Imperial China* (Stanford, CA: Stanford University Press, 2005); Gregory M. Pflugfelder, *Cartographies of Desire: Male-Male Sexuality in Japanese Discourse, 1600–1950* (Berkeley: University of California Press, 1999); Chen Yingfang, "Qingnian" yu Zhongguo de shehui bianqian (Beijing: Shehui kexue wenxian chubanshe, 2007), 1–22.

54. Tani Teruhiro, *Seinen no seiki* (Tokyo: Dōseisha, 2003), 29–31.

55. See Richard Evan Jobs and David M. Pomfret, "The Transnationality of Youth," in *Transnational Histories of Youth in the Twentieth Century*, ed. Jobs and Pomfret (London: Palgrave Macmillan, 2015), 3–4.

56. A large number of studies have been done on these groups. Some of the relatively recent ones include Anne E. Gorsuch, *Youth in Revolutionary Russia: Enthusiasts, Bohemians, Delinquents* (Bloomington: Indiana University Press, 2000); Timothy H. Parsons, *Race, Resistance, and the Boy Scout Movement in British Colonial Africa* (Athens: Ohio University Press, 2004); Michael H. Kater, *Hitler Youth* (Cambridge, MA: Harvard University Press, 2004); Richard Evan Jobs and David M. Pomfret, eds., *Transnational Histories of Youth in the Twentieth Century* (London: Palgrave Macmillan, 2015); Mark Roseman, ed., *Generations in Conflict: Youth Revolt and Generation Formation in Germany, 1770–1968* (New York: Cambridge University Press, 1995).

57. *Sai* is calculated according to the Chinese and Japanese lunar calendar. People began life as one sai and on every lunar New Year's Day, they gained another sai.

58. Nagano Hiroko, "Collective Maturation: The Construction of Masculinity in Early Modern Villages," trans. Anne Walthall, in *Recreating Japanese Men*, ed. Sabine Frühstück and Anne Walthall (Berkeley: University of California Press, 2011), 203–215.

59. Morris Low, "The Emperor's Sons Go to War: Competing Masculinities in Modern Japan," in *Asian Masculinities: The Meaning and Practice of Manhood in China and Japan*, ed. Kim Louie and Morris Low (New York: Routledge, 2003), 81–99; Theodore F. Cook Jr., "Making 'Soldiers': The Imperial Army and the Japanese Man in Meiji Society and State," in *Gendering Modern Japanese History*, ed. Barbara Molony and Kathleen Uno (Cambridge, MA: Harvard University Press, 2008), 259–294.

60. See Watanabe Yōko, *Kindai Nihon joshi shakai kyōiku seiritsushi* (Tokyo: Akashi Shoten, 1997). On the education of women in colonial Korea, see Kim Puja, *Shokuminchiki Chōsen no kyōiku to jendā* (Yokohama: Seori Shobō). On the seinendan for young women in colonial Taiwan, see Miyazaki Seiko, "Shokuminchiki Taiwan ni okeru josei no eijenshī ni kansuru ichi kōsatsu," *Jendā kenkyū* 6 (March 2003): 85–108; Miyazaki Seiko, "Taiwan ni okeru joshi no seinendan to shokojin no keiken (1939–45-nen)," *Gendai Taiwan kenkyū* 39 (March 2011): 62–83. For studies of rural women, see also Tamanoi, *Under the Shadow of Nationalism*; Simon Partner, *Toshié: A Story of Village Life in Twentieth-Century Japan* (Berkeley: University of California Press, 2004).

61. Waswo, "The Transformation of Rural Society," 451–605. Shin, *Peasant Protest*, esp. chapter 4; Ōkado Masakatsu, "Meibōka chitsujo"; Chih-Ming Ka, *Japanese Colonialism in Taiwan: Land Tenure, Development, and Dependency, 1895–1945* (Boulder, CO: Westview, 1995), esp. chapter 4.

62. Quote from Yoshimi Yoshiaki's interview by Ethan Mark. Yoshimi, *Grassroots Fascism*, 15.

63. Watanabe Tsutomu, "Dare ga heishi ni nattanoka (2)," *Kansei Gakuin Daigaku Shakaigakubu kiyō* 119 (October 2014): 19–36, esp. 19–21.

64. Barbara H. Rosenwein, *Emotional Communities in the Early Middle Ages* (Ithaca, NY: Cornell University Press, 2006); See also Barbara H. Rosenwein, "Problems and Methods in the History of Emotions," *Passions in Context: Journal of the History and Philosophy of the Emotions* 1, no. 1 (2010): 1–32. One might also think of the concept of "emotional regime," but this book does not investigate emotional rules, norms, and ideals imposed on youth. See Willian M. Reddy, *The Navigation of Feeling: A Framework for the History of Emotions* (Cambridge: Cambridge University of Press, 2001).

65. His extensive interview by the National Institute of Korean History appears in Kuksa P'yŏnch'an Wiwŏnhoe, *Chibang ŭl salda: Chibang haengjŏng, 1930-yŏndae esŏ 1950-yŏndae kkaji* (Kwach'ang-si: Kuksa P'yŏnch'an Wiwŏnhoe, 2006), 2–220.

1. NATIONAL TRENDS

1. The Greater Japan Seinendan Federation did not include six major cities (Tokyo, Yokohama, Nagoya, Kyoto, Osaka, Kobe) until 1935. Karafuto joined it in 1928. Kumagai Tatsujirō, *Dai Nihon Seinendanshi* (Tokyo: Nippon Seinenkan, 1942), 156–159, appendix 61–67.

2. On these formal changes in institutions, see Kumagai, *Dai Nihon Seinendanshi*, and various other publications by the Japan Youth Center. The seinendan reverted to village-centered organizations (although still headed by the Japan Youth Center) after the end of World War II.

3. For more detail on Yamamoto's upbringing and activism, see Tani Teruhito, *Yamamoto Takinosuke no shōgai to shakai kyōiku jissen* (Tokyo: Fuji Shuppan, 2011).

4. Less than 10% of the young male population served army conscription during Meiji, and this increased to 18%–22% between the 1910s and the early 1930s. See Katō Yōko, *Chōheisei to kindai Nihon* (Tokyo: Yoshikawa Kōbunkan, 1996), 65–67; Okada Yōji, "Seinendan undō no haha, Yamamoto Takinosuke no shōgai to shisō," in *Yamamoto Takinosuke zenshū*, Yamamoto Takinosuke (Tokyo: Nippon Seinenkan, 1985), 1: Tani, *Yamamoto Takinosuke*, 22–50.

5. Yamamoto Takinosuke, "Inaka seinen," in *Yamamoto Takinosuke zenshū*, Yamamoto, 1.

6. Yonehara Ken, *Tokutomi Sohō* (Tokyo: Chūō Kōronsha, 2003), 61–81. Tokutomi Sohō originally emphasized the importance of "country gentlemen" (*inaka shinshi*), but the main audience were those in school in the cities.

7. Kimura Naoe, *"Seinen" no tanjō: Meiji Nihon ni okeru seijiteki jissen no tenkan* (Tokyo: Shinyōsha, 1998), 43.

8. "Shin Nihon no seinen oyobi shin Nihon no seiji," *Kokumin no tomo* 6–9 (July–October, 1887): 1–15, 8–15, 10–17, 9–16, respectively. See David R. Ambaras, *Bad Youth: Juvenile Delinquency and the Politics of Everyday Life in Modern Japan* (Berkeley: University of California Press, 2006), 72–74.

9. Kimura, *"Seinen" no tanjō*, 131–205.

10. Yamamoto, "Inaka seinen," 3.

11. Ibid., 6, 9.

12. Ibid., 17.

13. Ibid., 49.

14. Various scholars have discussed Japanese agrarianism in more detail. See Thomas Havens, *Farm and Nation in Modern Japan: Agrarian Nationalism, 1870–1940* (Princeton, NJ: Princeton University Press, 1974); Stephen Vlastos, "Agrarianism without Tradition: The Radical Critique of Prewar Japanese Modernity," in *Mirror of Modernity: Invented Traditions of Modern Japan*, ed. Stephen Vlastos (Berkeley: University of California Press, 1998), 74–94; Carol Gluck, *Japan's Modern Myths: Ideology in the Late Meiji Period* (Princeton, NJ: Princeton University Press, 1985), 178–204; Kerry Smith, *A Time of Crisis: Japan, the Great Depression, and Rural Revitalization* (Cambridge, MA: Harvard University Asia Center, 2001), 94–113, for example.

15. Yokoi Tokiyoshi, "Nōhon shugi," (October 1897), 232, trans. and quoted in Havens, *Farm and Nation*, 101.

16. Havens, *Farm and Nation*, 104; Gluck, *Japan's Modern Myths*, 180.

17. Katō Kanji, "Kōkoku nōmin no jikaku to shimei" (1936), trans. and quoted in Havens, *Farm and Nation*, 292.

18. This was, of course, similar to many examples around the world. See Irvin Scheiner, "The Japanese Village Imagined, Real, Contested," in *Mirror of Modernity*, ed. Vlastos, 67–78.

19. Gluck, *Japan's Modern Myths*, 182. See also 178–186.

20. Yamamoto, "Inaka seinen," 9.

21. Ann Waswo, "The Transformation of Rural Society, 1900–1950," in *The Cambridge History of Japan*, vol. 6, *The Twentieth Century*, ed. Peter Duus (New York: Cambridge University Press, 1988), 543.

22. During Meiji, villages in Tōhoku had very low crop yields in 1869, 1875, 1876, 1879, 1886, 1888, 1889, 1890, 1902, 1905, 1910, 1913, and 1914. Shida Sonshi Hensan Iinkai, *Shida sonshi* (Miyagi: Shida-son, 1950), 143–154.

23. Okada, "Seinendan undō no haha," 2.

24. Robert MacDonald, *Sons of the Empire: The Frontier and the Boy Scout Movement, 1890–1918* (Toronto: University of Toronto Press, 1993), 4.

25. See Ambaras, *Bad Youth*.

26. G. Stanley Hall, *Adolescence: Its Psychology and Its Relations to Physiology, Anthropology, Sociology, Sex, Crime, Religion, and Education*, 2 vols. (New York: D. Appleton, 1904); John R. Gillis, *Youth and History: Tradition and Change in European Age Relations, 1770–Present* (New York: Academic Press, 1981), 95–184. The Japanese translation of Hall's work is Jī Sutanrē Hōru, *Seinenki no kenkyū*, trans. Nakajima Rikizō, Motora Yūjiro, et al. (Tokyo: Dōbunkan, 1910).

27. Ambaras, *Bad Youth*, 87–88.

28. Yanagita Kunio, *Meiji Taishōshi: Sesōhen* (1930; repr., Tokyo: Heibonsha, 1962), 301–302.

29. Isono Shōzō, "Shakai kyōiku no seiritsu to sono honshitsu no kansuru ichi kōsatsu, ni," *Kyōikugaku kenkyū* 24, no. 6 (1957): 29–30.

30. Kumagai, *Dai Nihon Seinendanshi*, 163.

31. Sheldon Garon, *Molding Japanese Minds: The State in Everyday Life* (Princeton, NJ: Princeton University Press, 1997), 7.

32. Many scholars in Japan have discussed the policies of the Local Improvement Movement and their implementation. For example, Miyachi Masato, *Nichi-Ro Sensōgo seijishi no kenkyū* (Tokyo: Tōkyō Daigaku Shuppankai, 1973), 1–127. Kasama Kenji, *Chihō kairyō undōki ni okeru shōgakkō to chiiki shakai* (Tokyo: Nihon Tosho Sentā, 2003).

33. Maeda Ujirō, *Chihō seinen no tebiki* (Tokyo: Taiseikai Shuppanbu, 1912), 84–85.

34. Ryōminsha, ed., *Chihō seinen no jikaku* (Tokyo: Rakuyūdō, 1911), 9. See a similar argument in Maeda, *Chihō seinen*, 11–14.

35. Ogawa Toshio and Hashiguchi Kiku, "Shakai kyōiku no seiritsu to sono honshitsu ni kansuru ichi kōsatsu, ichi," *Kyōikugaku kenkyū* 24, no. 4 (1957): 6–18.

36. Kasama, *Chihō kairyō undōki*, 113–115.

37. Ogawa and Hashiguchi, "Shakai kyōiku no seiritsu," 6–18.

38. The Japanese government had persistently avoided the term *society* (*shakai*) because it invoked the image of socialism.

39. Matsuda Takeo, "Norisugi Yoshihisa no shakai kyōikuron no keisei to sono toku-shitsu," in *Gendai Nihon shakai kyōiku shiron*, ed. Shinkai Hideyuki (Tokyo: Gakujutsu Shuppankai, 2002), 56–59.

40. On the politicization of rural problems between the 1890s and 1920s, see Miyazaki Ryūji, "Taishō demokurashī ki no nōson to seitō 1, 2, 3," *Kokka gakkai zasshi* 7/8, 9/10, 11/12 (1980): 1–67, 69–126, 77–145, respectively; Itō Masanao, Ōkado Masakatsu, and Suzuki Masayuki, *Senkanki no Nihon nōson* (Kyoto: Sekai Shisōsha, 1988), 18–26.

41. Richard Smethurst, *A Social Basis for Prewar Japanese Militarism: The Army and the Rural Community* (Berkeley: University of California Press, 1974); Ōe Shinobu, *Kokumin kyōiku to guntai* (Tokyo: Shin Nihon Shuppansha, 1974). See also Kubo Yoshizō, *Nihon fashizumu kyōiku seisakushi* (Tokyo: Meiji Tosho, 1969); Kanō Masanao, *Taishō demokurashī no teiryū* (Tokyo: Nihon Hōsō Shuppan Kyōkai, 1973), 95–154; Ōgushi Ryūkichi, "Seinendan jishuka undō no ayumi," *Gekkan shakai kyōiku*, March 1989, 88–95; Ōkado Masakatsu, "Meibōka chitsujo no henbō," in *Gendai shakai eno tenkei*, ed. Sakano Hiroshi et al. (Tokyo: Iwanami Shoten, 1993), 65–108.

42. Smethurst, *A Social Basis*, 1–21.

43. Tanaka Giichi, *Shakaiteki kokumin kyōiku* (Tokyo: Hakubunkan, 1915), 88.

44. Norisugi Yoshihisa, "Senji ni okeru Doitsu seinen o ronjite wagakuni no seinen ni oyobu," *Miyagi kyōiku* 235 (March 1917): 16–20.

45. Kawai Yorio, *Tanaka Giichi den* (Tokyo: Tanaka Giichi Den Hensansho, 1929), 306; Tanaka Giichi, *Ōshū Taisen no kyōkun to seinen shidō* (Tokyo: Shingetsusha, 1918). See Hira-yama Kazuhiko, *Seinen shūdanshi kenkyū josetsu II* (Tokyo: Shinsensha, 1978), 21–30 for Tanaka Giichi's intervention into seinendan policies. See also Smethurst, *A Social Basis*, 1–49.

46. On government officials' reactions against student activism, see Kubo, *Nihon fashi-zumu kyōiku*, 165–183.

47. Monbushō Futsū Gakumukyoku, ed., *Seinen kunren gikai* (Tokyo: Shakai Kyōiku Kyōkai, 1926). The youth training center absorbed the vocational training school and became the "youth school" (*seinen gakkō*) in 1935.

48. Hirayama, *Seinen shūdanshi*, 21–30. "Dai-37 teikoku gikai shūgiin giji sokkiroku dai-7 gō," 88, quoted at 29.

49. Tanaka, *Shakaiteki kokumin kyōiku*, 117–132.

50. Nagata Tetsuzan, *Kokka sōdōin no igi* (Tokyo: Aoyama Shoten, 1926), 190–193.

51. Hirayama, *Seinen shūdanshi*, 73–77.

52. Based on interviews with Xu Chongfa in Hengshan, Xinzhu province, on May 20 and 27, 2011.

53. Hirayama, *Seinen shūdanshi*, 82.

54. Moriya Eifu, *Chihō seinen no kyōyō* (Tokyo: Teikoku Seinen Hakkōjo, 1919), 20–21, quoted in Hirayama, *Seinen shūdanshi*, 30.

55. Maeda, *Chihō seinen*, 190.

56. Monbushō Futsū Gakumukyoku, *Zenkoku seinendan no jissai* (Tokyo: Minbushō, 1921), 32.

57. See Tani, *Wakamono nakama*. Onizuka Hiroshi, "Seinen shūdan ni miru chiiki shakai no tōsei to minshū ni yoru sono juyō no katei," *Rekishigaku kenkyū* 669 (March

1995): 19–36 examines the transition from the traditional youth group to a modern one in Shimoina village, Nagano.

58. Monbushō, *Kansai shokenka seinenkai jōkyō torishirabesho* (Tokyo: Monbushō, 1910).

59. See Hiroshima-ken, *Hiroshima kenka seinen dantai jōkyō torishirabesho* (Hiroshima: Hiroshima-ken Naimubu, 1910); Matsuo Kōzaburō, *Mohan seinendan no soshiki to shisetsu* (Tokyo: Kaihatsusha, 1911).

60. Gunma-ken, *Gunma-ken seinen yagakukai jōkyō shirabe* (Maebashi: Gunma-ken Naimubu, 1909); Gunma-ken, *Gunma-ken tōkeisho 1911–1925* (Maebashi: Gunma-ken, 1926), part III, "Population and Others," 9.

61. Shinjō Yagakukai, "Seinen yagaku kaisoku" (1909), archived in the Seinendanhō Ākaibusu, Tsuruga College.

62. Ibid.

63. "Gendai seinen yo!" *Yamane seishi kaihō* 30 (July 1, 1927): 1–2.

64. Ibid.

65. "Aru seinen no otakebi jinsei wa doryoku," *Yamane seishi kaihō* 32 (September 1, 1927): 1–2. Nakano sei, "Seikō wa doryoku kara," *Yamane seishi kaihō* 33 (October 1, 1927): 1–2.

66. Barbara Sato, "Commodifying and Engendering Morality: Self-Cultivation and the Construction of the 'Ideal Woman' in 1920s Mass Women's Magazines," in *Gendering Modern Japanese History*, ed. Barbara Molony and Kathleen Uno (Cambridge, MA: Harvard University Press, 2008), 99–130.

67. Tani Teruhiro, *Seinen no seiki* (Tokyo: Dōseisha, 2003), 60–85.

68. Ibid., 86–89; Shūyōdan, *Shūyōdan undō hachijūnenshi gaishi* (Tokyo: Shūyōdan, 1985), 76–82, 106–108.

69. Yamamoto Takinosuke, "Ryōsha no kankei," *Kōjō* (December 1922): 15–19.

70. The scholar Tani Teruhito digitized them and made them available at the Seinendanhō Ākaibusu, Tsuruga College, Fukushima. They are now housed in the Japan Youth Center in Tokyo.

71. Kimura, *"Seinen" no tanjō*, 173.

72. Tahata Ryōkichi, "Itoshiki kora no tameni 7," *Yamane seishi kaihō* 19 (August 25, 1926): 1.

73. Ishigaki Yūki sei, "Seikatsu no igi: Nanji wa nazeni ikite irunoka," *Yamane seishi kaihō* 19 (August 15, 1926): 1; Suzuki Jōichi, "Kibō wa seinen no inochi," *Akita-shi seinendan danhō* 3 (November 20, 1926): 1.

74. "Itari shushō Mushisorīni shi yori Nihon seinen danjo ni okurareshi meshisēji," *Yamane seishi kaihō* 19 (August 25, 1926): 2.

75. Kimura Ryūtarō, "Nōson seinen no shinro," *Yamane seishi kaihō* 23 (December 5, 1926): 3–4.

76. Quoted in Suzuki Masayuki, "Taishōki nōmin seiji shisō no ichi sokumen jō," *Nihonshi kenkyū* 174 (January 1977): 13, trans. and requoted in Waswo, "The Transformation of Rural Society," 592–593.

77. Ōgushi, "Seinendan jishuka undō no ayumi," 92.

78. Ibid.

79. For more detail on Shimoina Seinenkai's autonomy movement, see Ōgushi, "Seinendan jishuka undō no ayumi"; Hirayama, *Seinen shūdanshi*, 107–268; and Kanō, *Taishō demokurashī*, 95–154.

80. Dai Nihon Rengō Seinendan, *Danhō* 1 (July 1925): 40–94. Hirayama, *Seinen shūdanshi*, 92–93.

81. During the 1880s and 1890s, Meiji agrarians praised models of "experienced farmers" (*rōnō*) such as "Meiji Three Great Rōnō"—Nakayama Naozō, Nara Senji, and Funatsu Denjibei. They exemplified early agrarian ideals. However, according to a study conducted

by the seinendan, young farmers in the 1920s did not find their biographies as inspiring as those of other "successful" figures. See Takeda Kyōji, *Nihon nōson shugi no kōzō* (Tokyo: Sōfūsha, 1999), 86–97. Dai Nihon Rengō Seinendan Chōsaka, *Seinen yomimono ni kansuru chōsa II* (Tokyo: Dai Nihon Rengō Seinendan, 1929), 33–37.

2. FROM MOBILIZATION TO THE SOCIAL MOBILITY COMPLEX

1. See Itō Masanao, Ōkado Masakatsu, and Suzuki Masayuki, *Senkanki no Nihon nōson* (Kyoto: Sekai Shisōsha, 1988), 46–170.

2. See, for instance, Michael Lewis, *Becoming Apart: National Power and Local Politics in Toyama, 1868–1945* (Cambridge, MA: Harvard University Asia Center, 2000); Kären Wigen, *The Making of a Japanese Periphery, 1750–1920* (Berkeley: University of California Press, 1995); Martin Dusinberre, *Hard Times in the Hometown: A History of Community Survival in Modern Japan* (Honolulu: University of Hawai'i Press, 2012); Simon Partner, *The Mayor of Aihara: A Japanese Villager and His Community, 1865–1925* (Berkeley: University of California Press, 2009); Gail Lee Bernstein, *Isami's House: Three Centuries of a Japanese Family* (Berkeley: University of California Press, 2005).

3. Furukawa city became part of the larger Ōsaki city in 2005. These mergers are typical for remote areas with shrinking populations in today's Japan.

4. Shida Sonshi Hensan Iinkai, *Shida sonshi* (Miyagi: Miyagi-ken Shida-gun Shida-son, 1950), 44–46.

5. Nōrin Chūō Kinko Kikakubu, *Nōson jittai chōsa shiryō dai-2 shū: Miyagi-ken Shida-gun Shida-son* (unpublished; available at Tōhoku University Library, circa. 1948), 22. Shida Sonshi Hensan Iinkai, *Shida sonshi*, 2.

6. Sunaga Shigemitsu, ed., *Kindai Nihon no jinushi to nōmin: Suitō tansaku nōgyō no keizaigakuteki kenkyū, Nangō-mura* (Tokyo: Ochanomizu Shobō, 1966), 35–37.

7. Ibid., 192–197.

8. Shida village experienced low harvests frequently—1869, 1875, 1876, 1879, 1886, 1888, 1889, 1890, 1902, 1905, 1910, 1913, and 1914. Shida Sonshi Hensan Iinkai, *Shida sonshi*, 143–154.

9. Sunaga, *Kindai Nihon no jinushi to nōmin*, 192–197.

10. Hangai Seiju, *Shōrai no Tōhoku* (Tokyo: Maruyamasha Shosekibu, 1906), foreword 1–4.

11. Nakamura Kichiji, ed., *Miyagi-ken nōmin undōshi I* (Tokyo: Kokusho Kankōkai, 1982), 147.

12. On the detailed account on the roles of landlords and the Miyagi government on agricultural production, see Christopher Craig, "The Middlemen of Modernity: Local Elites and Agricultural Development in Meiji Japan" (PhD diss., Columbia University, 2014).

13. Miyagi Kengikaishi Hensan Iinkai, *Miyagi kengikaishi dai-1 kan* (Sendai: Miyagi Kengikai, 1968), 1–14. Even in the recent popular telling of the Meiji Restoration, Tōhoku represents the conservative, ignorant, and stubborn forces that did not appreciate the efforts of the founding fathers of the Meiji state. See, for example, the NHK historical drama series *Ryōma den*, broadcast between January and November 2010.

14. Sugawara Michiyoshi, "Tōhoku fushin ni taisuru konpon hōsaku," *Miyagi kenjin* 9:10 [*100-go kinen: Miyagi-ken no zenbō*] (October 1933): 1–5.

15. Shida Sonshi Hensan Iinkai, *Shida sonshi*, 146–147.

16. Hangai, *Shōrai no Tōhoku*, 10–11.

17. Ibid., foreword 15–17.

18. Go Chō sei, "Honken ni okeru shōgaku jidō no tokusei kanyō jō tokuni chūi subeki jikō narabini korega tekisetsu naru shisetsu hōhō ikan," *Miyagi-ken Kyōikukai zasshi* 192 (March 1913): 11–12.

19. Shōdenshi, "Honken ni okeru shōgaku jidō no tokusei kanyōjō tokuni chūi subeki jikō narabini korega tekisetsunaru shisetsu hōhō," *Miyagi-ken Kyōikukai zasshi* 191 (February 1913): 1.

20. Kasama Kenji, *Chihō kairyōki ni okeru shōgakkō to chiiki shakai* (Tokyo: Nihon Tosho Sentā, 2003), 85.

21. "Miyagi-ken gakumu zatsuji, Sengo to kyōiku," file M38 2–0026, Miyagi-ken Kōbunshokan.

22. D. Colin Jaundrill, *Samurai to Soldier: Remaking Military Service in Nineteenth-Century Japan* (Ithaca, NY: Cornell University Press, 2016), 116–119.

23. Harada Keiichi, *Kokumingun no shinwa: Heishi ni naru to yū koto* (Tokyo: Yoshikawa Kōbunkan, 2001), 32–34.

24. Katō Yōko, *Chōheisei to kindai Nihon* (Tokyo: Yoshikawa Kōbunkan, 1996), 20.

25. Kitamura Riko, *Chōhei, sensō to minshū* (Tokyo: Yoshikawa Kōbunkan, 1999), 1–37. The length of military service was reduced from three to two years in 1927. See Katō, *Chōheisei to kindai Nihon*, 46–50.

26. "Chōhei shobun o ukezaru mono," *Kahoku shinpō*, December 19, 1907, 2.

27. "Guntai no seishin," *Kahoku shinpō*, July 29, 1906, 1.

28. "Shida Shōgakkō Seinendan," *Miyagi-ken Kyōikukai zasshi* 148 (December 1908): 47–50.

29. Ibid.

30. "Seinen no mohan," *Miyagi-ken Kyōikukai zasshi* 134 (October 1907): 47–48.

31. Shida Sonshi Hensan Iinkai, *Shida sonshi*, 265.

32. See Hijikata Sonoko, *Kindai Nihon no gakkō to chiiki shakai: Mura no kodomo wa dōikitaka* (Tokyo: Tōkyō Daigaku Shuppankai, 1994), esp. 54, on how school education became the central focus of village administration in Meiji.

33. Since before the end of the Tokugawa period, land in rural villages in Miyagi had been accumulated in the hands of a small number of landlords. Many traditional landlords collapsed because of the financial burdens of the Boshin War as well. The heavy land taxes in Meiji, the 1880s deflation, and repeating natural disasters turned many self-cultivating small farmers into tenants. Many tenants also abandoned their land completely during the first four decades of Meiji. See Sunaga, *Kindai Nihon no jinushi to nōmin*, 55–56. In Shida, between 1890 and 1911, the number of landless peasants increased from 103 to 381. The lost land was absorbed by local moneylenders (or the landlord class). In 1907, Shida village had a landlord who owned more than fifty hectares. By the following year, there were four of them. Considering that the maximum amount of land that one family could cultivate by themselves was six to seven hectares, the owner of fifty hectares of land depended heavily on tenant farmers. See Shida Sonshi Hensan Iinkai, *Shida sonshi*, 17; and Sunaga, *Kindai Nihon no jinushi to nōmin*, 162.

34. The village administrative office was nothing more than a federation of hamlets at the beginning. But the modern administrative responsibility assigned to the landlords provided them with a legal backup of their dominance as well as a larger scale of land management. Sunaga, *Kindai Nihon no jinushi to nōmin*, 64–70.

35. Nakamura, *Miyagi-ken nōmin undōshi*, 205.

36. See Craig, "The Middlemen of Modernity," 114–230 on how landed notables extended their power and facilitated agricultural modernization.

37. "Seinen dantai," in "Miyagi-ken gakumu zatsuji, Sengo to kyōiku," file M38 2–0026, Miyagi-ken Kōbunshokan.

38. Shida Sonshi Hensan Iinkai, *Shida sonshi*, 22–31.

39. The collective cultivation itself was not new to hamlets. It was a usual measure to take in times of famine. But in the contract-based tenancy of common land, peasants were forced to produce rice for commercial use, not for self-use to directly alleviate

their hunger. It also accelerated the rice-centric agriculture and commercialization of rice, rather than diversifying products to reduce famine risks. For details of Meiji land reform in Miyagi villages and the complex character of village-owned common land, see Sunaga, *Kindai Nihon no jinushi to nōmin*, 201–208 and 282–302.

40. "Chihō zasshin, Shida-gun," *Kahoku shinpō*, February 5, 1911, 3.

41. Miyagi-ken Shida Gun'yakusho, *Dai 5-kai Meiji 43-nen Miyagi-ken Shida gunchi ippan* (Miyagi: Shida Gun'yakusho, 1912), 46.

42. Sunaga, *Kindai Nihon no jinushi to nōmin*, 9–10; Craig, "The Middlemen of Modernity," 175–230.

43. "Shida Shōgakkō Seinendan," *Miyagi-ken Kyōikukai zasshi* 148 (December 1908), 49–50.

44. Youth groups during this period also had a function to promote agricultural reform without heating up the power struggle of political parties. Government officials denounced the strategy of parties like Seiyūkai, which attempted to widely appeal to landlords' private interests. From the viewpoint of government officials, youth groups, by embodying the "harmony of the village" and "collective spirit," detached the issue of agricultural reform from party politics. On the tension surrounding the politicization of villages, see Miyazaki Ryūji, "Taishō demokurashīki no nōson to seitō 1," *Kokkagakkai zasshi* 93, no. 7/8 (1980): 445–511.

45. Tomeoka Kōsuke, "Seinen dantai no seishin teki kiso," *Miyagi-ken kyōiku zasshi* 118 (December 1911): 49–50. On Tomeoka's persona as an activist, see David Ambaras, "Social Knowledge, Cultural Capital, and the New Middle Class in Japan, 1895–1912," *Journal of Japanese Studies* 24, no. 1 (1998): 1–33.

46. Shida Sonshi Hensan Iinkai, *Shida sonshi*, 266.

47. Utsumi Teitarō, ed., *Miyagi-ken seinen kyōiku no ayumi* (Sendai: Miyagi-ken Kyōiku Iinkai, 1987), 49–50.

48. Fukutake Tadashi, *Fukutake Tadashi chosakushū dai-4 kan: Nihon nōson no shakaiteki seikaku, Nihon no nōson shakai* (Tokyo: Tōkyō Daigaku Shuppankai, 1975), 39. See also Satō Mamoru, *Kindai Nihon seinen shūdan kenkyū* (Tokyo: Ochanomizu Shobō, 1970), 17–193 on traditional hamlet youth associations in Tōhoku. The ethnographer Takeuchi Toshimi argued that the youth groups led by Meiji officials were modeled after traditions in the southwest region and did not fit the reality of Tōhoku: the southwest village youth groups emphasized horizontal ties, whereas Tōhoku's village communities were organized more hierarchically. Takeuchi Toshimi, *Mura to nenrei shūdan* (Tokyo: Meicho Shuppan, 1991), 33.

49. Gotō Ichizō, *Eien nari, mura no kokoro: [Miyagi-ken Ōsaki chihō] Meiji, Taishō, Shōwa no wakamono tachi* (Tokyo: Fumin Kyōkai, 1990), 24–26.

50. In some hamlets, *keiyakukō* itself indicated an (adult) age group that comes after *wakashūgumi*. Fukuda Ajio, *Nihon sonraku no minzokuteki kōzō* (Tokyo: Kōbunkan, 1982), 243–288.

51. Takeuchi, *Mura to nenrei shūdan*, 5–6.

52. "Seinen dantai ni kansuru chūi jikō," *Miyagi-ken Kyōikukai zasshi* 175 (October 1911): 53.

53. The nature of *keiyakukō* changed over time to match the changing social classes. One form of hamlet agreement, *tanomoshikō*, an agreement of financial cooperation for such occasions as holding a wedding ceremony and renewing the thatched roof, was particularly prevalent. In some cases, during the transitional landlord-tenant relationship in the first two decades of the 1900s, it functioned as a moneylending system from landlords to tenants and facilitated the concentration of land in landlords' hands. See Sunaga, *Kindai Nihon no jinushi to nōmin*, 58–59. In Shida village, tanomoshikō continued during World War II, and there were more than forty groups of tanomoshikō even in 1950. Shida Sonshi Hensan Iinkai, *Shida sonshi*, 226.

54. Gotō, *Eien nari*, 39.

55. Utsumi, *Miyagi-ken seinen kyōiku*, 57.

56. Takeuchi, *Mura to nenrei shūdan*, 33.

57. See Theodore F. Cook Jr., "Making 'Soldiers': The Imperial Army and the Japanese Man in Meiji Society and State," in *Gendering Modern Japanese History*, ed. Barbara Molony and Kathleen Uno (Cambridge, MA: Harvard University Press, 2005), 259–294. The Meiji Civil Code (1896), for example, made the first son of the main family the sole legitimate heir. Before this, inheritance had no gender specificity in many parts of Miyagi. Miyagi-ken Miyagi no Joseishi Kenkyūkai, *Miyagi no joseishi* (Sendai: Kahoku Shinpōsha, 1999), 12–17.

58. See Takeuchi, *Mura to nenrei shūdan*, 1–190, for the premodern and modern female organizations in Tōhoku hamlets. The young women's group was nominally established at the same time in 1905 in Shida, but there was no continuation from the traditional hamlet female associations, and any detail of the young women's group is absent from the record. The only brief reference is Shida Sonshi Hensan Iinkai, *Shida sonshi*, 268–269.

59. The *honke* consisted of only the legitimate line of the heir. The rest of the family members, including second and third sons, constituted a subordinate rank of farmers, akin to the status of nonrelated tenant farmers. On the other hand, tenant families usually maintained a close relationship with the *honke* for generations, and sometimes received a portion of land as branch families. Because of this blurred boundary between the family members with a blood relationship and others, the entire hamlet community often made up a large family-labor institution (*ie*). The labor relationship in such communities was usually described as that of "parent" and "child" (*oyakata, kokata*). Beginning in the mid-nineteenth century, however, this labor relationship gradually ended. Since the Meiji Civil Code presumed clearer lines between family members and those not part of the family, landlords who accumulated land as moneylenders sought a contract-based relationship with their tenant farmers. When the village administrative office replaced the private capacity of landlords, its tenancy (of common land) was contractual, rather than familial. This also led tenant farmers to form an alliance to fight rising rents. After the famine in 1905, tenant alliances spread in Miyagi. Tenant farmers in Shida village established a union in February 1908 to negotiate with the new type of landlord. See Ariga Kizaemon, *Ariga Kizaemon chosakushū IX: Ie to oyabun kobun* (Tokyo: Miraisha, 2001), 17–153; Nakamura, *Miyagi-ken nōmin undōshi*, 322. Satō Mamoru also emphasizes the importance of landlords in youth associations in Tōhoku. Satō, *Kindai Nihon seinen shūdan kenkyū*, 192–193.

60. Before the Meiji period, these apprentice-tenants who worked for landlord families were called *nago*. The nago system originated in the medieval era and continued to exist as a custom. In the Meiji era, the nago system was banned and apprentice-tenants became tenant farmers. But in the Tōhoku region, the custom remained for the time being because of the slow pace of change in economic renovation and the introduction of a monetary economy. For more detail, see Mori Kahē, *Ōu nago seido no kenkyū* (Tokyo: Hōsei Daigaku Shuppankyoku, 1984). In English, see Thomas C. Smith, *The Agrarian Origins of Modern Japan* (Stanford: Stanford University Press, 1959), but note that Smith's study is mainly about the western area.

61. Shida Sonshi Hensan Iinkai, *Shida sonshi*, 266, 302–303.

62. Ibid., 267.

63. "Shida Rengō Seinen Taikai," *Kahoku shinpō*, May 8, 1911, 5.

64. "Miyagi-ken seinendan hatsudanshiki," *Miyagi kyōiku* 232 (December 1916): 33–36, 45.

65. Utsumi, *Miyagi-ken seinen kyōiku*, 87–89.

66. Ban Shōshi, "Chōheisho zakkan," *Miyagi kyōiku* 240 (August 1917): 90.

290   NOTES TO PAGES 58–63

67. Shida Sonshi Hensan Iinkai, *Shida sonshi*, 286–287.

68. Ibid., 321–322.

69. Furukawa Shishi Hensan Iinkai, ed., *Furukawa shishi dai-9 kan shiryō IV: Kindai, gendai* (Miyagi: Furukawa-shi, 2005), 470.

70. Information in this paragraph and the following is based on an interview with Katō Haruhiko (Katō Einojō's son) in Ōsaki city on April 24, 2012, and Katō Einojō's memoirs, edited by Katō Haruhiko. Katō Haruhiko, ed., *Jinsei sanmyaku yume bōbō: Katō Einojō ikōshū* (Ōsaki, printed by editor, 1987). See also Gotō, *Eien nari*, 110–130; Shida Sonshi Hensan Iinkai, *Shida sonshi*, 289–290.

71. Katō Einojō, "Buttsukaranakyā," *Omoto* 1 (December 1931): 6–10.

72. Naoji, "Yabuhebi," *Omoto* 1 (December 1931): 20–21.

73. Gotō, *Eien nari*, 121–122.

74. See Sunaga, *Kindai Nihon no jinushi to nōmin*, 303–383; Itō, Ōkado, and Suzuki, *Senkanki no Nihon nōson*, 46–95.

75. Sunaga, *Kindai Nihon no jinushi to nōmin*, 378–379.

76. Yonekura Tatsujirō, *Miyagi kusa no ne undō no gunzō* (Sendai: Azuma Shobō, 1984), 80.

77. Ibid., 104–114. Saitō Yoshirō, *Monogatari Miyagi-ken nōmin undōshi chū* (Sendai: Hikari Shobō, 1985), 7–32.

78. Furukawa Shishi Hensan Iinkai, *Furukawa shishi*, 110–115.

79. For example, "Shamintō enzetsukai," *Kahoku shinpō* August 13, 1928, 6.

80. Furukawa Shishi Hensan Iinkai, *Furukawa shishi*, 102–111.

81. For example, Sandra Wilson regards the left-leaning young groups in Nagano as having an independent voice, as opposed to government-sanctioned ones. In such a view, the dichotomy between the left and the right was analogous to being "active" and "passive," respectively. Sandra Wilson, "Angry Young Men and the Japanese State," in *Society and the State in Interwar Japan*, ed. Elise Timpton (London: Routledge, 1997), 100–125.

82. Hirayama Kazuhiko gives an elaborate examination of how the seinendan turned to leftist activities during various social tensions in Shimoina village, Nagano prefecture. Hirayama Kazuhiko, *Seinen shūdanshi kenkyū josetsu II* (Tokyo: Shinsensha, 1978), 108–257.

83. Kataguchi Hiroshi, "Kome sōdō to seinendan," *Seikei daigaku seiji keizai ronsō shūkan kinen ronbunshū jōkan*, November 1968, 208–232. Michael Lewis, *Rioters and Citizens: Mass Protest in Imperial Japan* (Berkeley: University of California Press, 1990), 23–26.

84. Miyagi-ken Kyōiku Iinkai, ed., *Miyagi-ken kyōiku hyaku-nenshi dai-2 kan: Taishō, Shōwa zenki hen* (Tokyo: Gyōsei, 1977), 488. Female and male students usually did not attend the same classes, and many schools offered sewing and other skill-oriented classes for female students, too. This movement reflected a heated debate over the goal of education in the countryside—was it to create nation-conscious citizens with standardized education, or provide students with practical skills that were useful for their specific occupations? Generally moving toward an expansion of vocational training, many schools offered agricultural training programs to farm youth.

85. Shida Sonshi Hensan Iinkai, *Shida sonshi*, 286–289.

86. In some villages, youth groups' night classes became a substitute for supplementary vocational schools. By the late 1920s, more than 70% of agricultural populations received vocational training in these institutions. Okabe Kyōiku Kenkyūshitsu, *Nōson ni okeru seinen kyōiku: Sono mondai to hōsaku* (Tokyo: Ryūginsha, 1942), 28 and 34; Hijikata, *Kindai Nihon no gakkō*, 200.

87. Miyagi-ken Kyōiku Iinkai, *Miyagi-ken kyōiku hyaku-nenshi*, 493–494.

88. Utsumi, *Miyagi-ken seinen kyōiku*, 90–91. With the addition of the youth training center, the system of youth education became redundant and confusing. In three out of every ten villages, supplementary vocational schools virtually functioned as youth training centers. The national association of supplementary vocational schools filed an

official complaint with the government in 1927, saying that "in the regions where the youth training center was forcefully implemented against the supplementary vocational school, the cost rose tremendously and the administration became too troublesome. It not only generated numerous obstacles, but in extreme cases, it also gave double burdens to the youth and students." "Seinen kuren to jitsugyō hoshū gakkō tono kankei ni kansuru kengi," *Miyagi kyōiku* 338 (August 1927): 90. To streamline youth education facilities, the supplementary vocational school and the youth school were merged together to become the "youth school" (*seinen gakkō*) in 1935.

89. Akama Heikichi, "Hoshū kyōiku no kekkan to sono kairyō hōan," *Miyagi kyōiku* 315 (September 1925): 40.

90. Shimogōri Heiji, *Sennin kyōin nōson seinengakkō no keiei* (Tokyo: Dai-ichi Shuppan Kyōkai, 1939), 29.

91. Miyagi-ken Kyōiku Iinkai, *Miyagi-ken kyōiku hyaku-nenshi*, 497.

92. See Okabe Kyōiku Kenkyūshitsu, *Nōson ni okeru seinen kyōiku*, 106, chart 52.

93. Their résumés are filed in "Gakuji: Seinen kunrenjo shidōin kaishoku" 3-0016 (1927), "Gakuji: Seinen kunrenjo" 3-0016 (1928), "Gakuji: Shakai kyōiku, seinen kunenjo kankei" 3-0019 (1929) in Miyagi-ken Kōbunshokan.

94. The hourly rate was calculated based on the average of the monthly income of male substitute teachers. They received about thirty-five to thirty-eight yen every month. Miyagi Kenchiji Kanbō, *Shōwa 2-nen Miyagi-ken tōkeisho dai-1 kan: Gakuji* (Sendai: Miyagi-ken, 1929), 35.

95. The government spent 1.6 billion yen (nearly the amount of one year's national total revenue, mainly financed by national bonds) for public construction projects to rescue impoverished rural residents between 1932 and 1934. Kerry Smith calculated that in Fukushima, rural residents worked 25.5 days a year in village relief programs and earned seventeen yen doing so on average. Kerry Smith, *A Time of Crisis: Japan, the Great Depression, and Rural Revitalization* (Cambridge, MA: Harvard University Asia Center), 149. Teachers experienced a decrease in their salaries and delays in payments during the Depression. In Miyagi, forty-seven schools could not pay their teachers in June 1931. See Kubo Yoshizō, *Nihon fashizumu kyōiku seisakushi* (Tokyo: Meiji Tosho Shuppan, 1969), 183–194.

96. When the supplementary vocational school needed more teachers with practical skills, prefectural governments established vocational teachers training schools. This gradually opened up a window for elementary-educated village youth as well.

97. See the résumés of teachers in youth schools filed in 3-0007 (1936), Miyagi-ken Kōbunshokan.

98. Satō Kesao, "Tate," *Seinen to shojo* 5 (December 1928): 14–16.

99. Mori Shigeshi, "Tate nōson sei," *Seinen to shojo* 5 (December 1928): 9–11.

100. Kitamura, *Chōhei, sensō to minshū*, 75–120.

101. Watanabe Yōko, *Kindai Nihon joshi shakai kyōiku seiritsushi: Shojokai no zenkoku soshikika to shidō shisō* (Tokyo: Akashi Shoten, 1997), 33–35.

102. Ibid., 104–139.

103. Ibid., 407–434.

104. Amano Fujio, *Nōson shojokai no soshiki oyobi shidō* (Tokyo: Rakuyōdō, 1916), 1.

3. TOTALITARIAN JAPANIZATION

1. For example, see, Giulia Albanese and Roberta Pergher, eds., *In the Society of Fascists: Acclamation, Acquiescence, and Agency in Mussolini's Italy* (NY: Palgrave Macmillan, 2012); Martina Steber and Bernhard Gotto, eds., *Visions of Community in Nazi Germany*; Geoff Eley, *Nazism as Fascism: Violence, Ideology, and the Ground of Consent in Germany, 1930–1945* (London: Routledge, 2013); Paul Corner, ed., *Popular Opinion in Totalitarian Regimes: Fascism, Nazism, Communism* (Oxford: Oxford University Press, 2009).

2. See Louise Young, *Japan's Total Empire: Manchuria and the Culture of Wartime Imperialism* (Berkeley: University of California Press, 1999).

3. See Kerry Smith, *A Time of Crisis: Japan, the Great Depression, and Rural Revitalization* (Cambridge, MA: Harvard University Asia Center, 2001), 41–83; Sunaga Shigemitsu, ed., *Kindai Nihon no jinushi to nōmin: Suitō tansaku nōgyō no keizaigakuteki kenkyū, Nangō-mura* (Tokyo: Ochanomizu Shobō, 1966), 475–477.

4. See Shakaikyoku Shomuka Chōsagakari, *Chōsa shiryō dai-20 gō: Tōhoku chihō nōson hihei jōkyō dai-3 hen* (July 1930), 140, graph 219, repr. in *Kyōkōka no Tōhoku nōson II*, ed. Kusunoki Masahiro (Tokyo: Fuji Shuppan, 1984), 504.

5. Hosaka Masayasu, *Go ichigo jiken: Tachibana Kōzaburō to Aikyōjuku no kiseki* (Tokyo: Sōshisha, 1974), 327, trans. and quoted in Smith, *A Time of Crisis*, 81. See also Suematsu Tahei, *Watashi no Shōwashi* (Tokyo: Misuzu Shobō, 1963), 27–28, 82–83.

6. Mumeisha published a collection of newspaper articles (mainly from *Tōkyō Asahi nichinichi* and *Tōō nippō*). Mumyōsha, ed., *Shinbun shiryō: Tōhoku daikyōsaku* (Akita: Mumyōsha Shuppan, 1991).

7. "Kono hisanji! Urareta musume sengohyaku-mei: Kyōsaku ga honken nōgyoson ni oyoboshita eikyō," *Tōō nippō* May 3, 1933, repr. in Mumyōsha, *Shinbun shiryō*, 35.

8. "Bareisho mo kuitsukusu," *Kahoku shinpō*, August 1, 1932, 4.

9. "Sui, reigai no jūatsu ni kigasen ni tatsu nōmin," *Kahoku shinpō*, November 19, 1934, 8.

10. Nōmin Kyōiku Kyōkai, *Nōmin no shososhiki keitai ni kansuru kenkyū: Miyagi-ken Shida-gun Matsuyama-chō no jittai chōsa* (n.p.: Nōmin Kyōiku Kyōkai, 1958), 5.

11. "Nōmin akka no ichiin wa kore," *Kahoku shinpō*, May 5, 1930, 6. "Shida mura ni matamata kosaku sōgi boppatsu," *Kahoku shinpō*, January 28, 1931, 4.

12. Smith, *A Time of Crisis*, 16–17.

13. Ibid., 252.

14. Teikoku Nōkai, *Tōhoku chihō nōson ni kansuru chōsa jittaihen*, March 1935, 433–481, repr. in *Kyōkōka no Tōhoku nōson fukkokuban*, ed. Kusumoto Masahiro (Tokyo: Fuji Shuppan, 1984), 603–651.

15. Smith, *A Time of Crisis*, 112.

16. For details on this campaign in Miyagi, see Satō Nobuo, *Sensō no jidai no mura okoshi* (Sendai: Nanbokusha, 2007).

17. "Shida-mura Nihachikai kyō hakkaishiki," *Kahoku shinpō*, February 22, 1934, 8. For details on the revitalization campaign at hamlet and village level, see Smith, *A Time of Crisis*, 224–268.

18. Ōkado Masakatsu, *Kindai Nihon to nōson shakai: Nōmin sekai no henyō to kokka* (Tokyo: Nihon Keizai Hyōronsha, 1994), 313–314. "Seinen no chikara o motte Yanaizu-chō kōsei o hakaru," *Kahoku shinpō*, April 23, 1934, 8.

19. Ōkado, *Kindai Nihon*, 315.

20. Shida's neighbor Ōnuki, in the village's newsletters, often highlighted the central role of seinendan members in the village's social life. Itō Takuji, *Ōnuki-mura monogatari: Kutō no nōminshi* (Furukawa: Ōsaki Taimususha, 1978).

21. Itō, *Ōnuki-mura monogatari*, 67–68.

22. Ibid., 152.

23. For example, a teacher in Miyagi recalled, "When I opened the newspaper and read the accomplishments of the soldiers was the only time of the day when I found comfort" in the mid-1930s. Ōe Masao, "Manshū dayori," *Miyagi kyōiku* 523 (January, 1943): 67.

24. "Kenka yūben taikai," *Kahoku shinpō*, August 13, 1929, 4.

25. "Ichi seinen no funtō doryoku de mohan nōzeiku ga umareru," *Kahoku shinpō*, April 24, 1930, 4. "Heishi nana-mei no otegara," *Kahoku shinpō*, April 24, 1930, 4. "Yūryō seikunsei," *Kahoku shinpō*, May 5, 1930, 6. "Shūyō zadankai," *Kahoku shinpō*, September 9, 1930, 6.

26. Ōkado, *Kindai Nihon*, 315–316.

27. See Okui Ayako, "'Kindai kazoku' no taishūka ni kansuru ichikōsatsu," *Shakaigaku zasshi* 20 (2003): 190–203.

28. "Namida aratani kokyō e: Eirei wa eikyū ni nemuru," *Kahoku shinpō*, March 8, 1932, 4. "Suihai o kawashita dōkyō no yūshi," *Kahoku shinpō*, February, 2, 1933, 7. "Gaisen yūshi o mukaete miyo kakuchi no kyōkiburi," *Kahoku shinpō*, January 18, 1933, 8.

29. Between 1936 and 1937, the army expanded from 240,000 troops to 950,000. At the same time, volunteer soldier recruitment for the navy also expanded. In 1937, the number of recruits was 9,174, but the number increased from 28,004 in 1941, 63,629 in 1942, and 111,739 in 1943 to 208,660 in 1944. Watanabe Tsutomu, "Dare ga heishi ni nattanoka (1)," *Kansei Gakuin Daigaku Shakaigakubu kiyō* 119 (October 2014): 5 and 8.

30. "Hijō jikyoku han'ei: Shida-gun chōhei kensa kessho shigansha ni-mei," *Kahoku shinpō*, May 11, 1936, 8.

31. Itō, *Ōnuki-mura monogatari*, 107–108.

32. For example, "Gōgun, seikunsei tō roppyaku-mei: Sōretsuna sentō enshū," *Kahoku shinpō*, March 8, 1932, 4. "Eaigawa o hasande hakunetsusen tenkai," *Kahoku shinpō*, March 28, 1932, 4. "Sida, Tōda no kōchi o hasami sōretsunaru mogi enshū," *Kahoku shinpō*, March 3, 1935, 8.

33. "Taikyaku, shingeki o tsuzuke sōretsuna shigaisen tenkai," *Kahoku shinpō*, April 10, 1932, 4.

34. "Ōshii Yamato nadeshiko," *Kahoku shinpō*, December 12, 1935, 8.

35. Kikuchi Keiichi, *Nanasen-tsū no gunji yūbin: Takahashi Minejirō to nōmin heishi tachi* (Tokyo: Hakujusha, 1983) introduces seven thousand letters that soldiers sent to their village and the local leader. A newspaper article, "Chūtaichō no onjō ni kanpun no shōshūhei: Kataku musubu chihō to guntai," *Kahoku shinpō*, December 12, 8, also reveals the close ties deliberately built between villages and battlefronts.

36. See Ichinose Toshiya, *Kokyō wa naze heishi o koroshitaka* (Tokyo: Kadokawa Gakugei Shuppan, 2010) on the mechanism of the social pressure to die in battle emanating from home villages.

37. See Louise Young, *Beyond the Metropolis: Second Cities and Modern Life in Interwar Japan* (Berkeley: University of California Press, 2013), 141–187.

38. The emphasis on local characteristics in education originally began as liberal activism by schoolteachers, challenging standardization in the late 1920s. In Tōhoku, teachers in Akita launched a movement to teach local languages, histories, and characteristics in through the journal *Hoppō kyōiku* (Northern education) in 1930. "Kantōgen: Warera ga shimei," *Hoppō kyōiku* 1, no. 1 (February 1930): 1.

39. Manryū Mamoru, "Kyōdo no shizen to bunka toni rikkyaku suru seikatsu shidō 1," *Miyagi kyōiku* 353 (November 1928): 21, for example.

40. Nakata Jinjō Kōtō Shōgakkō, "Kyōdoai no kyōiku no jissai shisetsu," *Miyagi kyōiku* 368 (February 1930): 59–61.

41. Miura Mitsujirō, "Kokugo kyōiku jō kara mita hōgen to hyōjungo no mondai," *Miyagi kyōiku* 423 (September 1934): 33.

42. Nagato Raizō, "Seinen kunren shikō 3," *Miyagi kyōiku* 333 (March 1927): 30–32.

43. Kumagai Tatsujirō, *Dai Nihon Seinendanshi* (Tōkyō: Kumagai Tatsujirō, 1942), 109–112, 227–262.

44. See Andō Kōki, "Sengo seinendanron ni okeru 'wakamonogumi'zō ni kansuru kōsatsu: 'Seinendan = wakamonogumi botai'ron ni chakumoku shite," *Nihon Shakai Kyōiku Gakkai kiyō* 40 (2004): 13–22.

45. "Ōgon no nami yureru hōjōno Ōsaki heiya nōgyō Miyagi no ōza Shida-gun," *Kahoku shinpō Miyagi kenka ban*, August 31, 1936, 8.

46. "Chihō jichi no kōjō chūken seinen ni kitai," *Kahoku shinpō Miyagi kenkaban*, August 31, 1936, 8.

47. Okabe Kyōiku Kenkyūshitsu, *Nōson ni okeru seinen kyōiku: Sono mondai to hōsaku* (Tokyo: Ryūginsha, 1942), 589.

48. Hoshino Tatsurō, "Kyōdo kyōiku, kinrō kyōiku, kōmin kyōiku," *Miyagi kyōiku* 378 (December 1930): 22, 24.

49. Itō Hyōgo, "Kyōiku o kichō to shitaru Tōhoku shinkōsaku," *Miyagi kyōiku*, July 1937, 50–51.

50. Yamauchi Saiji, "Tōhoku seinen gakkō kyōkasho hensan kadode no kai," *Miyagi kyōiku*, November 1938, 95.

51. Nagato, "Seinen kunren shikō 3."

52. "Seikunshosei no shussekinan kaishō," *Kahoku shinpō*, July 10, 1934, 8.

53. "Totei kyōiku ni komarinuku kakuchi seinen gakkō," *Kahoku shinpō*, October 28, 1935, 8.

54. "Genkaku naru keirei: Rengō enshū mo zenkenteki na mononi seinen gakkō no shidō hōshin," *Kahoku shinpō*, February 25, 1941, 3.

55. "Tōhoku ichi no seiseki nyūkōritsu 99%," *Kahoku shinpō*, February 25, 1941, 3.

56. Shida Sonshi Hensan Iinkai, *Shida sonshi* (Miyagi: Miyagi-ken Shida-gun Shidason, 1950), 206–207.

57. "Honnendo wa sanbyaku-chōson go-kanen keikaku de kakudai: 'Hyōjun nōson' settei yōkō," *Kahoku shinpō*, April 8, 1943, 2.

58. "'Kunren no seikatsuka' Funaoka Seinendan no shisetsu keiei gaiyō: Tsukerareta kenka ichi no origami," *Kahoku shinpō*, January 16, 1935, 8. The phrase "kunren no seikatsuka" had already appeared in a 1927 publication endorsing youth training centers, but it referred more to the importance of vocational training over academic education. See Ishida Risaku, *Seinen kunrenjo no keiei* (Tokyo: Tōyō Tosho Kabushiki Gōshi Gaisha, 1927), 20–22.

59. "Imaya mizou no kokunan: Seinen no shimei omoshi," *Kahoku shinpō*, August 12, 1937, 8.

60. "Kokka sōdōin hijō jikyoku o kyōchō: Shida-gun seinendan taikai sengen," *Kahoku shinpō*, August 21, 1937, 8.

61. Okabe Kyōiku Kenkyūshitsu, *Nōson ni okeru seinen kyōiku*, 495.

62. Ibid., 72.

63. On dojo-style training and "integration of training and everyday life," see Terasaki Masao, ed., *Sōryokusen taisei to kyōiku: Kōkokumin 'rensei' no rinen to jissen* (Tokyo: Tokyō Daigaku Shuppankai, 1987).

64. "Hachiman dōjō: Shida sonchō seinen ni okuru," *Kahoku shinpō*, December 14, 1938, 4.

65. Saitō Tomi, "Gakkō no dōjōteki seikaku," *Miyagi kyōiku* 520 (October 1942): 2–9.

66. Karino Rikuzō, "Dōjō chūshin seinen rensei no jittai," *Miyagi kyōiku* 536 (November 1943): 45–48.

67. Shimogōri Heiji, *Sennin kyōin nōson seinengakkō no keiei* (Tokyo: Daiichi Shuppan Kyōkai, 1939), 43–44.

68. Sandra Wilson points out that scholars had perceived the problem of overpopulation as early as the 1880s, and that the government recognized the population problem in the late 1920s, establishing a "Board of Inquiry into Population and Food Problems" in 1927. Sandra Wilson, "The 'New Paradise': Japanese Emigration to Manchuria in the 1930s and 1940s," *International History Review* 17, no. 2 (1995): 251–255; Abe Hiroki, "Nōson no nayami," *Miyagi kyōiku*, October 1936, 32–33. See also Young, *Japan's Total Empire*, 307–351.

69. Young, *Japan's Total Empire*, 318–321.

70. Iida-shi Rekishi Kenkyūjo, ed., *Manshū imin: Iida Shimoina kara no messēji* (Tokyo: Gendai Shiryō Shuppan, 2007), 31–33.

71. See Sandra Wilson, "Bureaucrats and Villagers in Japan: *Shimin* and the Crisis of the Early 1930s," *Social Science Japan Journal* 1, no. 1 (1998): 121–140.

72. Young, *Japan's Total Empire*, 329.

73. Kimura Tadashi, "Manshū Shokumin Kyōkai Sendai Shibu ni tsuite" (June 28, 1931), in *Kimura Tadashi sensei kōenshū "Sonchō jūnen,"* ed. Kimura Tadashi Sensei Kōenshū Sonchō Jūnen Kankōkai (Sendai: Kimura Tadashi Sensei Kōenshū Sonchō Jūnen Kankōkai, 1937), 148–149, trans. and quoted in Wilson, "The New Paradise," 265.

74. "Nihon'ichi no iminmura Nangō ga 'bunson' o kensetsu," *Kahoku shinpō*, July 22, 1937.

75. "Manshū no tenchi ni Ōnuki-kyō kensetsu: Ōi ni imin netsu o aotte," *Kahoku shinpō*, May 21, 1937, 8.

76. Wilson, "The New Paradise," 269–271.

77. Iida-shi Rekishi Kenkyūjo, *Manshū imin*, 33.

78. Kumagai, *Dai Nihon Seinendanshi*, 381–382.

79. "Miyagi Seinen Mansen Kai," *Miyagi seinen* 2 (February 1933): 50. Kumagai's Seinendan history also lists study trips to Manchuria starting in 1926, but there are no details available on the program. Kumagai, *Dai Nihon Seinendanshi*, Seinendan hattatsu nenpyō, 23.

80. "Miyagi Seinen Mansen Kai," 49–52.

81. For example, see Miura Yoshinori, "Mansen kengakuki," a series of articles in *Miyagi seinen* between December 1935 and March 1936; "Manshū ijūchi shisatsu nisshi shō," *Miyagi kyōiku*, February 1940, 44–64.

82. Shin Toyonori, "Hirake! Warera no Manmō," *Miyagi seinen* 14 (July 1936): 9.

83. Hyun Ok Park, *Two Dreams in One Bed: Empire, Social Life, and the Origins of the North Korean Revolution in Manchuria* (Durham, NC: Duke University Press, 2005), 24–63.

84. Satō Yūtarō, "Genzai no Senjin ni tsuite," *Akita-shi Seinendan danhō* 3 (November 1926): 1.

85. Igu-gun Edano-mura Seinendan, *Danhō* 11 (April 1935): n.p.

86. Saitō Jūrō, "Seinen gakkō 'kyōdo' no ichikōsatsu," *Miyagi kyōiku*, June 1940, 21.

87. "Shinken na seinen nomi ima no tairiku wa kangei," *Kahoku shinpō*, November 2, 1939, 7.

88. Gosode, "Manchū imin gōdō shinzen kekkonshiki," *Miyagi seinen,* April 1937, 76–79.

89. See Reto Hofmann, *The Fascist Effect: Japan and Italy, 1919–1952* (Ithaca, NY: Cornell University Press, 2015).

90. "Nichidoku seishōnendan no kōkan," *Miyagi seinen* 37 (June 1938): 1.

91. "Matsukoto hisashiki meihō no tomo: Kinō Tōhoku no yūto Sendai hōmon," *Kahoku shinpō*, September 12, 1938, 1.

92. Furukawa Shishi Hensan Iinkai, ed., *Furukawa shishi dai 9-kan shiryō IV: Kindai gendai* (Sendai: Furukawa-shi, 2005), 148–149.

93. Interview with Yūki Tamiya in Ōsaki city, April 24, 2012.

94. Katō Haruhiko (Einojō's son) donated files of his certificates and appointment letters, among others, to the Furukawa Shishi Hensan Iinkai. These materials ("Katō-ke bunsho") are available for viewing at Ōsaki City Hall.

95. Some of them are reprinted in Furukawa Shishi Hensan Iinkai, *Furukawa shishi dai 9-kan shiryō IV.*

96. "Jinushisan ni makeruna," *Kahoku shinpō*, April 9, 1943, 4.

97. "Taisei Yokusankai Shidagun Shibu dai-3 kai kyōryoku kaigi," May 18, 1941, stored in Katō-ke bunsho, Ōsaki City Hall.

98. Shida-son Yokusan Sōnendan, "Shokuryō zōsan no chikai," May 28, 1944, stored in Katō-ke bunsho, Ōsaki City Hall.

99. Tominaga Yoshio, "Nōson ni gekisu," *Yomiuri hōchi*, September 17, 1944, 2. Found in Aratanome burakukai, "Taisei yokusan roku" notebook in Katō-ke bunsho, Ōsaki City Hall.

100. Ōkado Masakatsu, "Kodomo tachi no sensō, kodomo tachi no sengo," in *Iwanami kōza Ajia Taiheiyō sensō 6: Nichijō seikatsu no naka no sōryokusen*, ed. Kurasawa Aiko et al. (Tokyo: Iwanami Shoten, 2006), 96–101. The original quote is in Yamanaka Hisashi, *Bokura shōkokumin* (Tokyo: Henkyōsha, 1974), 266.

101. Satō Tadao, *Kusa no ne no gunkoku shugi* (Tokyo: Heibonsha, 2007), 9–29.

102. Itō, *Ōnuki-mura monogatari*, 94.

103. The shortage of food became a serious issue beginning in 1939 because there was a huge drop in imports of Korean rice in 1939 and of Taiwanese rice in 1940. Sunaga, *Kindai Nihon no jinushi to nōmin*, 494.

104. Furukawa Shishi Hensan Iinkai, *Furukawa shishi dai 9-kan shiryō IV*, 172.

105. Kurokawa Midori, "Chiiki sokai haikyū—toshi to nōson saikō" in *Iwanami kōza Ajia Taiheiyō sensō 6*, ed. Kurasawa et al., 32–34.

106. Nishi Furukawa Chiiki Zukuri Iinkai, *Furusato saihakken Nishi Furukawa no meisho to kyūseki* (Ōsaki city: Nishi Furukawa-chiku Shinkō kyōgikai, 2008), 25.

107. Watanabe, "Dare ga heishi ni nattaka (1)," 8–12; Ōe Shinobu, *Chōheisei* (Tokyo: Iwanami Shoten, 1981), 144.

108. Sunaga, *Kindai Nihon no jinushi to nōmin*, 488.

109. Shakaikyoku Shomuka Chōsagakari, *Chōsa shiryō dai-20 gō*, 139, repr. in *Kyōkōka no Tōhoku nōson II*, ed. Kusunoki, 503.

110. Nōrin Chūō Kinko Kikakubu, "Nōson jittai chōsa shiryō dai-2 shū: Miyagi-ken Shida-gun Shida-son" (unpublished, Nōrin Chūō Kinko Kikakubu, 1948), 22.

111. Shida Sonshi Hensan Iinkai, *Shida sonshi*, 46

112. Ibid., 174–187.

113. Katō Einojō's hamlet newsletter (*kairanban*), October 17, 1943, for example, archived in Katō-ke bunsho, Ōsaki City Hall.

114. Katō Einojō's hamlet newsletter (*kairanban*), September 2, 1943, archived in Katō-ke bunsho, Ōsaki City Hall.

115. The national body of the sōnendan, the Greater Japan Imperial Assistance Sōnendan, was led by Gotō Fumio, a main proponent of youth training in the government and a lifetime executive of the imperial seinendan. Other seinendan leaders also got involved in establishing and managing the national network of sōnendan, such as Tazawa Yoshiharu and Yamazaki Nobuyoshi. Tazawa argued that "the permanent mission of the sōnendan movement was the continuance of the seinendan." Tazawa Yoshiharu, "Sōnendan no kōkyūteki igi to tōmen no ninmu," Sōnendan 1 (January 1941): 4. Found in Ōno Rokuichirō bunsho, R204 (309)1803, in the National Diet Library of Japan.

116. "Idō rōryoku kappatsuka: Otome butai Fukushima e," *Kahoku shinpō*, June 8, 1939, 8.

117. For example, "Kono kyōryoku, kono kansha: Ōsaki zendo ni tatakau kyūmai engun," *Kahoku shinpō*, October 27, 1943, 4.

118. "Shigansha 3-bai toppa: Ōsaki chihō teishintai, otome no sekisei," *Kahoku shinpō*, February 29, 1944, 4.

119. One example, written for children, is Shirahagi no Kai, ed., *Obāsan kara mago tachi e: Miyagi no sensō* (Sendai: Miyagi Shirahagi no Kai Chūō Shibu, 2005).

INTERLUDE: OKINAWA'S PLACE IN THE NATION-EMPIRE

1. The historian George Kerr calls this era "a true 'colonial period.'" George Kerr, *Okinawa: The History of an Island People* (Tokyo: Tuttle, 2000), 408. The final year of the

period of the Preservation of Old Customs Policy varies depending on the scholar and the issue at stake.

2. Itani Yasuhiko, "Kyūkan onzonki ni okeru Okinawa no seinen dantai," *Waseda Daigaku Daigakuin Kyōikugaku Kenkyūka kiyō bessatsu* 18, no. 1 (2010): 55–57. The schooling rate remained extremely low—4.94% of school-age boys and .42% of school-age girls in Kunigami were enrolled in school as of 1887; enrollment reached nearly 90% around the Russo-Japanese War. Kunigami-gun Kyōikubukai, ed., *Okinawa-ken Kunigami gunshi* (Nago: Kunigami-gun Kyōikubukai, 1919), 160–161. Nago Shishi Hensan Iinkai, ed., *Nago shishi honpen 6: Kyōiku* (Nago: Nago Shiyakusho, 2003), 41.

3. Okinawa was ruled by the American occupation government until the island's "return" to Japan in 1972. Several U.S. military bases still remain in Okinawa.

4. Tomiyama Ichirō, *Kindai Nihon shakai to "Okinawajin": "Nihonjin" ni naru to yū koto* (Tokyo: Nihon Keizai Hyōronsha, 1990), 109–193.

5. Ōta Masahide, *Okinawa no minshū ishiki* (Tokyo: Shinsensha, 1995), 279–289.

6. Ibid., 296–303. Matayoshi Seikiyo, *Nihon shokuminchika no Taiwan to Okinawa* (Inowan, Okinawa: Okinawa Aki Shobō, 1990), 265–273.

7. Wendy Matsumura, *The Limits of Okinawa: Japanese Capitalism, Living Labor, and Theorizations of Community* (Durham, NC: Duke University Press, 2015).

8. Ryūkyū Seifu, *Okinawa kenshi*, vol. 4, *Kakuron-hen* 3 *kyōiku* (Tokyo: Kokusho Kankōkai, 1989), 606–607; see articles in *Ryūkyū kyōiku* and *Okinawa kyōiku* around 1902–1911.

9. Ōta Tennan, "Joshi kyōiku to honken," *Ryūkyū shinpō*, July 5, 1900, cited in Ōta, *Okinawa no minshū ishiki*, 101.

10. "Kinengō hakkan no ji," *Okinawa seinen kinengō* 7 (November 1909): preface.

11. Nishikihara-sei, "Okinawa no heijiteki kansatsu," *Okinawa seinen kinengō* 7 (November 1909): 140.

12. A number of newspaper reports on Nago Seinenkai (established in 1899 for the purpose of reforming old customs) between 1899 and the 1910s in *Ryūkyū shinpō* and *Ryūkyū kyōiku* discuss their goal of reforming old customs, for example.

13. Kusunoki-sei, "Ōgimi kyōiku," *Okinawa kyōiku* 75 (July 1912): 44.

14. "Haneji tsūshin," *Ryūkyū shinpō*, October 9, 1900, in *Nago shishi shiryō-hen 2, senzen shinbun shūsei 1*, ed. Nago Shishi Hensan Iinkai (Nago, Okinawa: Nago-shi), 62–63.

15. Iha Fuyū, "Toshokan nite no taiwa," in *Iha Fuyū zenshū*, vol. 11 (Tokyo: Heibonsha, 1976, originally 1921), 277–278.

16. On this point, see Itani, "Kyūkan onzonki," 55–65.

17. "Okinawa-ken kaku gunku seinenkai jōkyō," *Okinawa seinen* 103 (1915): 58.

18. There are many memoirs testifying to strict seniority among children. One example is Kijokashi Hensan Iinkai, *Kijokashi* (Ōgimi, Okinawa: Kijokashi Hensan Iinkai, 1996), 283.

19. The original report is "Okinawa kenmin no rekishiteki kankei oyobi ninjō fūzoku" (1922), quoted in *Nago shishi honpen 6*, ed. Nago Shishi Hensan Iinkai, 122.

20. In Kunigami county, three thousand students participated in the county-wide sports competition in 1894, four years before mandatory conscription began in Okinawa. Okinawa-ken Kunigami-gun Kyōikubukai, *Okinawa-ken Kunigami gunshi* (Kunigami, Okinawa: Okinawa-ken Kunigami-gun Kyōikubukai, 1919), 142–143.

21. Fukuoka Katsuhiro, "Motobu chōheisho bōdō jiken no saikenshō," *Urazoe Shiritsu Toshokan kiyō* 11 (March 2000): 109–122.

22. Ichi Seinentō, "Kunrei sareta seinenkai fujokai ni tsuite," *Ryūkyū shinpō*, August 17, 1910, 2.

23. A renowned Okinawan intellectual and writer, Higa Shunchō, also recalled the discrimination as "riki-jin" he experienced during his military service. Higa Shunchō, "Nengetsu to tomoni," in *Higa Shunchō zenshū*, vol. 4 (Naha: Okinawa Taimusu), 205.

24. Funatsu Yoshiaki, ed., "Hōgen ronsō o kyūmei suru," *Okinawa bunka kenkyū* 34 (March 2008): 289–419, esp. 360–361.

25. Ōta, *Okinawa no minshū ishiki*, 393–398.

26. "Enshū to jidō no kansō," *Ryūkyū shinpō*, January 25, 1914.

27. A series of articles on youth groups written by the prefectural educational consultant Kawabe Yūkichi in *Ryūkyū shinpō* are typical examples that used these phrases associated with youth education around Japan. Kawabe Yūkichi, "Seinenkai ni tsuite, (1)-(4)," *Ryūkyū shinpō*, July 24, 25, 26, and 27, 1915, in *Okinawa keinshi*, vol. 18, *Shiryō-hen 8: Shinbun shūsei kyōiku*, ed. Ryūkyū Seifu (Naha: Ryūkyū Seifu, 1966), 795–799.

28. Kawabe Yūkichi, "Seinenkai ni tsuite (4)," *Ryūkyū shinpō*, July 27 1915, in *Okinawa keinshi*, vol. 18, ed. Ryūkyū Seifu, 798–799.

29. Tomiyama, *Kindai Nihon shakai to "Okinawajin,"* 78–98.

30. "Nōson o misutete kengai ni tobidasu seinen danjo ga kono ichigatsuni 67-hyakumei ni noboru," *Okinawa asahi shinbun*, February 2, 1925.

31. Miyagi Harumi, "'Sensō zenya,' hitobito no kurashi: Keizai hatan to shinobiyoru ikusa no ashioto," *Okinawa-ken joseishi kenkyū* 2 (1998): 68.

32. Ōgane Kume-sei, "Muigina dekasegi o kitan seyo," *Sōzō seinen* (October 1928): 35.

33. Interview with Taira Eishō on April 31, 2012, in Toyohashi city, Aichi. Taira was the head of Ōgimi Village Seinendan in the mid-1930s. He has written briefly about the seinendan in his memoir. Taira Einoshō, *Kaisō: Fūsetsu ni taete* (self-pub., Toyohashi, Aichi, 1996), 38–39.

34. Okinawan laborers, for example, gathered and established a left-leaning "youth alliance" (*seinen dōmei*) in Ōsaka.

35. Nago Shishi Hensan Iinkai, *Nago shishi honpen* 6, 351.

36. On the Arashiyama Incident, see the compiled newspaper articles in Nago Shishi Hensan Iinkai, ed., *Nago shishi shiryō-hen 3 senzen shinbun shūsei 2* (Nago: Nago Shiyakusho, 1985), 189–198.

37. One of the main leaders of the Ōgimi Village Administration Reform Movement, Yamashiro Zenkō, published his memoirs. See Yamashiro Zenkō, *Yanbaru no hi: Shōwa shoki nōmin tōsō no kiroku* (Naha: Okinawa Taimususha, 1976).

38. Matsumura, *The Limits of Okinawa*, 173.

39. For more detail and testimonies, see Fukuchi Hiroaki, *Mura to sensō: Kijoka no Shōwashi* (Naha: "Mura to Sensō" Kankōkai, 1975); Fukuchi Hiroaki, *Nōheitai: Kuwa no shōnen senshi* (Naha: Naha Shuppansha, 1996); Fukuchi Hiroaki, *Hiroku Okinawa kessen bōeitai: Yunde ni takeyari, mete ni kuwa* (Naha: Okinawa Jiji Shuppan, 1985).

40. Nago Shishi Hensan Iinkai, *Nago shishi honpen* 6, 132–134.

41. Fukuchi, *Mura to sensō*, 188–194.

42. Ibid., 241–242.

4. COLONIAL INTELLECTUALS

1. Chen Yongzheng et al., eds., *Kang Youwei Liang Qichao sanwenxuan* (Hong Kong: Sanlian shudian, 1994), 220.

2. For a discussion of Ch'oe Nam-sŏn's impressions in Japan, see, Yun Se-jin, "'Sonyŏn' kwa 'Ch'ŏngch'un' kkaji, kŭndaejŏk chisik ŭi sŭp'ekt'ŏk'ŭl," in '*Sonyŏn' kwa 'Ch'ŏngch'un' ŭi ch'ang*, ed. Kwon Podŭre (Seoul: Ihwa Yŏja Taehakkyo Ch'ulp'anbu, 2007), 23–30.

3. Yun, "'sonyŏn' kwa 'Ch'ŏngch'un' kkaji," 23–30. The word *sonyŏn* indicated a young generation or a young man and was used interchangeably with *ch'ŏngnyŏn* in this period. *Ch'ŏngch'un* means a "spring" period in one's life, similar to adolescent or youthful years. Yi Kwang-su is a controversial figure in modern Korean literature. He is known as the founder of modern Korean literature but became infamous as a "pro-Japanese collaborator" in the postliberation period.

4. In *Hwangsŏng sinmun*, it increased from 12 in 1905 to 93 in 1908. The youth-related articles in *Taehan maeil sinbo* numbered 127 in 1908 and 177 in 1909. Kee-hun Lee (Yi Ki-hun), "Ilcheha ch'ŏngnyŏn tamnon yŏn'gu" (PhD diss., Seoul National University, 2005), 39–40.

5. "Sonyŏn ŭi Han'guk," *Taehan maeil sinbo*, July 1, 1910.

6. Yi Sun-jong, "Ch'ŏngnyŏn ŭi chagi," *Hwangsŏng sinmun*, March 4, 1905.

7. Kyeyangsanin, "Kwŏn'go Ch'ŏngnyŏn" *Hwangsŏng sinmun*, February 20, 1905.

8. Koju (Yi Kwang-su), "Kŭmil a Han ch'ŏngnyŏn ŭi kyŏngu," *Sonyŏn* 3, no. 6 (1910): 26–31.

9. "Ch'ŏngnyŏn Hakuhoe Ch'wijisŏ," *Sonyŏn* 2, no. 8 (1909): 14–16.

10. *Ch'inmokhoe, Cheguk Ch'ŏngnyŏnhoe*, for example. "Ponhŏe kŭmsŏk chigam," *Tae-han hŭnghakpo* 13 (November 1909): 1–6. Lee, "Ilcheha ch'ŏngnyŏn tamnon yŏn'gu," 37–38.

11. For example, "Ch'ŏnghoe kwŏnmyŏn," *Hwangsŏng sinmun*, November 8, 1905. Kyeyangsanin, "Kwŏn'go Ch'ŏngnyŏn"; "Sonyŏn'gye p'unggi ka yŏgyŏsi ho a," *Hwangsŏng sinmun*, August 14, 1909.

12. "Ne ch'aegim," *Hak chi kwang* [*Lux Scientiae*] 15 (March 1918): 1–6.

13. Another example is "Abando ch'ŏngnyŏn ŭi samyŏng," *Chosŏn ilbo*, April 27, 1921.

14. See Andre Schmid, *Korea between Empires* (New York: Columbia University Press, 2002), 171–198 for a discussion on how a Korean ethnic consciousness, particularly a history of *minjok*, developed between 1895 and 1919.

15. See Chōsen Sōtokufu Gakumukyoku, *Sōjō to gakkō* (Seoul: Chōsen Sōtokufu, 1920). See Erez Manela, *The Wilsonian Moment: Self-Determination and the International Origins of Anticolonial Nationalism* (New York: Oxford University Press, 2007) about the influence of Woodrow Wilson on the March First Movement.

16. Chōsen Sōtokufu Gakumukyoku, *Sōjō to gakkō*, 8–9.

17. Ibid., 1.

18. "Chŏn Chosŏn Ch'ŏngnyŏnhoe Yŏnhap Kisŏnghoe chojik," *Tonga ilbo*, June 30, 1920, 3.

19. Ibid. Other examples include Yi Tonhua, "Chosŏn Ch'ŏngnyŏnhoe Yŏnhaphoe ŭi sŏngnip e ch'wihaya," *Kaebyŏk* 7 (January 1921): 33, and Zenra-nandō Naimubu, *Seinenkai shidō hōshin* (Kwangju: Zenra-nandō, 1922), 1.

20. Including those with other labels, such as "self-cultivation groups," "abstinence clubs," "social groups," and "semireligious groups," these numbers went up to 985 in 1920, and nearly 3,000 in the following years. Chōsen Sōtokufu Keimukyoku, *Chōsen chian jōkyō* (Seoul: Chōsen Sōtokufu, 1922), 179–180.

21. "Chosŏn Ch'ŏngnyŏn Yŏnhaphoe ijunyŏn kinyŏm," *Tonga ilbo*, December 1, 1922, 3.

22. Tongnip Undongsa P'yŏnch'an Wiwŏnhoe, *Tongnip undongsa che 3-kwŏn* (Seoul: Tongnip Yugongja Saŏp Kigŭm Unyong Wiwŏnhoe, 1971), 889.

23. Kin Ikkan (Kim Ik-han), "Shokuminchiki Chōsen ni okeru chihō shihai taisei no kōchiku katei to nōson shakai hendō" (PhD diss., University of Tokyo, 1995), 261–264.

24. Kanamori Jōsaku, *1920-nendai Chōsen no shakaishugi undōshi* (Tokyo: Miraisha, 1985), 16–20.

25. Zenra-nandō Naimubu, *Seinenkai shidō hōshin*, 2; Kin, "Shokuminchiki Chōsen ni okeru chihō shihai taisei," 264–265. Kanamori, *1920-nendai Chōsen*, 15–20.

26. *Tonga ilbo*, June 18, 1920, cited in Tsuji Hironori, "Shokuminchiki jitsuryoku yōsei undō ni okeru renzoku to tenkan," *Chōsenshi Kenkyūkai ronbunshū* 37 (October 1999): 81.

27. Tsuji, "Shokuminchiki jitsuryoku yōsei undō," 18; Kin, "Shokuminchiki Chōsen ni okeru chihō shihai taisei," 261–269 makes a similar point.

28. See Kanamori, *1920-nendai Chōsen*, 17–18.

29. "Chosŏn Ch'ŏngnyŏn Yŏnhaphoe ijunyŏn kinyŏm." Most of the members were concentrated in South Kyŏngsang, South Hamgyŏng, and Hwanghae provinces. "Chosŏn Ch'ŏngnyŏnhoe Yŏnhaphoe chojik tanch'e illamp'yo," *Asŏng* 1 (March 1921): 103–106.

30. The preparatory group was established on June 28, 1920. For details on the establishment of the Korea Youth Group Association, see An Kŏn-ho, "1920-yŏndae chŏnban'gi Chosŏn Ch'ŏngnyŏnhoe Yŏnhaphoe e kwanhan yŏn'gu" (master's thesis, Sungsil University, 1993), 22–27.

31. O Sang-gŭn, "Chŏlsirhan kago ha esŏ wanjŏnhan tanch'e toegi rŭl yoham," *Kaebyŏk* 6 (December 1920): 43–44

32. Yi Ton-hwa, "Chosŏn ch'ŏngnyŏnhoe yŏnhaphoe ŭi sŏngni e ch'wihaya," *Kaebyŏk* 7 (January 1921): 36.

33. O Sang-gŭn, "Kŭmil ŭi munje: Chibang ch'ŏngnyŏn tanch'e palchŏnch'aek," *Tonga ilbo*, February 25, 1921.

34. "Chosŏn Ch'ŏngnyŏn Yŏnhaphoe ijunyŏn kinyŏm."

35. Chen Boyu, "Taiwan zhi qingnianjie," *(Hanwen) Taiwan riri xinbao*, October 28, 1905, 9.

36. Chen Wensong, *Zhimin tongzhi yu 'qingnian': Taiwan zongdufu de 'qingnian' jiaohua zhengce* (Taipei: Taida chuban zhongxin, 2015), 155–160.

37. Izumi Akira, "Taiwan tōmin ni tsugu," *Taiwan qingnian* 1, no. 1 (1920): 7.

38. Beginning with the opening words of the inaugural issue of *Taiwan qingnian*, it was repeatedly mentioned. "Kantō no ji," *Taiwan qingnian* 1, no. 1 (1920): 1.

39. Lin Chenglu, "Shinjidai ni shosuru Taiwan seinen no kakugo," *Taiwan qingnian* 1, no. 1 (1920): 29.

40. See Cai Peihuo, "Wagatō to warera," *Taiwan qingnian* 1, no. 4 (1920): 13–24; Cai Peihuo, "Hanzu zhi guyouxing," *Taiwan qingnian* 2, no. 3 (1921): 24–28.

41. Chen Duxiu, "Jinggao qingnian," *Taiwan minbao*, September 1, 1923, 3. *Taiwan minbao* was the successor of *Taiwanese qingnian* and *Taiwan*. It was published in Tokyo until August 1927, when it obtained permission to be published in Taiwan. The translation is from S. Y. Teng and J. K. Fairbank, eds., *China's Response to the West* (Cambridge, MA: Harvard University Press, 1954), 240.

42. Many well-known modernist activists and advocates of New Literature, including Lin Xiantang and Cai Huiru, continued practicing classical poetry. See Yokoji Keiko, *Wenxue de liuli yu huigui: Sanling niandai xiangtu wenxue lunzhan* (Taipei: Lianhe wenxue chubanshe, 2009), 185–187; Faye Yuan Kleeman, *Under an Imperial Sun: Japanese Colonial Literature of Taiwan and the South* (Honolulu: University of Hawai'i Press, 2003), 145–159. For details on the complex movements in modernizing the Chinese language, refer to Yurou Zhong, "Script Crisis and Literary Modernity in China, 1916–1958" (PhD diss., Columbia University, 2014).

43. Zhou Taoyuan, "Zen Ajia no taisei yori mitaru gen Taiwan seinen ni taisuru kyūmu," *Taiwan qingnian* 1, no. 3 (1920): 51–52.

44. See "Kantō no ji," 1; "Kyōjaku tōsō yori jiyū heiwa e," *Taiwan qingnian* 1, no. 4 (1920): 1; "Kantō no ji," *Taiwan qingnian* 2, no. 1 (1921): 1, for example. Although this was the dominant argument put forth by the main writers and editors of *Taiwanese qingnian* and *Taiwan minbao*, there were some exceptions, such as Ke Di, "Qingnian zizhitan," *Taiwan minbao*, October 1, 1924, 2.

45. For example, "Kantō no ji," *Taiwan qingnian* 2, no. 5 (1921): 1, and Jian Ru, "Guanyu Zhanghua sixiang wenti de kaoan," *Taiwan minbao*, September 11, 1924, 4–5.

46. Wu Keji, "Taiwan qingnian zijuelun," *Taiwan qingnian* 1, no. 4 (1920): 17.

47. Lu Yankun, "Bendao qingnian zhi juexing," *Taiwan minbao*, October 21, 1924, 10.

48. Xu Qingxiang, "Chihō seinendan o kanshō su," *Taiwan qingnian* 1, no. 5 (1920): 45–48.

49. Taiwan Sōtokufu Keimukyoku, ed., *Taiwan shakai undōshi; Taiwan Sōtokufu keisatsu enkakushi dai-ni hen: Ryōtai igo no chian jōkyō chūkan* (1939, repr. Tokyo: Ryūkei Shosha, 1973), 202.

50. Chen Wen Sung (Winston) (Chen Wensong), "Shokuminchi shihai to 'seinen': Sōtokufu no 'seinen' kyōka seisaku to chiiki shakai no henyō" (PhD diss., University of Tokyo, 2008), 277.

51. Similar study groups were formed by Taiwanese students in Japan as well. See reports in Taiwan Sōtokufu Keimukyoku, *Taiwan shakai undōshi*, 52.

52. "Qingnianhui yu dushuhui," *Taiwan minbao*, December 12, 1926, 3–4.

53. Taiwan Sōtokufu Keimukyoku, *Taiwan shakai undōshi*, 37–38, 583–585.

54. Ibid., 190.

55. For details of the internal struggle, see Taiwan Sōtokufu Keimukyoku, *Taiwan shakai undōshi*, 182–216.

56. "Bunka Kyōkai no ninmu," *Taiwan minbao*, October 16, 1927, 10.

57. "Kakchi ch'ŏngnyŏnhoe e taehaya (sang)," *Tonga ilbo*, March 11, 1921, 1.

58. Yi Kang, "Chōsen seinen undō no shiteki kōsatsu (4)," *Chōsen shisō tsūshin* 18, no. 472 (1927): 5.

59. Yi Kang, "Chōsen seinen undō no shiteki kōsatsu (1)-(15)," *Chōsen shisō tsūshin* 18, no. 469–484 (1917); An, "1920-yŏndae chŏnban'gi," 36–61; An Kŏn-ho, "1920-yŏndae chŏnban'gi Chosŏn ch'ŏngnyŏn undong ŭi chŏn'gae," in *Han'guk kŭnhyŏndae ch'ŏngnyŏn undongsa*, ed. Han'guk Yŏksa Yŏn'guhoe kŭnhyŏndae ch'ŏngnyŏn undongsa yŏn'guban (Seoul: P'ulpit, 1995), 69–79. There were several factions cooperating with or competing against one another among Korean socialists behind their negotiations with nationalists. On this point, see Pak Ch'ŏl-ha, "1920-yŏndae chŏnban'gi sahoejuŭi ŭi ch'ŏngnyŏn undong kwa Koryŏ Kongsan Ch'ŏngnyŏnhoe," *Yŏksa wa hyŏnsil* 9 (June 1993): 242–273.

60. On age consciousness for the Komsomol, see Matthias Newmann, "'Youth, It's Your Turn!': Generations and the Fate of the Russian Revolution (1917–1932)," *Journal of Social History* 46, no. 2 (2012): 273–304. The Koryŏ Communist Youth Alliance in exile set up an upper age limit at thirty years old. This group, established in Shanghai in 1921, exerted significant power over many of the Socialist youth groups operating in Korea with its status as a branch organization of the Communist Youth International. Pak, "1920-yŏndae chŏnban'gi sahoejuŭi ŭi ch'ŏngnyŏn," 249–252.

61. An Kŏn-ho and Pak Hye-ran, "1920-yŏndae chunghuban ch'ŏngnyŏn undong kwa Chosŏn Ch'ŏngnyŏn Ch'ongdongmaeng," in *Han'guk kŭnhyŏndae ch'ŏngnyŏn undongsa*, ed. Hanguk Yŏksa Yŏn'guhoe Kŭnhyŏndae Ch'ŏngnyŏn Undongsa Yŏn'guban (Seoul: P'ulpit, 1995), 98. Most restrictive was the Kyŏngsŏng Youth Group led by the Puksŏng Socialist Group, which advocated age twenty-five as the upper limit. "Once people turn over twenty-five years old, their activities become political. . . . They could take advantage of the pure youth under twenty-five as much as they want, and trick these youth groups as they please," claimed Song Pong-u, a leading figure of the Puksŏng group. He adopted a strict sense of youth defined by a physiological age, not by youthful qualities that older leaders claimed to have. Song Pong-u, "Yŏllyŏng chehannon: Isibose rŭl chu-jang," *Ch'ŏkhudae imsi-ho*, July 5, 1924, 1, cited in Kee-hun Lee (Yi Ki-hun), "1920-yŏndae sahoejuŭi inyŏm ŭi chŏn'gae wa ch'ŏngnyŏn tamnon," *Yŏksa munje yŏn'gu* 13 (December 2004): 305.

62. Pak, "1920-yŏndae chŏnban'gi sahoejuŭi ŭi ch'ŏngnyŏn," 249–251.

63. This use of age as a weapon lost its appeal after this particular generation, however. Once the language of class struggle gained a dominant position in anticolonial discourse in the late 1920s, mentions of youth in leftist writings quickly diminished. Especially after the last attempt to unite the leftist and nationalist forces through the establishment of Sin'ganhoe took place in 1927, they could no longer describe youth as warriors in the class struggle. Lee, "1920-yŏndae sahoejuŭi inyŏm," 308–311.

64. An, "1920-yŏndae chŏnban'gi," 70–71.

65. Some of the examples include "Kŭmhae ch'ŏngnyŏn hyŏksin," *Tonga ilbo*, February 26, 1925; "Samsipse ro chehan hyŏksin ch'onghoe esŏ hoech'ik to kaejŏng hae," *Tonga ilbo*, March 12, 1925; "Kyŏngsŏng ch'ŏngnyŏn hyŏksin," *Tonga ilbo*, April 2, 1925.

66. Tsuji, "Shokuminchiki jitsuryoku yōsei undō," 93–96. The rate of schooling (public, private, and *sŏdang*) of all school-age children in 1925 was 25%. That of the populations in the countryside and female children was significantly lower. This was calculated based on the numbers provided in Kim Puja, *Shokuminchiki Chōsen no kyōiku to jendā* (Tokyo: Seori Shobō, 2005), 371. A national survey in 1930 estimated the literacy rate for the first time and found that 80% of Korean populations were illiterate either in Korean or Japanese.

67. See Gi-Wook Shin, "Agrarianism: A Critique of Colonial Modernity in Korea," *Comparative Studies in Society and History* 41, no. 4 (1999): 784–804; Clark Sorensen, "National Identity and the Construction of the Category 'Peasant' in Colonial Korea," in *Colonial Modernity in Korea*, ed. Michael Robinson and Gi-Wook Shin (Cambridge, MA: Harvard University Press, 1999), 288–310.

68. Young Hoon Kang, "Personal Reminiscences of My Japanese School Days," in *Korea's Response to Japan: The Colonial Period, 1910–1945*, ed. Eugene Kim et al. (Kalamazoo: Western Michigan University, 1974), 288.

69. For a quick survey of the peasant literature movement in the 1930s, see Ho Ung Jung (Chŏng Ho-ung), "Nongmin munhak yŏn'gu ŭi hyŏnhwang kwa ap'ŭro ŭi panghyang," *Han'guk hakpo* 10, no. 4 (1984): 4155–4187.

70. Albert L. Park, *Building a Heaven on Earth: Religion, Activism, and Protest in Japanese Occupied Korea* (Honolulu: University of Hawai'i Press, 2015).

71. See Chu P'ong-no, "1920-yŏndae 'Chosŏn Nongminsa' ŭi nongmin sahoe kyoyuk hwaltong e kwanhan yŏn'gu," (PhD diss., Tan'guk University, 1990), 81–136.

72. Mongmyŏk Sanin, "Nongch'on ch'ŏngnyŏn ege ponenŭn kŭrwŏl," *Kaebyŏk* 6, no. 1 (1925), 20–22.

73. These articles appeared in July almost every year in the 1920s. Some examples include "Ha hyu chung kwihyang hanŭn haksaeng chegun ege," *Kaebyŏk* 5, no. 7 (1924): 56–69 and "Hahyu e kwihyang hanŭn haksaengdŭl ege," *Nongmin* 1, no. 3 (1930): 2–6.

74. Taiwan Sōtokufu Keimukyoku, *Taiwan shakai undōshi*, 199.

75. For more details, see Chen Nanhong, "Rizhishiqi nongmin xiaoshuozhong di jingyingzhuyi yu nongmin xingxiang (1926–1937)" (master's thesis, National Cheng Kung University, 2007); Zhang Huiqi, "Rizhishiqi Taiwan nongcun xiaoshuo yanjiu" (master's thesis, National Chung Cheng University, 2008).

76. See Huang Qichun, "Rizhi shiqi shehui zhuyi sichaoxia zhi xiangtu wenxue lunzheng yu Taiwan huawen yundong," *Zhongwai wenxue*, February 1995, 56–74. For the most comprehensive account on the first debate on nativist literature, see Yokoji, *Wenxue de liuli yu huigui*.

77. Yang Kui, "Bunpyōshō shinsa iin shoshi ni atau," *Bungaku hyōron* 3, no. 3 (1936), cited in Chen Nanhong, "Rizhishiqi nongmin xiaoshuozhong," 45. On Yang Kui's work, see Kleeman, *Under an Imperial Sun*, 160–174.

78. Kang, "Personal Reminiscences," 288.

79. On Bunkyōkyoku, see Chen Wen Sung (Winston) (Chen Wensong), "Seinen no sōdatsu: 1920-nendai shokuminchi Taiwan ni okeru seinen kyōka undō–Bunkyōkyoku setsuritsu o chūshin ni shite" (master's thesis, University of Tokyo, 2000).

80. See Mori Ariyoshi, *Seinen to ayumu Gotō Fumio* (Tokyo: Nippon Seinenkan, 1979) for Gotō's involvement in seinendan associations.

81. For example, Taiwan Sōtokufu Naimukyoku Bunkyōka, *Zentō seinenkai sonota shakai kyōkateki dantai* (Taipei: Taiwan Sōtokufu, 1926). Taiwan Sōtokufu Bunkyōkyoku, *Zentō seinendan, shojokai, kachōkai, shufukai shirabe* (Taipei: Taiwan Sōtokufu, 1926).

82. Chen Wen Sung, "Seinen no sōdatsu," 38–43, 45–51.

83. Taihoku-shū Rengō Dōfūkai, *Gendai seinen dokuhon: Nōson no kan jō* (Taipei: Taiwan Nichinichi Shinpō, 1926), 14.

84. Chen, "Seinen no sōdatsu," 54–55. Miyazaki Seiko, *Shokuminchiki Taiwan ni okeru seinendan to chiiki no henyō* (Tokyo: Ochanomizu Shobō, 2008), 144–163.

85. Kon Wajirō, *Chōsen buraku chōsa tokubetsu hōkoku* (Seoul: Chōsen Sōtokufu, 1924), 4.

86. Ibid., 34

87. For example, Odauchi Michitaka, a Japanese specialist on rural living and education, conducted a study on the slash-and-burn peasants in the Korean countryside in 1923. Odauchi Michitaka, *Chōsen buraku chōsa hōkoku: Kadenmin raijū shinajin* (Seoul: Chōsen Sōtokufu, 1924).

88. Zenshō Einosuke's research results include *Chōsen no kei* (1926), *Chōsen no jinkō genshō* (1927), *Chōsen no saigai* (1928), *Chōsen no hanzai to kankyō* (1928), *Chōsen no sei* (1934), and three massive volumes of *Chōsen no shūraku* (1933–1935), all published as research material (*chōsa shiryō*) by Chōsen Sōtokufu. His studies still serve as the most comprehensive research on Korean villages in prewar years. The focus on Korean customs and traditions by these researchers coincided with a growing appreciation of Korean folk art and culture by Japanese cultural critics. Yanagi Muneyoshi pioneered this field in the 1910s and 1920s, establishing a Korean folk art museum in 1924. Both these series of rural research and the folk art movement developed in close relation and rivalry with Korea's cultural nationalism. This stimulated the academic study of colonial ethnography in Japan. Kim Brandt, *Kingdom of Beauty: Mingei and the Politics of Folk Art in Imperial Japan* (Durham, NC: Duke University Press, 2007), 7–37.

89. On the idea of local culture (local color), see Kate McDonald, *Placing Empire: Travel and the Social Imagination in Imperial Japan* (Berkeley: University of California Press, 2017), 103–134; Sayaka Chatani, "The Ruralist Paradigm: Social Work Bureaucrats in Colonial Korea and Japan's Assimilationism in the Interwar Period," *Comparative Studies in Society and History* 58, no. 4 (2016): 1004–1031.

90. One example of the emphasis on social education and moral suasion is Matsumura Matsumori, "Gakkō o chūshin tosuru shakai kyōka," *Chōsen,* June 1921, 99–104.

91. Kasama Kenji, *Chihō kairyō undōki ni okeru shōgakkō to chiiki shakai* (Tokyo: Nihon tosho sentā, 2003), 11–12. Examples in Korea include Chōsen Sōtokufu Gakumukyoku, *Gakkō o chūshin to suru shakai kyōiku jōkyō* (Seoul: Chōsen Sōtokufu, 1922).

92. Zenra-nandō Naimubu, *Seinenkai shidō hōshin*, 5–6.

93. Ibid., 5–11. Chōsen Sōtokufu Naimukyoku Shakaika, *Chōsen shakai jigyō yōran* (Seoul: Chōsen Sōtokufu, 1923), 184–185.

94. See Tomita Akiko, "Nōson shinkō undōka no chūken jinbutsu no yōsei," *Chōsenshi Kenkyūkai ronbunshū* 18 (March 1981): 148–173.

5. FINDING RURAL YOUTH IN TAIWAN

1. Much of the scholarship emphasizes the developmental aspect of the colonial policies in the early periods, referring especially to Gotō Shinpei's adoption of "biological" principles. A classic study on this point is Chang Han-Yu and Ramon H. Myers, "Japanese Colonial Development Policy in Taiwan, 1895–1906: A Case of Bureaucratic Entrepreneurship," *Journal of Asian Studies* 22, no. 4 (1963): 433–449.

2. Zhong Qinghan, *Nihon shokuminchika ni okeru Taiwan kyōikushi* (Tokyo: Taga Shuppan, 1993), 120.

3. The reasons that Taiwanese avoided Japanese schools in early years were also listed in Taiwan Sōtokufu Minseibu Gakumubu, *Taiwan gakuji yōran* (Taipei: Taiwan Sōtokufu, 1919), 3–8.

4. Hayashi Genzaburō, "Jidō kyōiku to seinen kyōiku," *Taiwan Kyōikukai zasshi,* January 1903, 6–16.

5. For example, Xie Jieshi, a graduate of the earliest Japanese-language school who came back from China and Tokyo, was exalted as a successful diplomat and "a special

figure within Xinzhu's youth sector." Xie Jieshi becomes famous because he changed his Japanese nationality to that of the Republic of China in 1915 and became Manchukuo's ambassador to Japan in 1935. "Qingnian zhi jie," *(Hanwen) Taiwan riri xinbao*, September 9, 1909, 5; "Duandujianshi," *(Hanwen) Taiwan riri xinbao*, January 22, 1910, 4.

6. "Sheqingnianhui," *(Hanwen) Taiwan riri xinbao*, July 22, 1911, 3.

7. It is difficult to get an accurate number for population size because the administrative units changed over time. In 1895, Beipu-dazi had 800 residents, reaching nearly 2,940 in the 1930s. Including the neighboring hamlets, the number reached 9,320 by 1933. Fan Minghuan, ed., *Beipu yinxiang xiangzhi shang* (Xinzhu-xian: Beipu-xiang gongsuo, 2005), 253. Shinchiku-shū, *Shōwa 8-nen Shinchiku-shū dai-13 tōkeisho* (Xinzhu city: Shinchiku-shū, 1935), 33; Shinchiku-shū, *Shōwa 13-nen Shinchiku-shū dai-18 tōkeisho* (Xinzhu city: Shinchiku-shū, 1940), 13; Shimabukuro Kangi, *Hoppo kyōdoshi* (Beipu: Hoppo Kōgakkō, 1935), 66–69. The village's main agricultural goods were (rag) paper, rice, and tea as of 1935. The village first became famous for producing high-quality oolong tea and still produces an award-winning tea, Oriental Beauty, today. In the 1930s, Japanese people considered Beipu a picturesque site recommended for holiday visits. The Japanese named nearby Mount Wuzhi (Mount Five-Fingers) one of the twelve most scenic places in Taiwan, where "the magnificent view on the summit and the spiritual site with its many temples on the mountainside never cease to attract visitors." Chikutō Gun'yakusho ed., *Chikutō gunsei yōran* (Zhudong, Xinzhu: Chikutō Gun'yakusho, 1937), 22–24; Ōzeki Yoshio, "Chikutō yoitoko," *Shinchiku-shū jihō* 1 (June 1937): 104.

8. Ethnic Hakka currently compose one-fifth (about 4.5 million) of the Han population in Taiwan. Outside Taiwan, Hakka people spread in various areas throughout southern China, Southeast Asia, and Pacific islands. Because of their history and scale of migration, people sometimes refer to them as "Jews in Asia," whether they like this or not. Although ethnic borderlines lack a pencil-drawn clarity, their own language, customs, and legends (all with variations), as well as a belief that they originated from the Central Plains in the Yellow River Basin still characterize the Hakka as a distinctive ethnic group. ROC Executive Yuan website, *Republic of China Yearbook 2016*. https://english.ey.gov.tw/cp.aspx?n=A98EE53BDE2EF371, 10 and 44.

9. Tai Kokuki (Dai Guohui), *Tai Kokuki chosakusen 1: Hakka, Kakyō, Taiwan, Chūgoku* (Tokyo: Miyagi Shuppan, 2011), 110. "Holo" (福佬; Romanized also as "Hoklo") and "Minnan" (閩南) refer to the same ethnic group originally coming from the (southern) Fujian region and the language (or the dialect) they speak.

10. The Jiang family originally came from Huizhou, China, arriving at the Hongmao Port in 1737, then moving to Jiuxionglin forty years later. Wu Xueming, *Jinguangfu kenai yanjiu II* (Xinzhu city: Xinzhu xianli wenhua zhongxin, 2000), 9–56.

11. For more details on the development of the township, refer to Wu Xueming, *Jinguangfu kenai yanjiu I & II* (Xinzhu city: Xinzhu xianli wenhua zhongxin, 2000).

12. See Zhong Zhaozheng, *Jiang Shaozu zhuan* (Taipei: Jindai Zhongguo chubanshe, 1984).

13. Shinchiku-shū, *Shōwa 8-nen Shinchiku-shū dai-13 tōkeisho* (Xinzhu city: Shinchiku-shū, 1935), 33.

14. Not only did all the administrative functions that the Jiang family and other families had developed remain intact during the early years of Japanese rule, but their power continued to grow through their collaborating with the Japanese authorities. In 1899, the GGT gave a title of honor to the anti-Japanese hero Jiang Shaozu's cousin, Jiang Shaoyou, as a gesture of reconciliation. Jiang Zhengan, Jiang Shaozu's nephew, not only expanded his family business and enhanced the family's authority in Beipu but also was soon appointed as an adviser to the Xinzhu provincial government in 1912 and retained the position well into the 1920s. Jiang Shaozu's only child, Jiang Zhenxiang, also obtained

many official titles under the colonial ruling system, including an advisory position to the GGT, developing close ties with both the Japanese rulers and other ruling-class Taiwanese. Wang Xing'an, "Zhimindi tongzhi yu difang jingying: Yi Xinzhu, Maioli diqu wei zhongxin, 1895-nian–1935-nian" (master's thesis, National Taiwan University, 2000), 23. Ōzono Ichizō, *Taiwan jinbutsushi* (Taipei: Tanizawa Shoten, 1916), 140–141; Sugano Hideo, *Shinchiku-shū enkakushi* (Xinzhu city: Shinchiku-shū Enkakushi Kankōkai, 1938), 30–121; Lin Jinfa, ed., *Taiwan kanshin nenkan* (Taipei: Minshū Kōronsha, 1933), 40; Gomita Hiroshi, *Shinchiku-shū no jōsei to jinbutsu* (Xinzhu city: Suga Takeo, 1938), 257.

15. *Baojia* is a system in which the Qing government organized ten households as one unit, and ten units as one *jia*, and ten *jia* as one *bao*, in order to enforce local security and order. Under Japanese colonial rule, Gotō Shinpei adopted it as "Qing's tradition" to reinforce collective responsibility in maintaining law and order. See Hui-yu Caroline Ts'ai, *Taiwan in Japan's Empire Building: An Institutional Approach to Colonial Engineering* (New York: Routledge, 2009), 93–118.

16. Shimabukuro, *Hoppo kyōdoshi*, 152–153.

17. Huang Rongluo, "Xunzhao lao Taiwan: Yiwei weida Ribenren jiaoyujia," *Taiwan shibao*, April 10, 1993.

18. On the Beipu Incident, see Abe Shōsaku, *Hoppo jiken no taiyō to kōgakkō no kankei* (1907) reprinted in Chen Jiakang, *Beipu qinghuai* (self-pub., Beipu, Xinzhu, 2008), 95–123; Kimura Chiten, "Hoppo no bōdō," *Taiwan nichinichi shinpō*, November 17 and 19, 1907; "Ōtsubo no sangai" and "Hoppo jiken," *Taiwan nichinichi shinpō*, November 19, 1907; "Hoppo bōdō no gen'in," *Taiwan nichinichi shinpō*, December 20 and 21, 1907; "Hoppo jihen keisatsu no kōdō," *Taiwan nichinichi shinpō*, December 24, 25, and 26, 1907; Shiba Yoshitarō, *Taiwan no minzokusei to shidō kyōka* (Taipei: Taiwan Nichinichi Shinpōsha, 1927), 198–201. For recent discussions, see Yang Jingting, *Neifeng haojie: Beipu shijian miwen* (self-pub., Xinzhu, 1982); Huang Rongluo, *Beipu shijian wenji* (Xinzhu city: Xinzhu-xian wenhuaju, 2006); Yang Jingting, ed., *Beipu shijian yibai zhounian jinian zhuankan* (Xinzhu city: Xinzhu-xian wenhuaju, 2008).

19. "Aiyūsen kaifuku," *Taiwan nichinichi shinpō*, November 19, 1907.

20. Interview with Huang Yuanxing in Beipu on May 9, 2011.

21. Tai, *Tai Kokuki chosakusen*, 108.

22. Ibid., 112.

23. Many of the prominent leaders in Beipu during its development died quite young. Jiang Xiuluan's heir Jiang Ronghua died at age forty-six (1877), his brother Jiang Rongfu died the following year at thirty-two, Jiang Ronghua's son Jiang Shaoan had died at eighteen before his father passed away, and Jiang Ronghua's adopted heir Jiang Shaoji died when he was twenty-eight (1889). The anti-Japanese hero Jiang Shaozu died at age twenty (1895). Jiang Shaoji's close supporter Zeng Xuexi died when he was forty-three (1890). Wu Xueming and Xiu Xianming, "Lishi diaocha yanjiu," in *Xinzhu-xian xiandingguji: Beipu Jiang Axin guzhai xiufu diaocha yanjiu*, ed. Xue Qin (Xinzhu city: Xinzhu-xian wenhuaju, 2005), 1–2. Chen Zhihao, "Zhuqian neizhan de difang jiazushi yanjiu: Yi Beipu Zeng Xuexi jiazu wei li," *Xinzhu wenxian* 35 (December 2008): 45.

24. "Ikanishite shiteikinenbi o shukusuruka," *Taiwan nichinichi shinpō*, May 28, 1915, 7.

25. "Yexue kaihui," *(Hanwen) Taiwan riri xinbao*, September 26, 1915, 6.

26. "Seinendan saikai," *Taiwan nichinichi shinpō*, September 7, 1919, 4.

27. Ibid.; "Seinenkai kaisan," *Taiwan nichinichi shinpō*, October 15, 1919, 2.

28. Shimabukuro, *Hoppo kyōdoshi*, 26.

29. Ibid., 55. Matsuo Shōji, "Seinen shidōan," in *Seinendan shidō ronbunshū*, ed. Shinchiku-shū (Xinzhu city: Shinchiku-shū, 1932), 3.

30. Zhang Shigu's background can be found in Lin, *Taiwan kanshin nenkan*, 199.

31. "Xinzhu kai qingnianhui," (Hanwen) Taiwan riri xinbao, March 3, 1921, 6.

32. "Chikuseikai hakkaishiki," Taiwan nichinichi shinpō, May 27, 1921, 3. "Xinzhu tongxin," Taiwan kyōiku 230 (July 1921): Chinese pages 4–5. "Xinzhu tongxin," Taiwan kyōiku 231 (August 1921): Chinese pages 2–3.

33. Taiwan Sōtokufu Keimukyoku, ed., Taiwan shakai undōshi, Taiwan Sōtokufu keisatsu enkakushi dai-ni hen: Ryōtai igo no chian jōkyō chūkan (1939, repr. Tokyo: Ryūkei Shosha, 1973), 151. "Xinzhu qingnian zhi huoyue," Taiwan minbao, June 11, 1925, 5. "Qingnianhui de huodong," Taiwan minbao, January 9, 1927, 5.

34. Xinzhu C sheng, "Dui Xinzhu dushuhui de xiwang," 11.

35. "Qingnianhui yu dushuhui," Taiwan minbao, December 12, 1926, 3.

36. "Xinzhu zaikai wenhua jiangyan," Taiwan minbao, March 13, 1927, 6; "Xinzhu sifa jingguan de baozhuang," Taiwan minbao, May 15, 1927, 7, for example.

37. "Zuzhi sangyi gailianghui," Taiwan minbao, March 20, 1927, 8; "Zhu qingnianhui zuzhi zangyi gailianghui," (Hanwen) Taiwan riri xinbao, November 16, 1927, 4; "Xinzhu qingnianhui lihui," (Hanwen) Taiwan riri xinbao, December 20, 1927, 4. Similar reports on March 5, June 20, July 22, 1928.

38. "Xinzhu duanxun (2)," Taiwan minbao, April 10, 1927, 7.

39. Ibid. The characteristic as elite clubs was obvious especially because the Xinzhu youth group associated themselves mainly with graduates of middle schools or above, not with working youth in the city. "Xuesheng dakenqinhui," Taiwan minbao, August 14, 1927, 6.

40. Xinzhu C sheng, "Dui Xinzhu dushuhui de xiwang," 11.

41. "Xinzhu: Qingnianhui zonghui," Taiwan minbao, July 2, 1928, 6; "Xinzhu qingnianhui jiesan," Taiwan minbao, March 31, 1929, 2.

42. "Xinzhu zhi qingniantuan yu zhonglaozu fenli," (Hanwen) Taiwan riri xinbao, March 8, 1929, 4; "Xinzhu qingnianhui jiesan," Taiwan minbao, March 31, 1929, 2; "Xinzhu: Dushuhui jiesan," Taiwan minbao, March 25, 1928, 6.

43. Shimabukuro, Hoppo kyōdoshi, 82.

44. It also offered a "youth library," among other things. Taiwan Sōtokufu Naimukyoku, Zentō seinenkai sonota shakai kyōka teki dantai (Taipei: Taiwan Sōtokufu, 1925), 7.

45. "Beipu Citiangong saiqianxiang," (Hanwen) Taiwan riri xinbao, March 30, 1927, 4. The Xinzhu youth group also advocated to renew the customs surrounding religious festivals, trying to end the use of pillories and the burning of paper offerings as well. "Xinzhu Zhusheng juhui," (Hanwen) Taiwan riri xinbao, May 31, 1925, 2.

46. Shimabukuro, Hoppo kyōdoshi, 62–66.

47. Taiwan Sōtokufu Naimukyoku, Zentō seinenkai, 8; Taiwan Sōtokufu Bunkyōkyoku, Zentō seinendan, shojokai, kachōkai, shufukai shirabe (Taipei: Taiwan Sōtokufu, 1926), 10; Shinchiku-shū, Shinchiku-shū shakai kyōiku (Xinzhu city: Shinchiku-shū, 1931), 32. Lin Jinfa, Taiwan jinbutsu hyō (Taipei: Sekiyōsha, 1929), 118. Also based on interviews with Huang Yuanxing and his friends in Beipu on May 30 and August 18, 2011.

48. "Kaihō: Rakuseishiki to shukugakai kyokō no Hoppo Shin'yō kumiai," Taiwan no sangyō kumiai 44 (February 1930): 97–98.

49. Shimabukuro, Hoppo kyōdoshi, 55.

50. "Shinchiku-shū shusai no gakkō seinendan undōkai," Taiwan nichinichi shinpō, November 5, 1925, 2.

51. Shimabukuro, Hoppo kyōdoshi, 55.

52. Ibid., 55–56.

53. "Xinzhu qingniantuan," (Hanwen) Taiwan riri xinbao, May 18, 1929, 4. "Shinchiku seinendan ketsudanshiki," Taiwan nichinichi shinpō, May 26, 1929, 5.

54. "Shinchiku-shūka no seinendan ketsudan," Taiwan nichinichi shinpō, October 12, 1934, 2; Taiwan Sōtokufu Naimukyoku, Zentō seinenkai, 1. Taiwan Sōtokufu

Bunkyōkyoku, *Zentō seinendan*, 1; Taiwan Sōtokufu, *Taiwan shakai kyōiku gaiyō* (Taipei: Taiwan Sōtokufu, 1929), 3. Taiwan Sōtokufu Bunkyōkyoku, *Taiwan shakai kyōiku gaiyō* (Taipei: Taiwan Sōtokufu, 1932), 13. Shinchiku-shū Naimubu Kyōikuka, *Shinchiku-shū kyōiku tōkei yōran* (Xinzhu city: Shinchiku-shū, 1932), 94–100. Shinchiku-shū Naimubu Kyōikuka, *Shinchiku-shū kyōiku tōkei yōran* (Xinzhu city: Shinchiku-shū, 1933), 74–78. The overall number of youth group members (both male and female) peaked around 1926, and shrank in the early 1930s, but this trend was more evident in Gaoxiong and Tainan provinces. In Xinzhu, the increase was steadier, although slower.

55. Miyazaki Seiko, *Shokuminchiki Taiwan ni okeru seinendan to chiiki no henyō* (Tokyo: Ochanomizu Shobō, 2008), 133.

56. Ibid., 135–136.

57. Miyajima Yutaka, "Hontō nōson seinendan shidō no jissai," in *Seinendan shidō ronbunshū*, ed. Shinchiku-shū, 119.

58. Ibid., 120–125.

59. Matsuo, "Seinen shidōan," 8, 43.

60. The number of unemployed was 1 in Beipu, 67 in Zhudong county, 1,236 in Xinzhu province, and 18,129 in Taiwan at large in the 1930 survey. Taiwan Sōtoku Kanbō Rinji Kokusei Chōsabu, *Shōwa 10-nen kokusei chōsa kekkahyō* (Taipei: Taiwan Sōtokufu, 1932), 666–669.

61. Edgar Wickberg, "The Taiwan Peasant Movement, 1923–1932: Chinese Rural Radicalism under Japanese Development Programs," *Pacific Affairs* 48, no. 4 (1975–1976): 558–582. Left-leaning authors, such as Yang Kui and Lai He (Loa Ho), started taking on the theme of the exploitation of Taiwanese peasants in the 1930s. Colonial social activists often discussed the rural problem in the journal *Shakai jigyō no tomo* around 1929. Also refer to Taiwan Sōtokufu Keimukyoku, ed., *Taiwan shakai undōshi*, 999 for the number of tenant disputes between 1924 and 1929.

62. Matsuo, "Seinen shidōan," 43.

63. Miyajima, "Hontō nōson seinendan shidō no jissai," 120.

64. Ibid., 121–123.

65. For a discussion of how Beipu's village society was organized before the Japanese colonial period, see Wu Xueming, "Riben zhiming tongzhi xia Taiwan xiangcun shehui de bianqian," *Taipei wenxian* 107 (March 1994): 23–67.

66. Miyajima, "Hontō nōson seinendan shidō no jissai," 128.

67. Ibid., 126–127.

68. Ibid., 126.

69. Hashinabe Kazuyoshi, "Hontō ni okeru seinendan shidō no jissaian," in *Seinendan shidō ronbunshū*, ed. Shinchiku-shū, 97.

70. Miyajima, "Hontō nōson seinendan shidō no jissai," 133.

71. Hashinabe, "Hontō ni okeru seinendan shidō no jissaian," 62–63.

72. Shimabukuro, *Hoppo kyōdoshi*, 27–55. For the entire school district, the schooling rate was a lot lower: around 38%–44% of male and 12%–18% of female school-age children in the school district attended the school between 1930 and 1934. This is slightly lower than the averages for Zhudong county and Xinzhu province, most likely because the Beipu school district covered remote mountainous areas from which it was difficult for children to commute.

73. Interview with Huang Yuanxing in Beipu on May 9, 2011.

74. In 1901, one of the very first night classes in Xinzhu city provided Japanese-language education to uneducated workers, made possible only in cooperation with schoolteachers. "Shinchiku no yagakkō," *Taiwan nichinichi shinpō*, May 23, 1901, 1. The teachers were core members of the Xinzhu youth group who provided Japanese classes at night schools in the

early 1920s. Naturally, these night classes took place in the facilities of elementary schools. Dai Tianfei, "Shinchiku tsūshin," *Taiwan kyōiku* 231 (August 1921): 2.

75. "Beipu qingniantuan huodong," *(Hanwen) Taiwan riri xinbao*, March 30, 1929, 6.

76. Shimabukuro, *Hoppo kyōdoshi*, 58–60.

77. "Shinchiku-shū Kyōka Taisaku Zadankai jōkyō," *Taiwan kyōiku* 381 (April 1934): 134.

78. Shibayama Takenori, "Sōshun no inaka o aruku, Shinchiku-shū no gakuen o meguru," *Kunpū* 34 (March 1935): 16–17.

79. Matsuo, "Seinen shidōan," 48–49.

80. For example, Shinchiku-shū, *Shinchiku-shū kyōiku tōkei yōran* (Xinzhu city: Shinchiku-shū, 1932), 95–100.

81. Matsuo, "Seinen shidōan," 5.

82. "Yūryō seinendan no hyōshō," *Taiwan kyōiku* 356 (March 1932): 113–114.

83. Matsuo, "Seinen shidōan," 6.

84. Ibid., 10–12.

85. Ibid., 46–47.

86. "Shinchiku Seinendan no jitensha tōnorikai," *Taiwan nichinichi shinpō*, January 29, 1931, 5. "Shinchiku Seinendanin hokubu jitensha ryokō," *Taiwan nichinichi shinpō*, January 30, 1931, 2.

87. "Shinchiku-shū no kōtsū seiri," *Taiwan nichinichi shinpō*, October 2, 1931, 3.

88. For example, see "Chūnanbu chihō o fukumu rajio hōsō kokugo fukyū no yūbe," *Taiwan kyōiku* 363 (October 1932): 92–93; "Chūnanbu chihō o fukumu rajio hōsō kokugo fukyū no yūbe," *Taiwan kyōiku* 368 (February 1933): 97–98. On Xinzhu youth's performance in the show, see Yazawa Hideo, "Sangatsu jūsannichi kokugo fukyū rajio hōsō ni shutsuen sareta Shinchiku-shi no minasama ni: Nihonjin nara nihongo de hanase," *Taiwan kyōiku* 357 (April 1932): 133–135.

89. Some youth groups affiliated with the Cultural Association had already adopted amateur plays to attract a wide audience in the 1920s. They had proved the effectiveness of entertaining youth plays, not only to reach various audiences but also to transform the youth who practiced and performed them. Xinzhu's Xinguang Tutuan performed enlightenment-theme plays almost professionally, for example. See Taiwan Sōtokufu Keimukyoku, ed., *Taiwan shakai undōshi*, 158, 223. There are a number of anecdotes about the popularity of amateur youth plays recorded by researchers. See Chen Wensong, *Zhimin tongzhi yu "qingnian,"* 335, for example.

90. *Kunpū* 30 (November 1934), appendix. The Zhongli rural youth group from Xinzhu province presented their own play at the All-Taiwan Japanese Language Competition, similarly advertising to abolish the custom of arranged marriage. Chūreki Seinendan, "Seinengeki: Taue uta," *Kunpū* 32 (January 1935): 24–27.

91. Taiwanese elite three decades earlier had refused to send their children to elementary school because these schools practiced singing songs. Taiwan Sōtokufu Minseibu Gakumubu, *Taiwan gakuji yōran*, 4.

92. Cai Qingzi, "Kinken no seinen," *Kunpū* 30 (November 1934): 18–19.

93. "Daishinsai nyūsu," *Kunpū* 36 (May 1935): 37.

94. The damage in Beipu was not as devastating, but twenty-five members of the Beipu Seinendan immediately gathered to collect information and maintain the village's social order. "Shushōnari seinendan," *Kunpū* 36 (May 1935): 4–34. Seinendan members in Xinzhu and Taipei provinces engaged in prolonged volunteer work, accompanying the injured and delivering food and goods to the victims. "Shinpo Seinendan no jihatsuteki hōshi," *Taiwan nichinichi shinpō*, April 27, 1935, 3. "Daitōtei Seinendan kara kyūgohan ga shutsudō," *Taiwan nichinichi shinpō*, April 28, 1935, 2.

95. Nakayama Yū, "Hohoemu aozora," *Kunpū* 47 (March 1936): 1–13.

96. Miyazaki, *Shokuminchiki Taiwan*, 173–180.

6. EMOTIONAL BASIS FOR JAPANIZATION

1. Xu Peixian, "Riben tongzhi moqi Xinzhu shinei de jiaoyu zhuangkuang," *Zhuqian wenxian* 43 (July 2009): 43.

2. On the focus on emotional communities, see Barbara H. Rosenwein, "Problems and Methods in the History of Emotions," *Passions in Context: Journal of the History and Philosophy of the Emotions* 1, no. 1 (2010): 1–32. See also Stephanie Olsen, ed., *Childhood, Youth, and Emotions in Modern History* (New York: Palgrave Macmillan, 2015).

3. Many have written personal experiences in the Hitlerjugend, for example. See Michael H. Kater, *Hitler Youth* (Cambridge, MA: Harvard University Press, 2004); Jurgen Herbst, *Requiem for German Past: A Boyhood among the Nazis* (Madison: University of Wisconsin Press, 1999). When historians discuss the emotions of teenagers, they tend to describe them as "children" rather than "youth." See the ambiguous categories of children and youth in chapters of Olsen, *Childhood, Youth, and Emotions in Modern History*.

4. See Leo T. S. Ching, *Becoming "Japanese": Colonial Taiwan and Politics of Identity Formation* (Berkeley: University of California Press, 2001); Miyata Setsuko, *Chōsen minshū to "kōminka" seisaku* (Tokyo: Miraisha, 1985); Ch'oe Yu-ri, *Ilche malgi singminji chibae chŏngch'aek yŏngu* (Seoul: Kukhak Charyŏwŏn, 1997).

5. "Seinendan shūka kara 350-mei o atsume kyūichikō kōdō de," *Taiwan nichinichi shinpō*, September 8, 1937. "Rengō Seinendanin ga kenshō o kigan Shinchiku Jinja ni sanpai," *Taiwan nichinichi shinpō*, September 18, 1937.

6. Miyazaki Seiko, *Shokuminchiki Taiwan ni okeru seinendan to chiiki no hen'yō* (Tokyo: Ochanomizu Shobō, 2008), 88, 217–219, 257–263, 311–353. The *seinen gakkō* increased in number in 1943 and there was a plan to make it mandatory. It provided premilitary training for elementary school graduates. The one in Xinzhu city was established in 1939. My interviewees did not remember if there was a seinen gakkō in Beipu.

7. "Danjo seinen o zenbu seinendan ni: Shinchiku-shū no Seishin Sōdōin Undō," *Taiwan nichinichi shinpō*, October 19, 1937.

8. The numbers are from Shinchiku-shū Kyōikuka, *Shinchiku-shū kyōiku tōkei yōran* (Xinzhu city: Shinchiku-shū, 1936–1939).

9. "Seinen shūrenjō ni okeru Akahori chiji kunji," *Dōkō* 181 (October 5, 1938): 3.

10. "Sensei," *Kunpū*, August 1938, 7.

11. Kobayashi Seizō, "Seinen ni tsugu," *Kunpū,* May 1938, 7.

12. According to the official statistics, an average of 48.47% of school-age children went to school (63.84% of male and 33.10% of female children) in 1938. Shinchiku-shū, *Shōwa 13-nen Shinchiku-shū dai-18 tōkeisho* (Xinzhu city: Shinchiku-shū, 1940), 35.

13. Tanaka Ichirō, "Honshū seinendan kyōka saru," *Shinchiku-shū jihō* 39 (August 1940): 32–35.

14. See Hui-yu Caroline Ts'ai, *Taiwan in Japan's Empire Building: An Institutional Approach to Colonial Engineering* (New York: Routledge, 2009), 145–166, for a discussion on creating "the local," which became the center of colonial rule and developed into wartime mobilization.

15. "Hōkō undō genchi hōkoku: Genni imashimubeshi hōkō undō no chūshōka," *Shinkensetsu,* July 1943, 28.

16. Barak Kushner, *The Thought War: Japanese Imperial Propaganda* (Honolulu: University of Hawai'i Press, 2006).

17. "Hōkō undō genchi hōkoku," 28.

18. Ibid., 29.

19. "Taihoku-shū ga Shirin ni nōgyō shūrenjo o secchi shūka no wakaki mohan nōson seinen o senbatsu nōson shidōsha o yōsei no hōshin," *Taiwan nichinichi shinpō*, November 25, 1931; "Zentō teki ni hokoru ni taru Taihoku-shū nōgyō shūrenjo nōgyō keiei nohan o ippan ni shiji subete kyūhi ikkanen de sotsugyō," *Taiwan nichinichi shinpō*, December 7, 1931.

20. "Dai ikkai Zentō Nōson Chūken Seinen Shidō Kōshūkai," *Kunpū* 33 (February 1935): 33–35.

21. "Tokushoku aru seinen dōjō Shinchiku-shūritsu Nōgyō Denshūjo: Suki to kama de jicchi tanren shite mohan nōson seinen o zōsei," *Taiwan nichinichi shinpō*. July 20, 1935.

22. Kishiwa Tadashi, "Joshi shidōsha renseikai" (unpublished report, May 1943, provided by Xu Chongfa) briefly describes the difficulty that Xinzhu officials had in getting a permit from the GGT. Participating youth constructed a new shūrenjō building in Matsugane in the backyard of the Shinchiku Shrine in late 1943.

23. The very first term trained twenty young men for thirty days. Women's training for the first few years was twenty days.

24. "Iyoiyo kaishi o kettei shita Shinchiku-shūritsu Seinen Shūrenjō," *Shinchiku shinpō*, August 1, 1938.

25. Peng Qingshun and Liao Dayan, "Nikki," *Dōkō* 181 (October 5, 1938): 5.

26. "Shūritsu Seinen Shūrenjō kuniku no jissai," *Dōkō* 181 (October 5, 1938): 1.

27. "Dai 13-ki shūren gyōji yoteihyō," 23 (unpublished, 1941, provided by Xu Chongfa).

28. Interview with Jiang Zhaoying in Qionglin, Xinzhu province, on June 29, 2011.

29. "Dai 12-ki shūrensei ni kansō o kiku," *Dōkō* 244 (May 20, 1941): 6.

30. Ibid.

31. "Taibō no joshi shūrensei iyoiyo chikaku nyūjō," *Dōkō* 199 (July 5, 1939): 1.

32. Kishiwa, "Joshi shidōsha renseikai."

33. "Shirayuri nikki," *Dōkō* 200 (July 20, 1939): 5.

34. "Buraku no myōjō, tsuchi no senshi, shūrenjō shūryōsei Huang Kunxuan kun o tou," *Dōkō* 185 (December 5, 1938): 6.

35. "Miyo!! Wakōdo no moyuru tōshi o!! Shinshin no shūren ni, kokugo buraku no kensetsu ni kekki seru Sekitō seinen bundan," *Dōkō* 186 (December 20, 1938): 4.

36. Okumura Ryōtarō, "Seinen shūrenjō no shūryōsei o kataru," *Dōkō* 186 (December 20, 1938): 7.

37. Letter from Chen Fengjie (twelfth-term female trainee) to Xu Chongfa, December 11, 1943 (provided by Xu Chongfa).

38. Ibid.

39. Letter from Liu Chunzi to Xu Chongfa, August 15, year unknown (most likely 1943 or 1944) (provided by Xu Chongfa).

40. "Okāsan e," *Dōkō* 184 (November 20, 1938): 5.

41. "Okāsan ni 3-kanen keikaku de kokugo kyōju hajimemashita," *Dōkō* 189 (February 5, 1939): 7.

42. "Kimi ga yo shōjo!!" *Dōkō* 203 (September 5, 1939): 8.

43. The elementary school consisted of two parts: the first was six years of primary education, and the second was two or three years of the upper-level program. Many elementary schools in Taiwan established the upper-level program in the 1920s. After graduating from the primary program, children could go to either the upper-level program or other secondary education, including middle schools, agricultural schools, and normal schools.

44. All based on interviews with Huang Yuanxing in Beipu on May 9, 20, 30, and August 18, 2011.

45. "16-nendo ni okeru Kingyō Hōkoku Seinentai no kunren," *Chihō gyōsei*, June 1941, 25.

46. Ōta Toshio, "Hontō seishōnen no kunren ni tsuite," *Chihō gyōsei*, June 1941, 6.

47. Miyao naimu buchō, "Kingyōhōkoku seinentai ni toku," *Dōkō* 217 (April 5, 1940): 1.

48. "Seinen shokun wa mazu dantai kyōiku o ukeyo," *Dōkō* 218 (April 20, 1940): 1.

49. Qiu Xionghao, "Taiken o kataru kangeki aratanaru dōjō seikatsu," *Dōkō* 191 (March 5, 1941): 5.

50. "Shimin no uwasa, shūrensei wa 'heitaisan no yōda," *Dōkō* 182 (October 20, 1938): 5–6.

51. "Dai 4-ji kingyō hōkoku seinentai kaitai hōkokushiki ni okeru chiji kakka kunji yōshi," *Dōkō* 243 (May 5, 1941): 3.

52. Xu Chiongfa's diary during the Labor Corps, October 1, 1941.

53. Miyajima Yutaka, "Hontō nōson seinendan shidō no jissai," in *Seinendan shidō ronbunshū*, ed. Shinchiku-shū (Xinzhu city: Shinchiku-shū, 1932), 132; Ts'ai, *Taiwan in Japan's Empire Building*, 56.

54. Interview with Huang Yuanxing in Beipu on May 9 and 30, 2011.

55. Interview with Huang Rongluo in Zhudong, Xinzhu province, on May 3, 2011.

56. Interview with Jiang Zhaoying in Qionglin, Xinzhu province, on June 29, 2011.

57. "Kingyō hōkokutai yori genki na tayori," *Dōkō* 220 (May 20, 1940): 7.

58. "Hōkoku seinentai no Shinchiku shūtai kaeru," *Taiwan nichinichi shinpo*, May 28, 1940. "Dai 2-kai Kingyō Hōkoku Seinentai ni taisuru Miyagi chiji no kunji," *Dōkō* 227 (September 5, 1940): 3

59. Xu Chongfa's diary, July 12, 1941.

60. Interview with Huang Yuanxing in Beipu on May 9, 2011.

61. Ibid.

62. "Zadankai kingyō hōkoku o kataru," *Dōkō* 221 (June 5, 1940): 6.

63. Ibid.

64. Many of the letters from female graduates to Xu Chongfa, as well as an interview with Jiang Zhaoying in Qionglin, June 29, 2011, mention how impressive the dark, skinny, strong bodies of male trainees were.

65. Xu Chongfa's diary, June 9, 1941.

66. Huang Xiuying's letter to Xu Chongfa around late February 1945.

67. Wu Wentong "Shūrenjō no shosensei ni," *Dōkō* 199 (July 5, 1939): 6. The graduates received everyone's address after the graduation. A couple of letters to Xu Chongfa also say that the graduates continued to exchange letters.

68. Xu Chongfa's diary and many of the letters he received.

69. His marriage partner was decided by his parents, outside the youth training circle, however. He recalled that "then I thought I should let these female graduates know that I already got married."

70. Miyazaki, *Shokuminchiki Taiwan*, 293.

71. Interview with Huang Rongluo in Zhudong on August 15, 2011. He lived in Nanzhuang, Miaoli, in Xinzhu province. Since his grandfather encouraged his sons and grandsons to obtain higher education, Huang Rongluo also decided to attend the agricultural school and aspired to go to college later. He was "not interested in local seinendan activities," although he knew they were gathering in the elementary school.

72. For example, Wu Zhuoliu, *Ajia no koji* (1956, repr. Tokyo: Shinjinbutsu Ōraisha, 1973) and Zhong Zhaozheng, *Zhuoliu* (Taipei: Yuanjing chuban, 2005).

73. I collected thirty-one names of those who attended the shūrenjō from Beipu and had Huang Yuanxing discuss their family backgrounds. Most of them, although their families originally lived near the mountains, ran small shops by the late 1930s in Beipu town. Interviews with Huang Yuanxing in Beipu on August 18, 2011, and Wen Qingshui in Beipu on August 23, 2011.

74. In 1926, when the Ugaki Kazushige cabinet introduced the youth training center (*seinen kunrenjo*) in Japan and planned its establishment in the colonies, for example, Taiwanese and Korean colonial governments went against the cabinet's decision and postponed it indefinitely, for the reason that without military service in effect, pre-military training was inappropriate for colonial societies. Kōbun ruijū 2A-11-rui 1587, "Shokuminchi ni okeru seinen kunren ni kansuru ken," cited in *Sōryokusen to Taiwan*, Kondō Masami (Tokyo: Tōsui Shobō, 1996), 39.

75. Taiwan Sōtokufu Kanbō Jōhōka, *Warera no chōheisei* (Taipei: Taiwan Sōtokufu, 1943), 33–34 in Kondō, *Sōryokusen to Taiwan*, 40–41.

76. For instance, the Shinchiku seinendan had a gym teacher of the Xinzhu middle school give drills to the members for three weeks in 1929 in preparation for its inauguration ceremony. They continued practicing army drills as part of training in the 1930s. "Shinchiku Seinendan gunji kyōren," *Taiwan nichinichi shinpō*, April 14, 1929, 5.

77. Kondō, *Sōryokusen to Taiwan*, 39–55. For more details, see Zhou Wanyao (Chou Wan-yao), "Riben zaiTai junshi dongyuan yu Taiwanren de haiwai canzhan jingyan," *Taiwanshi yanjiu* 2, no. 1 (1995): 85–126.

78. Kondō, *Sōryokusen to Taiwan*, 44–45.

79. Ibid., 34–45.

80. "Shiganhei seido no jisshi o yōbō: Tōmin wa nessei o hirō seyo," *Taiwan shinminpō*, August 10, 1940.

81. "Iwasa chūsa ni yoru seinendan taikai saetsu," *Dōkō* 187 (January 5, 1939): 5.

82. "Joshi seinendan no kyōren ni tsuite," *Dōkō* 187 (January 5, 1939): 6.

83. Tanaka Kiyoshi, "Taiwan tokubetsu shiganheisei to kunren," *Taiwan nichinichi shinpō*, July 3 and 4, 1941.

84. Based on Japanese governmental statistics, 126,750 Taiwanese *gunzoku* and 80,433 Taiwanese soldiers were sent abroad between 1937 and 1945. See Kashikuma Osamu, "Taiwan jūmin senbotsusha no izoku nado ni taisuru chōikin no hōritsu," *Taiwan Kyōkaihō* 400 (January 15, 1988): 5.

85. Figures showed that 22.2% of the Taiwanese civilian military employees died, whereas 2.7% of Taiwanese soldiers died on the battlefield. Ibid.

86. Kondō, *Sōryokusen to Taiwan*, 351–354.

87. Taiwangun Shireibu, *Shina Jihen to hontōjin no dōkō* 1 (Taipei: Taiwangun Shireibu, October 1, 1937), and 3 (December 1, 1937). See Kondō, *Sōryokusen to Taiwan*, 353–354.

88. Kobayashi Seizō, *Shina Jihen to Taiwan* (self-pub., Taipei, 1939), 12, says that as of 1939, there were XX000 Taiwanese translators (the actual number was hidden for intelligence purposes.)

89. Yang Jingting, "Qilao fangtan," *Xinzhu wenxian* 4 (December 2000): 18.

90. Kashikuma, "Taiwan jūmin senbotsusha."

91. The Japanese military deliberately kept the recruitment processes of the translators unclear for strategic reasons during the war but announced the number of Agricultural Corps openly.

92. Taiwan Sōtokufu Shokusankyoku, ed., *Taiwan Nōgyō Giyūdanshi* (Taipei: Taiwan Sōtokufu, 1942), 37–40, 87–116, 169–222.

93. Ibid., 270–273.

94. Zou Yunyan, "Kama wa watashidomo no jūken de aru," *Dōkō* 212 (January 20, 1940): 8, for example.

95. "Honshū shusshin no seinen butai 9-nin sorotte suki no senshi," *Dōkō* 227 (September 5, 1940): 4.

96. "Senchi dayori," *Dōkō* 220 (May 20, 1940): 7.

97. "Dai issen yori," *Dōkō* 227 (September 5, 1940): 6.

98. Out of 150 men who participated in the second-term Agricultural Corps from Xinzhu, 110 remained in China after the conclusion of their program, whereas only a quarter of the youth from the other provinces (155 out of 599) did. Taiwan Sōtokufu Shokusankyoku, ed., *Taiwan Nōgyō Giyūdanshi*, 246–247.

99. Ibid., 374. A similar example is discussed in Miyazaki Seiko, "Moto-Taiwanjin tokubetsu shiganhei ni okeru 'shokuminchi keiken,'" in *Sengo Taiwan ni okeru "Nihon": Shokuminchi keiken no renzoku, henbō, riyō*, ed. Igarashi Masako and Mio Yūko (Tokyo: Fūkyōsha, 2006), 61–92.

100. Ichiyō sei, "Shiganhei, kenpeiho, kangofu, shūka seinen no sōshingun," *Shinchiku-shū jihō* 58 (March 1942), 72–73.

101. Yang(shi) Qianhe, "Nisshōki no motoni: Josei no tachiba kara," *Shinkensetsu* 5 (March 1943): 50–51.

102. "Shiganhei o shigan senu seinen towa kekkon sezu," *Taiwan nichinichi shinpō*, January 14, 1942, 3.

103. Zhou Jinpo, "Shiganhei," in *Shū Kinpa [Zhou Jinpo] Nihongo sakuhinshū*, ed. Nakajima Toshio and Huang Yingzhe (Tokyo: Ryokuin Shobō, 1998), 14–37.

104. See *Taiwan shaoniangong de gushi: Lü de haipingxian, Shonenko*, directed by Guo Liangyin and Fujita Shūhei (2006; Taiwan, distributed by Taipei-shi wenhuaju) as well as Wang Xiqing, "Ji Riju moqi fu Riben wei 'haijun gongyuan' zhi Taiwan shaonian xinsuan-shi," *Taiwan wenxian* 48 (February 1997): 115–145.

105. "Tekiki matamata raishū," *Taiwan minpō*, January 4, 1945, 1. "Tada junchūmuni no ichinen: Waga riku no wakazakura taran, tekishūka hatsu no chōhei kensa hajimaru," *Taiwan shinpō*, January 16, 1945, 2.

106. For example, "Shinchiku-shi o jūtan bakugeki," *Taiwan shinpō*, June 18, 1945, 2.

107. Interviews with Beipu residents in Beipu on May 9, 2011.

108. Ōsawa Sadakichi, "Chōheisei no tsugini kyōkon ga kuru," *Shinkensetsu* 14 (November 1943): 17.

109. "Zadankai: Kokugo seikatsu no shinkensetsu," *Shinkensetsu*, February 1944, 28.

110. Interview with Huang Yuanxing in Beipu on May 30, 2011.

111. Chen Jiakang, *Beipu qinghuai* (self-pub., Beipu, Xinzhu, 2008), 21.

112. Interview with Huang Yuanxing in Beipu on May 30, 2011.

113. Chen Wensong, *Zhimin tongzhi yu 'qingnian': Taiwan zongdufu de 'qingnian' jiao-hua zhengce* (Taipei: Taida chuban zhongxin, 2015), 262–268.

114. Ōsawa Sadakichi, *Rikugun tokubetsu shiganhei annai* (Taipei: Kōmin Hōkōkai, 1942), 3.

115. Nagata Tomiki, "Kōgakkō kyōin no nayami," *Shinchiku-shū jihō* 46 (January 1941): 73–74.

116. Tai Kokuki (Dai Guohui), *Tai Kokuki chosakusen 1: Hakka, Kakyō, Taiwan, Chūgoku* (Tokyo: Miyagi Shuppan, 2011), 112.

117. Ibid., 93.

7. MODEL RURAL YOUTH IN KOREAN VILLAGE

1. Nonsan became an administrative county in 1914.

2. "Nonsan p'yŏngya nŭn Namsŏn e yusu 1," *Tonga ilbo*, September 27, 1927, 4.

3. Nonsan Siji P'yŏnch'an Wiwŏnhoe, *Nonsan siji II: Yŏksa wa munhwa yujŏk* (Non-san: Nonsan Siji P'yŏnch'an Wiwŏnhoe, 2005), 278. Rare for this mountainous peninsula, 60% of the Nonsan region is less than one hundred meters above sea level, making it a prominent agricultural production site even today. Yee Jae-Yeol (Yi Chae-yŏl), Kang Hee-Kyung (Kang Hŭi-gyŏng), and Seol Dong-Hoon (Sŏl Tong-hun), *Ch'ungch'ŏng chiyŏk ŭi sahoe ŭisik kwa chiyŏk chŏngch'esŏng* (Seoul: Paeksan Sŏdang, 2004), 39.

4. It became the commercial center after the Imjin War in the late sixteenth century. Nonsan Siji P'yŏnch'an Wiwŏnhoe, *Nonsan siji I: Chiri wa maŭl iyagi* (Nonsan: Nonsan Siji P'yŏnch'an Wiwŏnhoe, 2005), 274–275.

5. Chŏng Yŏn-t'ae, "Nittei no chiiki shihai, kaihatsu to shokuminchiteki kindaisei," in *Kindai kōryūshi to sōgo ninshiki II: Nittei shihai ki*, ed. Miyajima Hiroshi et al. (Tokyo: Keiō Gijuku Daigaku Shuppankai, 2005), 5–9.

6. Ibid., 13.

7. Ibid., 10.

8. Jun Uchida argues that colonizers viewed Korea as a colony of settlement, much like Hokkaido. She also makes the analogy of pioneers in the New World. Jun Uchida,

Brokers of Empire: Japanese Settler Colonialism in Korea, 1876–1945 (Cambridge, MA: Harvard University Asia Center, 2011), 59 and 62.

9. For example, in the 1930 colonial census, Nonsan county had an average of 231.6 people per square kilometer, whereas the national average was 95.4. Chōsen Sōtokufu, *Shōwa 5-nen, Chōsen kokusei chōsa hōkoku, dōhen Chūsei nandō* (Seoul: Chōsen Sōtokufu, 1930), 2.

10. In 1911, the number of Japanese agricultural settlements reached 2,132 families (6,892 people). Among 1,129 Japanese farming families in South Ch'ungchŏng, 677 were landlords, 114 were owner-cultivators, 196 both owned and rented land, and 115 were tenants as of 1932. Japanese-owned land was 21,137 *chō* of rice paddies and 10,868 *chō* of fields in the same year. Minjok Munje Yŏn'guso ed., *Ilche ha chŏnsi ch'ejegi chŏngch'aek saryo ch'ongsŏ 55: Chiwonbyŏng, chingbyŏng 1* (Kyŏnggi-do Koyang-si: Han'guk Haksul Chŏngbo, 2001), 255, 290, 294.

11. Tomimura Rokurō, ed., *Chūnan Ronzan hattenshi* (Tokyo: Kihara Jun'ichirō, 1914), 1.

12. Ibid., "Miyake Suejirō" photo caption.

13. Nonsan Siji P'yŏnch'an Wiwŏnhoe, *Nonsan siji II*, 28.

14. Tomimura, *Chūnan Ronzan hattenshi*, 9–16.

15. Chŏng Yŏn-t'ae, "Nittei no chiiki shihai," 43–46

16. See Nonsan Siji P'yŏnch'an Wiwŏnhoe, *Nonsan siji II*, 25–223 for a more detailed history of this region. Sŏ Sun-hwa, "Ch'ungch'ŏng chiyŏk chumin ŭisik ŭi sahoesachŏk ilgoch'al," in *Hosŏ chibangsa yŏn'gu*, ed. Hosŏ Sahakhoe (Seoul: Kyŏngin Munhwasa, 2003), 437.

17. Out of a total of 430 households. The numbers were based on the Statistics of People's Registration (1909), cited in Nonsan Siji P'yŏnch'an Wiwŏnhoe, *Nonsan siji II*, 226–229. The (overlapping) number of farming families was 308. The total population was 2,063. But the numbers of unregistered households and farming families were large in statistics compiled in 1909. The 1930 census recorded 1,570 households and 8,148 residents.

18. Ch'ungch'ŏng Namdoji P'yŏngch'an Wiwŏnhoe, *Ch'ungch'ŏng-namdoji* (Taejŏn: Ch'ungch'ŏng-namdoji P'yŏngch'an Wiwŏnhoe, 1965), 264.

19. This criticism remained strong even in the 1920s, particularly in *Tonga ilbo*. Uchida, *Brokers of Empire*, 208–209.

20. Many local ruling families expanded their holding of farms in the sixteenth and seventeenth century. Lee Hae-Jun (Yi Hae-jun), *Chōsen sonraku shakaishi no kenkyū*, trans. Inoue Kazue (Tokyo: Hōsei Daigaku Shuppankyoku, 2006) gives an excellent, deeply historical study of the social relationships between the local ruling elite, peasant communities, and the state.

21. Japanese migrants aggressively expanded their land ownership through purchase, loan business, or programs of the Oriental Development Company. By 1935, there were 40 Japanese households and 172 Japanese residents in Kwangsŏk. Nonsan-gun, *Kwangsŏk* (Nonsan: Nonsan-gun saemaŭl-kwa, 1992), 24. As shown in the same statistics, the total number of residents in Kwangsŏk rose to 9,429, a more than fourfold increase since the survey conducted in 1909. This might be result of more thorough recording measures in the 1930s. By the 1930s, in the Nonsan plain, the Japanese settlers set up eight large farming companies. Nonsan Siji P'yŏnch'an Wiwonhŏe, *Nonsan siji II*, 279. Gragert argues that Japanese settlement, however, did not change the existing patterns of landholding and small-scale agricultural production. Edwin Gragert, *Landownership under Colonial Rule: Korea's Japanese Experience, 1900–1935* (Honolulu: University of Hawai'i Press, 1994), 109–110.

22. Nonsan-gun, *Kwangsŏk*, 30.

23. As individuals (not a company), the Yun family owned the second-largest land area in Nonsan county, a few times bigger than farms owned by Japanese landholders. Nonsan Siji P'yŏnch'an Wiwŏnhoe, *Nonsan siji II*, 281–282.

24. The Yun family in Kwangsǒk was a branch of the P'ap'yǒng Yun family, a promi-
nent yangban clan in South Ch'ungch'ǒng. Nonsan-gun, *Kwangsǒk*, 31. Kuksa P'yǒnch'an
Wiwǒnhoe, *Chibang ǔl salda: Chibang haengjǒng, 1930-yǒndae esǒ 1950-yǒndae kkaji*
(Kwach'ǒn-si: Kuksa P'yǒnch'an Wiwǒnhoe, 2006), 9. Interview with Kim Yǒng-han in
Taejǒn on February 13, 2012.

25. Nonsan-gun, *Kwangsǒk*, 81–82, 92, 107–108.

26. Edmund de Schweinitz Brunner, "Rural Korea: A Preliminary Survey of Economic,
Social, and Religious Conditions," in *The Christian Mission in Relation to Rural Problems*,
ed. International Missionary Council (New York: International Missionary Council,
1928), 135–136.

27. The yangban was based more strictly on blood heritage and functioned primarily
as literati-bureaucrats than the Japanese landlord system. Lee Hae-Jun and many others argue that the strictly patriarchal family organization of the Korean yangban class
developed only in the late seventeenth century, when the central Chosǒn government
promoted neo-Confucian ideology. For ruling yangban families, patriarchal lineage was
a means to prevent the fragmentation of the limited landholding, as well as to maintain
local ties when peasant communities under their rule obtained more autonomy. See Lee,
Chōsen sonraku shakaishi no kenkyū.

28. On ture, see Ch'oe Chae-sǒk, *Kankoku nōson shakai kenkyū*, trans. Itō Abito and
Shima Mutsuhiko (Tokyo: Gakuseisha, 1979), 276–278.

29. Lee, *Chōsen sonraku shakaishi no kenkyū*, 81–92.

30. As in Meiji Japan, the emphasis on the old (hamlet) communities was made in
Korea in order to compensate for the 1914 policy of transferring administrative power
from hamlets to village (*myǒn*).

31. Ohara Shinzō, "Chihō shinkōkai no sōsetsu," in *Chōsen tōchi no kaiko to hihan*, ed.
Kida Chūei (Seoul: Chōsen Shinbunsha, 1936), 55–58.

32. "Chūsei-nandō ni okeru shinkōkai," *Chōsen* 101 (September 1923): 117.

33. "Chūsei-nandō shinkōkai no kokoroe sono-ichi," *Chōsen* 82 (December 1921): 103;
"Chūsei-nandō shinkōkai no kokoroe sono-ni," *Chōsen* 83 (January 1922): 26.

34. Hǒ Chong, "Ilche sigi Ch'ungnam chiyǒk ǔi ch'ǒngnyǒn undong," in *Ch'ungnam
chiyǒk maǔl yǒn'gu: Pigyo wa chonghap*, ed. Kim P'il-tong (Seoul: Minsogwǒn, 2011),
89–91.

35. "Nonsan ch'ǒngnyǒn kurakpu chojik," *Tonga ilbo*, May 8, 1920, 4; "Kongju
ch'ǒngnyǒnhoe," *Tonga ilbo*, July 6, 1926, 4; "Nonsan ch'ǒngnyǒnhoe," *Tonga ilbo*, September 29, 1927, 4.

36. "Kanggyǒng ch'ǒngnyǒnhoe chojik," *Tonga ilbo*, May 30, 1920, 4.

37. Ji Soo-gol (Chi Su-gǒl), "Ilche sigi Ch'ungnam Puyǒ, Nonsan-gun ǔi yuji chiptan
kwa hyǒksin ch'ǒngnyǒndan," *Han'guk munhwa* 36 (December 2005): 207.

38. When they taught, they offered classes on Hangǔl, the Chinese classics, math, Japanese, English, accounting, law, and economics to the urban populace. Teachers from colonial elementary schools usually took charge of them. "Yangch'on ch'ǒngnyǒnhoe yahak-
hoe, *Tonga ilbo*, February 7, 1922, 4; "Kanggyǒng ch'ǒngnyǒnhoe yahak sǒllip," *Tonga ilbo*,
February 7, 1923, 4, Hǒ, "Ilche sigi Ch'ungnam chiyǒk," 93–97.

39. For example, see "Mindae Nonsan-gunbu," *Tonga ilbo*, May 30, 1923, 4.

40. "Nonsan p'yǒngya nǔn Namsǒn e yusu 3," *Tonga ilbo*, September 29, 1929, 4.

41. "Minuhoe p'okheng sakǒn," *Tonga ilbo*, October 3, 1926, 4, for example.

42. "Yun-ssi ǔi kyoyungnyǒl," *Chosǒn ilbo*, January 2, 1923, 4; "Kwangsǒk-myǒn e
nodong yahak," *Chosǒn ilbo* October 16, 1923, 3.

43. No documents prove the validity of this information. This is testimony of Kim
Yǒng-han, a friend of Yun's family and a local historian of Nonsan. Interview in Taejǒn
with Kim Yong-han on November 23, 2011.

44. Sayaka Chatani, "The Ruralist Paradigm: Social Work Bureaucrats in Colonial Korea and Japan's Assimilationism in the Interwar Period," *Comparative Studies in Society and History* 58, no. 4 (2016): 1004–1031.

45. Uchida, *Brokers of Empire*, 150–151

46. Ibid., 143–187.

47. "Naisen yūwa no kōtenkei: Ronzan no Aoki Kihachi shi," *Chōsen* 100 (July 1923): 207.

48. Kin Yikkan (Kim Yik-han), "Shokuminchiki Chōsen ni okeru chihō taisei no kōchiku katei to nōson shakai hendō" (PhD diss., University of Tokyo, 1995), 125–129.

49. Kim Yŏng-hŭi, *Ilche sidae nongch'on t'ongje chŏngch'aek yŏn'gu* (Seoul: Kyŏngin Munhwasa, 2002), 475–476.

50. Zenra-nandō Naimubu, *Seinenkai shidō hōshin* (Cholla-namdo: Zenra-nando Naimubu, 1922), 20.

51. "Kwangsŏk-myŏn chinhŭnghoe palchŏn," *Chosŏn ilbo*, December 8, 1923, 4; "Yumanghan chinhŭnghoe," *Chosŏn ilbo*, January 27, 1923, 4.

52. Chōsen Sōtokufu Gakumukyoku Shakai Kyōikuka, *Chōsen shakai kyōka yōran* (Seoul: Chōsen Sōtokufu, 1937), cited in *Ilche ha chŏnsi ch'ejegi chŏngch'aek saryo ch'ongsŏ 47: Hwangguk sinminhwa chŏngch'aek 18*, ed. Minjok Munje Yŏn'guso (Kyŏnggi-do Koyang-si: Han'guk Haksul Chŏngbo, 2000), 29–30.

53. Ibid., 162–163. See Gi-Wook Shin and Do-Hyun Han, "Colonial Corporatism: The Rural Revitalization Campaign, 1932–1940," in *Colonial Modernity in Korea*, ed. Gi-Wook Shin and Michael Robinson (Cambridge, MA: Harvard University Press, 1999), 70–96.

54. "Nōsan gyoson shinkō undō no zenbō," *Chōsen* 224 (January 1934): 17.

55. Ibid. and "Nōsan gyoson shinkō keikaku no jisshi gaikyō," *Chōsen* 224 (January 1934), 4–111. See also Kim Yŏng-hŭi, *Ilche sidae nongch'on t'ongje*, 73–86.

56. Ugaki Kazushige, *Chōsen o kataru* (Tokyo: Jitsugyō no Nihonsha, 1935), 132–134, trans. and cited in Uchida, *Brokers of Empire*, 331.

57. As early as 1913, Governor-General Terauchi issued a decree on the protection of small farmers to promote owner-cultivators against the vested interests of Japanese settlers; see Uchida, *Brokers of Empire*, 125.

58. Chūsei-nandō, *1930-nen chōsa kosaku kankō chōsa* 2 (Konju: Chūsei-nandō, 1931), 324–329.

59. Gi-wook Shin, *Peasant Protest and Social Change in Colonial Korea* (Seattle: University of Washington Press, 1996), 54–73. A newspaper reported that there were more than three thousand disputes in nine months, an average of twenty a day, in 1935. "Ch'ungnam-do sojak chaengŭi 9-kaewŏl kan 3-ch'ŏn kŏn," *Chosŏn chungang ilbo*, November 9, 1935 (evening edition).

60. *Tonga ilbo*, March 24, 1932, quoted in Shin, *Peasant Protest and Social Change*, 69.

61. Paku Sopu (Pak Sŏp), *1930-nendai Chōsen ni okeru nōgyō to nōson shakai* (Tokyo: Miraisha, 1995), 177–211. He argues that the GGK could enact the tenancy law in 1933 before Japan did because Korean tenancy customs were extremely unfair to tenants, the absence of legislative bodies allowed the government to ignore the pressure from landlords, and some Korean landlords supported the law to rescue fellow Koreans.

62. "Seinen dantai no sōdōin miawase," *Osaka asahi shinbun furoku Chōsen asahi*, August 16, 1932.

63. "Kokumin jiriki kōsei no aki sekkyokuteki ni seinendan yūdō," *Keijō nippō*, September 10, 1932.

64. Tomita Akiko, "Nōson shinkō undōka no chūken jinbutsu no yōsei," *Chōsenshi Kenkyūkai ronbunshū* 18 (March 1981): 158; Keijō Nipponsha, *Shōwa 15-nendo Chosen nenkan* (Seoul: Keijō Nipponsha, 1940), 600–601.

65. Kwangsŏk did not exist as an administrative village until 1914, so Kim's great-grandfather was the head of a smaller village (*myŏn*) that came into being in 1900.

66. In Korea, elementary schools were legally allowed to set up the upper-level program (*kōtōka*) in 1922, but the practice did not spread as in Japan or Taiwan.

67. The model graduate program reflected a broader change in the field of education beginning in 1924, from academic knowledge toward agricultural training. See O Sŏng-ch'ŏl, *Singminji ch'odŭng kyoyuk ŭi hyŏngsŏng* (Seoul: Kyoyuk Kwahaksa, 2000), 297–310. Schools first established vocational (or agricultural) programs to teach farming techniques and the use of new fertilizers. Toyota Shigekazu, "Jikka kyōiku ni tsuite," *Chōsen chihō gyōsei*, December 1925, 38–58 gives a list of programs that a number of schools initiated in 1924. This coincided with the debate on educating local culture and practical skill in Japan proper. Advocates for agricultural training often positioned themselves against the nationalists' movement to establish a university. It was more "democratic" education than higher education, they argued, and "if the state was going to spend a massive amount of money [for university education], we feel that it should be spent for lower-level [education]." Hayashibara Norisada, "Chōsen ni okeru kyōiku gyōsei mondai 1," *Chōsen chihō gyōsei*, June 1925, 25.

68. For more on the graduate guidance program, see Tomita, "Nōson shinkō undōka no chūken jinbutsu"; Yi Ki-hun, "Ilche ha nongch'on pot'ong hakkyo ŭi 'ch'orŏpsaeng chido,'" *Yŏksa munje yŏn'gu* 4 (April 2000): 269–306; Yahiro Ikuo, "Sotsugyōsei shidō to nōson shinkō saku 2," *Chōsen chihō gyōsei*, June 1932, 27.

69. Kuksa P'yŏnch'an Wiwŏnhoe, *Chibang ŭl salda*, 20–24.

70. Tomita, "Nōson shinkō undōka no chūken jinbutsu," 161; see Shin, *Peasant Protest and Social Change* for the general trend of farming in Korea.

71. Masuda Shūsaku, "Chōsen ni okeru buraku chūshin jinbutsu ni tsuite no ichi kōsatsu," *Chōsen* 257 (November 1936): 93–96.

72. Ibid., 102.

73. Yahiro Ikuo, "Sotsugyōsei shidō to nōson shinkōsaku 1," *Chōsen chihō gyōsei,* May 1932, 27–28.

74. Yahiro Ikuo, "Sotsugyōsei shidō to nōson shinkōsaku 2," *Chōsen chihō gyōsei*, June 1932, 28–30.

75. Masuda, "Chōsen ni okeru buraku chūshin jinbutsu," 91–92.

76. Yun Chang-ŏp, *Jissenjō kara mita seinendan soshiki to keiei* (Seoul: Seinendansha, 1939), 7–8. The other two factors are customs of early marriage, and the lack of development of shrines.

77. Tomita, "Nōson shinkō undōka no chūken jinbutsu," 162.

78. Kuksa P'yŏnch'an Wiwŏnhoe, *Chibang ŭl salda*, 23. Interview with Kim Yŏng-han in Taejŏn on November 23, 2011.

79. Tomita, "Nōson shinkō undōka no chūken jinbutsu," 159–164.

80. Among 9,116 villagers, 7,289 could not read either Korean or Japanese, according to the 1930 census (South Ch'ungch'ŏng), 46. In official statistics, the national average of elementary school enrollment was 17.3% (male: 28%, female: 6.2%) in 1930 and 23.4% (male: 36.7%, female: 9.8%) in 1935. O, *Singminji ch'odŭng kyoyuk*, 133.

81. The national average of the schooling rate of school-age children in the early 1930s was barely 20% (male: 28%–30%, female: 7%–8%). In cities, it was more than 50% (male: 70%, female: 23%–31%). Chōsen Sōtokufu Gakumukyoku, *Chōsenjin gakurei jidō shūgaku no jōkyō* (Seoul: Chōsen Sōtokufu, 1935). See also O, *Singminji ch'odŭng kyoyuk*, 133.

82. Kuksa P'yŏnch'an Wiwŏnhoe, *Chibang ŭl salda*, 16–20.

83. Ibid., 24–25.

84. Interview with Kim Yŏng-han in Taejŏn on November 23, 2011.

85. Kim Yŏng-han remembered that the main feature of *kyōrei kumiai* groups, which the government specified as the most closely supervised groups in the Rural Revitalization Campaign, was encouraging women to engage in agriculture. Shinkō seinendan youth were their instructors. Chūsei-nandō, *Shinkō no Chūnan* (Taejŏn: Chūsei-nandō, 1935), 85–127.

86. Interview with Kim Yŏng-han in Taejŏn on November 27, 2011.

87. The scholar Kim Yŏng-hŭi argues that the degree of generational conflict varied from village to village, and generally speaking, clan-based communities (*tongsŏng burak*) tended to have more cooperation than confrontation. Kim Yŏng-hŭi, *Ilche sidae nongch'on t'ongje*, 476–479.

88. Interview with Kim Yŏng-han in Taejŏn on November 23, 2011.

89. Yahiro Ikuo, "Sotsugyōsei shidō to nōson shinkō saku 2," *Chōsen chihō gyōsei*, June 1932, 31.

90. Cho Wŏn-hwan, "Seinen shidō ni tsuite," *Chōsen chihō gyōsei*, April 1934, 39.

91. Chūsei-nandō, *Chūsei-nandō kyōiku yōkō* (Taejŏn: Chūsei-nandō, 1937), 442–447.

92. Interview with Kim Yŏng-han in Taejŏn on November 23, 2011.

93. Kuksa P'yŏnch'an Wiwŏnhoe, *Chibang ŭl salda*, 119.

94. Many of the arrested youth were put into reformatory programs that forced their ideological conversion (*tenkō*). As of 1935, the government reported that out of 1,353 thought criminals in South Ch'ungch'ŏng, 781 became "converts" and another 118 were in the process of being converted. In Nonsan country, 155 people (85 Japanese and 70 Koreans) were designated as "thought reformers" in 1930 to facilitate conversion. Some of these youth could recover their upper mobility only after their conversion. Kōtō Hōin Kenjikyoku Shisōbu, "Chūsei-nandōka no shisō gaikyō narabi dōkō: Ronzan, Fuyo, Seiyō, Reizan oyobi Karatsu-gun kaku shisō zendō kikan no katsudō jōkyō," *Shisō ihō* 9 (December 1936): 13–50.

95. Kim Puja, *Shokuminchiki Chōsen no kyōiku to jendā* (Kanagawa: Seori Shobō), 115–138. See 163–271 on the situation for women's schooling.

96. He remembers that the literary magazine *Samch'ŏlli* was relatively popular among young villagers. Those who understood Korean Han'gŭl often read the novels in the magazine for those who could not.

97. Chūsei-nandō, *Chūsei-nandō kyōiku yōkō*, 649–650.

98. Paku Sopu, *1930-nendai Chōsen*, 163–165.

99. "Ch'ungnam-do hangnyŏng adong sipkuman ch'on yŏmyŏng!" *Chosŏn chungang ilbo*, February 22, 1936 (evening edition), 1.

8. OPPORTUNITIES AND LOOPHOLES

1. Takashi Fujitani, *Race for Empire: Koreans as Japanese and Japanese as Americans during World War II* (Berkeley: University of California Press, 2011); Brandon Palmer, *Fighting for the Enemy: Koreans in Japan's War, 1937–1945* (Seattle: University of Washington Press, 2013).

2. Chōsen Sōtokufu Gakumukyoku Shakai Kyōikuka, *Chōsen shakai kyōiku yōran* (Seoul: Chōsen Sōtokufu, 1937), 99–100.

3. "Chōsen ni hajimete no nōji kunrenjo," *Chōsen* 219 (August 1933), 140.

4. Furushō Itsuo, "Chūsei-nandō nōson joshi kōshūjo o shisatsu shite," *Jiriki kōsei ihō* 19 (March 1935): 7; "Chihōchō kōbun," *Chōsen Sōtokufu kanpō* 2195 (May 8, 1934).

5. Later, the length of training became eleven months. Yi Tae-gyu, "Chūnan yūryō nōsan shisatsu shokan ni," *Chōsen chihō gyōsei*, January 1938, 144. Officially the age range was set between eighteen and twenty-five, but the head of the Yusŏng center recruited those age twenty to thirty. Kobayashi Rinzō, "Jujō Nōson Seinen Kunrenjo o miru," *Chōsen nōkaihō* 5 (May 1936): 63.

6. Furushō Itsuo, "Chūsei-nandō Nōson Seinen Kunrenjo o shisatsu shite," *Jiriki kōsei ihō* 18 (February 1935): 5–6; "Chihōchō kōbun," *Chōsen Sōtokufu kanpō* 2238 (June 19, 1934).

7. "Chihōchō kōbun," *Chōsen Sōtokufu kanpō* 2690 (January 4, 1936); "Chihōchō kōbun," *Chōsen Sōtokufu kanpō* 2797 (May 13, 1936). These centers also offered two-month training for elementary school graduates.

8. Kobayashi, "Jujō Nōson Seinen Kunrenjo o miru," 62. Shinozaki Denzaburō, "Busshin ichigen, shinshin ichijo," *Chōsen* 251 (April 1936): 2–7.

9. Ibid.

10. Yi Pam-ik, "Chūnan no shinden kaihatsu undō," *Chōsen* 252 (May 1936): 77–86.

11. "Jikyoku ni saikaishi zen-Sen chūken seinen taikai kaisai saru," *Jiriki kōsei ihō* 49 (October 1937): 43.

12. Ōno Ken'ichi, "Kokumin no kunren to soshikika ni kansuru hiken," *Bunkyō no Chōsen*, March 1938, 36–54.

13. Kim Yŏng-han, who later supervised human resources of local offices, recalled that "so many talented people went to rural youth training centers and became *myŏn* secretaries." An interview with Kim in Taejŏn on November 23, 2011.

14. For a rare interview with a former graduate and instructor in Kyŏngi province's rural youth training center, see Aono Masaaki, Chōsen nōson no 'chūken jinbutsu,'" *Chōsen gakuhō* 141 (October 1991): 39–68.

15. Shinozaki, "Busshin ichigen, shinshin ichijo," 7.

16. "Waga dō no kinrō hōshi undō, Zenra-nandō," *Chōsen* 282 (November 1938): 38.

17. Furushō Itsuo, "Chūsei-nandō Nōson Koshi Kōshūjo o shisatsu shite," *Jiriki kōsei ihō* 19 (March 1935): 7.

18. Yuasa Katsuei, "Rupotāju onshō no shujusō," *Chōsen gyōsei* 232 (February 1942): 14.

19. Interview with Kim Yŏng-han in Taejŏn on November 27, 2011. Kim also told me a story of his friend who went to an agricultural school. When he graduated, he waved the diploma and shouted, "This is worth two thousand *yen!*" indicating the tuition his family had paid for five years. School diplomas and family wealth were directly connected.

20. Interview with Kim Yŏng-han in Taejŏn on November 27, 2011.

21. Matsumoto Takenori, *Chōsen nōson no shokuminchi kindai keiken* (Tokyo: Shakai Hyōronsha, 2005), 105.

22. Matsumoto finds examples in the journal *Chōsen chihō gyōsei*. Matsumoto, *Chōsen nōson*, 106–109. Another source of the youth's psychology is a 1930 diary written by O Chŏnbok residing in Hwasun county, South Cholla. He could not finish the upper-level elementary program and came back to his village. He worked as a farmer but gradually became depressed. His life turned upward when he got a job in the village administrative office. Hong Sŏngch'an, "Ilche ha kohangnyŏk 'sirŏp' ch'ŏngnyŏn ŭi nongch'on saengh-wal kwa ch'eje p'yŏnip," *Han'guk kyŏngje hakpo* 12, no. 1 (2005).

23. Matsumoto, *Chōsen nōson*, 104. Because the examination to become a village secretary conferred a qualification, rather than placement in a specific post, successful examinees could freely transfer between different offices too. An interview with Kim Yŏng-han in Taejŏn on November 23, 2011.

24. Interview with Kim Yŏng-han in Taejŏn on November 23, 2011.

25. Ibid., November 27, 2011.

26. Ibid., February 13, 2012.

27. Excerpts from *Chōsen chihō gyōsei*, cited in Matsumoto, *Chōsen nōson*, 122.

28. Hong, "Ilche ha kohangnyŏk," 382.

29. Matsumoto, *Chōsen nōson*, 119.

30. Kuksa P'yŏnch'an Wiwŏnhoe, *Chibang ŭl salda: Chibang haengjŏng 1930-yŏndae esŏ 1950-yŏndae kkaji* (Kyŏnggi-do, Kwach'ang-si: Kuksa P'yŏnch'an Wiwŏnhoe, 2006), 88.

31. Nakamura Kosei, "Taigen shōgen: Men shokuin ni seinenkai o mōkeyo," *Chōsen chihō gyōsei*, February 1930, 78; Shin Pok-kyun, "Taigen shōgen: Men shoki wa sono men jūmin taru mohan seinen o motte menchō yori suisen seshime saiyō subeshi," *Chōsen chihō gyōsei*, August 1930, 113.

32. "Seinendan no kyōka fukyū," *Chōsen* 268 (September 1937): 153–154.

33. "Seinendan no fukyū narabi ni shidō ni kansuru ken," *Chōsen shakai jigyō*, May 1936, 68–70.

34. "Akibare ni iki takarakani taikai narabi ni hatsudanshiki o ageta Keihoku Rengō, Chōsen Rengō Seinendan ni sanka shite," *Chōsen chihō gyōsei*, November 1938, 54–58.

35. "Seinendan shidō hōshin ni shin seishin o orikomu," *Chōsen nippō*, March 12, 1938.

36. After 1938, these volunteer labor groups were called the Patriotic Labor Corps (Kinrō Hōkokutai), organized at various levels of seinendan associations. It does not seem that their activities were as centralized as those of the Taiwan's Volunteer Labor Corps.

37. "Rengō Seinendan no funki," *Chōsen mainichi shinbun*, April 9, 1939.

38. Interview with Kim Yŏng-han in Taejŏn on November 23, 2011.

39. Ibid.

40. Kuksa P'yŏnch'an Wiwŏnhoe, *Chibang ŭl salda*, 24–25. Interview with Kim Yŏng-han in Taejŏn on November 23, 2011.

41. "Seinen kunrenjo no nintei ni tsuite," *Bunkyō no Chōsen*, December 1928, 8–9.

42. See Keijō Nippōsha, *Chōsen nenkan*, (Seoul: Keijō Nippōsha, 1933–1942), 1933: 551–552, 1934: 410, 1938: 591, 1941: 558, and 1942: 460–461.

43. Chōsen Sōtokufu, *Chōsen Sōtokufu Jikyoku Taisaku Chōsakai shimon'an sankōsho: Naisen ittai no kyōka tettei ni kansuru ken* (Seoul: Chōsen sōtokufu, September 1938, 26.

44. The speed of expansion exceeded the original plan of 140 additional centers a year. Ibid., 26–28. Chōsen Sōtokufu Jōhōka, *Chōsen jijō shiryō dai-4 gō: Rensei suru Chōsen* (Seoul: Chōsen Sōtokufu, 1944), 9. Chōsen Sōtokufu Gakumukyoku Shakai Kyōikuka, *Chōsen shakai kyōiku yōran* (Seoul: Chōsen Sōtokufu, 1941), 39–41.

45. Chōsen Sōtokufu Jōhōka, *Rensei suru Chōsen*, 8.

46. "Naisen ittai wa Kudara no mukashi ni kaere," *Keijō nippō*, June 4, 1938, 1.

47. Naimushō, *Taiheiyō senka no Chōsen oyobi Taiwan* (1944), in Miyata Setsuko, *Chōsen minshū to "kōminka" seisaku* (Tokyo: Miraisha, 1985), 62.

48. Palmer, *Fighting for the Enemy*, 89.

49. Miyata, *Chōsen minshū*, 50–56; Palmer, *Fighting for the Enemy*, 44–47. The shortage of military manpower was more closely felt after 1942, when Japan faced increasingly severe battles.

50. In 1932, coinciding with the start of the Rural Revitalization Campaign, the Chōsengun considered the future possibility of soldier recruitment in Korea. Chōsengun Sanbōchō, "Chōsenjin shiganhei mondai ni kansuru ken kaitō" (Seoul: Chōsengun, November 1937), 236, available at http://www.koreanhistory.or.kr. Ugaki directly expressed his desire to introduce Korean military service, remarking that "Koreans should start serving in the military as soon as possible" in 1934. Ugaki Kazushige, *Ugaki Kazushige nikki II* (Tokyo: Misuzu Shobō, 1970), 981–982. As early as 1927, when he requested building the standing army in Korea and when he temporarily served as a deputy governor-general in Korea, Ugaki had already considered the need for a conscription system among Koreans. Ugaki Kazushige, *Ugaki nikki* (Tokyo: Asahi Shinbunsha, 1954), 11.

51. Chōsengun Shireibu, "Chōsenjin shiganhei seido ni kansuru iken" (Seoul: Chōsengun Shireibu, June 1937), 255, available at http://www.koreanhistory.or.kr.

52. Chōsengun Sanbōchō, "Chōsenjin shiganhei mondai," 242.

53. Military officers and GGK officials claimed that since 1931 "the Korean people had become increasingly patriotic in their attitudes toward Japan." Fujitani, *Race for Empire*, 42.

54. See Jun Uchida, *Brokers of Empire: Japanese Settler Colonialism in Korea, 1876–1945* (Cambridge, MA: Harvard University Asia Center, 2011), 319.

55. Chōsengun Shireibu, "Chōsenjin shiganhei seido," 262–263.

56. Chōsen Sōtokufu Keimukyoku, *Dai-73 kai Chōsen Sōtokufu Teikoku Gikai setsumei shiryō I* (1937, repr., Tokyo: Fuji Shuppan, 1994), 292.

57. Ibid., 293.

58. It was shortened to four months in 1941.

59. The translation is from Fujitani, *Race for Empire*, 261.

60. Their daily routines are elaborated in "Chōsen Shiganhei Kurenjo sankanki," *Chōsen no kyōiku kenkyū* 121 (October 1938): 69–91. Kuramoto Hiroshi, "Senbō no mato kunrenjo seito no ichinichi (shōzen)," *Chōsen* 284 (January 1939): 88–99.

61. The famous *aikokuhan* was similar to Japanese *tonarigumi* in enforcing collective responsibility to each unit of around ten households in tax payment, volunteer labor, and so on. Kim Yŏng-hŭi, *Ilche sidae nongch'on t'ongje chŏngch'aek yŏngu* (Seoul: Kyŏngin Munhwasa, 2002), 234–242.

62. The government estimated that only one-third of all applicants "truly volunteered." Chōsen Sōtokufu, *Dai-79 kai Teikoku Gikai setsumei shiryō*, December 1941, 104, cited in Palmer, *Fighting for the Enemy*, 77. See Palmer, 74–83 on the coercive nature of the volunteerism.

63. Interviews with Kim Yŏng-han in Taejŏn on November 23 and 27, 2011, and February 13 and 29, 2012.

64. "Wakaki hantōjin senshi nihyaku yomei rekishiteki dai-ippo o fumu," *Keijō nippō*, June 16, 1938 (evening edition), 1; "Shiganhei Kunrenjo no kaishoshiki ni atarite," *Chōsen nippō*, June 15, 1938, in *Chōsen tsūshin* 145 no. 3635 (1938): 1.

65. "Chōsen Shiganhei Kurenjo sankanki," 78–79.

66. Ibid., 72–73.

67. "Hantō minshū no shidōteki tachiba to kokka jigyō no tantōteki chii!" *Keijō nippō*, January 30, 1938.

68. Kuramoto Hiroshi, "Shigansha kunrenjo hōmonki," *Chōsen chihō gyōsei*, December 1938, 44.

69. "NaiSen ittai wa Kudara no mukashi ni kaere," 1.

70. "Chōsen shiganhei kurenjo sankanki," 86.

71. Kuramoto Hiroshi, "Shigansha kunrenjo hōmonki," 44.

72. "Chiwŏnbyŏng Yi kun: Yukkun kongkwa e hapkyŏk," *Chosŏn ilbo*, December 19, 1939, 2, for example.

73. Palmer, *Fighting for the Enemy*, 44–45.

74. Kaida Kaname, "Shiganhei seido no genjō to shōrai eno tenbō," *Konnichi no Chōsen mondai kōza* 3 (Seoul: Ryokki Renmei, 1939): 27–28.

75. "Shiganhei ōbosha 7 man 9 sen," *Chōsen tsūshin* 166, no. 4120 (1940): 4–6.

76. Kuksa P'yŏnch'an Wiwŏnhoe, *Chibang ŭl salda*, 209.

77. "Chedae hu chiwŏnbyŏng chigŏp ŭl udae," *Chosŏn ilbo*, January 20, 1938, 2.

78. Interview with Kim Yŏng-han in Taejŏn on November 27, 2011.

79. Kuksa P'yŏnch'an Wiwŏnhoe, *Chibang ŭl salda*, 29. About half the Korean volunteer soldiers were put in the reserves. Palmer, *Fighting for the Enemy*, 89.

80. The league was renamed the Korean League for Total National Power (Kokumin Sōryoku Chōsen Renmei).

81. Kokumin Seishin Sōdōin Chōsen Renmei, *Chōsen ni okeru kokumin seishin sōdoin* (Seoul: Kokumin Seishin Sōdōin Chōsen Renmei, 1940), 1–58.

82. For example, see Chūsei-nandō, *Kyōka iin hikkei* (Taejŏn: Chūsei-nando, 1940), 4–9.

83. See Higuchi Yūichi, *Senjika Chōsen no nōmin seikatsushi 1939–1945* (Tokyo: Shakai Hyōronsha, 1998), 205–217.

84. See the series of articles on Chōsen nōgyō no saihensei in *Chōsen* 330 (November 1942): 14–90.

85. Watanabe Toyohiko, "Nōmin dōjō wa nōmin no heiei," *Kokumin sōryoku*, November 1942, 28–33.

86. The "(male) youth" section was divided into three categories: (1) students of seinen kurenjo, (2) those age fourteen to twenty and not students of the seinen kunrenjo, and (3) those between the ages of twenty and thirty. Children between ten and fourteen years old who were not attending school also formed the "boys" section. The Chōsen Seinendan, unlike the former federation, did not become part of the Japanese organization (the Greater Japan Seishōnendan). A brief discussion on this point is in Ōgushi Ryūkichi, *Seinendan to kokusai kōryū no rekishi* (Tokyo: Yūshindō, 1999), 163–164.

87. Chōsen Sōtokufu Gakumukyoku Shakai Kyōikuka, *Chōsen shakai kyōiku yōran* (Seoul: Chōsen Sōtokufu, 1941), 27–39. Similar details can be found in Chōsen Sōtokufu Gakumukyoku, "Seinendan no shintaisei kaisetsu," *Bunkyō no Chōsen* 188 (April 1941): 51–77.

88. The national average for elementary school enrollment was 41.6% (male: 60.8%, female: 22.2%) in 1940 and 47.4% (male: 66.1%, female 29.1%) in 1942. O Sŏng-ch'ŏl, *Singminji ch'odŭng kyoyuk ŭi hyŏngsŏng* (Seoul: Kyoyuk Kwahaksa, 2000), 133.

89. Chōsen Sōtokufu Gakumukyoku Shakai Kyōikuka, *Chōsen shakai kyōiku yōran*, 35.

90. Interview with Kim Yŏng-han in Taejŏn on November 27, 2011.

91. "Seinendan kaiso to ryūgen higo," *Maeil sinbo* editorial, in *Chōsen tsūshin* 4497 (May 29, 1941): 1–3.

92. Tanaka Takeo, "Koiso sōtoku jidai no tōchi gaikan," *Chōsen kindai shiryō kenkyū shūsei* 3 (May 1960): 243.

93. Mitarai Tatsuo, *Minami Jirō* (Tokyo: Minami Jirō Denki Kankōkai, 1957), 433–435. See Higuchi Yūichi, *Senjika Chōsen no minshū to chōhei* (Tokyo: Sōwasha, 2001), 28–33.

94. According to Tanaka Takeo, then vice governor of Korea, the Government-General in Taiwan insisted that it would implement universal elementary education sooner than Korea, which pressured the GGK to match that speed. Tanaka, "Koiso sōtoku jidai," 219–222.

95. Higuchi, *Senjika Chōsen no minshū to chōhei*, 58.

96. Chōsen Sōtokufu Gakumukyoku Renseika, "Chōheisei no jisshi to Chōsen seinen no tokubetsu rensei," *Bunkyō no Chōsen* 84 (February 1943): 27–32.

97. Higuchi, *Senjika Chōsen no minshū to chōhei*, 58.

98. In total, 273,139 draft notices were sent out, 206,057 underwent the military exams, and 55,000 were placed on active duty. Palmer, *Fighting for the Enemy*, 112–117.

99. Ibid., 117–136. For example, in one incident in 1944, even high-ranking Korean military officers rebelled against the Japanese army, organizing a group desertion of Korean conscripts. Also see Higuchi, *Senjika Chōsen no minshū to chōhei*, 205–208.

100. "Hantō ni chōheisei," *Kokumin sōryoku* 4, no. 6 (1942): 4–6.

101. In 1937, out of 598 *gunzoku*, 391 were drivers and 111 were interpreters. Higuchi Yūichi, *Kōgun heishi ni sareta chōsenjin* (Tokyo: Shakai Hyōronsha, 1991), 13.

102. The exact number is not known but combined with the forced labor, Higuchi estimates twenty thousand went to Southeast Asia and islands in the Pacific. Higuchi *Senjika Chōsen no minshū to chōhei*, 177.

103. Interview with Kim Yŏng-han in Taejŏn on November 27, 2011.

104. Higuchi, *Senjika Chōsen no nōmin seikatsushi*, 100. For close calculation, see Kang Sŏng-ŭn, "Senjika Nihon teikokushugi no Chōsen nōson rōdōryoku shūdatsu seisaku," *Rekishi hyōron* 355 (November 197): 37–41.

105. Chōsen Nōkai Chōsaka, "Nōka no rōdō jōken ni kansuru ichi chōsa," *Chōsen Nōkaihō*, February 1944, quoted in Higuchi, *Senjika Chōsen no nōmin seikatsushi*, 98.
106. Kuksa P'yŏnch'an Wiwŏnhoe, *Chibang ŭl salda*, 114.
107. Ibid., 44.
108. Ibid., 116.
109. Interview with Kim Yŏng-han in Taejŏn on November 27, 2011.
110. Interviews with Kim Yŏng-han in Taejŏn on November 27 2011, and February 13, 2012.
111. Since the early 1930s, many young people had left their villages of their own volition to go to Japan or Manchuria. In a study on the population movement conducted in Talli hamlet in Ulsan, South Kyŏngsang, in 1935, those between the ages of sixteen and twenty-five tended to leave the village more than any other age group. The study showed that Japan was the first choice for those in the upper- and middle-class villagers whereas the lower-class peasants migrated within Korea. Manchuria was a choice for "the upper-class with significant capital who would want to do their own business," "middle-class people with technical skill but could not go to Japan," and "those from the upper and middle class who went bankrupt and turned themselves into agricultural immigrants." The researchers also found that nearly all elementary school graduates left the village because "Korean rural villages and agriculture do not have the power to attract them culturally or economically. . . . The power of young 'new' people is suppressed under the older generations and customs, and their desire to devote themselves to the construction of rural culture is also hindered by the authorities." Nichi-Man Nōsei Kenkyūkai Tōkyō Jimusho, *Chōsen nōson no jinkō haishutsu kikō* (Tokyo: Nichi-Man Nōsei Kenkyūkai, 1940), 12–26.
112. Shirohara Jō, "Man-Mō Kaitaku Seinen Giyūtai ni tsuite," *Bunkyō no Chōsen* 223 (June 1944): 45–50. See also Higuchi, *Senjika Chōsen no nōmin seikatsushi*, 140–141.
113. Interview with Kim Yŏng-han in Taejŏn on February 13, 2012. Kuksa P'yŏnch'an Wiwŏnhoe, *Chibang ŭl salda*, 30.
114. Kagawa Tomomi, "Chōsen Nōgyō Hōkoku Seinentai o genchi ni miru," *Chōsen* 327 (August 1942): 55.
115. Kagawa Tomomi, "Chōsen Nōgyō Hōkoku Seinentai (shōzen)," *Chōsen* 329 (October 1942): 93. Kagawa Tomomi, "Chōsen Nōgyō Hōkoku seinentai o genchi ni miru," *Chōsen* 327 (August 1942): 63.
116. Chōsen Sōtokufu Nōrinkyoku Nōseika, *Nōgyō Hōkoku Seinentaiki* (Seoul: Chōsen sōtokufu, 1942), 13–50.
117. Ibid., 51–54.
118. Interviews with Kim Yŏng-han in Taejŏn on November 23 and 27, 2011, and February 13 and 29, 2012. Although many Korean people chose to maintain silence regarding their eager participation in Japan's war effort, some offered the reflection that participation was natural, especially for children and youth. One example is Pak Ch'ang-hŭi's comment; he considered collecting scrapped iron and pine oil a good thing to do when he was a child, and he doubts how Koreans could have retained a sense of nationhood if there had been no August 15 liberation. Tanaka, "Koiso sōtoku jidai," 248–249.
119. "World Briefing. Asia: South Korea: Crackdown on Collaborators," *New York Times*, May 3, 2007. Andrew Wolman, "Looking Back While Moving Forward: The Evolution of Truth Commissions in Korea," *Asian-Pacific Law and Policy Journal* 14, no. 3 (2013): 39–41. One example of the class-based definition of collaborators and victims is the reinvestigation of war criminals. In November 2006 the Truth Commission in South Korea reexamined the cases of convicted class B and C Korean war criminals and voided their guilty verdicts. It deliberately left out those who were

armed police and high-ranking officials because the commission assumed that they had "volunteered." "Kangje tongwŏn 'Chosŏnin chŏnbŏm' omyŏng pŏsŏtta," *Sŏul Sinmun*, November 13, 2006.

120. For a discussion on the problem of the concept of collaboration in the East Asian context, see Konrad Mitchell Lawson, "Wartime Atrocities and the Politics of Treason in the Ruins of the Japanese Empire, 1937–1953" (PhD diss., Harvard University, 2012), 15–23.

9. AS YOUNG PILLARS OF THE NATION-EMPIRE

1. "Dai 1-kai Dai-Tōa Seishōnen Shidōkaigi kaigiroku" (November 12 and 13, 1943); "Dai 2-ji Dai-Tōa Seishōnen Shidōkaigi ketsugian" (October 9, 1944), the archives of the Japan Youth Center.

2. Aaron William Moore, *Writing War: Soldiers Record the Japanese Empire* (Cambridge, MA: Harvard University Press, 2013).

3. Nakaji Sei, "Gotairei no miyako ni noborite," *Chōsen shakai jigyō*, December 1928, 33–38.

4. Suzuki Yoshiaki, "Gotaiten hōshuku Dai Nihon Seinendan dai 4-kai taikai ni sankashite," *Chōsen shakai jigyō*, February 1929, 42–48.

5. Ibid.

6. "NichiManShi seinen tamashiino yakudō! Dai Nihon Seinendan dai 15-kai taikai narabi NichiManShi seinen kōkankai," *Nihon seinen shinbun*, September 17, 1939, 1.

7. Ibid.

8. Ibid.

9. KY-sei, "Chōsen zaikai nisshi," in *Shōwa 14-nen 9-gatsu 13-nichi, Dai 15-kai taikai nisshi*. Nagano-kenritsu Rekishikan (Nagano Prefectural Museum of History), toguchi, shakai shūdan, seinen shūdan, shō-ken S, 1939–1940.

10. A diary in *Shōwa 14-nen 9-gatsu 13-nichi, Dai 15-kai taikai nisshi*.

11. She mentions this individual in Miyazaki Seiko, *Shokuminchiki Taiwan ni okeru seinendan to chiiki no hen'yō* (Tokyo: Ochanomizu Shobō, 2008), 237.

12. On the "eventful" approach, the author is informed by Rogers Brubaker et al., *Nationalist Politics and Everyday Ethnicity in a Transylvanian Town* (Princeton, NJ: Princeton University Press, 2006).

13. Sasaki Kameo, "Gotairei no naichi e 1," *Shakai jigyō no tomo* 4, no. 3 (1929): 49–56; Sasaki Kameo, "Gotairei no naichi e 2," *Shakai jigyō no tomo* 4, no. 4 (1929): 92–98.

14. Interview with Xu Chongfa in Shakeng, May 20, 2011.

15. The content of Xu Chongfa's report in *Dōkō* remains only partially known as a quote in a letter of Xu's student. Letter from Huang Xiuying, September 8, 1942.

16. Statistics between 1931 and 1939 are in "Tennichi ikuei shikin nōgyō jisshūsei haken jōkyō," *Bunkyō no Chōsen* 180 (August 1940): 52.

17. "Chōsen Kyōikukai tennichi ikuei shikin: Naichi haken nōgyō jisshūsei zadankai," *Bunkyō no Chōsen* 177 (May 1940): 70.

18. These points appear over and over in the printed diaries and reports published as "Tennichi ikuei shikin: Naichi haken nōgyō jisshūsei nisshi" or "Chōsen Kyōikukai tennichi ikuei shikin: Naichi haken nōgyō jisshūsei no katsudō jōkyō," in *Bunkyō no Chōsen* between August 1933 and September 1938, as well as in a roundtable discussion: "Chōsen Kyōikukai tennichi ikuei shikin: Naichi haken nōgyō jisshūsei zadankai," *Bunkyō no Chōsen* 177 (May 1940): 67–75.

19. Chong Su-yŏn, "Tennichi ikuei shikin: Naichi haken nōgyō jisshūsei nisshi," *Bunkyō no Chōsen* 98 (October 1933): 103.

20. "Chōsen Kyōikukai tennichi ikuei shikin: Naichi haken nōgyō jisshūsei zadankai," *Bunkyō no Chōsen* 177 (May 1940): 75.

21. Okabe Makio, "Shokuminchi fashizumu undō no seiritsu to tenkai: Manshū Seinen Renmei to Manshū Kyōwatō," *Rekishigaku kenkyū* 3, no. 406 (1974): 3.

22. Ibid., 1–15.

23. Kawasaki Murao, "Manshū no seishōnen undō," *Shin Manshū* 4, no. 4 (1940): 26–29.

24. Miyazawa Eriko, "Manshūkoku ni okeru seinen soshikika to kenkoku daigaku no kensetsu," *Ajia bunka kenkū* 21 (March 1995): 62.

25. Kawasaki, "Manshū no seishōnen undō," 27. Ronald Suleski, "Reconstructing Life in the Youth Corps Camps of Manchuria, 1938–45: Resistance to Conformity," *East Asian History* 30 (December 2005): 70, 89.

26. Ronald Suleski, "Northeast China under Japanese Control: The Role of the Manchurian Youth Corps, 1934–1945," *Modern China* 7, no. 3 (1981): 351–377. See also Louis Young, *Japan's Total War: Manchuria and the Culture of Wartime Imperialism* (Berkeley: University of California Press, 1999), 404–405.

27. Okutsu Kaoru, "Minzoku kyōwa wa Nihon seishin de," *Shin Manshū* 4, no. 1 (1940): 35.

28. Suleski, "Reconstructing Life in the Youth Corps," 80; Suleski, "Northeast China under Japanese Control," 361.

29. Hōno Nisoji, "Manshū no tomodachi," *Kaitaku* 5, no. 2 (1941): 95.

30. The quotes are from interviews in Imai Ryōichi, "'Manshū' Kaitaku Seinen Giyūtai kyōdo chūtai ni okeru nōgyō kunren," *Jidō kyoikugaku kenkyū* 31 (March 2012): 123–137. Daily life at the camps is also detailed in Suleski, "Reconstructing Life in the Youth Corps Camps of Manchuria." See also Young, *Japan's Total War*, 399–411.

31. Imai, "'Manshū' Kaitaku Seinen Giyūtai," 128.

32. Higuchi Yūichi, *Senjika Chōsen no minshū to chōhei* (Tokyo: Sōwasha, 2001), 110; Kondō Masami, *Sōryokusen to Taiwan* (Tokyo: Tōsui Shobō, 1996), 372. Not all of them were deployed in the military, however.

33. For statistics on Taiwan, refer to Kashiwaguma Osamu, "Taiwan jūmin senbotsusha no izokutō ni taisuru chōikintō no hōritsu," *Taiwan Kyōkaihō* 400 (January 15, 1988): 5. The numbers of Korean soldiers and military employment are based on those disclosed by the Japanese government in 1953. For a discussion on the changes in official statistics in the 1960s, refer to Takeuchi Yasuto, "Chōsenjin gunjin gunzoku no kyōsei dōinsū," *Ōhara Shakai Mondai Kenkyūjo zasshi* 686 (December 2015): 17–32.

34. Takashi Fujitani discusses the records of Korean prisoners of war, governmental and army reports, and interviews that show the procedures and reactions of Korean soldiers in the Japanese military. See Takashi Fujitani, *Race for Empire: Koreans as Japanese and Japanese as Americans during World War II* (Berkeley: University of California Press, 2011), 239–298. Brandon Palmer also provides some discussion on various motivations behind Korean youth's volunteering. He introduces a few accounts that show the motive to learn how to use weapons for the independence of the Korean nation. Brandon Palmer, *Fighting for the Enemy* (Seattle: University of Washington Press, 2013), 78–79.

35. NHK "sensō shōgen" purojekuto, *Shōgen kiroku: Heishitachi no sensō 5* (Tokyo: NHK Shuppan, 2011), 76–77. On the same point, see an interview in Hayashi Eidai, *Chōsenjin kōgun heishi: Nyūginia-sen no tokubetsu shiganhei* (Tokyo: Takushoku Shobō 1995), 153.

36. Hayashi, *Chōsenjin kōgun*, 96 and 200.

37. Utsumi Aiko, *Chōsenjin "kōgun" heishitachi no sensō* (Tokyo: Iwanami Shoten, 1991), 9.

38. Utsumi Aiko, *Chōsenjin BC-kyū senpan no kiroku* (Tokyo: Keisō Shobō, 1982) 16, 138–139.

39. NHK "sensō shōgen" projekuto, *Shōgen kiroku*, 71.

40. Kim Ki-bong, "Watashi to 1945-nen 8-gatsu 15-nichi," *Kikan gendaishi*, November 1973, 101. One survivor of the first group of volunteer soldiers in Taiwan put the ambi-

guity in a short sentence: "It was not coercion, nor was it enthusiastic volunteering." See Miyazaki, *Shokuminchiki Taiwan*, 290.

41. Hayashi, *Chōsenjin kōgun*, 92–93.

42. The phrase *model youth* remains key to some survivors' memories of application. See Hayashi, *Chōsenjin kōgun*, 28, 132–133.

43. Rikugunshō, "Chōsen shusshinhei toriatsukai kyōiku no sankō shiryō sōfu ni kansuru ken rikugun ippan e tsūchō." Ref. C1007819700, 1943. Riku-mitsu-S18-1-1, JACAR, Bōei Kenkyūjo.

44. "'Kōgun' heishi ni natta Chōsenjin," *Kikan gendaishi* 4 (August 1974): 146 and 150; NHK "sensō shōgen" purojekuto, *Shōgen kiroku*, 75 and 79.

45. Tei Shunga (Zheng Chunhe), *Taiwanjin motoshiganhei to Dai Tōa Sensō* (Tokyo: Tentensha, 1998): 230–231.

46. "Lin Zhendong xiansheng fangwen jilu," in *Taipei-shi Taiji Ribenbing chafang zhuanji: Rizhi shiqi canyu junwu zhi taimin koushu lishi*, ed. Chen Yiru and Tang Xiyong (Taipei: Bei-shi wenxianhui, 2001), 157.

47. Palmer, *Fighting for the Enemy*, 73, 131–136; "'Kōgun' heishi ni natta Chōsenjin," 146–151.

48. Tei, *Taiwanjin motoshiganhei*, 219–220, 231.

49. Utsumi, *Chōsenjin BC-kyū*, 9–11; A similar point was made in "'Kōgun' heishi ni natta Chōsenjin," 143.

50. Palmer, *Fighting for the Enemy*, 128.

51. "'Kōgun' heishi ni natta Chōsenjin," 147.

52. Ibid., 140–151.

53. Fujitani, *Race for Empire*, esp. 21–28.

54. One example of vulgar racism haunting the life of ranked Korean officers is shown in an interview: Pak Kap-ch'ŏl, "Chiwŏnbyŏng podamdo kkŭllyŏ kan kŏyŏ," in *Kapcha, Ŭlch'uksaeng ŭn kinin e kaya handa*, ed. Ilche Kangjŏm ha Kangje Tongwŏn P'ihae Chinsang Kyumyŏng Wiwŏnhoe (Seoul: Ilche Kangjŏm ha Kangje Tongwŏn P'ihae Chinsang Kyumyŏng Wiwŏnhoe, 2006), 32–44.

55. Perhaps their desire to establish a sense of superiority was strengthened by the simple fact that colonial volunteer soldiers were, frankly, more qualified as soldiers than regular Japanese conscripts. A former Taiwanese volunteer soldier reflects that he always felt that he was "above" the Japanese soldiers in the same troop. Miyazaki, *Shokuminchiki Taiwan*, 291.

56. "'Kōgun' heishi ni natta Chōsenjin," 146. A similar reflection is in NHK "sensō shōgen" purojekuto, 79; Kim, "Watashi to 1945-nen 8-gatsu 15-nichi," 106–107.

57. "'Kōgun' heishi ni natta Chōsenjin," 143.

58. See Palmer, *Fighting for the Enemy*, 128; Minato Ken'ichi, "Kaigun tokubetsu rikusentai, Kainantō: Taiwan shusshinhei tono kizuna," in *Rōku taiken shuki*, ed. *Heiwa Kinen Tenji Shiryōkan*, http://www.heiwakinen.jp/shiryokan/heiwa/10onketsu/O_10_384_1.pdf.

59. Hayashi, *Chōsenjin kōgun*, 110–111.

60. Ibid., 139. A similar account is at 179.

61. Ibid., 182.

62. Ibid., 183–184.

63. Ibid., 161, 208.

64. Takeuchi, "Chōsenjin gunjin gunzoku," 18; Kashiwaguma, "Taiwan jūmin senbotsusha," 5; Kōsei Rōdōshō, "Senbotsusha ireijigyō no jisshi jōkyō" (press release, August 7, 2015).

65. Kim, "Watashi to 1945-nen 8-gatsu 15-nichi," 96–98.

66. Quote in Pak Kyŏng-sik, "Nihon no haisen to Chōsen no kaihō," *Kikan gendaishi* 3 (November 1973): 69.

67. Kim, "Watashi to 1945-nen 8-gatsu 15-nichi," 98–99.
68. O Rim-jun, "Dai Nihon Teikoku shiganhei toshite," *Ushio* 144 (September 1971): 224–231.
69. Muramatsu Takeshi, *Chōsen shokuminsha: Aru Meijijin no shōgai* (Tokyo: Sanseidō, 1972), 219–22.
70. "Kyū shokuminchi no yūbinkyoku eno chokin, 1900-man kōza, 43-oku en nokoru," *Nihon keizai shinbun*, August 18, 2010.
71. Tanaka Hiroshi, "Rin Suiboku kokka hoshōtō seikyū jiken ni tsuite no ikensho," *Keizaigaku ronshū* 42, no. 5 (2003): 19–33.
72. The bereft families received 2.6 million yen and the surviving former soldiers with severe injuries received 4 million yen based on the 2001 law, "Heiwa jōyaku kokuseki ridatsushatō de aru senbotsusha izokutō ni taisuru chōikintō no shikyū ni kansuru hōritsu," http://www.shugiin.go.jp/internet/itdb_housei.nsf/html/housei/h147114.htm.

EPILOGUE: BACK IN VILLAGES

1. "Gunshidan sennin shokuin rirekisho tsuzuri," a file found in the storage of the Miyagi Youth Center.
2. "Seinen dantai shakai kyōiku ni kansuru tsuzuri" (1947), a file found in the archives of the Japan Youth Center.
3. Sheldon Garon, *Molding Japanese Minds: The State in Everyday Life* (Princeton, NJ: Princeton University Press, 1998), 158.
4. Ibid., 159–160.
5. Tani Teruhiro, *Seinen no seiki* (Tokyo: Dōseisha, 2003), 189–191.
6. *Brief Histories of Seinendan (Youth Association) and Nippon Seinenkan (Japan Youth Foundation)*, 11, archives of the Japan Youth Center.
7. Andō Kōki, "Sengo ni okeru senzenki seinendan shidōsha no 'fukken' to 'kyōdōshugi,'" *Nihon Shakai Kyōiku Gakkai kiyō* 46 (2010): 1–10; Miyasaka Kōsaku, "Nihon no shakai kyōiku ni okeru shidōsharon no keifu," *Gekkan shakai kyōiku* 6, no. 3 (1962): 24–32.
8. Donald M. Typer, "Nippon Seinenkan rijikai hyōgiinkai no kaisai ni atatte: Tazawa seishin o yomigaeraseyo," in "Seinen dantai shakai kyōiku ni kansuru tsuzuri" (1947), the archives of the Japan Youth Center.
9. Nihon Seinendan Kyōgikai, *Nihon Seinendan Kyōgikai 20-nenshi* (Tokyo: Nippon Seinenkan, 1971), 58–59, 70–71. Tani, *Seinen no seiki*, 161. The CIE established the Institute for Training and Educational Leadership to promote group work theories.
10. Sunaga Sadao, "Mura ni okeru seinen katsudō," in *Kenka chiiki seinendan no gaiyō*, ed. Miyagi-ken Kyōiku Iinkai and Miyagi-ken Seinendan Renraku Kyōgikai (circa. 1959), 26–28, archives of the Japan Youth Center.
11. Kitagawa Kenzō, *Sengo no shuppatsu: Bunka undō, seinendan, sensō mibōjin* (Tokyo: Aoki Shoten, 2000), 83.
12. Imai Toyozō, "Seinen yagakukai no ugoki," *Gekkan shakai kyōiku* 10, no. 2 (1966): 84–90.
13. *Shimoina seinen* (August 1946), quoted in Kitagawa, *Sengo no shuppatsu*, 76.
14. Quoted in Kitagawa, *Sengo no shuppatsu*, 80–81.
15. Quoted in ibid., 79.
16. Kitagawa, *Sengo no shuppatsu*, 90–95.
17. Interview with Katō Haruhiko in Ōsaki city on April 24, 2012; Katō Einojō, *Jinsei sanmyaku yume bōbō, Katō Einojō ikōshū* (self-pub. by Katō Haruhiko, Ōsaki, Miyagi, 1987), 25–35.
18. See "sonze" of 1950 in Shida Sonshi Hensan Iinkai, *Shida sonshi* (Miyagi: Miyagi-ken Shida-gun Shida-son, 1950), 49.

19. "Ōsaki nōmin daigaku kankei shorui tsuzuri" (1946–1949), Katō-ke bunsho, owned by Ōsaki City Hall, history compilation section.

20. Katō, *Jinsei sanmyaku*, 98

21. Nippon Seinenkan Miyagi-ken Shibu, "Shomu" (Showa 20-nen 9-gatsu yori), a file found in the storage of the Miyagi Youth Center.

22. "Shōwa 27-nen 28-nen seinen gakkyū kankei tsuzuri: Dai 1-shu," archives of the Japan Youth Center.

23. Yoshikawa Hiroshi, "'Seinen gakkyū' no shisakuka katei ni kansuru ichikōsatsu," *Yokohama Kokuritsu Daigaku kiyō* 37 (November 1997): 261–279.

24. Miyahara Seiichi, "Seinendan to seinen gakkyū," in "Shōwa 27-nen 28-nen seinen gakkyū kankei tsuzuri: Dai 1-shu," archives of the Japan Youth Center.

25. Danno Nobuo, "Dōnaru kotoshi no nōson, nōson shitsugyōsha: Mura zentai de toriageyō," *Asahi shinbun*, February 26, 1951.

26. Nihon Seinendan Kyōgikai, *Nihon Seinendan Kyōgikai 20-nenshi*, 99–100, 119–120, 138–140.

27. "Hataraku seishōnen no shidō," *Asahi shinbun* (editorial), June 26, 1953; "Futatsu no seishōnen taikai," *Mainichi shinbun* (editorial), May 17, 1953.

28. "Chiiki seinen no undō ni nozomu," *Asahi shinbun* (editorial), May 14, 1953; Hashiura Mamoru, "Watashitachi seinendan no genjō to mondaiten," in *Kenka chiiki seinendan no gaiyō*, ed. Miyagi-ken Kyōiku Iinkai et al., 18–21.

29. Sunaga, "Mura ni okeru seinen katsudō."

30. Koshikawa Rokurō, "Seinendan katsudō ni taisuru chikumin no kangae," in *Kenka chiiki seinendan no gaiyō*, ed. Miyagi-ken Kyōiku Iinkai et al., 24–28.

31. Xu Chongfa's letter to graduates of the Shinchiku seinen shūrenjō, September 4, 1945. Xu's personal archives.

32. Ibid.

33. Interviews with Xu Chongfa in Shakeng, Xinzhu province, on May 20 and 27, 2011.

34. Interview with Huang Yuanxing in Beipu on May 30, 2011.

35. Ibid.

36. Interview with Jiang Zhaoying in Qionglin, Xinzhu province, June 29, 2011.

37. Ibid.

38. Wu Zhuoliu, *Wuhuaguo* (Taipei: Caogen chuban, 1995), 136–137.

39. Jiang Yongjing, "Sanminzhuyi qingniantuan yu kangzhan jianguo," *Jindai Zhonguo* 92 (December 1992): 51–67. Cao Xin, "Shei you qingnian, shei you jianglai: Kangzhan qijian Guomin zhengfu zhengqu qingnian de nuli yu cuozhe," *Liang'an fazhanshi yanjiu* 6 (December 2008): 71–107; Ka Girin (Ho I-Lin), *Ni nihachi Jiken: "Taiwanjin" keisei no esunoporitikusu* (Tokyo: Tokyo Daigaku Shuppankai, 2003), 62–63.

40. Kristin Mulready-Stone, *Mobilizing Shanghai Youth* (London: Routledge, 2015), 62–85.

41. Kondō Masami, *Sōryokusen to Taiwan* (Tokyo: Tōsui Shobō, 1996), 469–483.

42. Ka, *Ni nihachi Jiken*, 112; Chen Cuilian, "Sanminzhuyi qingniantuan yu zhanhou Taiwan," *Fazheng xuebao* 6 (July 1996): 75.

43. Ka, *Ni nihachi Jiken*, 111–115.

44. Wu Xinrong, *Wu Xinrong Huiyilu* (Taipei, Qianwei chubanshe, 1989), 248–249, cited in Ka, *Ni nihachi Jiken*, 117.

45. Ka, *Ni nihachi Jiken*, 115–117.

46. Zhang Yanxian, Xu Mingxun, Yang Yahui, and Chen Fenghua, *Xinzhu fengcheng 228* (Xinzhu: Xinzhu-shi zhengfu, 2002), 151–152.

47. Zhang et al., *Xinzhu fengcheng 228*, 152–153.

48. Chen Suzhen, "Liu Jiarong Shounanji," *Xinzhu wenxian* 5 (March 2001): 31.

49. Interviews with anonymous Beipu residents, May 6, 2011.

50. Chen Jiakang, *Beipu qinghuai* (self-pub., Beipu, Xinzhu, 2008), 64.

51. Ka, *Ni nihachi Jiken*, 96–98.

52. Interview with Xu Chongfa in Shakeng, Xinzhu province, May 27, 2011.

53. Interview with Huang Yuanxing in Beipu, Xinzhu province, May 30, 2011.

54. Ibid.

55. "Seinensetsu kakuchi no moyooshi," *Taiwan xinshengbao*, April 2, 1946, 4. There are a number of articles describing the activities of Youth Day in *Taiwan xinshengbao* published between March 26 and April 2, 1946.

56. "Disan jie qingnianjie zhuxi xungao qingnian," *Taiwan xinshengbao*, March 29, 1946, 2.

57. Zhang et al., *Xinzhu fengcheng 228*, 150–151. Wang Shiqing, "Sanminzhuyi qingniantuan tuanyuan yu 228 shijian (chutan)," *Shilian zazhi* 21 (December, 1992): 12. Kaibara Mitsuyo, "Taiwan nashonarizumu no haikei to shinjō," *Taiwanshi kenkyū* 12 (March 1996): 1–19. Many oral histories and memoirs give firsthand details of people's impressions of GMD officials and soldiers in Taiwan.

58. See Ka, *Ni nihachi Jiken*, 208–229 for details of the rising tensions between Taiwanese locals and GMD authorities.

59. Li Youbang, "Taiwan qingnian de xinketi," *Taiwan xinshengbao*, January 1, 1947, 11.

60. Lai Zehan, *228 shijian yanjiu baogao* (Taipei: Shibao chubanshe, 1994), 48–56.

61. Wang, "Sanminzhuyi qingniantuan tuanyuan," 14. Chen, "Sanminzhuyi qingniantuan," 81–85.

62. Ka, *Ni nihachi Jiken*, 239.

63. Zhang Yanxian, et al., *Xinzhu fengcheng 228*, 154.

64. Interview with Xu Chongfa in Shakeng, Xinzhu province, May 27, 2011. On how those who had served in the Japanese military were spontaneously remobilized to confront the Guomindang during the 228 Incident, see Victor Louzon, "From Japanese Soldiers to Chinese Rebels: Colonial Hegemony, War Experience, and Spontaneous Remobilization during the 1947 Taiwanese Rebellion," *Journal of Asian Studies* 77, no. 1 (2018): 161–179.

65. Interview with Huang Yuanxing in Beipu, Xinzhu province, May 30, 2011.

66. Ke Yuanfen, "Taiwan zai jiaoyu," *Taiwan xinshengbao*, March 29, 1947, 4.

67. Ka, *Ni nihachi Jiken*, 271.

68. Shangguan Yeyou, "Yinianlaide Taiwan qingnian fuwutuan," *Taiwan xinshengbao*, March 29, 1951, 6.

69. For details of Jiang Jingguo's leadership in sanqingtuan in China, see Wang Liangqing, "'Xinren' yu 'qijia': Jiang Jingguo xiansheng de jueqi yu sanminzhuyi qingniantuan," in *Zhongguo xiandaishi zhanti yanjiu baogao* (20), ed. Zhonghua minguo shiliao yanjiu zhongxin (Taipei: Republic of China shiliao yanjiu zhongxin, 1999), 339–392.

70. "Zongtong haozhao qingnian dajie he juezu qingnian jiuguotuan," *Taiwan xinshengbao*, March 29, 1952, 1. See Li Taihan, "Cong Qinglianhui dao Jiuguotuan chengli de guocheng," *Taiwan Historica* 56, no. 3 (2005): 129–156.

71. Youshi chubanshe, *Zhongguo qingnian fangong jiuguotuan* (Taipei: Youshi chubanshe, 1952), 6–9.

72. See Li Taihan, "Zhanhou Taiwan de 'zai zhandouhua': Yi 1953-nian 'shuqi qingnian zhandou xunlian' wei li," *Shihui* 5 (August 2001): 69–85.

73. Many Taiwanese people today believe that Hakka people have a strategic alliance with the GMD. On the psychology of Hakka populations, refer to Horie Shun'ichi, "Futatsu no Nihon: Hakka minkei o chūshin to suru Taiwanjin no 'Nihon' ishiki," in *Sengo Taiwan ni okeru "Nihon": Shokuminchi keiken no renzoku, henbō, riyō*, ed. Igarashi Masako and Mio Yūko (Tokyo: Fūkyōsha, 2006), 93–121.

74. Lin Boyan, "Botao, liuyun, qingchun: Cong shaonianbing dao Zhongguojun de Zhang Shulin," *Xinzhu wenxian* 6 (2001): 141.

75. See Bruce Cumings, *The Origins of the Korean War*, vol. 1, *Liberation and the Emergence of Separate Regimes, 1945–1947* (Princeton, NJ: Princeton University Press, 1981), 68–318.

76. Interview with Kim Yŏng-han in Taejŏn on November 27, 2011.

77. Song Nam-hŏn, *Haebang 3-yŏnsa* 1 (Seoul: Kkach'i, 1990), 57.

78. Ryu Sang-yŏng, "8.15-ihu ch'oiuik ch'ŏngnyŏn danch'e ŭi chojik kwa hwaltong," in *Haebang chŏnhusa ŭi insik*, ed. Chŏng Hae-gu et al., vol. 4 (Seoul: Han'gilsa, 1989), 55; Kim Haeng-sŏn, *Haebang chŏngguk ch'ŏngnyŏn undongsa* (Seoul: Sŏnin, 2004), 32–33.

79. Cumings, *The Origins of the Korean War*, vol. 1, 74–76. Kim, *Haebang chŏngguk*, 31–36.

80. Ji Soo-gol (Chi Su-gŏl), "Ilche sigi Ch'ungnam Puyŏ, Nonsan-gun ŭi yuji chiptan kwa hyŏksin ch'ŏngnyŏn chiptan," *Han'guk munhwa* 36 (December 2005): 223, fn. 107.

81. Ji, "Ilche sigi Ch'ungnam," 238; "Ch'ungnam chibang silchŏng chosa pogo," reprinted in *Hyŏndaesa charyo ch'ŏngsŏ 1 Migun CIC Chŏngbo pogosŏ 1: RG319 Office of the Chief of Military History*, ed. Chŭngang Ilbo Hyŏndaesa Yŏn'guso (Seoul: Sŏnin Munhwasa, 1996), 551 and 589. The estimated period of RG319 materials is 1946–1951.

82. Cumings, *The Origins of the Korean War*, vol. 1, 73, 276–280. Kim, *Haebang chŏngguk*, 37–48.

83. Yi Man-gyu, *Yŏ Un-hyŏng Sŏnsaeng t'ujaengsa* (Seoul: Minju Munhwasa, 1947): 18–22.

84. On the details of youth politics of this period, refer to Kim, *Haebang chŏngguk*.

85. Ryu, "8.15-ihu," 62–68; Kim, *Haebang chŏngguk*, 79–189.

86. Ryu, "8.15-ihu," 86.

87. Ibid., 69–76, 88–99; Kim, *Haebang chŏngguk*, 191–332, 379–449.

88. Interview with Kim Yŏng-han in Taejŏn on November 27, 2011.

89. "Ch'ungnam chibang silchŏng," 587–593; Ji, "Ilche sigi Ch'ungnam," 234–242.

90. Cumings, *The Origins of the Korean War*, vol. 1, 332–344.

91. Ibid., 351–371.

92. Bruce Cumings, *The Origins of the Korean War*, vol. 2, *The Roaring of the Cataract, 1947–1950* (Princeton, NJ: Princeton University Press, 1990), 237–259.

93. Charles K. Armstrong, *The North Korean Revolution, 1945–1950* (Ithaca, NY: Cornell University Press, 2003), 62–64.

94. Suzy Kim, *Everyday Life in the North Korean Revolution, 1945–1950* (Ithaca, NY: Cornell University Press, 2013), 114; Armstrong, *The North Korean Revolution*, 100.

95. Armstrong, *The North Korean Revolution*, 99–106; Kim, *Everyday Life*, 119–135.

96. Interview with Kim Yŏng-han in Taejŏn on November 27, 2011.

97. Sŏnu Ki-sŏng and Kim P'an-sŏk, *Ch'ŏngnyŏn undong ŭi ŏje wa naeil* (Seoul: Hwaetpulsa, 1969), 27.

98. See Bruce Cumings, *The Korean War: A History* (New York: Modern Library, 2010), 165–203; Don-Choon Kim, *The Unending Korean War: A Social History*, trans. Sung-ok Kim (Larkspur, CA: Tamal Vista, 2000), 143–178.

99. Cumings, *The Korean War*, 183–185. See also Kim, *The Unending Korean War*, 201–202.

100. Hayashi Eidai, *Chōsenjin kōgun heishi: Nyūginia-sen no tokubetsu shiganhei* (Tokyo: Takushoku Shobō 1995), 227–244.

ON THE ARCHIVES AND SOURCES

I consulted multiple national, local, and personal archives in various locations during my research for this book. There exist rich materials to explore in the field of Japan's prewar and wartime youth training, and a lot of them have become readily available through reprints, microfilms, and digital databases. At the same time, the search for personal and village histories made me realize that a substantial amount of local sources are not archived in any institution.

A large number of the primary sources on the policies, surveys, contemporary theories, and guidelines on youth education in Japan have been reprinted in *Kindai Nihon seinenki kyōiku sōsho* by Nihon Tosho Sentā. The official Seinendan Federation's magazines, *Seinen* and *Teikoku seinen,* have also been available through Fuji Shuppan's microfilm sets. The Japan Youth Center has published multiple versions of the history of the seinendan. Some include such useful details as the minutes of annual conventions, related laws, and newspaper reports. I had access to these reprints in the libraries of Columbia University and Waseda University.

As of 2011, Professor Tani Teruhiro at Tsuruga Junior College hosted the massive collection of village *seinendanhō* (seinendan newsletters), including some from Manchuria, Okinawa, and Taiwan, but it has been transferred to the Japan Youth Center in Tokyo since then. Again, as of 2011, the archives of the Japan Youth Center were not cataloged, but consisted of boxes of random sets of documents, *The Youth Cards*, youth newspapers, and other various materials. Some of the documents were about local seinendan branches as well. They were available for viewing when I made a request.

Many other nation- and local-level sources, including for colonial policies, are available at government archives and libraries in Tokyo. Ōno Rokui-chirō materials at the Modern Japanese Political History Materials (Kensei Shiryōshitsu) in the National Diet Library, for example, include policies on youth mobilization in colonial Korea. In addition to sources at government institutions, a big collection on colonial Korea is at the Yūhō Bunko of the Tōyō Bunka Kenkyūjo (Research Institute for Oriental Cultures) in Gakushūin University. The library of the Taiwan Kyōkai in Tokyo has rare historical publications that were not available anywhere else. To find sources on Okinawa, the Hōsei University Institute for Okinawa Studies is probably the best place in Tokyo.

The robust tradition of local history compilation across Japan, particularly that in Miyagi, provides researchers with many gems. The Miyagi Prefectural Archives houses extensive original documents dating from the Meiji period, of which I found those on education particularly rich. All the census data and local history chronicles are readily available there, too. Miyagi's important regional newspaper, *Kahoku shinpō*, can be accessed in microfilms at the Miyagi Prefectural Library. Unfortunately, however, the prints between August 1912 and June 1918 are permanently lost (likely because of air raids) and thus are unavailable in microfilms, too. The library of Tōhoku University has an impressive collection on the regional history. There I made use of the entire original copies of *Miyagi kyōiku* (or former *Miyagi Kyōikukai zasshi*). The Miyagi Seinen Kaikan also keeps boxes of documents related to prefecture seinendan activities in storage, although they were not preserved well or cataloged at all. For details on Katō Einojō, I obtained the help of the local history office of Ōsaki City Hall. Katō's family donated his personal archives to the city and I was allowed to view them in their office. Shida village meeting minutes were also available for viewing. Some of these sources are reprinted in Furukawa city history chronicles. The local historian Gotō Ichizō offered me a copy of Katō Einojō's youth group journal, *Omoto*, via Osaki city officials. These local officials helped me visit and interview Katō Haruhiko (Katō Einojō's son) as well. The staff of the Furukawa-Shida district community center also helped me contact a few elderly men residing in the area for interviews on the village seinendan.

In Okinawa, too, the prefecture and municipalities have strong local historical sections. The Okinawa Prefectural Library has the best collection of regional newspapers in addition to rare primary and secondary sources. The University of the Ryukyus Library houses a number of original copies of youth group journals. As in the rest of the country, local officials have compiled detailed village and town histories, and many include oral histories. They were particularly helpful, given that many sources were lost during the war. After consulting the published local histories, I visited Nago City Library, the

Nago city history office, and the Ōgimi village history office to view more local sources, including many self-published memoirs and autobiographies. Introduced by the community center, I was able to interview a number of elderly residents in Ōgimi village. I found the residence of Taira Einoshō, a former seinendan leader of Ōgimi village, in Aichi prefecture and visited him for an interview as well.

Both Taiwan and South Korea have faced political upheavals that made it risky to keep personal and local historical documents. But movements to compile local histories have been emerging. In Taiwan, I found a periodical by local historians, *Xinzhu wenxian*, particularly useful. Through that journal I contacted a local historian, who provided information about another historian in Beipu, who introduced me to Huang Yuanxing, who took me to Xu Chongfa. Xu's personal archive of the Xinzhu Province Youth Training Institute was beyond anything I had expected. It included many issues of *Dōkō*, personal letters from students to Xu, attendance records, photo albums, teachers' notes, his diaries, and other materials, all of which are completely unique data. Through Huang and Xu, I met other Beipu residents and former seinendan members. Beipu's local background was relatively easy to find thanks to the heavy-lifting work of local historians. Histories of the Jiang family and ethnographical research on Hakka life in Beipu are particularly rich. I also obtained help from researchers at National Chiao Tung University (Jiaotong University) and National Central University to gain access to a Saisiyat community. I interviewed a Saisiyat-descendant family and obtained memoirs about Japanese rule, although I did not include a section on aboriginal society in this book.

In Taipei, the largest collection of sources on Japanese colonial rule is located in the Taiwan Research Center of the National Taiwan Library in Yong'an. There I browsed through many sources and narrowed down my case study to Xinzhu. The center's website offers databases of digitized images of publications from the colonial period (available offsite after initial registration). The digital archive of *Taiwan nichinichi shinpō* (*Taiwan riri xinbao*) was available in many major libraries. For other newspapers and primary sources, I visited the libraries of the National Taiwan University and Academia Sinica.

Village and personal histories of the colonial period were more difficult to gain access to in Korea. After browsing many municipal history volumes and consulting a number of researchers, I first decided to examine the case of Naju city in South Chŏlla. With the help of Naju city officials, I interviewed several old residents. The Naju officials also offered me many volumes of their historical research that I could not find in Seoul. Unfortunately, in the end, I acquired very little information about youth mobilization there. I then decided to find Kim Yŏng-han, whose interview appears in *Chibang ŭl salda* (Living the local), published by the National Institute of Korean History. I visited his residence in Taejŏn a number of times to interview him and borrowed his personal photos and documents. His home village, Kwangsŏk, does not have a history compilation section in the administration. I walked around and talked to village residents on the street, but the mega-scale relocation during the Korean War made this tactic unproductive. However, Kim Yŏng-han's personal archives and materials available at the National Archives (Kukka Kirŏgwŏn) and libraries in Seoul provided me with sufficiently rich information on the background of the village and the region.

In Seoul, my primary go-to place for sources was the National Library of Korea. Its website also offers a great range of colonial-period publications in digital form. The libraries of Seoul National University and Yonsei University also had rare newspapers and other primary sources from the colonial period. The website of Korean History Database (Han'guksa teit'ŏ beisŭ; http://db.history.go.kr) offers a massive amount of digitized sources on different periods of Korean history, including those of the Japanese colonial period. Official documents and multiple periodicals, including the entire issues of *Tonga ilbo* between 1920 and 1962, are searchable and downloadable through their website.

Index

Adolescence concept, in Japan, 28–29, 41, 45, 68
"Advice to Youth" (*Capital Gazette*), 109
Agrarianism/agrarian nationalism, in Japan, 15–16; migration to Manchuria and, 81–85; seinendan and, 25–28; totalitarian Japanization and, 77–78; urban hegemony and, 11–12
Agrarianism/agrarian nationalism, in Korea, 122–25, 127, 180, 181, 186, 189, 193, 203–4, 208–9
Agrarianism/agrarian nationalism, in Taiwan, 124, 130, 145, 148–49, 151–52, 179
Agricultural Corps, in Taiwan, 172–73, 178
Aikokuhan (patriotic units), in Korea, 219–20
Akamatsu Katsumaro, 62
All Korea Local Pillars of Youth Training Session, 205
All Korea Youth Party Convention, 120, 205
All-Nation Youth General Alliance, in Korea, 266
Anticolonial intellectuals: in Korea, 4, 107–8, 111, 113–14, 120–23, 124–25, 200; in Taiwan, 4, 107–8, 114–17, 119–20, 124, 129
Arashiyama Incident (1931–1932), 101
Aratanome 4-H Club, 17, 45, 59–62, 71, 86
Arbeitsdienst (German Labor service), adopted in Korea, 210
Army Reservist Associations (*zaigō gunjinkai*), in Japan, 32, 33
Army Special Volunteer Soldier Program Act, in Taiwan, 170
Asahi shinbun, 255
Assimilationist principles, racism and nation-empire concept, 4–9
Association of Social Work, in Taiwan, 138
Atsumi Kanzō, 118

Baden-Powell, Robert, 28
Beipu Seinendan, 140
Beipu Youth Group, 136, 138–39, 140, 144
Blood-signed military applications, 2, 76, 175, 215
Boshin Imperial Rescript (1908), 30, 57, 96
Boshin War, 48

Boy Scouts, in Britain, 28, 38
Britain, colonial administration and, 7
Brunner, Edmund de Schweinitz, 185
Bunkyō no Chōsen journal, 237, 238

Cai Peihuo, 116, 119–20
Cai Qingzi, 147
"Call to Youth" (Chen), 118
Chaenyŏng county, Korea, 112–13, 122
Chang Tŏk-su, 113, 120
Chen Boyu, 114–15
Chen Cheng, 259, 261
Chen Duxiu, 116, 118, 119
Chen Wen Sung, 118
Chen Yi, 261
Chiang Kai-Shek, 258, 260
China: national imperialism and, 5; post-war Taiwan and, 256–63; Taiwanese youth and, 115–17
China Incident (1937), 80, 210
China Youth Anti-Communist Corps (CYC), 262–63
Chinese Youth Anti-Communist Anti-Soviet League, 262
Ching, Leo T. S., 8–9
Chi Su-gŏl. *See* Ji Soo-gol
Chŏndogyo Youth Party, 123
Ch'oe Nam-sŏn, 109, 111
Ch'oe Tal-sun, 187–88
Ch'ŏngch'un (Youth) magazine, 109
Ch'ŏngnyŏn (Korean concept of youth), 109–11
Chōsen chihō gyōsei journal, 208
Chōsen journal, 192
Chōsengun (standing army in Korea), 215–16
Chōsen Seinendan Federation, in Korea, 210–11, 217, 220
Chosŏn chungang ilbo newspaper, 201
Chosŏn ilbo newspaper, 112, 201
Cho Tong-sun, 189, 191–92, 265
Chūō Hūtokukai, 29
"Circumstances of Korean Youth Today" (*Sonyŏn*), 110
"City fever" (*tokainestsu*), 30, 37

Hayashi Genzaburō, 132
Henry, Todd A., 9
Hikita Eikichi, 33–34
Hirayama Kazuhiko, 34
Hirohito, Emperor, 77, 234, 257
Hitler Youth, 71, 85, 273
Hodge, George R., 264, 267
Ho I-Lin, 259
Hong Hyo-min, 122
Hōtoku agrarian morality, 30, 74, 237
Hōtokukai (Society of Repaying Virtue), 29–30, 41, 51, 88, 187
Hŭk (Yi Kwang-su), 122
Huang Jitu, 259
Huang Kunxuan, 159
Huang Rongzhe, 159
Huang Wancheng, 259
Huang Yiuying, 169
Huang Yuanxing, 17, 151, 161–63, 165, 167–68, 170, 176–77, 178, 181, 204, 226, 250; in post-war era, 257, 260, 262, 263
Hwangsŏng sinmun (Capital Gazette), 109
Hyŏksin (progressive reform) movement, in Korea, 187, 188, 191
Hyung Ok Park, 83–84

Ie no hikari (magazine), 82
Iha Fuyū, 97
Imperial Agricultural Association, in Japan, 73
Imperial Rescript on Education (1890), in Japan, 51
Inaka seinen (Rural youth) (Yamamoto), 23–25, 27, 40–41
Independence Club Movement (1896–1899), in Korea, 110
"Inner territories," defined, 16
"Internalization of a state ideology," use of term, 10
Ishiwara Kanji, 82, 206
Italy, 9
Iwabuchi Toshio, 56
Iwasa Hiroshi, 171
Izumi Akira, 115

Japan, 6, 11, 39–40, 121; agrarian nationalism in, 11–12, 15–16, 25–28, 77–78, 81–85; "colonial legacy" of, 250–51, 270–75; concept of adolescence in, 28–29, 41, 45, 68; "ideologies of democracy," 35; "integration of training and everyday life," 80; invasion of Taiwan in 1895, 6, 114, 130, 131; Korean farm youth sent to, 225–26; post-war era in, 251–56; reactions in to surrender, 246–48; Taiwanese youth view as oppressor, 117;

urban-rural binary in, 11–12. *See also Seinendan* (village youth associations); Totalitarian Japanization; "Young pillars of the empire"
Japan Seinendan Convention, 252, 255
Japan Youth Center, 22, 252
Japan Youth Newspaper, 83
Jiang Axin, 138–39, 172
Jiang family, in Taiwan, 133–35, 138–39, 161, 167, 262
Jiang Ruichang, 138, 260
Jiang Shaozu, 133
Jiang Weishui, 119–20
Jiang Xiuluan, 133
Jiriki kōsei ihō (Self-revitalization news), 193
Ji Soo-gol, 187–88, 267

Kabo reforms (1894–1896), in Korea, 110
Kadowaki Yoshio, 58, 63
Kaebyŏk journal, 123
Kagawa Tomomi, 225
Kahoku shinpō, 50, 73, 75, 78, 79, 80, 85, 86–87
Kalsan Shinkōkai, 190
Kanno Sukeo, 84
Kanō Masanao, 32
Kapsin Palace Coup (1884), 110
Katō Einojō 66, 68, 138, 139, 189; Aratanome 4-H Club and, 17, 45, 58–61, 62; in post-war era, 254; in totalitarian Japanization era, 71, 72, 86–88, 89; wartime deaths and, 90
Katō Hiroyuki, 5
Katō Hisanosuke, 59, 61, 74, 80
Katō Kanji, 26, 82
Keiyakukō-based youth governance, 54
Kim Chong-won, 269
Kim Il-Sung, 267, 268
Kim Ki-bong, 246–47
Kim Ku, 267
Kim Myŏng-sik, 113, 120
Kim Puja, 200
Kim Sa-guk, 113
Kim To-hyŏn, 122
Kimura Naoe, 24, 38
Kimura Tadashi, 82
Kim Yŏng-han, 273; background, 17–18; exemption from labor conscription, 203–4, 223–24; military mobilization and preparation and, 211, 219, 221, 223, 226–28; in post-war era, 264, 267, 268, 270; rhetoric of Japanese nationalism and, 226; social mobility complex and, 181, 194–99, 200–202, 207–8; volunteer soldier training program and, 217, 219
Kitagawa Kenzō, 253

youth" and, 3; local and national tensions of 1930s and, 76–79; masculinity and, 14; migration to Manchuria and, 81–84; military influence, 31–35, 42–43; newsletters of, 38–39; night study groups and, 36–37; in post-war era, 251–56; rapidity and scale of expansion, 35–36; rural-centered imperialism and, 71; social theories as youth reforms, 28–29; standardization of, 37–40; state goals for, 2–3, 21–23; and tenants' demands in 1920s, 61–62; Yamamoto Takinosuke and, 23–25, 27, 35; young women and newsletters of, 69; youth as new social category, 40–43. *See also* Social mobility complex

Seinendan Chūōbu, 22, 29

"Self-revitalization" (*jiriki kōsei*) campaign, in Japan, 73–74

Shibusawa Eiichi, 207

Shida village, 44, 68; described, 46; elementary school youth group, 50–53, 56; employment opportunities, 45, 63, 65–68; rice-centered economy of, 46–47, 48, 52; self-reliance during Great Depression, 74; village youth groups and, 53–56; youth's increased leverage against established authority, 45, 58–62; youth training schools in, 63

Shida Village Seinendan, 56

Shikenkai (Exam world) journal, 196

Shimoina county youth group, 40–41, 42

Shinchiku Seinendan, in Taiwan, 137, 140, 145, 146

Shinganhei (Volunteer soldier) (Zhou), 175

Shinjō seinendan, 36–37

Shinkensetsu (New Construction) journal, 153, 176

Shinkōkai, and modernization attempts in Korea, 180–81, 186–87, 190–93

Shinkō seinendan, in Korea, 193, 194, 196–98, 200–201, 203, 205, 206–14, 221

Shojokai (maidens' groups), 69, 81

Shūrenjō (youth training institute), 154–65, 178

Shufang schools, in Taiwan, 131–32, 135

Shūyō (self-cultivation), 33, 37–38, 42; in Japan, 29–31, 51, 63, 75; in Korea, 194; in Okinawa, 99; in Taiwan, 125, 141, 145–46, 154; women and, 69

Sim Hun, 122

Sino-Japanese War (1895), 133, 183, 215

Sinŭiju Incident, 268

Smethurst, Richard, 11, 32, 42

Smith, Kerry, 73

Sŏdang (private schools), in Korea, 185, 191, 194, 207

Sōnendan (adult associations), 86, 87, 90, 296n115

Social Darwinism, 5, 28, 107, 111, 117

Social dynamics, nation empire and, 10–11

Social education (*shakai kyōiku*), 30–31, 33, 42

Social Education Law (1949), in post-war Japan, 251–52

Social mobility complex: in Korea, 181, 203–4, 206–9, 226, 248–49, 272; Taiwan and, 148–49, 169–70, 178, 248–49, 272; use of term, 15

Social mobility complex, in Japan: collapse of, during era of totalitarian Japanization, 72, 89–92; during Great Depression, 75; impact of, 270–71; women and, 69; youth training and alteration of young men's social prospects, 45–46, 63–69

Social National Education (Tanaka), 32

Sonyŏn (Youth) magazine, 109, 110

South Korea: "colonial legacy" of Japan and, 274; in post-war era, 264–68, 269, 270

Soviet Union, 9, 10, 121, 127

Sugawara Michiyoshi, 48

Sun Yat-Sen, 258

Suzuki Yoshiaki, 234–35

Syngman Rhee, 267–68, 269

Taehan maeil sinbo (Korea Daily News), 109

Taishō Democracy, 29, 31–34, 90, 115

Taiwan, 7, 11, 69, 129–50; agrarian nationalism and, 124, 130, 145, 148–49, 151–52, 179; anticolonial intellectuals in, 4, 107–8, 114–17, 119–20, 124, 129; assimilationist principles and, 6, 7, 8; colonial government and, 125–26, 127; "colonial legacy" of Japan and, 274; delegates to seinendan conventions, 234; education in, 130–35, 140–44, 152, 165, 167, 242, 271; interethnic mistrust in youth, 130, 131–35; invaded by Japan in 1895, 6, 114, 130, 131; middling class in, 15, 170; 1930s Japanese migration to, 83, 84; in post-war era, 256–63; reactions in to Japanese surrender, 246–48; seinendan, rural youth, and agrarian nationalism, 145–49; seinendan and education, 140–44; socialist youth groups and age concerns, 119–22; social mobility complex and, 148–49, 169–70, 178, 248–49, 272; "volunteer fever" in, 1–2; volunteer soldiers' experiences, 241–46; war's consequences and, 246, 249; Xinzhu and Beipu youth organizations, 136–39

Studies of the
Weatherhead East Asian Institute
Columbia University

Selected Titles

(Complete list at: http://weai.columbia.edu/publications/studies-weai/)

Idly Scribbling Rhymers: Poetry, Print, and Community in Nineteenth-Century Japan, by Robert Tuck. Columbia University Press, 2018.

Forging the Golden Urn: The Qing Empire and the Politics of Reincarnation in Tibet, by Max Oidtmann. Columbia University Press, 2018.

The Battle for Fortune: State-Led Development, Personhood, and Power among Tibetans in China, by Charlene Makley. Cornell University Press, 2018.

Aesthetic Life: Beauty and Art in Modern Japan, by Miya Mizuta Lippit. Harvard University Asia Center, 2018.

China's War on Smuggling: Law, Economic Life, and the Making of the Modern State, 1842–1965, by Philip Thai. Columbia University Press, 2018.

Where the Party Rules: The Rank and File of China's Authoritarian State, by Daniel Koss. Cambridge University Press, 2018.

Resurrecting Nagasaki: Reconstruction and the Formation of Atomic Narratives, by Chad Diehl. Cornell University Press, 2018.

China's Philological Turn: Scholars, Textualism, and the Dao in the Eighteenth Century, by Ori Sela. Columbia University Press, 2018.

Making Time: Astronomical Time Measurement in Tokugawa Japan, by Yulia Frumer. University of Chicago Press, 2018.

Mobilizing without the Masses: Control and Contention in China, by Diana Fu. Cambridge University Press, 2018.

Promiscuous Media: Film and Visual Culture in Imperial Japan, 1926–1945, by Hikari Hori. Cornell University Press, 2018.

The End of Japanese Cinema: Industrial Genres, National Times, and Media Ecologies, by Alexander Zahlten. Duke University Press, 2017.

The Chinese Typewriter: A History, by Thomas S. Mullaney. The MIT Press, 2017.

Forgotten Disease: Illnesses Transformed in Chinese Medicine, by Hilary A. Smith. Stanford University Press, 2017.

Borrowing Together: Microfinance and Cultivating Social Ties, by Becky Yang Hsu. Cambridge University Press, 2017.

Food of Sinful Demons: Meat, Vegetarianism, and the Limits of Buddhism in Tibet, by Geoffrey Barstow. Columbia University Press, 2017.

Youth For Nation: Culture and Protest in Cold War South Korea, by Charles R. Kim. University of Hawai'i Press, 2017.

Socialist Cosmopolitanism: The Chinese Literary Universe, 1945–1965, by Nicolai Volland. Columbia University Press, 2017.

Yokohama and the Silk Trade: How Eastern Japan Became the Primary Economic Region of Japan, 1843–1893, by Yasuhiro Makimura. Lexington Books, 2017.

The Social Life of Inkstones: Artisans and Scholars in Early Qing China, by Dorothy Ko. University of Washington Press, 2017.

Darwin, Dharma, and the Divine: Evolutionary Theory and Religion in Modern Japan, by G. Clinton Godart. University of Hawai'i Press, 2017.

Dictators and Their Secret Police: Coercive Institutions and State Violence, by Sheena Chestnut Greitens. Cambridge University Press, 2016.

The Cultural Revolution on Trial: Mao and the Gang of Four, by Alexander C. Cook. Cambridge University Press, 2016.

Inheritance of Loss: China, Japan, and the Political Economy of Redemption After Empire, by Yukiko Koga. University of Chicago Press, 2016.

Homecomings: The Belated Return of Japan's Lost Soldiers, by Yoshikuni Igarashi. Columbia University Press, 2016.

Samurai to Soldier: Remaking Military Service in Nineteenth-Century Japan, by D. Colin Jaundrill. Cornell University Press, 2016.

The Red Guard Generation and Political Activism in China, by Guobin Yang. Columbia University Press, 2016.

Accidental Activists: Victim Movements and Government Accountability in Japan and South Korea, by Celeste L. Arrington. Cornell University Press, 2016.

Ming China and Vietnam: Negotiating Borders in Early Modern Asia, by Kathlene Baldanza. Cambridge University Press, 2016.

Ethnic Conflict and Protest in Tibet and Xinjiang: Unrest in China's West, coedited by Ben Hillman and Gray Tuttle. Columbia University Press, 2016.

One Hundred Million Philosophers: Science of Thought and the Culture of Democracy in Postwar Japan, by Adam Bronson. University of Hawai'i Press, 2016.

Conflict and Commerce in Maritime East Asia: The Zheng Family and the Shaping of the Modern World, c. 1620–1720, by Xing Hang. Cambridge University Press, 2016.

Chinese Law in Imperial Eyes: Sovereignty, Justice, and Transcultural Politics, by Li Chen. Columbia University Press, 2016.

Imperial Genus: The Formation and Limits of the Human in Modern Korea and Japan, by Travis Workman. University of California Press, 2015.

Yasukuni Shrine: History, Memory, and Japan's Unending Postwar, by Akiko Takenaka. University of Hawai'i Press, 2015.

The Age of Irreverence: A New History of Laughter in China, by Christopher Rea. University of California Press, 2015.

The Knowledge of Nature and the Nature of Knowledge in Early Modern Japan, by Federico Marcon. University of Chicago Press, 2015.

The Fascist Effect: Japan and Italy, 1915–1952, by Reto Hofmann. Cornell University Press, 2015.

The International Minimum: Creativity and Contradiction in Japan's Global Engagement, 1933–1964, by Jessamyn R. Abel. University of Hawai'i Press, 2015.

Empires of Coal: Fueling China's Entry into the Modern World Order, 1860–1920, by Shellen Xiao Wu. Stanford University Press, 2015.

Lightning Source UK Ltd.
Milton Keynes UK
UKHW010318121019

351412UK00002B/324/P